DR CLIVE YOUNG is an Edinburgh-bor[illegible]efore retiring in 2023, was the Head of P[illegible]rsity College London. He taught as an As[illegible]rsity for a decade and directed many UK a[illegible]ects

For over 25 years Clive has been fascinated by the fate of the Scots language he learned as a bairn in East Central Scotland. He created one of the first Scots websites in 1996, coined the word *wabsteid*, and curates an archive of Scots in the media. He is the author of a range of resources for Scots learners and is now working on a follow-up to *Unlocking Scots*, tracing how the language is spoken nowadays across Scotland and in Ireland.

Clive graduated as a botanist from the University of St Andrews, gained a PhD researching seaweed on the Isle of Man and worked for the NHS in Glasgow before realising he was an educator at heart.

He now lives in Glasgow with his wife Deb and a lurcher dog called Cooper.

Unlocking Scots

The secret life of the Scots language

CLIVE YOUNG

Luath Press Limited
EDINBURGH
www.luath.co.uk

To my Mancunian mother, Muriel, who lang syne fell in love with Scotland.

First published 2023
Revised edition 2025

ISBN: 978-1-80425-234-5

The author's right to be identified as author of this book
under the Copyright, Designs and Patents Act 1988 has been asserted.

This book is made of materials from well-managed,
FSC®-certified forests and other controlled sources.

MIX
Paper from
responsible sources
FSC® C011748

Printed and bound by
Ashford Colour Ltd., Gosport

Typeset in 11.5 point Sabon by
Main Point Books, Edinburgh

Contents

Preface

THE SCOTS LANGUAGE is the hidden treasure of Scottish culture. For many of us it is still how we speak to each other, how we express our feelings, our humour, even our Scottishness. It not only connects us to our communities at an emotional level but also links us to our past. Scots was created by millions of voices coming together to share words, phrases and jokes; to understand, act on (and often laugh at) the world around them. Such is its power to unite, it was ruthlessly supressed and all but erased from our schools, our media and our public life. Unsupported and unloved by the anglophones in authority, its traditional cohesion started to fragment, almost turning Scots into the dialect (or dialects) of English that historically it never had been. Countless school bairns were shamed and physically beaten for speaking the language of their families, surely one of the most wretched episodes in Scotland's story. Speakers were even denied literacy in their own tongue so it could all the more easily be mocked as 'bad English' or 'slang'. Many speakers internalised this contempt and began to despise their own language. Scots became trapped in a strange 'culture of silence'.

Yet the anglophone elites couldn't quite kill our defiant tongue. In a spectacular expression of Scottish autonomy, during the 2011 Census over a million and a half people took the unprecedented opportunity to declare they still spoke Scots. Of course, nowadays most of us speak Scots in a dynamic mix with Scottish English, but so what? Enough of the 'old' Scots remains in everyday Scottish vernacular to give those words their power to connect and sometimes confront. Poets and performers have appropriated these rebellious traits for their own ends, but Scots is not just a heritage curio for artists, tea towels and witty social media memes. Scots is a living tongue, with as much right to be treated as a minority language as Gaelic, Irish or Welsh.

Over two decades ago the UK government signed up to the European Charter for Regional or Minority Languages (ECRML). The Charter declared that 'the right to use a regional or minority language in private and public life is an inalienable right'. It emphasised 'the need for resolute action to promote regional or minority languages in order to safeguard them'. Scots, along with its dialect Ulster Scots, was at last recognised officially as a minority language, together with Gaelic, Irish and Welsh. But Scots was always treated as second class and never received anything like the care or protection the others have enjoyed since then. Only in 2023 did the Scottish Government, for the first time, reference Scots in legislation through the Scottish Languages Bill. Enacted in 2025, the Bill recognised Scots as a language in its own right and acknowledged the stigma its speakers often face. This book therefore starts with the basic premise of ECRML, that Scots is a minority language and rightfully should be supported and revitalised as such. The tongue is now undeniably at risk, gradually losing both vocabulary and grammar, but the resultant blending of Scots with Scottish English in everyday speech should be seen as a sign only of its long-term neglect and not an excuse to scorn it even more.

When anyone starts exploring the Scots language as a speaker, scholar, teacher or creative writer, the culture of silence surrounding the language makes it easy to assume we are all at 'ground zero'. That could hardly be further from the truth. Since the 18th century, the nature and future of Scots has attracted the attention of many exceptional thinkers and writers. Unfortunately, very little of this lengthy, multi-voice debate is easily accessible. Much is hidden in obscure and dense scholarly articles, dusty library books, newspaper archives, government documents, long-forgotten position papers and reports and, nowadays, social media posts. But even there you will not find a singular, definitive tale. This is Scotland, and we like to argue. I offer my own account here as a starting point, but my real aim in writing *Unlocking Scots* is to help you appreciate, reconnect with and hopefully participate in this rich discussion. As the inspirational writer and broadcaster Billy Kay reminded us, disagreement is almost obligatory when talking about Scots.

> It is a veritable tinder box of a subject, for although only a tiny group of people have had the opportunity to study it, everyone has very strong opinions on the matter.[1]

The reason is simple, those who study Scots are by necessity self-taught. Learning resources are sparse, and often focus on dialectical difference rather than Scots as a cohesive language system. The strong identity of local dialect traditions sometimes undermines a collective vision of Scots as a shared and shareable linguistic tradition, a 'public good' for all. The patchy academic scholarship on the subject, far from providing an objective perspective, often still frames Scots as a subordinate dialect to English. Many commentators from the British nationalist tradition oppose any expression of autonomous

1 Kay 1993:177

Scottish culture, so public discussion of the Scots language invariably triggers social media toxicity.

We still lack a communal perspective, so I have approached my task cautiously. I include many direct quotes from as wide a range of voices as I can, including writers, speakers, researchers, historians, linguists, academics, journalists, bloggers and tweeters. The wee footnotes are there so you can find the originals. To extend the argument, I have also included new ideas from sociolinguists, social theory, cultural studies, language rights and minority language revitalisation. If we can overcome some of the jargon, these disciplines can bring fresh and constructive outlooks that may challenge our long-fossilised attitudes and biases.

That said, I am not a historian, professional linguist or even a Scots language activist. I am simply a former, and now very rusty, native speaker. To borrow a quotation from the indefatigable Scots lexicographer William Graham, 'a much better-known authority should have been entrusted with the task of compiling such a work'.[2] Alas, in the meantime, you'll have to make do with me.

2 Graham 1977:8

Introduction

> The Scots language is a mark of the distinctive identity of the Scottish people; and as such we should be concerned to preserve it, even if there were no other reason, because it is ours. This statement requires neither explanation nor apology.[1]

IF SCOTS IS HISTORY'S GIFT to the Scottish people, it is a gift not always appreciated. I was lucky enough to be brought up in Scots-speaking areas of East Lothian, Fife and Perthshire in the late 1960s and early 1970s. All the wee bairns around me spoke Scots, as did most of the adults. I learned Scots naturally alongside Scottish English, usually mixing them, as was the habit in those parts. Scots was 'just the way we spoke', but it was always something more, too. Many of us mastered the skill of fine-tuning the density of our Scots and Scottish English mix on the fly; more Scots or more English depending on the circumstances. One Fife teacher even called us 'bilinguals'. She said we used one language in the classroom and another in the playground. I liked that idea.

My interest in Scots is not nostalgic, though, but political. As an adult I discovered that the everyday language of my childhood had been supressed and all but expunged from any serious debate about Scottish culture and politics. I might never have realised this at all, but in the early 1990s I spent much time in Barcelona. There I learned how Catalan, itself once proscribed, could be revitalised and restored to something like normality. Of course, post-Franco Spain was not the same as pre-devolution Scotland, but I slowly began to see my other native tongue in a new light.

Let us take a simple example. The *Manual of Modern Scots*, the first comprehensive grammar of the language, reached its centenary in 2021.[2] The *Manual* established the very foundation of our understanding of Scots as a language distinct from English. Its authors, William Grant and James Main Dixon, analysed the rich use of spoken Scots in 18th and 19th century Scottish literature. They described a structure and vocabulary that can still be recognised, albeit faintly at times, in modern Scottish vernacular. No native Scots speaker can read the *Manual* without feeling the joy of realising that the language they use (or used to use) every day has roots deep in Scotland's history.

1 McClure 1988, 1997

2 Grant and Dixon 1921

I know, you've never heard of the *Manual of Modern Scots*. Scots is still trapped in what the radical Brazilian educator Paulo Freire once called a 'culture of silence'; a silence caused by oppression. The subjugation of Scots was not primarily violent, though we know Scots-speaking school children were beaten for using their native tongue, but by something more insidious. Bairns had it drummed into them that their normal Scots speech was inferior and deficient. Novelist Val McDermid remembered her own experience.

> At school, we were told off when we slipped into Scots. Dialect words collided with the red pencil if they appeared in our written work and the only time they were permitted in our speech was in January, when we were practising our recitations for Burns Night [...] Inside the classroom, we tidied up our diction. But outside, I spoke guid braid Fife, ken.[3]

Learning standard English was beneficial for McDermid and the rest of us. But in that mission generations of bairns were denied knowledge of their native tongue. Its history and social significance were ignored, and the language they spoke at home often derided. In such repressive conditions people can internalise negative feelings about their language, and maybe even about themselves.

The language has become estranged from its speakers, and many feel alienated from their own way of speaking. Some do not believe their tongue is 'separate or even worthy of survival'.[4]

> Indeed, it is one of the saddest experiences of field work to find speakers of extremely 'dense' Scots refer to their language as 'slang'.

Another researcher, Johann Unger viewed the long-term stigmatisation of Scots as a 'social wrong'. He explained it as follows:

1. There is generally (even within Scotland) a lack of awareness that Scots can be regarded as a language (or even a legitimate language variety) that differs from English. Instead it is seen as 'just a dialect' (of English) or as 'bad English'.
2. Scots suffers from low prestige both amongst its speakers and amongst non-speakers, especially in most registers of its written varieties and in written contexts.
3. There has to date been a high level of discrimination against

3 McDermid 2021

4 Millar 2011:2

> Scots speakers in all areas of Scottish society and in many cases this is (knowingly or unknowingly) sanctioned by institutions and supported or at least allowed by official language policies.[5]

As a minority, non-official tongue, Scots is far from alone in suffering this type of injustice. Yet in recent decades many countries, especially in Europe, have taken significant steps to counter linguistic marginalisation, stigmatisation and discrimination. Generally speaking, 'authorities across the EU now tend to see linguistic diversity as a strength'.[6] In Scotland, official support for Scotland's other indigenous tongue, Gaelic, has been transformed, but not for Scots. Even though a third of the population speak Scots to some extent, the language remains largely ignored, and left to fragment and fade. A social wrong indeed.

5 Unger 2013:2

6 Leask 2021

CHAPTER ONE

How Scots Works

What is 'Scots' anyway?

> The single thing that always tells me I am home is when I hear Scots around me – in the street, on the bus, in the shops, in the pubs.[1]

SCOTLAND HAS A unique soundscape. It is usually the first thing noticed by new visitors and returnees alike. One guidebook put it, 'the Scots speak English with a varying accent – in places like Glasgow and Aberdeen, it can often be indecipherable'.[2] Practically all Scots speak Scottish English, characteristically accented, but recognisably a variant of English. However, about a third of the population can also use Scots, a quite distinctive form of speech. Scottish spoken language can sometimes seem like a dialect of English laced with 'Scotticisms',[3] but when people are chatting together informally, it sometimes shifts into what sounds to outsiders at least like a different language. As that is what it is.

> [W]hen Scots speakers use the full canon of their dialect, not only the sounds and words, but also the syntax and grammar, differ greatly from the English equivalent.[4]

Nonetheless, 'full canon' Scots is not the norm.

> Relatively few people speak unequivocal Scots on some occasions and unequivocal English on others […] The much commoner situation

1 McDermid, 2021

2 *Lonely Planet*, 2017

3 Scottish words and phrases

4 Kay 1993:17

> is that the language of a given individual will sometimes contain a greater and sometimes a lesser number of Scots forms.[5]

The mix itself is dynamic, and sometimes described as a 'continuum', or a scale with Scots at one end and English at the other.[6]

> It is quite possible – indeed necessary under most conditions – to speak about a continuum between dense varieties of Scots and the most standard forms of Scottish Standard English [...] Most Scots [...] 'commute' along this continuum on a day-to-day basis depending on context.[7]

Compare this with Gaelic speakers who can switch cleanly to English and back again, using either one language or the other. The Scots language, though, typically works alongside English on a 'more-or-less' basis. While in some areas speakers may be able to switch abruptly from broad Scots to fairly standard Scottish English (I have heard this in Shetland, for example), in the Central Scots area where I grew up the Scots component tended to fade in and out as needed.

A continuum implies the existence of both English (no-Scots) and Scots (no-English) poles. However, these two ends are not equivalent. The English end is taught formally and examined in Scottish schools. Scots vocabulary and grammatical structure are picked up haphazardly from family members, friends and the surrounding community. In the spoken language, therefore, knowledge and skills in Scots tend to be highly variable and usually locally inflected.

Scots is far more than a spoken variety. Until fairly recently, oral skills were backed up by knowledge of traditional Scots writing, poems and songs. Scots has a celebrated literary tradition that has long inspired a strong sense of autonomous identity, indeed its very 'languageness'. Something called Scots has been recognised for centuries, with thousands of words distinct from standard English. The *Concise Scots Dictionary*[8] alone contains 40,000 entries. Though even the most proficient Scots speaker nowadays would only know a fraction of them, the eminent Scots scholar J Derrick McClure was probably correct in saying, 'all of us know, or know roughly, or have some idea, of what is meant by "Lowland Scots"'.[9]

---

5 McClure 1979:27
6 Eg Aitken 1979
7 Millar 2018:3
8 Scottish Lang. Dictionaries 2017
9 McClure 1980:11

The assumed ability to define Scots, albeit loosely, underpinned a question in the 2011 UK Census that asked Scottish people to self-assess their abilities to speak, read and write Scots. When the results revealed that 1.5 million people claimed to be able to speak Scots, the obvious question arose, 'What does "speaking Scots" actually mean?'. Earlier Census researchers had provided a useful working definition.

> A person classified as speaking with a Scots accent would use the same words as an English-speaker but sound different; a person speaking with a dialect would choose words that are local variants of the 'mainstream' language; a person whose speech was classified as being a different language would use constructions of the language as well as vocabulary.[10]

The way that Scots is pronounced, as well as some words themselves, differs across regions. Local patterns of speech are grouped into 'dialects' such as Shetland/Shetlandic, Doric and Glaswegian, and these often evoke strong feelings of pride. Some claim such varieties are 'not Scots', but all Scots dialects are mutually comprehensible, and even the much-maligned urban varieties retain Scots roots in their words and structure.

Scots is unique to Scotland apart from an offshoot in nearby Ulster. It is spoken from the northern isles of Shetland and Orkney down the eastern coast, through the major central belt cities to the coast and rolling hills of Ayrshire, and all the way down to the Borders. Scots' southern limit corresponds to the country's frontier with England. The people on the other side may speak in their own distinctive manner but, despite sharing words with their northern cousins, few would consider what they say to be Scots. In comparison, Ulster Scots bears its unmistakably Scots origins with pride.

But is Scots really a language?

The question of whether Scots is a language or 'merely' a dialect of English, 'bad' English or even, a current favourite, 'slang', has disrupted discussions around Scots for a long time. According to Dick Leith, labelling Scots as a dialect (or worse) is just part of its marginalisation.

> The notion that Scots is at most a dialect of English has been communicated to most Scottish people [and] many Scottish people, like some speakers of English-based creoles, may feel that their tongue

10 Máté 1996:6

> is not different enough from English to justify calling it a separate language. In other words, it is linguistic criteria that are uppermost in their minds (as they are in the minds of most English people in their attitude to Scots): Scots sounds, grammar and vocabulary are close to those of English in a way that those of Gaelic, say, are not.[11]

So, what *is* the current expert opinion? In late 2019 The Open University (OU), published a two-part online course *Scots Language and Culture*.[12] With contributions from 16 prominent experts in the field and covering 20 topics, the course represents a snapshot of how the language/dialect/whatever debate has progressed over recent decades. The first thing of note is that Scots is treated throughout the course as a language. According to of one its authors, Simon Hall, 'most linguists and academics agree that Scots is a language in its own right'.[13] The claim was validated the following year when Peter Trudgill, the leading authority on the dialects of English, wrote: 'The indigenous languages of Britain are English, Scots, Welsh, and Scottish Gaelic'[14], confirming unambiguously, 'Of the non-English UK languages, Scots has the largest number of speakers, with 1.5 million'.

In the OU course, Hall listed reasons why Scots is now considered a language.

1. Along with Welsh, Scottish Gaelic, and Irish, Scots and Ulster Scots were formally classified as UK minority languages when the UK Labour administration ratified the European Charter for Regional or Minority Languages (ECRML) in 2001. Since then UK governments, Conservative and Labour alike, have acknowledged Scots as a language in regular ECRML reports. The Scottish Parliament also routinely uses the term 'language' to designate Scots, for example releasing its own *Scots Language Policy* in 2015.
2. Scots has a vast vocabulary, a range of unique grammatical features, a huge store of idiomatic expressions and sounds uncommon in English. Trudgill confirms, 'its pronunciation, grammatical structures, orthography, and vocabulary are significantly different from English', adding 'and so is its history'.[15]
3. Scots indeed has a long independent history. One of the 20th century's

11 Leith 1997:157

12 The Open University 2019

13 Hall 2019

14 Trudgill 2021a

15 Trudgill 2021b

leading Scots scholars, Jack Aitken, wrote of the 'ancient belief' dating back to the 15th century that 'there is an entity with some form of separate existence called the Scots language'.[16] Hall adds, 'It is the language of a magnificent, centuries-old literature, and was once a language of state used by kings, politicians and ordinary people alike'.[17]

4. Scots has its own 'dialects', including varieties used in the cities of Dundee, Edinburgh and Glasgow. Hall emphasises, 'It is important not to confuse these dialects of Scots with dialects of English, or to imagine that Scots is a dialect of English. So, the dialects of Caithness, Orkney or Shetland are varieties of Scots. The language used in the North East of Scotland and known as the Doric is a variety of Scots.'

Trudgill explains why definitions are so important.

> The status of a linguistic variety as a language or dialect is often more of a political, cultural and historical than linguistic matter, so to an extent it is a matter of perception.[18]

The idea is neatly summed up in the well-known maxim 'a language is a dialect with an army and navy', attributed to the scholar of Yiddish, Max Weinreich. It should be added though that academic linguists are nowadays wary of hierarchical labels like language and dialect, preferring the neutral term 'variety'.

What about the 'linguistic criteria', cited by Leith above? He was referring to 'mutual intelligibility', a staple of folk or popular linguistics, claiming that when two varieties are commonly understandable, they should be thought of as dialects rather than separate languages. Hence Gaelic and English are obviously different languages, but what about Scots and English? The first thing to consider is that the criterion of mutual intelligibility is problematic. The Scandinavian languages Swedish, Danish and Norwegian are largely comprehensible between each other and likewise Gaelic is partially intelligible to Irish speakers. Reflecting on the intelligibility criterion, Edinburgh-based linguist Graeme Trousdale believed Scots' relationship to English to be, 'a particularly good example of the problem', adding, 'It is the case that some speakers of Scots are not fully intelligible – even if they speak slowly – to some speakers of English'.[19] Trudgill, however, concludes that the Scots

16 Aitken 1982, 2015:2

17 Hall 2019

18 Trudgill 2021b

19 Trousdale 2010:6

versus English intelligibility criterion is meaningless anyway.

> Scots and English are historically closely related and linguistically similar – just as Norwegian and Danish are related and similar – and both pairs of languages are mutually intelligible to a fair degree.

As an aside, the website Elinguistics.net[20] hosts an intriguing 'genetic proximity calculator' comparing 170 languages. Lower proximity index figures represent linguistic closeness. The English–Scots pairing scores 10.2, Danish–Norwegian (Bokmal) is only 3.7 and Gaelic–Irish is 7.3. Even closer language pairs are Croatian–Serbian: 2.8, Afrikaans–Dutch: 2.9, Russian–Ukrainian: 3.4, Hindi–Urdu: 4.3 and Czech–Slovak: 5.7.

McClure summed up the case for Scots' linguistic autonomy:

> [S]ince Scots has at least as good a claim to be called a language as many other speech forms which are regularly so called, those who wish it to regard it as a language are fully entitled to do so; and the onus is on those who would deny it this status to prove that another classification is more appropriate.[21]

What kind of language is Scots?

Classifying 'full canon' Scots as a language on historical, political and linguistic grounds is perhaps the easy part. It is more challenging to try to describe how Scots functions as a language today, as it is not generally spoken in the 'idealised form'[22]. While Scots words and phrases can be heard in much of everyday Lowland Scottish speech, they are almost always mixed in various combinations with the dominant tongue, Scottish English. The *Concise Scots Dictionary* tries to capture this complexity.

> The language of contemporary Scotland can fairly be described as fluid. It is marked by a wide and highly variable range of speech-styles, ranging from the broad Scots of some fishing and farming communities, through various intermediate 'mixtures of Scots and English', to a variety of standard English spoken in a Scottish accent (ie SSE) [Scottish Standard English]. Even the last of these usages retains obvious affiliations with the more fully Scottish speech styles

20 Elinguistics.net 2021

21 McClure 1998:11

22 Millar 2020:6

> – in the accent with which it is pronounced [and] in the speakers' frequent recourse to repertory of Scotticisms…[23]

We are just not used to thinking about 'languages' operating in that way, and in the face of such formidable fuzziness, there has been a temptation to label all Lowland vernacular speech as 'Scots'. For example, in 1997 the Scottish National Dictionary lexicographer Iseabail Macleod stated that:

> [Scots] covers everything from dialects that the English – or other Scots – wouldn't understand, to the way we're speaking right now, which is English with a Scottish accent.[24]

If you are compiling lists of Scotticisms, an all-inclusive definition may be reasonable, but it undermines the case just made for Scots being a separate language system. An over-permeable classification also allows other scholars to label exactly the same complex that Macleod described as 'Scottish English'.[25]

We will explore mixing in more detail later, but in my view, hazy terminologies run the risk that the term 'Scots' becomes a nebulous descriptor rather than the name of a discrete language. To consider Scots as a normal minority language we require far more precise terminology, one that unambiguously identifies the Scots language components of Scottish Lowland vernacular. To this end, three distinct patterns of Scottish speech can be identified, drawing from the definitions above.

- *The Scots language*: Several (closely) related spoken dialects underpinned by a literary tradition employing established and prestigious (pan-dialect) orthographic conventions.[26] This is 'dictionary' Scots written or spoken at full canon. The use of the 'The' definite article here is significant.
- *Scottish Standard English (SSE)*: English pronounced with a Scottish accent and including a few Scotticisms.[27] Trudgill calls SSE, 'the local form of an originally non-local language which has become institutionalised and is spoken with a distinctive pronunciation and some distinctive words and grammatical structures'.[28]

23 Macleod and Cairns 2017:xiv
24 Quoted in Dossena 2005:15
25 Eg Stuart-Smith 2018
26 Eg Eagle 2011
27 Melchers and Shaw 2011
28 Trudgill 2021b

> *Scottish language*: The range of spoken mixtures forming a continuum between two poles, broad vernacular/dialectal Scots at one end, and SSE the other. Sometimes called *Scots language* but in both cases without the all-important 'The' definite article.

These terms are often used, but they are not typically defined in this precise way (or indeed in any way). The third definition maybe stands out. Surprisingly, there is no common term for the everyday dynamic mix of Scots and Scottish English. We lack a label such as *Spanglish*, which refers to a Spanish and English mix. The only term to hand is *Scottish* (or *Scots*) *language*. It is not very satisfactory, but at least has some authority, being the phrase favoured in the Scots language policy of Creative Scotland in 2015. The official body conspicuously dropped the 'the', stating, 'We recognise that Scots language is an integral part of Scotland's identity and cultural life'.[29] While this term may be taken as referring to the spoken mix, it is not actually defined as such.

By applying this type of clear classification, the 'languageness' of Scots as a recognisable component in vernacular Scottish language mix is made more distinct without denying the fluidity of the spoken blend. 'The Scots Language' still remains recognisable as a cohesive linguistic system, even if only used intermittently, if at all, in its entirety.

The 'no standards' myth

With these definitions in mind, I will next explore three areas often portrayed as problematic when discussing Scots as a language. These are *standards* (or lack thereof) for written Scots, *literacy* and *dialect variation*. All three are interconnected, as illustrated by this wonderful quote from Sir James Wilson, an unsung early pioneer of Scots linguistic field research. In the foreword to one of his monographs in 1915, Wilson observed as follows.

> [T]he Lowland dialects are not at all sharply divided from each other, so that there is little apparent ground for dealing with each of them separately. The tendency has been to consider Scottish speech as a whole, instead of as a collection of dialects, a view which has been greatly assisted by the use of a more or less standard form for literary purposes.[30]

29 Creative Scotland 2015a:2

30 Wilson 1915: Foreword

Writing at a time when Scots was arguably at its peak in terms of speaker numbers and general literacy, Wilson made two significant points. He notes firstly the cohesion of the spoken dialects and secondly that the sense of Scots as a unified national language was underpinned by a widely read literature written in something approaching a standard. Over the intervening century those core principles underpinning the languageness of Scots have been undermined, sometimes by its own champions. Let us start with the standards issue, seen variously over the years as a geeky irrelevance, an authoritarian menace to creatives, a death-sentence for dialects or an essential step for survival.

Despite its governmental recognition, Scots is rarely used in official settings. Last time I looked, even the Scottish Parliament in Edinburgh did not have any signage in the Scots language. The main justification for Scots' institutional invisibility is that it has 'no standards'. The mantra is repeated in almost all discussions around Scots. The ground-breaking *Scots Language and Culture* course opened with, 'As opposed to English and Gaelic, Scots is a non-standard language'.[31] *Scots Warks: Support and Guidance for Writing*, published by the authoritative Scots Language Centre (SLC) in 2021, makes the same point. 'Scots has no standardisation', it decalares, though adding it is 'something that has been debated for decades in the Scots language community'.[32]

While it is a truism to say that the Scots language has no *official* standard form, it seems a stretch to assert it has 'no standardisation' or even that it is 'a non-standard language'. History and common sense suggest quite the opposite. The *Manual* was published just six years after Wilson's quote above, and there was certainly a notion of a Scots standard at that time. A century later, a wide range of modern literature in Scots, supported by dictionaries, grammars and so on, still act as potential models of modern Scots. Do these publications have 'no standardisation'? Obviously, they do, but James Costa explained the nuance.

> While there is no Scots standard *de jure*, numerous debates have come to shape sets of expectations, if not of norms, as to what Scots should *de facto* look like [...] the writing of Scots is constrained by a number of covert rules, stratified through decades of academic and scholarly conversations.[33]

31 Warnecke 2019

32 Scots Language Centre 2021

33 Costa 2017:50

So, although there is no 'official' standard in the strict *Académie française* sense, after hundreds of years of printing Scots texts a soft standard has emerged. This covers spelling and structure but also recognises some dialectical and other variants. The standard is more subjective, diffuse and opinion-focused than we would think of as normal for a language, but written Scots certainly has conventions and traditions aplenty. As with any other language, such conventions can be respected or ignored. The SLC guidance confirms this; 'We do have well known spellings that are favoured and patterns of grammar and syntax that are uniquely ours'. Again, it is useful to distinguish *the* Scots language in its written form as the target for standardisation, rather than the vernacular Scottish language mix in all its richness and variety. There has never been any call to standardise spoken and dialectical Scots, an act generally considered neither desirable nor possible.

In my view, we should celebrate the communal 'soft standardisation' of written Scots just a little more, but where did these 'norms' come from? As we know from the opening section, the linguistic structure of literary and spoken Scots has been well documented for over a century. The first Scots dictionaries were published in the 19th century, and scholars began to chronicle the spoken and written language systematically in the early 20th century. More than 40 years ago, William Graham published the first edition of *The Scots Word Book*, a Scots-English and more significantly English-Scots wordlist[34] that would eventually find its realisation 20 years later in *The Essential Scots Dictionary*. In parallel, there have been various expert-led initiatives to 'harden' the traditional standards by suggesting stricter orthographic (spelling) rules.[35] Without governmental support these were easy to ignore.

Should Scots have an official standard written form anyway? It would not be difficult to stabilise and strengthen the existing soft standards. Much of the groundwork was done in the late 1990s to build on existing dictionary conventions. Apart from enabling official use of Scots, standardisation would formalise, clarify and document the 'linguistic distance' between Scots and (Scottish) English, so ratifying its languageness. Illustrating this very point, at the beginning of his textbook *An Introduction to English Sociolinguistics*, Trousdale challenged his readers.

> Consider the following language varieties: 'German', 'English', 'Scots', 'American'. Which of these are languages? Most people are of the opinion that German and English are definitely languages,

34 Graham 1977

35 Scots Spellin Comatee 1998

> American definitely not, and Scots is hard to classify [...] Because there is little consensus on the formal and functional differences between Scots and English, some people erroneously consider Scots to be 'bad English'.[36]

Standardisation, and its systematic official implementation, would go a long way towards ending this confusion, at least regarding the status of the Scots language itself. As a useful by-product, some long-overdue standardisation of Scottish English might be useful, too. We will revisit Scottish English in Chapter Six.

The loss of literacy

> Scots is too often seen as just an oral language, which suggests that it is not something you can be literate in. However, when you think about it, all languages are oral except for sign language.[37]

> But recently, for the first time, I've seen contemporary Scottish literature written in Scots. If people read a book in Scots and they see it legitimately written on a page in print, then we can start having discussions about how it's so connected to people's lives, often in ways they don't realise.[38]

A major part of Scots' claim for languageness is its written form. Widespread literacy in the language was implied in the 1915 quote from Wilson in the previous section. Half a century later, I learned to read Scots informally at home via the then-ubiquitous comics *Oor Wullie* and *The Broons* at much the same time as I learned to read standard English at school. But Scots was not entirely absent from our 1960s primary school classrooms either. We memorised poems by Burns and other Scots writers, most of which were written in the *Manual* style. In fact, Scots reading books containing stories, songs, and poetry were still being printed for schools until the early 1970s. However, the unbroken tradition of informal and folk literacy around Scots that had survived for centuries began to be weakened in the late 1960s and was all but obliterated over a couple of generations. The cost was not just 'literacy' in the technical sense, *Manual*-style Scots is still easily readable, but literacy as a broad cultural and shared community activity. I work in

36 Trousdale 2010:8

37 Briggs 2021:6

38 Len Pennie, quoted in Hinds, 2021

education, so it should come as no surprise that I am a big fan of all forms of literacy. You don't have to be a radical like Paulo Freire to recognise the importance of literacy to empower individuals and communities. By the same token, illiteracy can be seen as a weapon of social control.

But what happened to Scots in the 1960s? Just as language was becoming a powerful symbol of defiance and decolonisation in Catalonia and elsewhere, the cohesive literary identity of Scots began to be undermined. Eccentric *ad hoc* written representations of Scottish speech were promoted in both elitist poetry and popular comedy. Long-familiar print conventions, the very foundation of Scots dictionaries, were scorned in favour of avant-garde or amusing 'eye-dialect' spellings. These deliberately exoticised the written form and disconnected speakers from longstanding writing traditions. While often claiming to be anti-establishment, 'authentic' and radical, this literary trope had the real effect of further disempowering and marginalising Scots and its speakers. The written representation of Scots began to descend into DIY chaos and many Scots speakers who went to school from the 1970s onwards seem unaware that a consistent written form ever existed. The 1970s have been described as 'probably the nadir of education in Scots'.[39]

Here, I believe, is the origin of what Robert McColl Millar, a leading academic expert on the Scots language, refers to as *dislocation*, a disempowering separation of written and spoken forms of the language. Illiteracy was repackaged as authenticity; dictionaries were distained, and standardisation efforts condemned as fogeyish finger-wagging. Moreover, as fewer people spoke Scots regularly in its purest forms anymore, written texts that amplified the Scots components appeared forced or unnatural, especially to a new generation of readers who had rarely, if ever, seen full canon Scots in print.

One other reason for dislocation is more nuanced, and it stems from a century of discrimination between rural 'good Scots' and urban 'bad Scots' variants. Although this distinction has largely faded, it continues to cast a long shadow. Some writers dismiss 'dictionary' Scots as an idealised, rigid or purist form of the language, disconnected from both regional dialect and the fluid mixing of most vernacular speech. This positioning typically rejects any form of standardisation. It is difficult to overstate how bizarre this attitude is. Almost all other endangered minority languages, including Gaelic, view standardisation and expansion of the language as quite normal and indeed crucial for survival.

39 Commentary on Aitken 1981, 2015

What about the Scots dialects?

While written representations are essential in a highly literate society, written language always derives from speech, and gains its vitality from spoken forms. Linguists rightly talk about the 'primacy' of spoken language and, equally, speakers nowadays tend to judge any writing on their personal experience of spoken Scots. The Scots Language Centre guidance for Scots writers advises, 'listen to your own Scots voice: How does it sound when you say a phrase or sentence?'.[40] That voice is likely to have local tones. If the persistence of Scots as a recognisable component of Scottish vernacular speech is remarkable, just as noticeable is the distinctiveness of local varieties.

> I tell people in England or America that if you go out of Edinburgh into East Lothian or Fife, the accent and language changes. It's to Scotland's credit that such a small country can produce such diversity.[41]

Thus, as Millar said, 'there is no one way to speak Scots'.[42] Vernacular Scots is usually grouped into five main dialects: Insular (Orkney and Shetland), Northern (North-East Scots 'Doric'), Central (including the major urban dialects), Southern (mainly the Borders) and Ulster. Writer Thomas (Tammas) Clark believed Scots' very survival was a result of the tenacity of these local linguistic identities.

> So whit kept it alive fae then tae nou? Naethin but the spoken dialects o the wirkin classes. Borders Scots, Glesga Scots, Dundonian an Doric an Orkney Scots; these were the life-support machines that saved the tongue fae oblivion. These are the reasons wiv a language left tae talk aboot.[43]

Unfortunately, there is a downside. The decline in literacy, together with minimal media exposure, negligible political action and a lack of official standardisation have all undermined the holistic linguistic identity of Scots.

> Scots has been fragmented as a language and, with the dearth of broadcasting in the remaining dialects, very few people have first-hand experience of the spectrum of Scots which is spoken across the country.[44]

40 Briggs 2021:7

41 Irvine Welsh quoted in Trainer 2021

42 Millar 2018:198

43 Clark, T 2016

44 Kay 1993:133

Scots language champions sometimes fear people might have lost the idea that Scots ever existed as a national language. For example, after reminding visitors of the language status of Scots, the Scots Language Centre website continues:

> Scots is the collective name for Scottish dialects known also as 'Doric', 'Lallans' and 'Scotch' or by more local names such as 'Buchan', 'Dundonian', 'Glesca' or 'Shetland'.

It is hard to imagine equivalent Gaelic or Welsh resource centres describing their languages as 'a collection of dialects', though it is just as truthful for those tongues. A natural consequence of this misconception is a claim that the Scots dialects are so different from each other they should be considered as different languages. North-East Scots is widely called (The) Doric nowadays and, as Billy Kay remarks, half-jokingly, 'appears to have declared UDI from Scots',[45] UDI here being a unilateral declaration of independence.

From a linguistic standpoint, the various dialects, when spoken in a reasonably pure form, are distinctive phonetically and in terms of local words used, but remember back in 1915 Wilson observed they were, 'not at all sharply divided from each other'. After a century of dialect erosion and population movement, it is hard to imagine the dialects are any more divergent now. Andy Eagle made the same point more recently regarding the underlying cohesion of current spoken Scots.

> [T]he differences between the (broad) Scots dialects are not as 'striking' as they may at first appear, all Scots dialects share the same underlying phonological system and much the same syntactical and morphological conventions. The different pronunciations of the same general Scots words are largely predictable, the differences are more often than not on the level of accent, particularly among the Central Scots dialects spoken south of the Tay.[46]

Kay is particularly critical of the 'myth' that Scots is only intelligible within a small local area and that, 'one dialect speaker cannot communicate with another one from a different area'. This has served to reduce the public use of Scots and reinforce 'the local rather than the national identity with the tongue'.[47] In the OU course mentioned earlier, Bruce Eunson appreciated

45 Kay 1993:157

46 Eagle 2011

47 Kay 1993:157

the 'passion and feeling of pride' evoked by Scots dialects, but also saw the downside of only highlighting the local.

> Whilst recognition of this element of Scots language is essential to properly grasp the sense of identity Scots speakers from different parts of Scotland have, the over-emphasis placed by Scots speakers on the diversity aspect of the language is one of the reasons for the division that keeps Scots language from truly uniting as a language with a community of 1.5 million speakers, and may hinder the chances of the figure rising in the future.[48]

Later in the OU course, Ashley Douglas implied there may even be a 'divide and rule' political rationale behind this.

> In the past, some politicians have been more likely to view Scots as a disparate group of dialects, as opposed to a coherent national language. They are also often more likely to be supportive to a regional dialect – such as Doric.[49]

Scots as 'nobody's child'

Turning to politics, civic activism to promote Scots is noticeably weaker than that of most other minority languages including, of course, Gaelic. There are four reasons I can think of for this.

1. Nowadays, Scots is mainly spoken in working-class and rural communities who may lack the resources and social capital to self-organise. By contrast, Gaelic has a determined and organised cadre of middle-class champions able to campaign for it. A self-sustaining Gaelic infrastructure, providing services associated with Gaelic culture and language, has gradually been built up over decades, supported by public funding. None of this exists for Scots.
2. Gaelic also benefits from having a readily available template for Celtic minority language revitalisation, derived from Welsh and Irish. Gaelic is therefore promoted not just because it is the right thing to do (which it is) but also because the government knows *what* to do. Scots is more complex, still stigmatised and is spoken in that perplexing mix with

48 Eunson 2019:21

49 Douglas 2019:13 (In her breakthrough 2016 study on the politics of Scots, Douglas coined the resonant term 'naebody's bairn', possibly an echo of Scottish singer Sydney Devine's famously maudlin 1974 hit 'Nobody's Child', a poignant metaphor for abandonment.)

Scottish English. Without a revitalisation roadmap for Scots, and in the absence of popular agitation to demand one, Scots requires 'top-down' governmental action. In this regard, Scots faces yet another barrier, this time political.

3. The lack of political support is the most limiting factor for Scots. The unionist parties (Labour, Conservatives and Liberal Democrats), who have collectively dominated Scottish politics for most of my lifetime, have a history of voting down Scots-positive policies, maybe fearing such a potent symbol of Scottish identity. The Scottish National Party (SNP), once the natural champions of Scots, are nowadays ambivalent. Their former enthusiasm waned noticeably when so many people declared themselves to be Scots speakers in the 2011 Census. Perhaps the party began to consider the potential economic costs of support for Scots, and thus the political benefits of maintaining their own culture of silence. Only now, at the time of writing, is some political interest stirring again with the Scottish government's 2022 consultation on proposed legislation to ensure the long-term growth of Gaelic and Scots.[50]
4. Scots does not follow traditional notions of a 'normal' language bound by purity and regularity. This has consequences not only for describing the language, but also for its use in education and government. According to Millar, 'the lack of a strong idea of what Scots is probably leads to non-linguists shying away from too much discussion of the matter'.[51]

The outcome of such cloudy, competing and contradictory notions of Scots has been political and policy paralysis. Existing government action is ineffective, underfunded and slow to implement, often appearing cynical or tokenistic. Policies and statements may refer to Scots as a minority language on occasion, but far more frequently it is framed as a hazily defined cultural asset or creative resource. Even if public and political interest is resurfacing, vague and varied views on what Scots is and what to do with it undermine any attempts at consistent and ambitious action, especially when such initiatives run the risk of being scrutinised by a hostile press and possibly sceptical public.

The existential threat

In 2021 Scots was named on a list of 12 UK and European languages that are at risk of extinction.[52] The ranking was based on the UNESCO system with

50 Scottish Government 2022

51 Millar 2005:195

52 Hebditch 2021

its six levels to determine how at-risk each language is. Rather than being decided by the number of speakers, classifications are mostly determined by the 'intergenerational transmission' of a language, that is whether older speakers pass on the language to their offspring. As Millar put it: 'Everything flows from this relationship'.[53] He reports that even in its supposedly North East heartlands, the bairns are simply not learning Scots from the people around them.

The reasons are both social and economic. Older people, who in previous generations would have passed on their spoken language to their grandchildren, are now more isolated. Use of Scots in the workplace is disappearing as locally-based manual labour declines. Leisure is increasingly anglicised; English-only radio, cinema, and television have long been thought of as dangers to Scots, and online social media is overwhelmingly in English. At the Scots end of the continuum, the distinctive grammar, vocabulary, pronunciation and expressions are in decline. Simply put, adults now use fewer Scots structures and do not pass on what they do know to their bairns. With little exposure to Scots in schools and the media to counterbalance it, Scots terms are becoming less common and thus less useful. After all, it is pointless to use Scots words and phrases if you think no one 'gets' them. To save face, the natural tendency is to shift your speech habits to the English end of the continuum.

Will Scots become a hobby language like Manx ? On the Isle of Man the last native speaker of Manx died in 1974 and the language is now preserved by enthusiasts. Scots will not perish just as dramatically as that. As Millar put it:

> [S]heer numbers of speakers mean that there is unlikely to be a time when a 'no speaker' outcome will be possible. That these varieties will be less Scots and have more affinities with colloquial forms of (Standard) English is extremely likely.[54]

He notes that spoken Scots usages compete with and are influenced by the ubiquitous and dominant vernacular forms of English. Millar is concerned that, with the loss of its Scots components, colloquial Scots language and maybe, by extension, Scots itself will become dialectised. It may mutate into the 'real' dialect of English that it never was historically. If this continues, Scots may one day be reduced to just an accent, and even accents are vulnerable to globalisation. By the end of the century, our distinctive Scottish soundscape may be reduced to a faint murmur in the wind.

53 Millar 2020:13

54 Millar 2020:189

'Ye'r no deid yet!'

Before we fall completely into despondency, the 'death of Scots' has long been predicted. Yet the language miraculously, defiantly, survives.

> The Scots language can be heard in almost every community in Scotland. For many it is an integral part of Scottish life and is heard on a daily basis in the workplace, at sports and communal events, in shops and in the family.[55]

When the UK government finally conceded to include a question on Scots in the 2011 Census, one suspects they were secretly hoping that the 'inconvenient tongue' was dead, or nearly so. If so, the outcome was a shock. Over one and a half million people in Scotland identified themselves as Scots speakers, indeed more speakers than all other indigenous UK minority languages combined. Some had assumed that Scots had retreated to heartland areas such as Aberdeenshire and Shetland, but the Census revealed that Scots is still spoken all over Scotland, from the cities to the Highlands. At last there was real data to prove 'beyond doubt' that the Scots language remained a significant part of many people's lives.[56]

The release of the Census figures in 2013 should have been a cause for celebration, a joyous affirmation of Scottish identity and culture. Unfortunately, the timing could hardly have been worse. In the period leading up to the 2014 independence referendum, Scottish identity was politicised and the Census results were suppressed. The official response was to belittle Scots speakers' ability to rate their own abilities, and then to try to dismiss the inconvenient result as 'bad data'.

Scots speakers have a right to expect a lot more. Any language that has endured seven centuries, most of them without government backing or money, ignored by politicians and scorned by educators, deserves a little more love, and a little more understanding.

What next for Scots?

> Scots is certainly not a dialect, for the simple reason that it includes numerous different dialects; but with equal certainty it is not a language in the full sense of that English and French are languages.[57]

55 Fitt 2019:1.2

56 Fitt 2019:8

57 McClure 1998:11

For all the official and scholarly declarations of the language status of Scots, it still languishes in a linguistic limbo; not a dialect, slang or bad English, but not quite a language either. What McClure means by 'full sense' in the quote above is that Scots has not yet been developed and used as an official language with official standards. The German linguist Heinz Kloss infamously labelled Scots as a *Halbsprache* ('half language'). Writing in 1967, Kloss made a distinction between *Abstand* languages and *Ausbau* languages. *Abstand* languages are 'standalone' due to their inherent linguistic individuality (eg English versus Gaelic) while *Ausbau* languages are built up by a conscious effort of language planning and especially standardisation (eg Norwegian versus Swedish). In his original binary model, varieties that are neither *Abstand* nor *Ausbau* were classed as dialects. Scots, predictably, does not fit into simple binary distinctions and in 1984 Kloss came up with the *Halbsprache* concept for limbo varieties like Scots and Luxembourgish. In my view, 'half' seems rather uncharitable, given Scots' linguistic richness and literary standards. Perhaps *Fastsprache* (almost language) would have been more accurate term. Ironically, Scots' fellow *Halbsprache*, Luxembourgish, achieved official *Ausbau* status and since 1984 has been developed to be used both officially and in education.

Many of its supporters believe Scots should be treated as a full minority language like Gaelic, with at least some of the status, educational structure, speaker rights and financial support that entails. The recently formed Oor Vyce campaign group lists its demands, 'tae increase the provision and fundin fir Scots and pit forrit the presence o the Scots leid in Scotland's cultur and public life'.

- Giein the leid offeecial status wi a Scots Leid Act providin for the foonin o a statutory Scots Leid Board.
- Contributin tae public policy and political processes tae mak sure that Scots is taen tent o in futur leid policies.
- Giein Scots a position as a ilkaday wirkin, livin and eedicational leid at the hairt o Scottish society wi equal status tae the English, the Gàidhlig and the British Sign leids.
- Giein Scots a position as an offeecial national leid o Scotland, baith in law an fact.

If we really want to save this unique aspect of our culture, and, in Oor Vyce's words, 'mak siccar that Scots' lang history hauds forrit in the 21st century an ayont', Scots speakers and non-speakers alike must find a way to 'unlock' Scots from the cage of ignorance and bias that we have allowed it to rot in for far too long. And do it quickly, as time is always the enemy of any minority language, especially one labelled 'at risk'.

As we will see, it is not difficult to envisage a pragmatic and workable revitalisation strategy to stabilise and develop the Scots language by applying the basic principles discussed so far. But that is not the point. More importantly, we must strengthen our linguistic attachment to a tongue that has received so little affection over the last three centuries. We need to better understand its strengths and address its weaknesses. It is easy to agree Scots is a language, but what kind of language do we want it to be? What do we want to achieve with it? What does Scots mean to our linguistic and national identity? These are challenging questions; to unlock Scots fully we may end up having to unlock far more than our language.

CHAPTER TWO

The Social Life of Scots

Scotland, 'we have a problem'

ON A RAINY morning in January 2016, something strange and, to some, shocking was spotted in Scottish newsagents. *The National*'s front-page headline read 'Stairhead rammy: Labour faw apairt efter Blairites get their jotters'. For the first time in nearly a century, a mainstream(ish) national newspaper was using the Scots language for fairly normal purposes. The pro-independence tabloid had not 'went aw Scots,' as was later claimed, but was simply publicising a new column in Scots by author Matthew Fitt. In his own words:

> But jings or whit! A Scottish newspaper prentin somethin in the Mither Tongue and it isnae a poyum or a cartoon. Either Scots is teeterin on the verge o awmaist bein taen seriously, or it has been decidit by a cabal o heidbummers somewhaur that the auld leid is feenished, politically haunless and could nae langer herm a hornie golach sae why no embrace it? I hae a sleekit feelin it micht be tae dae wi the recent shooglin o seismic proportions in the foonds o Scotland but whit dae I ken? Whitever the wey o it, it's guid tae be here.[1]

Fitt's first article outlined the nature and history of Scots, concluding:

> Scots isnae sae much a minority language as a miracle language, in that it's a miracle it's no deid.

The newspaper's boldness triggered an unexpectedly emotionalised response. From that Thursday to the following weekend, I followed Twitter and social media traffic. Most messages were broadly supportive, but aggressive

1 Fitt 2016a

anti-Scots trolling quickly poisoned the discussion.

Many Tweeters performed the classic Scottish Cringe; 'what an absolute embarrassment', 'unbelievably cringey', 'what a joke', 'WotDaHell is wrong with you cretins'. Others were dismissive; 'That is not a language that is the corruption of language by ignoramuses', 'I genuinely thought this was a spoof', 'the nonsense purporting to be the Scots language', 'The phenomenon of Scottish people pretending this is 'Scots' is so odd', 'Stop trying to legitimise slang', 'There's Scots slang and then there's this!!!!'. A few people on Twitter appeared to be genuinely distressed; 'spoiled the only paper I read... No paper tomorrow then – no such language', and others seemed to be almost in denial; 'I'm NO cringing and Scots is NO a language I've never even met anybody who speaks Scots', 'Nobody in Scotland talks like that. Not a single soul. Embarrassing', 'Only slang and that's hard on the ears'.

Self-styled experts weighed in with arguments only marginally more nuanced; 'a reminder that what people call "Scots" these days is (mostly) a dialect, not a language', tweeted journalist Alex Massie, later warming to his theme, 'No. Scots can be a language; the Scots most people think of as Scots is not a language'. Another DIY linguist declared, 'It's perfectly comprehensible to any English speaker. This still falls within dialect boundaries'. 'It's slang, people,' proclaimed unionist pundit Stephen Daisley.

Others attempted to criticise Fitt's and the newspaper's actual language as bad Scots; 'This looks more like a mish-mash of local dialects', 'Hybrid and inconsistent, mixing together various regional forms and English borrowings', 'They confuse Scots with bad English. Their Tweet referring to "the morrow's" paper was toe-curling', 'Actually using the expressions stairheid rammy or get their jotters isn't really Scots, it's just novelty, if anything it mocks the language'. The utility of Scots was inevitably aired; 'Dialects are hard for others to understand, Scotland needs to look outward', 'If Scots want to do business overseas, we need to speak standard English', 'People who think Scots is a language: tell a job interviewer you're bilingual. Then tell me about the amazing job you didn't get'. Perhaps the most wretched keyboard warriors used their own limited knowledge of Scots to disparage it; 'Pure keech', 'Haw, yoose, that's jist a pyoor riddy. Who's yir Editor, OorWullie?

I wasn't the only was taken aback by the torrent of toxicity. David Leask of the *Sunday Herald* reflected:

> Whether it is road signs in Gaelic, or our sister paper, *The National*, printing articles in Scots, there is something about native languages

> that enrages a certain kind of unionist. This is not surprising: linguistic differences, even relatively small ones, tend to provoke a visceral response in ethnic nationalists of any stripe, anywhere in the world. And that, of course, includes British ones.[2]

'But why', asked Leask, 'do so many of us seem to despise our native tongues?'. The baggage of centuries of 'linguistic oppression', he argued, was not the only issue. Perhaps even more disheartening was that 'nobody seems to be remotely interested in the actual languages involved or the academic discipline of linguistics'. The Twitter tsunami exposed that many people lacked the basic vocabulary to discuss Scots in anything other than heightened emotional tones. Tweeting the following year, Leask found himself, 'fascinated and increasingly alarmed by attacks on once oppressed indigenous languages, Gaelic & Scots, after a period of consensus'. Gangs of online bullies had attempted to shame an everyday component of many people's Scottish identity, the way they speak. Leask concluded:

> This is not at all healthy. Of course, people live with the baggage of historic state-sanctioned prejudice against local speech. And, of course, such prejudice is intertwined with crude class snobbery (Scots in particular is associated with urban poor or rural folk). Combine this bigotry – because that is what it is – with poor levels of general linguistic knowledge & we have a problem.[3]

Scots language champion Billy Kay had recognised the same problem.

> With no grounding in their culture, objective assessment of its worth is well-nigh impossible and frequently people react with a passion which astonishes outsiders.[4]

The dismal affair should have punctured any 'guid conceit' of Scotland as an open-minded and progressive country. Many societies have long since moved beyond such primitive linguistic bigotry. The European Charter for Regional or Minority Languages (ECRML) expresses its progressive position succinctly.

> Regional or minority languages are part of Europe's cultural heritage

2 Leask 2016a

3 Leask 2017

4 Kay 1993:176

> and their protection and promotion contribute to the building of a Europe based on democracy and cultural diversity.

Scotland in the 21st century appears to be lagging way, way behind.

Groundhog Day

Sadly, writing this in late 2021 an award-winning young Scottish poet, Len Pennie, felt she had to leave Twitter, where she had over 100,000 followers after year-long 'vile abuse' from internet trolls. St Andrews student Pennie, who had sprung to popularity online for her 'Scots Word of the Day' and performances of her poetry, had been targeted, 'often by older men and anonymous Twitter accounts, leaving her on the receiving end of misogynous hate'. Pennie was also attacked by unionist Twitter users, 'who have suggested her use of her native Scots is contrived and promotes separatism'.[5] Many fellow artists came to her defence. The Scottish folk singer Iona Fyfe, for example, cited similar tales of online aggression throughout the year. She said she did not tend to receive abuse for singing in Scots but, 'when she speaks or writes social media updates in the language, that's when her Twitter feed is hit hard'.[6]

While some of the attacks on both artists appeared to be misogynistic, it was usually the use of Scots that triggered hostility.

> There's something strangely repetitive about the history of the Scots language in modern Scotland. In every generation, it seems that some Scots begin to grasp the truth that the working-class language they hear around them is not just an incorrect and sloppy form of English, but the fragmented legacy of a Scots tongue that was once, 500 years ago, the proud language of the entire Scottish state, reflecting the whole range of human affairs from law, religion, philosophy and romance, to the flyting (arguing) and comedy we now tend to associate with it. Yet in every generation it seems that that recognition flickers, only to fade again; and to talk to the young Scots-language poet Len Pennie about her work, is to realise that some of the old dismissive myths and assumptions about the Scots tongue have barely shifted in half a century.[7]

5 Meighan 2021

6 Mackie 2021

7 McMillan 2021

To tackle a few of these myths, we will need to look 'under the bunnet' to see how Scots works in modern Scottish society. The following sections are a quick beginner's guide to some useful perspectives from sociolinguistics. We will then revisit a few of the more difficult issues raised in Chapter One armed with this knowledge.

The sociolinguistics of The Proclaimers

As we saw in the last chapter, Scots does not play nicely with conventional notions of language, so we will need to turn to sociolinguistics, the study of how language works in society, to help us untangle things and improve our linguistic knowledge. Despite its uninviting academic label, I have found this branch of language study to be down-to-earth, practical and appealingly human-centred.

Why not start with a song? Most Scottish people will know 'Throw the 'R' Away', the 1987 hit by the Scottish duo The Proclaimers. The song's main premise is that the pronunciation of the R at the end of words like 'car' indicates Scottish vocal identity. Dropping the R to say something like 'cah' implies submission to southern English cultural norms, where the so-called *post-vocalic R* sound is rarely voiced. Simple differences in pronunciation (they mention *vowel flattening*, too) carry so many social implications that the twins could write an entire song about them. Uncovering these connections is the mission of sociolinguists, and Scotland turns out to be a pretty good place to study it.

> For sociolinguists living in Scotland, life is exhilarating and exhausting. Step out on the streets of Lerwick, Aberdeen, Glasgow, Edinburgh, Skye and be prepared for the 24/7 assault on your researcher ear.[8]

Sociolinguistics as a discipline emerged only in the 1960s. William Labov, an American linguist, was among the first to recognise how the then novel technology of the portable tape recorder could help researchers discover the ways people really spoke. In his most famous study, he recorded how people from various social classes behaved in downtown New York. The same post-vocalic R that The Proclaimers would sing about a generation later was also sometimes voiced in that city. However, unlike in England, 1960s New Yorkers thought sounding the R was classy. Labov discovered that when speakers were paying attention to their style – he made them read out word lists – they pronounced the R more distinctly. They used it far less when

8 Lawson 2014:xiii

telling an animated personal story. In formal settings, then, New Yorkers attempted to make their speech sound more prestigious. By listening to just a few specific sound differences, researchers soon discovered that everyone modifies their speech depending to whom they are speaking, and the social situation they find themselves in. The formality of the context, gender, education, local factors and, most importantly, class all have significant impacts on people's patterns of speech.

This descriptive tradition still dominates much of academic sociolinguistics in Scotland. A good example is Glasgow University's, Sounds of the City project that tracked sound changes in isolated elements of Glasgow speech.[9] 'Throw the 'R' Away', however, is less concerned with the sound itself than the social and political forces that drive change. Why do Scottish people feel the need to adopt imported speech norms? This type of question characterises 'a sociolinguistics of people'.[10] Here linguistic change is not assumed to be neutral or 'natural', but an outcome of unequal power dynamics between linguistic groups. When working with minority languages like Scots, some sociolinguists believe the inquiry should always go beyond simple description and try to uncover how social and historical factors shape and limit our language use. Only by exposing often-hidden ideologies can we hope to address linguistic inequalities.

Trainspotting and the dynamics of Scots

To illustrate the everyday dynamics of language choice, Miriam Meyerhof includes a fictional Scots speaker early in her 2010 US textbook *Introducing Sociolinguistics.*

> Take the case of Jennifer, who grew up in a small traditionally fishing village in the north-east of Scotland, but spent many years teaching English in Greece. Jennifer can draw on a number of different styles or ways of speaking depending on who she's talking to. If her interlocutor is a member of her family, she still uses a variety of Scots which is virtually incomprehensible to other native speakers of English. She says 'fit' instead of 'what'; 'na' instead of 'don't'; 'doon' instead of 'down'; 'be'er' instead of 'better', and so forth. But in Greece she quickly learnt that she needed to adopt a less regionally marked way of speaking if her students were going to understand her.[11]

9 Glasgow University 2014

10 Costa et al 2017:1

11 Meyerhoff 2006:1

We all do this, knowingly or not. Sociolinguists look for patterns in the way we use words, phrases and syntax in everyday conversation. They concentrate on forms with recognised alternatives, so-called linguistic *variables*, such as 'doon' and 'down' in the example above. Following Labov's initiative, researchers soon found that people in all language communities use a wide range of pronunciations, vocabulary, grammar and styles (formal and informal) on a regular basis, referred to as their linguistic repertoire. This means they can communicate roughly the same information in a variety of ways, depending on the social context. The informal crack of the home or a pub is very different from the formal style or register of the workplace. We learn the trick very early in school when our teachers warn us that our playground banter is unacceptable in the classroom. In formal settings, bairns must learn to use different words, idioms and even grammar. The linguistic taming continues into adulthood. One of Ronald Macaulay's interviewees in his 2005 study on everyday Scottish language described feeling that, in official contexts, 'You've got to [...] match them, sort of style', but then added, 'when I'm among my ain, I just talk whatever wey that suits me.[12] Using Scots in a Scottish language mix is a real, if underappreciated, skill and some people become very good at it. In his 1993 novel *Trainspotting*, Irvine Welsh played with the sociolinguistic potential of deliberate language manipulation. In one memorable scene the Edinburgh Scots-speaking hero Renton, in court for shoplifting, employs formal legalistic language such as 'I am no longer indulging in self-deception' with the magistrate to feign repentance. In linguistic terms, Renton was able to draw on his repertoire of Edinburgh Scots and formal English vocabulary. He was clearly able to differentiate both forms, use the prestigious legalese and at the same time eliminate the Scots variables from his speech.

Sociolinguists often describe this type of language as *style shifting* or *code switching*. Shifting is associated with styles or registers within a language and switching with multilingual communities where individuals can jump between quite distinct varieties or languages. Several studies have shown, though, that in practice style shifting and code switching overlap.[13] So-called switchers can also shift gradually and mix the two varieties. Thus, terms like *language crossing, language mixing and translanguaging* have all been coined to describe the subtle and sophisticated interchange between styles, varieties and languages.

Jennifer turns to standard English with her students to communicate outside her language community. Her motivation to shift or switch is clear.

12 Macaulay 2005:157

13 Eg Smith and Durham 2012

Inside a language group, the motivation is more subtle. Renton manipulated language to create a specific impression on the judge. The way we speak, whether consciously or unconsciously, conveys not just information but a shared social meaning to the listeners. Skilled raconteurs like Renton can exploit these features to express and negotiate identity in 'real time' while they speak. In a formal space such as a courtroom people are expected to use a formal style, so any informal speech is noticeable (or, as linguists say, *marked*) and could be construed as being deliberately disrespectful. Not everyone is as able (or willing) to play this linguistic game. In a famous case the same year as Welsh's book was published, a Sheriff held an 18-year-old lad in contempt for repeated use of the emblematic Scots word 'aye' in his court.[14]

A closely linked sociolinguistic notion is *solidarity*. Returning to our *Trainspotting* example, in everyday speech Renton uses the informal vernacular of Edinburgh to express solidarity with his pals, but in the courtroom employs more formal English to establish cultural solidarity with the magistrate. Solidarity here implies belonging to the same social group, with an assumption of shared values, attitudes and cultural references. It can represent a bond of familiarity and camaraderie, or occasionally the opposite: social distance, strangeness or unequal status. Solidarity is a language dynamic particularly relevant to Scots. Our speech patterns tend to converge in groups when we want to show a degree of social commonality with our audience, so-called *accommodation*. Conversely, conscious linguistic divergence can emphasise difference in status or identity. Subtle modifications in style, code or language can thus be used deliberately to imply or reinforce a social identity or status markedly different from that of the audience.

At an individual level then, sociolinguistic theory would predict that in Scotland, as elsewhere, individual speakers who have the skills may switch and shift between one variety and another in a predictable way. In the past, though, scholars assumed such choices were largely arbitrary, even chaotic.

> [B]efore the advent of modern sociolinguistic research, many linguists had believed variation in language to be unstructured, with random groups of speakers retaining random pronunciations.[15]

Such views may be due for an update.

A person's language choices are clearly moulded by the wider speech community to which they belong, and certain words and phrases tend to

14 *The Scotsman* 2002

15 Trousdale 2010:107

become associated with, or even vital for, specific social settings or *domains*. Informal domains are home, family, friends, and formal ones are schools, work, and official business. For minority tongues like Scots, language choices or patterns of use in separate domains become particularly meaningful. Marginalised (ie non-official) languages are typically relegated to the domestic, family and informal spheres, and are excluded, neglected and even forbidden in more formal settings like schools and courtrooms.

Diglossia: You'll take the high road and I'll take the low road

This idea of a division of linguistic roles, *diglossia*, dates back to the work of Charles Ferguson in 1959.[16] In its most basic form, diglossia implies that a community speaks two distinct varieties or languages, one with high prestige (often called H) and the other with low prestige, predictably named L. H is preferred in formal contexts and L is avoided, and vice versa. Education and the media reinforce the association of H with authority and modernity. Sociolinguist Janet Holmes states that diglossia is based on an uneven power dynamic, and 'this situation tends to characterise colonised countries with a clear-cut social class division: ie the elite speak one language and the lower classes another'.[17] In Scotland, anglicisation has often been described as a form of 'cultural colonisation'.[18]

> As an imposed language, English has a symbolic value clearly different from that of the minority languages. On one hand, as the official language of a power often regarded as alien and remote, it has often been redolent of authority and high social status. It also became, of course, the language of social aspiration and economic advancement.[19]

In such societies the H variety, in our case Scottish English, has also acquired a more technical or formal vocabulary and is standardised via officially endorsed grammars, dictionaries and education. In diglossic societies, L is always more variable, is maybe unstandardised and is principally a spoken form. Holmes observes pointedly, 'people generally do not think of the L variety as worth describing'.[20] Counterbalancing this, L is generally

16 Ferguson 1959
17 Holmes 2008:31
18 Eg Kay 1993:13
19 Leith 1997:151
20 Holmes 2008:29

considered richer in domestic and feelings-based or affective expressions and may have a special value in the community in conveying authenticity, emotion and social solidarity. L therefore lends itself to humour and sentimentality, not coincidentally the way Scots is usually framed by the media.

Is Scottish language really diglossic? Scots is unquestionably an informal L variety (sometimes termed *code*), with Scottish (Standard) English as the H variety, but Millar is cautious.

> [T]he last century has seen the former diglossia broken down in Scotland with a rather more confused and confusing pattern of usage being realised. Instead of code shifting between Scottish Standard English and Scots, many – perhaps most – speakers code mix, employing features of both the varieties in an apparently random way which quite probably suggests that that the two codes are no longer kept separate in speakers' minds. [21]

We will explore the whole notion of 'randomness' in the next section, but in the meantime, Holmes contends that in diglossic situations the notion of discrete varieties is rather idealised. As with other areas of linguistics, differences are usually a matter of degree. Whether speakers are aware which variety they are speaking may not be particularly important. Note also that Millar's implication of linguistic deficit is also a common theme in describing Scottish language, and one we will come across frequently.

Diglossia seems to me a useful model for describing Scottish language and the interplay between Scots and Scottish English. A powerful example is the 2012 study by Elizabeth Eustace on diglossic power relationships in the Scottish service industry. She observed that in corporate environments the distinctive Glasgow speech style of her interviewees was not 'associated with service excellence'. A consequence was that unemployed Glaswegian respondents said they avoided retail and hospitality work. Glaswegians who were employed in this sector tended to adopt various coping strategies to overcome discrimination. One individual she interviewed crossed fluidly to English in the presence of senior management and another learned standard English service scripts but continually worried about 'slipping up', ie, using Scots. In general, Eustace found employees had to:

> regulate themselves to perform linguistically depending on context and situation and the perceived status of the speakers, possibly to

21 Millar 2018:10

> achieve solidarity or positive face (to be liked by others), but at a cost of subsuming Scots identity.

For one interviewee the constant subservience was too stressful, claiming 'ye shouldnae try tae chynge'. As the researcher describes it:

> [Her] sense of worth in her social working class identity as a Glasgow Scots dialect speaker is validated as she repudiates claims to change her speech style [...] she defies them and in so doing defines herself as taking control of the situation, refusing to be scripted or regulated to represent middle class 'polite' or 'cultured' society.

Class attitudes and views on Scots are closely entwined, as we will see soon.

Dinna nix the mix

Scots scholar Marina Dossena considers the Scots-Scottish English complex to be 'one of the most distinct cases of linguistic co-existence'.[22] Nevertheless, it is still oddly under-researched when compared with equivalent translanguaging situations elsewhere. One reason may hark back to the old notion of *linguistic deficit*, with the possible implication that Scottish vernacular language is so flawed it barely warrants serious study. Consider the author's use of 'improper' in the following.

> [T]he coexistence of the Scots dialects with StE [Standard English] can be described as improper bilingualism, since speakers of both varieties cannot be said to operate with two linguistic systems, but rather with a variable bi-polar linguistic system, or dialect-standard continuum.[23]

The view that Scots and Scottish English mixing is somehow unsatisfactory or even unseemly is still widespread. Even renowned Scots scholar Jack Aitken suggested mixing may be considered defective; 'the situation is a continuum, so there are intermediate varieties, much room for idiosyncratic variation, and much obvious inconsistency in performance'.[24]

A related reason for the lack of research into the Scots continuum could be the unfavourable contrast often made between the language behaviour

22 Dossena 2005:2

23 Macafee 1981:7

24 Aitken 1981, 2015:74

of rural speakers, *switchers* and urban *drifters*. Mixing was often viewed, again, as inferior to switching. Aitken remarked as follows:

> [S]ome speakers can switch cleanly from one to the other – these people have been called dialect-switchers. Others again cannot or do not chose to control their styles in this way, but they do shift styles in a less predictable and more fluctuating way – these people we may call style-drifters.[25]

McClure made a similar point:

> [T]he author's impression, though he has no experimental evidence, is that speakers of the rural dialects often exhibit conscious bilingualism [ie diglossia] making a definite shift according to sociolinguistic circumstances between dialect and standard English, whereas speakers of urban dialects are less polarised in their speech, exhibiting variations which are more random, less consistent and less easy to relate to external circumstances.[26]

David Muirson was even harsher:

> Scots and English forms are jumbled up haphazardly so that a clear and consistent pattern can no longer be traced, as systematic grammar has gone out of the window.[27]

Linguistic research on other languages would suggest such chaos is possible, but not likely. What is undeniably true, however, is that language mixing is generally seen as shameful. Spanish, for example, is sometimes mixed with English to produce Spanglish, with Portuguese to make Portunhol and with Catalan, creating Catañol or Catanyol. In each case, speakers of both mother tongues regard such mixes as contaminated, deficient, low prestige, uneducated or 'slang' forms. To be fair on the earlier writers above, it is only recently that sociolinguists have begun to uncover and recognise the subtle structuring, skills and social value of such practices.

Writing 40 years ago, however, Billy Kay noticed that the continuum may not be just as chaotic as fellow scholars claimed.

---

25 Aitken 1979:86

26 McClure 1995:13

27 Muirson 1977:56

> [E]ven among older people who speak a much more conservative form of Scots than anyone of my generation, the more usual form of communicating... would be in a mixture of the two registers, *with the balance depending on the circumstances*.[28]

Dossena provides examples of such circumstances as 'the speakers' attitude, their relationship with the interlocutor, the topic etc',[29] and adds:

> Speakers do not just seem to code-switch between one and the other; their stylistic adjustments to context, topic and interlocutor encompass different aspects of both codes at the same time.

She explains, 'speakers and writers convey meaning by means of a careful, though spontaneous, selection of individual traits'. Dossena believes that an individual may opt to use alternative Scots or Scottish English variables, (sometimes termed *items*) in a conversation, depending on their knowledge of Scots and maybe, as suggested by Aitken below, habit.

Aitken developed a widely cited model of Scottish speech mixing. He divides speaker capability and practice into five categories, which he called *sociolects*, with Scots or 'broad Scots' at one end and English or what he termed 'Educated Scottish Standard English' at the other. While Aitken implies that people habitually stick to one category, he adds:

> [S]ome speakers of groups 2–4 [the middle categories] display a tendency to 'drift' in the direction of the more prestigious, fully English, variety by more frequently (though not necessarily inevitably) preferring an English item [from the 'English' categories] when addressing 'English-speaking' interlocutors.[30]

This dynamic is exactly what more recent translanguaging studies would predict. Furthermore, in the article Aitken also noticed the phenomenon of accommodation, which he labelled *convergence*.

> As well as this common 'upwards convergence' phenomenon (towards the more socially prestigious, variety [...] Educated Scottish Standard English), the situation also offers opportunities for 'downwards convergence' and, no doubt occasionally of 'divergence'.

---

28 Kay 1993:18 (my italics)

29 Dossena 2005:15

30 Aitken 1984, 2015:7

As mentioned earlier, field research into these phenomena is disappointingly sparse. The little evidence I found came via investigations into dialect loss, a process we will return to later. An example is a 2012 study[31] exploring the suspected loss of the distinctive Shetland dialect of Scots among young people in Lerwick, the island capital. Researchers discovered that when speaking with a local interviewer, some local speakers employed more Shetland dialect elements than when speaking with an outsider. Half did not (or could not) and spoke to both interviewers in standard Scottish English. The researchers concluded, 'dialect obsolescence is well advanced in this community' and that bidialectism (others might term it bilingualism) was a symptom of this decline. In 2016 a similar study took place in the Borders town of Hawick,[32] at the other end of Scotland but another assumed stronghold of Scots speakers. The research found that three of the five interviewees significantly changed the language features they used depending on whether the interviewer was a local or an outsider. Of the other two, both working class, one spoke mostly Scots and the other mostly Scottish English, the latter having lived and worked away from Hawick. The lower middle-class speakers were considered genuinely bidialectal and able to change their speech patterns. In contrast to the Lerwick study, this researcher concluded that bidialectism was not a precursor to language loss, but a way of maintaining local speech. Both studies focus on the dialect-like characteristics of Scots, hence the use of terms such as bidialectism rather than bilingualism. We will challenge this 'dialect' view of Scots next.

Lost in the blend?

In the first chapter we saw that Scots is now commonly described as a language, both officially and academically. However until quite recently the language mixing of vernacular Scots led to strikingly inconsistent views as to the nature of Scots among scholars. A notable theme among some academics has been to lump everything spoken in Scotland together, variously labelled as 'Scots' or 'Scottish English', or just 'English'. Even English with a Scottish accent has been dubbed by some as 'Scots' and Aitken himself blurs the distinction between Scots and English at times. In a 1982 paper[33] he describes, 'what some call Scots English, others Scots, others just English', adding, 'in fact the way most people in Scotland speak and indeed have spoken since the seventeenth century'. While recognising the 'Scottish

31 Smith and Durham 2012

32 Rawsthorne 2016

33 Aitken 1982, 2015:1

component to the English speech of Scotland as a whole', in that paper he views Scots as 'no more than a distinctive component in the total body of Scottish language, which can fairly be called a highly distinctive national variety of English'. In that same vein, Charles Jones perhaps provocatively entitled his 2002 monograph *Scots: The English Language in Scotland.*[34] Nevertheless, Jones also recognised 'the linguistic manifestations of Scots should be seen as a type of scale or cline, encompassing a very broad range of usage and formal characteristics'. How can we reconcile such apparently contradictory academic positions?

Regarding Scots and Scottish language as a dialect of English is not 'wrong'; it is a functional paradigm and can result in some insightful, indeed delightful, descriptive work. As English dialectology is a long-established field, a conventional view of Scots may help research get published in mainstream academic journals. Nonetheless, it should also be recognised that Scots-as-a-dialect is *ipso facto* an ideological position, implying subordination of Scottish language practice within a 'greater English' whole. Moreover, the term dialect implies a deviation from the prestigious or standard language form of the dominant group. The intention may not be political, but sociolinguist John Edwards describes the net result: 'differences are regularly translated into deficiencies'[35], and as a consequence:

> [T]he speech patterns of regional speakers, of ethnic minority-group members, of lower- or working-class populations – categories that frequently overlap, of course – elicit negative evaluations in terms of perceived status, prestige and levels of skill and education.[36]

Self-stigmatisation, even linguistic self-hatred among speakers, may follow.

> [T]hose whose speech includes nonstandard or stigmatised forms are typically their own harshest critics [...] a linguistic manifestation of social dominance/ subordination and, some would argue, of more blatant social control.

Dialectology is also primarily a descriptive discipline, as dialect change is portrayed as passive, 'neutral' and inevitable, usually leading to eventual *dialect death*. Nor is the static Scots-as-a-dialect model particularly useful if our goal is to reverse language shift. In my opinion, the model of a dynamic

34 Jones 2002

35 Edwards 2009:68

36 Edwards 2009:93

continuum between Scots and Scottish English proposed in this book is more suited for revitalising our language. It acknowledges that mixing in ordinary speech is a response to sociolinguistic and political influences. Mixing is not defective, therefore, but rather a skill and habit that may be developed. Individual speakers have control ('agency') over the amount of mixing they use and can raise the Scots language component in their vernacular speech and writing if they so desire. To be fair, contradictory and messy interpretations of the nature of Scottish language are understandable. The continuum model suggests two different linguistic systems are operating in tandem, but with much interplay between them. Millar reminds us again that 'Neither Scottish Standard English nor Scots exist in a vacuum in contemporary Scotland [...] there is considerable leakage – and confusion – between the two'.[37]

In this context, is it ever possible to untangle Scots and SSE components of Scottish language? Referring to written Scots (but applying to spoken language, too), McClure explains the problem.

> Any Scots text is likely to contain words of three classes: (a) words found regularly in standard literary English; (b) words that have obvious cognates in standard English, differing from them as a result of the independent development of pronunciation in the two languages; (c) words unique to Scots. Yet it is essential to understand that *words in all these categories are equally part of the Scots language and equally Scots.*[38] (His emphasis.)

Many very common Scots words such as 'time', 'by', 'face' and so on are identical to their English equivalents, so are they English or Scots words? McClure would claim them as Scots. At higher registers and technical domains a wide range of multi-syllable conceptual words such as 'education' and 'ability' are essentially the same, as they are French or Latin borrowings anyway. In written Scots, such terms are sometimes given a Scots spelling, such as 'eddication' or 'abeelitie', indicating they are indeed regarded as part of the Scots lexicon.

A few other complicating factors relating to vocabulary may further muddy perceptions especially of the spoken Scots-Scottish English mix, and lead to mistaken descriptions of 'randomness'.

- Individual speakers may have a limited Scots repertoire, so resort to English even though Scots equivalents are available.

37 Millar 2018:3

38 McClure 1998:17

- Speakers may be unsure of the Scots abilities of a new audience so may mix in both Scots and Scottish English alternatives to test for comprehension by trial and error. Thus, for example, they may intersperse both, 'I don't know' and 'A dinna ken' in, what may sound to an external or inexperienced researcher, an apparently random way.
- If the stranger speaks what is perceived as a different dialect of Scots, there may likewise be some reluctance to use Scots at all. I remember being accused of mocking Doric speakers when I spoke my own Central Scots with them.
- As Dossena suggested, people jump between Scots and English for symbolic reasons, eg to show authority, for humour, to display emotional authenticity and maybe just for fun. Such *metaphorical switching* (see below) may seem haphazard from a grammatical standpoint but could be deliberate and meaningful in context.
- Author L Colin Wilson observes how 'English-like' pronouns can be used in Scots for emphasis (*I* instead of *A*, for example) and this tendency can be applied across the continuum. English words may be dropped into a conversation to stress importance, or to ensure the desired meaning is conveyed.[39]

Vocabulary is not the only factor. Grammar is key in framing the mix. An unusual feature of the Scots-Scottish English complex is a lack of *constraint* at the point where Scots and English may be switched. Constraints are of much interest to linguists, as they influence the dynamics of code switching. Holmes suggests switches can only occur within phrases where the grammars of both languages line up.[40] While by no means identical, Scots and English grammars run in parallel, especially in sentence structure and word order.[41] Thus, switching can occur inside sentences or spoken phrases. Almost any Scots word can be swapped for an English one or, within the vocabulary limitations above, vice versa. I can personally compare switching between Catalan and Spanish. In casual conversation among groups who have mixed linguistic backgrounds, switching is common enough but occurs almost always at the ends of phrases. Although the Catalan and Spanish grammar structures also run in parallel, and preschool children mix the languages freely, Catalan education strongly encourages purism. Hispanicisms are frowned upon as corruptions or *barbarismes*.[42]

39 Wilson 2012

40 Holmes 2008:45

41 Purves 1997,2002, Robinson 2012

42 Eg Ruaix i Vinyet 2011

Scots and English switches have no such schooled-in constraints and no concept of barbarisms. Some combinations may be more likely than others, but it is hard to think of completely unacceptable mixtures. McClure again provides a useful illustration.

> The question immediately arises, therefore, of where Scots ends and English begins. *I'll not be going home till eleven o'clock tonight* is obviously English; *A'll no be gaun hame ti aleevin a 'cloak the nicht* is obviously Scots, and both are perfectly possible utterances. But what about *I'll no be going home till eleven o'clock the night*, *I'll no be gaun home to eleven o'cloak the night*, or any of several other equally possible permutations of Scots and English forms?[43]

The creative potential for this fluid type of interchange in more complex expressions is almost limitless.

> Each of the codes represents or symbolises a set of social meanings, and the speaker draws on the associations of each [...] Skilful code-switching operates like metaphor to enrich the communication [...] I prefer the term metaphorical switching [...] *switches are very well motivated in relation to the symbolic or social meaning of the two codes.*[44]

McClure recognised it could therefore be a 'matter of debate' whether someone was talking (or writing) in Scots or not. It clearly depends on degree and perception. The meaningful question then is not 'is it Scots?' but 'how Scots is it?'.

Holmes' concept of metaphorical switching suggests that the two-dimensional continuum model is always going to be an abstraction of a much more complex reality. Metaphors may have multiple layers of meaning and Warren Maguire cautions us not to oversimplify Scottish language.

> Any particular variant might be assigned all sorts of meanings, for example: Scots, SSE, Scotland-but-not-England, working-class, educated, local, Glasgow-and-not-Edinburgh, cool, different, old-fashioned, Catholic. None of these alternative meanings need have any reference to abstract notions of Scots and SSE, and it is more enlightening to think of Scottish speakers, like speakers everywhere else,

43 McClure 1979:27

44 Holmes 2008:45 (my italics)

> as operating in a multi-dimensional sociolinguistic variation space. Only some parts of this will equate with traditional notions of Scots and SSE, and neither of these terms may be relevant for many speakers.[45]

The notion of a multi-dimensional sociolinguistic variation space is attractive, and Holmes herself refers to such intricacy as *polyglossy*. On the other hand, it can overcomplicate, too. McClure remarked that all of us know, roughly, what is meant by Scots[46] and it comes as no surprise that Scots-speaking interview and focus group participants are reported as being easily able to distinguish their Scots from English.[47] Remember, the Scottish people were asked to identify the supposedly 'abstract' conceptions of Scots and Scottish English in the 2011 Census. The results were consistent, showing that the Scots and Scottish English distinction had a real meaning that in this context overwrote the important, but it seems secondary, identities listed by Maguire above.

Discrimination: 'the vowel system of the oppressed'

> We rarely talk about accents when we talk about discrimination, but it's something that can deeply affect people. When you feel like you have to force yourself to tone down or change your accent, it can change how you come across and what you say.[48]

The Eustace study discussed earlier illustrated some of the everyday impacts of language discrimination in the Glasgow workplace. Speakers' attitudes to their language and that of others drive the dynamics of switching, shifting, diglossia and related phenomena.

> [O]ver a century of mass education in English has led many people to see not only that the path to advancement leads through Standard English, but also that Scots itself is merely a corrupt dialect of the standard. A view held by Scots speakers as much as by those who do not speak the variety, this prejudice is extremely difficult to break through.[49]

45 Maguire 2012:3

46 McClure 1980:11

47 Eg Macaulay 2005, Unger 2013

48 Chloe Irvine quoted in Hay 2021

49 Millar 2005:195

Anti-Scots prejudice is real and perpetuated by what Millar called 'opinion-forming elements, such as educators and other figures of authority [...] whether consciously or not'.[50] The consequences are grim and imply a far deeper problem than a few ugly tweets. Language rights researcher Lionel Wee argued that prejudice always leads to discrimination, and that discrimination is always politically motivated.

> [L]anguage and other cultural practices are suppressed by a dominant group intent on eliminating any marker of distinctiveness in both public and private domains, perhaps via a process of forced assimilation.[51]

French sociolinguist Philippe Blanchet believed low-level language discrimination still blights the lives of far too many people.[52] He coined the term *glottophobia* to describe linguistic prejudice, drawing a comparison to homophobia, xenophobia and other forms of discrimination. Glottophobia was defined as 'contempt, hatred, aggression, rejection and exclusion of people' associated with negative discrimination of the 'incorrect, inferior, or bad' linguistic forms they use, be they languages, dialects or general language use. Luxembourg-based Jean Jacques Weber used a starker term: *linguistic racism*. Linguistic discrimination, like ethnic racism, he believed, was based on 'a hierarchical relation of inequality between (dominant versus dominated) social groups'. Speakers of the dominant (ie H) variety who have never encountered the issue may be unaware of the problem and those discriminating may not always be fully aware of the impact on their victims. Scottish historian Cairns Craig, however, regarded linguistic discrimination in Scotland as profoundly ideological. For any ambitious Scots aspiring to the 'role of fully achieved civilised Britishness' there was a barrier:

> It is not by our colour, of course, that we have stood to be recognised as incomplete within the British context, it is by the colour of our vowels: the rigidity of class speech in Britain.[53]

According to Craig, Scots speakers live within the 'vowel system of the oppressed', resulting in what has been described as *linguistic insecurity*, that is, negative prestige maybe even leading to linguistic self-hatred.

---

50 Millar 2018:165

51 Wee 2011:4

52 Blanchet 2016

53 Craig 1996:12

In the late 1990s Ronald Macaulay found almost three quarters of Glasgow teachers and more than half of the employers he interviewed commented on the inarticulateness of Scottish children and young adults, particularly in comparison with their English counterparts. 'Harsh', 'ugly', 'course', 'rough', 'guttural', 'slovenly', 'uncouth' and 'revolting' were some of the epithets teachers used to describe Glasgow speech.[54] Eilidh Bateman used similar interview-based research to explore attitudes towards Scots in Selkirk, using recordings of Scots and Scottish English as a starting point. She noted that in that Borders town, 'a number of interviewees rated the Scots, heard on the recording, as 'good' when basing their opinion on linguistic identity, and as 'bad' when considering social acceptability'.[55] Although they attached their own labels to language such as 'posh' for Scottish English and 'slang' for Scots, Bateman reported they sometimes did not seem to realise when they themselves were speaking Scots. Many of the participants even denied knowledge of Scots, 'despite conducting the entire interview using it'. Bateman concluded that Scots in some domains, 'is viewed as less estimable by the very citizens who speak it'. Terms like *oppression* and *language racism* may feel somewhat forced when applied to Scots, but Weber explained the rationale for using such loaded words.

> Through the sheer force of repetition, the core language racist tenets and assumptions have been naturalized, as it were. Implicitly or explicitly, they are ubiquitous in political and media discourse, as well as on the Internet, where they are disseminated faster than ever through social media such as Facebook and Twitter. They are perceived as commonsensical, their deep implication in racism has become increasingly invisible. Indeed, for many people, something that seems 'normal' is not subjected to critical thinking.[56]

According to radical educator Paulo Freire, it is exactly this pervasive, low-intensity oppression that leads to a 'culture of silence' where the existence of discrimination is not acknowledged.[57]

54 Macaulay 1997:50–53
55 Bateman 2000
56 Weber 2015:74
57 Freire 1968

Is there virtual linguistic apartheid in Scotland?

> You probably do know people who speak Scots as their first language (Scottish Gaelic as well) but just don't know it because they default to English in certain situations.[58]

The long-term and systematised stigmatisation of Scots makes 'neutral' surveying quite a problem. Critics of Scots revitalisation efforts often cite the 2010 Scottish Government poll *Public Attitudes Towards the Scots Language* that reported 64 per cent of adults did not actually consider Scots a language.[59] Predictably overlooked by such cynics was the finding that 30 per cent strongly disagreed with the survey's rather loaded 'not a language' question. Moreover, in the report views on Scots' languageness seemed to differ markedly according to how frequently it was spoken by the respondents.

> [T]he most frequent speakers are least likely to agree that it is not a language and those never speaking Scots most likely to do so.

The Census two years later revealed some 30 per cent of the Scottish population reported they were able to speak Scots. It could be reasoned by comparing the two data sets that those who speak Scots tend to think it is a language, and those who do not, do not. This seems to imply a kind of linguistic apartheid, where the two language communities do not interact. How is that even possible in a modern interconnected society?

Scotland's strange linguistic split, if that is what it is, could be the product of both the stigmatisation and accommodation described earlier. If you're one of the lucky 30 per cent who speaks Scots, you may consider that it is a language of some sort. Much of your natural conversation will (or could) be made up of Scots words and phrases, even if you only speak the more full-strength variant with your close relatives and friends. If you are one of the unfortunate 70 per cent who does not speak Scots and does not reside in a Scots-speaking community, Scots may never be directly spoken to you in any concentrated form. Fearing discrimination or embarrassment, Scots speakers will usually accommodate you by speaking to you in Scottish English. They assume you don't speak Scots. If you hear Scots at all, it will be in a heavily diluted version, reduced to isolated phrases and an accent for your benefit. In other words, to non-speakers Scots may sound like a dialect or an accent.

58 Lee 2021

59 Scottish Government 2010

This mistaken perception likely gained additional traction when the number of Scots speakers declined to less than half of the population, increasing the 'risk' of speaking Scots with strangers. It's understandable that people might start to avoid employing stigmatised forms. Johann Unger found that his interview participants who were using 'a considerable amount' of Scots words, pronunciation and structures expressed concern about how much spoken Scots he understood and adapted their speech to accommodate his assumed limited abilities.[60]

Another clear message buried by the 'not a language' stushie of the 2010 survey was that a substantial majority (over 85 per cent) agreed that Scots was an important part of the history and culture of Scotland. Two thirds of those polled said it was important that Scots was *used* in contemporary Scotland. The respondents' overwhelming view was that Scots plays a significant role in Scotland's identity, culture and legacy, 'even amongst those not considering it important, or not using it themselves'. This solid public support for Scots, like the language itself, is also conveniently overlooked by the critics of Scots revitalisation.

Bad Scots, good Scots

Adding to the convoluted attitudes towards the language, Scots, like most languages, has long had a prestige or high-status form, commonly referred to as *Good Scots*. During much of the 20th century, commentators regularly made a distinction between rural Good Scots (or Braid Scots) and urban *Bad Scots* variants. As we saw in the response to *The National*'s front page earlier, the remnants of this idea are still identifiable in discussions about Scots today. Another example is one journalist's recent take on the use of Scots in his newspaper, *The Herald*:

> [W]hy are some Scots terms more respectable than others? We would have no problem using carnaptious or dreich or indeed daft but would be unlikely to use a more modern term such as bawheid. Therein lies the crux. To some, using Scots words is akin to using slang. To others it means much more.[61]

'Carnaptious' and 'dreich' are examples of Good Scots, whereas 'bawheid' is not. The spoken and written variations of Good Scots were based on historic literary and probably idealised spoken country forms. If these were

60 Unger 2013:136

61 Allan 2021

considered 'good', it was tempting to label other kinds as 'bad'. Although this bias has long since faded among serious scholars, it continues to cast a pernicious shadow in the public mind. In the summer of 2021 a young Scots poet, Erin Boyle, performed her poem about Scotland's football team qualifying for the Euro competition, 'Fae The Scheme Tae The First Team', on a BBC social media site. Within hours, the piece provoked a storm of online abuse criticising the poet's accent and use of Scots words. So far, so predictable, but then the Education Convener of the Robert Burns World Federation decided to pitch in with a series of harsh tweets about Boyle's work.[62] This affair was an unhappy reminder of writer Colin Burnett's point:

> There is this socially accepted notion that it is OK to view Scots as high culture on one night of the year, Burns Night. But every other day it is deemed as low culture.[63]

Aitken raised and partially skewered the phenomenon in an entertaining 1982 paper entitled, 'Bad Scots: some superstitions about Scots speech'.[64] Drawing on historical accounts, he parodied the supposed contrast.

> Good Scots, wherever it can be found (if anywhere) is genuine, authentic, pithy, expressive, forceful, rich, fine, lovely and often old or good old. Bad Scots on the other hand is degraded, corrupted, degenerated, vulgarised, debased, perverted, slovenly, slipshod, uncouth, gibberish, jumble and so-called Modern Scots.

Aitken identified two components of so-called 'Bad Scots' both connected to the derogatory view of mixing as described earlier. The first is the replacement of older Scots forms with 'vulgar' urban slang, and the second the thinning out of Scots with Scottish English or, worse, some other colloquial form of English. Bad Scots is routinely associated with the working-class speakers of Scotland's urban centres, particularly Glasgow. McClure gives an example:

> But what about the Glasgow docker? His idiolect compared with [a Peterhead] fisherman and [a Selkirk] farmer would probably contain very few Scots words: the distinctive vocabulary of Scots has largely disappeared from the cities.[65]

62 Anderson 2021

63 Burnett 2021

64 Aitken 1982, 2015

65 McClure 1979:28

Distinct phonological forms such as 'hame' and 'mak' might be missing too. McClure asked, 'is the docker speaking Scots? Are the poems of Tom Leonard Scots?'. Aitken also warns us in his 1982 paper that:

> [P]ejorative expressions ultimately represent a response not to their qualities as language but to the social evaluation of the sort of people who speak them.

He then spends some time debunking the criticisms and, in the process, advocating 'dialect tolerance'. As he notes, 'it is probable that the majority of Scots speakers' speech varieties lie indeterminately between the archetypes of acceptable English, Good Scots and Bad Scots'. Aiken again acknowledged the prevalence of Scots language mixing that we are now familiar with, but his observation raises some further questions.

Firstly, where did Good Scots come from, and why? One argument is that the whole idea harks back to British ideologies of 18th century prescriptivism and purism. Maybe it was a response to the vigorous standardisation of 'ideal' English at the time and that we will look at in the next chapter. According to Aitken, Good Scots is 'fully Scots in every possible respect'; so, when available, the Scots vocabulary and idiomatic and grammatical options on the continuum are always chosen. He continued:

> This imaginary and uncorrupted Good Scots is thought to be spoken by some elderly rural peasants or, if this is not so, is believed to have been spoken by Scots generally in the not too distant past.

Given the dialect differences across Scotland, we might wonder how speech practice could have adhered to a standard if it was never taught formally. True, Scots dictionaries had been available since the 19th century, and we know several descriptive monographs on Scots and its dialects were published around the turn of the 20th century. Nevertheless, there was nothing like the flood of overtly prescriptive guides for the general public as existed for English. On the other hand, as pointed out in Chapter One, literacy was quite high by the late 19th century, and most people had exposure to Scots songs and poetry books both at school and at home. Macmillan describes how a series of Scots readers were distributed by the Burns Federation, 'to provide Scottish boys and girls with a continued course of reading in Scots'[66] and collections such

66 MacMillan 1972:Preface

as *Readings in Modern Scots*[67] and *Scotch Readings, Recitations & Sketches*[68] were widely available in the first half of the 20th century. Many urban bairns would also have had the chance to blether with older Scots-speakers from rural communities. One of the endearing storylines in the Scots-rich comic strip The Broons, started in the 1930s, involved regular visits to the countryside where the family owned a but an' ben cottage.

Having said that, I believe Aitken was correct in concluding that Good Scots was always something of a myth, and probably promoted for psychological or ideological reasons. Good Scots became an unattainable gold standard that could be used to devalue and dismiss any modern vernacular speech. A useful trope for opponents to Scots, it was also employed by sympathisers who felt they could rationalise their inaction by declaring the language damaged beyond redemption. The idea of Good Scots seems to have been resurrected inside the Scots language community in the 1960s and 1970s as an initially negative response to the upstart vernacular-styled writing of that period. McClure's reference above to the Glasgow-dialect poet Tom Leonard, who deliberately rejected traditional Scots spelling conventions for artistic effect, hints at this cultural standoff.

Some Scots writers' continuing opposition to standardisation is maybe another fading echo of the old division, but the original Good Scots/Bad Scots conflict appears to have dissipated or at least progressed over the last 30 years. As far back as 1983, a collection of papers *Scotland and the Lowland Tonguez,*[69] edited by McClure with a foreword by Aitken, attempted an overdue reconciliation between the various strands of Scots scholarship and language. In the volume, poet Edwin Morgan wrote of 'the acceptable emergence of Glasgow speech, both as an object of linguistic study and a medium for serious writing', condemning the earlier bias against the city dialect as 'not only improperly moralistic but strangely incurious'. A decade later the cultural commentator Joy Hendry felt the publication's 'accolade of academic respectability' was something of a watershed for Scots.

> There was a coming together of on all fronts, more or less, in favour of the language. This latest mini revolution, like so much else, began with the writers.[70]

Modern prose writing and dictionaries, especially *The Essential Scots*

67 Mackie 1913
68 Paterson 1925
69 McClure ed 1983
70 Hendry 1993:22

Dictionary in 2005 continued the trend of bringing together urban and older rural forms.

We should remind ourselves just how much 'Scots' remains in urban speech. Guidebooks, wordlists and the popular local newspaper quizzes relating to Glaswegian, Dundonian and other city dialects are always full of mainstream non-dialectal Scots words and *syntax* (ie, grammar structures).

> [T]he syntax of the language of speakers in urban areas like Edinburgh and semi-urban areas such as East Lothian is very similar to the syntax recorded in descriptions of Broad Scots produced at the beginning of the century. In particular one description by Sir James Wilson published in 1915 based on the older inhabitants of Dunning in Perthshire provides evidence that the syntax of Scots has remained quite stable over the past one hundred and thirty years.[71]

In 2020 Michael Dempster, Director of The Scots Language Centre, published a remarkable series of videos outlining the grammar of spoken Scots, highlighting the substantial 'braid' Scots elements still evident in his everyday West Central Scots speech.[72] Although it is encouraging to confirm so much remains, speakers and scholars alike still agree that there has been a steady loss of distinctive vocabulary, phrases and grammatical structure from the Scots end of the continuum. The process is so gradual it may barely be noticed, so if we ever want to combat the decline, it is worth exploring how the mechanism of linguistic erosion works.

How can you lose a language?

Scots has long been relegated to informal, generally leisure and familial, domains, and Scottish English is becoming the norm even in social areas where Scots was until recently quite common. Scots then is pushed back into ever safer domestic settings, disappearing totally from public use. Catalan linguists call this relentless domain-by-domain erosion of a minority language *substitution*. In addition to domain substitution, the structure of the language itself wears away. Varieties with no (or only partial) written standards to stabilise them are particularly prone to attrition. England-based journalist Ian Jack, writing in 2017, reflected that back in his native Scotland:

71 Miller 1998:54

72 Dempster 2020

> [A] place of strong dialects that some now argue amount to a separate language, vocabulary as well as accent was worn away. I can't ever remember using words that my parents used: *bairn* for child, *bide* for stay, *blate* for shy, *breeks* for trousers, *brig* for bridge (to name a few of the Bs).

Linguist Paul Kerswill describes two processes of language loss.[73] The first is *levelling* where distinctive but low-prestige local features, such as Jack's list of Scots words above, are ironed out when speakers encounter people from outside their community. We have seen this process earlier; convergence leads to accommodation around the prestige, usually standard, variant. The second process leading to loss of diversity is termed *diffusion*, when new (usually H) features spread out from a culturally dominant centre. The French linguist Louis-Jean Calvet refers to the broad process by which a subordinate language slowly blends into the dominant language as *absorption*.[74] The absorption starts with the grammar, then progresses though vocabulary to pronunciation. Although the grammar of broad Scots is quite distinct[75], the grammar of English continues to make substantive inroads into the mix of spoken Scottish language. The 'Scots' you often hear may in fact only be individual Scots words connected by standard English syntax. Over the years, as it is not formally taught, the distinct vocabulary itself begins to shrink. Eventually the only trace of the absorbed language is the phonology (ie accent). Finally, according to Calvet, 'certain phonological contrasts in a language tend to disappear, to be replaced by a haphazard alternation (or 'fluctuation') a fact which is evidence of the destruction from within of the whole system'.

Thus, it is not just words but pronunciation and accent that are at risk. Jack returns to our earlier example of the post-vocalic R:

> [H]aving grown up in Scotland, I sound the 'R'. People in England tend to skip the 'R' as the final consonant and [for 'ear'] say 'ee-uh' or 'ee-ah'.

Alarmingly, in 2005 it was reported the English 'invasion' on Scottish speech patterns was encroaching so fast that, 'language experts believe the Glaswegian guttural "R", pronounced at the end of words, could be lost within a generation'.[76] The researcher, 'also noticed a decline in the

---

73 Kerswill 2003

74 Calvet 1998:104–109

75 Eg Purves 1997/2002, Robinson 2012

76 Seenan 2005

aspirating "h" sound, with some young Scots committing the cardinal sin of pronouncing loch as lock'.

Linguistic intrusion does not have to result from personal contact; anglophone mass media can also have an impact. In 2013 Glasgow University linguists found that Glaswegian fans of the then very popular TV soap *East Enders* were picking up London English pronunciations such as 'f' for 'th' in words like 'three', and an 'oo' vowel in place of 'l' in words like milk and people.[77] As an aside, the famous glottal stop ('wa'er', 'bu'er' etc) is a distinctive feature of both Cockney and Glasgow speech, but seem to have originated separately and has been frowned upon in both cities since the 19th century. So, *East Enders* cannot be blamed for that one.

Scots' secret weapon: linguistic loyalty

So far, so bad. Most accounts of Scots adopt the same gloomy tone of decline we have just seen – what linguistic anthropologist and Gaelic champion Emily McEwan-Fujita dubbed 'discourses of death'.[78] But we should also remember that, while loss is undoubtedly occurring, there has not yet been the catastrophic wipe-out that commentators have prophesised for a century or more. Scots is still faring far better, for example, than the dialects of English, now disappearing in most parts of England. It is important therefore to strike a balance between fatalistic lamentations of loss and a more positive recognition of linguistic loyalty. As the 2010 attitudes survey made clear, the social and cultural value many Scottish people, including non-speakers, place on the language defies the relentless pressure to homogenise.

> In a strange, by no means straightforward, way, Scots act as a powerful marker of Scottishness, not just as in many areas where local dialects are associated with strong regional pride – in speech, but also in a long, albeit patchy, written heritage. At the very least its employment can be seen as a rather impotent challenge to hegemonic forces; in some incalculable way he can also be a means of 'imagining' the Scottish community.[79]

Macaulay reminded us of the fact that, 'Most Scots have no desire to speak "English English"'.[80] Eustace explained why; 'A point constantly raised

77 McKinlay 2013
78 McEwan-Fujita 2006, 2011
79 Millar 2005:190
80 Macaulay 1997:27

by respondents: that to speak the English language with a Scottish accent brought nationality labelling as English'.[81] Before anyone labels this as crude nationalism, such linguistic resistance, in Macaulay's words, stems from, 'the desire of a minority group to maintain its distinctiveness from the dominant majority group'.[82] A person's language, dialect and accent provide immediate evidence for social identity. A lifetime of aural socialisation makes us very acute to the linguistic indicators of community affiliation. Hearing a syllable or two enables us to interpret (rightly or wrongly) one another's social background: Scottish, Dundonian, working-class, etc.

> By their accent, their vocabulary, their discourse patterns, speakers identify themselves and are identified as members of this or that discourse community. From this membership, they draw personal strength and pride, as well as a sense of social importance and historical continuity from using the same language as the group they belong to.[83]

In Scotland, as everywhere, language is an intimate component of our personal, social and national identity. Billy Kay reminds us, 'language is central to people's being'.[84] Llamas and Watt explain why:

> [P]eople's choice of languages, and ways of speaking, do not simply reflect who they are, but make them who they are [...], they signal social belonging.[85]

The authors build on postmodern theoretical approaches that suggest identity is not essential, ie is not something we *have* or *are*, but rather it is something we *do* in a social context. In a well-known 1999 *Herald* piece, author William McIlvanney captured the idea of on-the-fly construction.

> Identity, personal or national, isn't merely something you have like a passport. It is also something you discover daily like a strange country. Its core isn't something solid, like a mountain. It is something molten, like magma.[86]

81 Eustace 2012:344
82 Macaulay 1997:3
83 Kramsch 1998:66
84 Kay 1993:117
85 Llamas and Watt 2010:9
86 Cited in McCrone 2009:151

This everyday discovery plays out within a fluid Scottish cultural and linguistic framework,

> [A] place of dialogue, between self and other, between inner and outer, between pasts and present, between invented pasts and discovered pasts and value systems past and future.[87]

To some extent, we can choose what our Scottish identity is like, linguistic or otherwise, but not completely.

> [T]hat choice will be formulated and to some extent constrained by the ways in which Scottish identity has been constructed in the past and also by the ways in which others perceive it.[88]

Negotiating this tension is both comforting and restricting but is what makes us truly human and, if we want to be, truly Scottish.

Affiliation to language communities therefore becomes a vital 'psychosocial anchor'[89], relieving the individual from, in the gloomy words of Kramsch, 'oblivion, anonymity, and the randomness of nature'.[90] Membership of groups can 'define and regulate the role of the individual within the social unit'[91], but also forms a part of an individual's concept of themself and therefore carries real emotional heft. This is why dialects and languages have such a powerful social and political function. Llamas and Watt explain, 'they are still what bind together communities, from the family to the nation [...] they carry our personal and community stories' and 'in transmitting the memory of who is not part of us, they transmit the meaning of who we are'.

How does this emotional weight impact on people's feelings about their language and identity? In her 2000 survey, Bateman reported a 'discernible insecurity' among her interviewees as they tried to explain the importance of language to their Scottish identity. 'Although they often spoke of pride when giving their reactions to the recording, the feeling was one of inferiority with respect to English'. In 2013 Bechhofer and McCrone surveyed people's opinions of symbols of national culture in Scotland. They found that three out of every ten Scottish respondents mentioned language as a symbol of Scottishness. That 30 per cent figure may ring a bell. In Bateman's survey

87 Craig 1996: 117
88 Douglas 2009:9
89 Edwards 2009:2
90 Kramsch 1998:6
91 Llamas and Watt 2010:10

above, almost 32 per cent of the participants said they favoured Scots above Scottish Standard English although only a quarter said they spoke it. She noted that at the time of her research, shortly after devolution, Scotland was, 'caught up in an emotional dialogue between two camps; the reinvention of Scottish nationalism and the attempt to restore faith in British identity in Scotland'. She considered emotion to be a fundamental issue, 'as identity and allegiance are available to be commandeered by whoever is most successful at invoking an emotive response'. Bechhofer and McCrone found in their own survey there was a tendency for Scots who include 'some sense of being British in their identity' to downplay the importance of language.

Scots, class and power

> The Scots language is penalised for one reason and that is because the language is routinely associated with the working class. Whereas standard English is written and spoken more widely amongst the middle classes in the country. Language is the signpost that divides us along class lines. And this fact is abundantly evident when you consider the cultural struggles between the Scots and English language.[92]

Author Colin Burnett above highlighted the issue of class that underlies much of the discussion so far. Bearing in mind Maguire's observation earlier that a particular variant might carry many polyglossic meanings apart from Scots and SSE, it is the issue of class loyalty that often permeates discussion about Scots, the Good Scots/Bad Scots division perhaps being the most conspicuous example.

Labov suggested back in the 1960s that class would always be significant in the formation of linguistic attitudes and, according to Macaulay, this is particularly relevant in Scotland where national and class identity often intersect.

> While most Scots reveal their Scottishness through the speech, it is the lower-class speakers who display the most marked features. It may not be a coincidence that working-class solidarity is much stronger in Scotland than in England (eg, in the trade union movement and in voting patterns). The lower-class speakers thus have a double reason for their form of speech: 1) to assert their Scottishness and separateness from the English; and 2) to confirm their working-class loyalty and rejection of middle-class values.[93]

92 Burnett 2021

93 Macaulay 1997:4

The link between speaking Scots and the class of most of its speakers is a major theme in the history of Scots, from the anglicisation of the Scottish upper classes in the 18th century to the emergence of the 'urban voice' in the late 20th century. Nonetheless, with a few notable exceptions such as Tom Nairn[94], cultural commentators on the left in Scotland have generally disparaged or ignored Scots language issues. This has resulted in a political disengagement from a significant component of Scottish culture and the power relations behind it. Even acknowledging the 'difficult dialogue' between Marxism and nationalism[95], leftist writers have all too easily fallen into conservative and 'inferiorist' positions about the Scots language. For example, in his otherwise radical *The Origins of Scottish Nationhood*, Neil Davidson adopted a surprisingly conservative position on, 'the myth of Scots', claiming, 'there never has been a "Scots" language other than Gaelic'; what is spoken in Scotland is part of the 'totality of English', and is therefore the equivalent of Scouse, Geordie or Cockney.[96] Fast forward 20 years and the left-wing British nationalist rhetoric remains virtually intact. In 2022, a prominent Scottish 'lefty lawyer' (his Twitter description) made a bizarre assault on Scots in a blog post[97] subsequently reported by the press. He alleged that Scots had been confected and weaponised by the Scottish Government for 'racist' purposes, namely, to discourage 'refugees with brown or black skins' from settling in Scotland. According to the author, who was once associated with the Labour Party; 'There is no such thing as "Scots" as a language. It is a dialect of English'. The post continued:

> If you look at who promotes the idea of 'Scots' being a language you quickly reach the conclusion that they are invariably white middle aged, and older, men on the blood and soil wing of the SNP.

A young female Scots writer, who had publicly expressed her disgust at these remarks was later called a 'white nationalist'. [98] To be fair on other Scottish 'leftys', some seem to have updated their views marginally to: 'There is debate about whether Scots is a language different from English'.[99] Nevertheless, such is the apparently deep-rooted linguistic prejudice among some on the Scottish left that it has fallen to English thinkers such as Marnie Holborow

94 Nairn 1977, 2015

95 Eg Munck 1986

96 Davidson 2000:56

97 Smart 2022

98 Hunter 2022

99 Fotheringham 2021:298

to establish more nuanced Marxist approaches to language diversity.

> [I]n the 19th century, the ideology of Standard English was part of a wider ruling-class project to extend the hegemony over a growing working class.[100]

Indeed, since the 1970s, radical linguists have used methods such as *critical discourse analysis* (CDA) to reveal how language is manipulated to create and preserve power relationships in society. Such approaches challenge power imbalances, with obvious initial targets being racist and sexist language. CDA is an unusually interventionist form of academic research, 'a sociolinguistics of people', as Costa put it. According to left-wing English sociologist Norman Fairclough, one of the founders of CDA:

> [T]he widespread societal promotion of standard varieties of a language, and the related derogation of vernacular varieties, is a specific example of the hegemony or domination that the critical discourse analyst should expose and challenge.[101]

We are reminded that political ideology is embedded not only in language itself, but how we think about it. The profoundly social aspect of language means that ideas held about language 'are interlaced with wider views about society'.[102] Billy Kay opened *The Mither Tongue* with a similar observation: 'politics determines the way we view language and culture and in time influences how we view ourselves'.[103]

Holborow, Leith and Kay agree that the ways we think about language are influenced by competing ideologies. French linguist Calvet criticised fellow scholars for failing to define the 'linguistic' concepts such as language and dialect in relation to social power.[104] In his 1998 book *Language Wars* he described how languages or varieties compete against each other within a single state. The dominant group usually attempts to impose its own language and culture on peripheral cultures for reasons of economic control, political 'unity', arrogance, ignorance, prejudice or sometimes to undermine alternative centres of identity and therefore power. Millar agreed that the aim of cultural homogenisation is always political domination:

100 Holborow 1999:185

101 Quoted in Holmes 2008:398

102 Holborow 1999:151

103 Kay 1993:11

104 Calvet 1998:54

> At the heart of monolingualism lie power differentials. Those who have more power (whether economic or political, or both) are able – whether consciously or not – to impose their language on those with less power (or, in a democratic age, less access to the centres of power). Those with less power may also move towards the use of the majority language by compulsion or, as regularly, by a sense of demoralisation about their native languages and cultures.[105]

Millar explained, 'varieties are dialectised under a neighbouring variety associated with political economic and cultural power'.[106] For all its languageness, Millar described Scots as a 'near-perfect example of a dialectised language'. He concludes, 'The Scots-speaking world presents a useful portrait of what laissez-faire attitudes and policies towards a socially disadvantaged kin tongue produces'.[107] Phillipson believed dialectisation is part of an old discourse in Britain, rooted in the state's colonial past.

> Two of the most central labels in colonialist cultural mythology are tribe and dialect. They both express the way the dominant group differentiates itself and stigmatises the dominated group. They therefore form part of an essentially racist ideology. The rule is that we are a nation with a language, and they are a tribe with a dialect.[108]

105 Millar 2005:27
106 Millar 2018:2
107 Millar 2018:219
108 Phillipson 1992:38

CHAPTER THREE

From Union to Devolution

Scots is an argument

El castellà és una llengua, el català és una polèmica.
Spanish is a language, Catalan is an argument.[1]

THE HISTORY OF Scots is in some part a long debate about what Scots is. As we saw at the end of the last chapter, the opposing labels 'language' and 'dialect' in particular imply very different meanings, attitudes and narratives. Such discourses shape how we think about our language and determine not only what questions are asked but even if the subject is raised at all. Until recently, Scots was rarely discussed seriously in public; it was ignored by mainstream history and social science studies, supressed in schools, neglected in the media and barely featured on the curriculum of Scottish universities.

As a result, Scots remains dislocated from the wider history of Scotland. Although historical contexts are frequently cited as explanations for Scots' fate, language is almost never mentioned as a causal factor, even obliquely, in mainstream Scottish history. Conventional accounts of Scotland's past almost never ask any kind of 'Scots language question'. Indeed, most historians and sociologists do not appear to consider language to be an important aspect of Scottish culture and identity. Such scholars are mostly anglophones who, according to one critic, 'appear to view aspects of the situation from a middle-class perspective'[2], a viewpoint, 'not shared by many of those Scots whose speech is further removed from the standard version of southern British English'.[3]

The lack of public discussion and hence understanding of Scots history is

1 Rojals 2016
2 Macaulay 2005:21
3 Macaulay 2005:153

paradoxical, given that writers and researchers have published a plethora of books and articles on the subject. The language's early beginnings, emerging from the Anglican dialect of Old English sometime before the 12th century to its present state of 'decline' in the early 21st century have been explored in scholarly detail. Treatments range from popular accounts[4] to academic approaches[5], the most recent being Robert McColl Millar's 2018 *Modern Scots: an analytical survey* and his *A Sociolinguistic History of Scotland*, published in 2020. Most, however, adopt that discouragingly gloomy tone of decline. But is this negativity still justified?

One of the revelations of the 2011 Census was the that more Scottish people speak a form of Scots now than at the time of the Union. The speech of virtually all the Lowland population in 1707 was likely to be 'full Scots', used across most communicative domains, including the law.[6] Scotland's population at the beginning of the 18th century was roughly one million, of whom about a third spoke Gaelic. If the rest spoke full Scots, the Scots language community of the time was about 750,000 people, largely illiterate. In the 2011 census, over twice that number declared themselves Scots speakers with seven out of ten of those claiming literacy. While the Scots of 2011 and the Scots of the early 18th century are unarguably different, the orthodox story of the Union destroying Scots as a living language starts to look, to use a good Scots word, shooglie.

During his Scottish tour in 1773, Samuel Johnson quipped, 'languages are the pedigree of nations'. Pedigree, nationhood and language are closely entwined in the history of Scots. The way that versions of Scots' origin story are told and re-told so frequently in academic and popular writing tells of the cultural importance of such tales. The histories of languages are 'socially situated narratives', and 'can thus be seen as a site of ideological production'.[7] In other words, they are important to our sense of self. We have an urge to delve back into history to establish the ancestry and therefore the credentials of Scots as a national language. Aitken writes of, 'the ancient belief – dating from 1494 – that there is an entity with some form of separate existence called the Scots language'.[8]

The story of Scots, at least up to the early 20th century, is very well documented and my goal in this chapter is not reiterate or revise the outstanding work of Scots language historians. Nonetheless, I believe the

4 Muirson 1977, McClure 1988, Kay 1986, 1993

5 Eg Aitken 1985, Jones 2002, Görlach 2002

6 Aitken 1985, 2015

7 Costa 2009:1

8 Aitken 1982, 2015:2

2011 Census findings, showing Scots as a still-living language, throws a very different light on the usual tale of 'decline', especially from the late 20th century and on to current times. My focus is on Modern Scots, the variety (more or less) used today. Modern Scots can be said to begin with the Treaty of Union of 1707, when the previously independent Scottish parliament was terminated, and Scottish parliamentarians took the high road to Westminster to establish the single political entity that, at the time of writing, we still live under.

Origin stories and the road not taken

The birth of Modern Scots is unavoidably linked to the demise of Scotland as an independent nation. The language can symbolise an underlying narrative around loss of political autonomy and cultural identity. Consequently, scholars often contrast the post-Union linguistic 'catastrophe' with the older Scots eras that preceded it, lasting by convention from the mid-15th century to the early 18th. This period is often considered the golden age of Scots as an official, national tongue. Adding to the weight of representing Scotland's culture, many accounts indicate a certain melancholy for the road not taken.

> Had Older Scots retained its former autonomy from English, we might have had in Britain today a language situation resembling that of modern Scandinavia, with Scots occupying a position like that of, say, Swedish and (Standard) English that of Danish; or (perhaps a closer parallel) Scots might be occupying the position of Catalan, (Standard) English that of Castilian Spanish.[9]

Against this romantic benchmark, post-Union Modern Scots could only ever disappoint. On the other hand, the early origin story of Scots suggests an alternative history was at least possible.

Anglo-Saxon arrived as a language in the British Isles in the 5th century and its northern Anglian dialect seems to have been present in lowland Scotland since the 7th century. By the 11th century, Gaelic had spread throughout Scotland, including the hitherto Anglian-speaking Lothians. However, during the following century Gaelic began to be pushed back by Anglian across the lowlands and up the east coast. This was due to the establishment of towns (burghs) by large numbers of Anglo-Norman settlers invited in by King David I and his successors. In just two centuries the variety, known initially as *Inglis* and from 1494 also as Scots, became the

9 Aitken 1984, 2015:3

main spoken tongue east and south of the Highland Line. Writing identified as an early form of Scots first appeared as commentaries to Latin and French documents in the 14th century, and John Barbour's Scots epic *The Bruce* was written about this time. By the late 15th century, a distinctive Middle Scots orthography had emerged. Immigration and commerce added new vocabulary from French, Gaelic and Middle Dutch. More words came in from Latin, replaced by Scots as the main literary and official language of the nation by about 1500. From this time, and throughout the 16th century, there were therefore two official languages used on the island of Great Britain: Tudor English and its closely related but far from identical sibling, Older Scots.

Printing and Protestantism: Scots before the Union

Most scholars agree Scots was already under pressure from English before 1707. The three traditional culprits cited are the Reformation from 1560 onwards, the Union of the Crowns in 1603 and the growth of English-language printing. Religious reformers spread vernacular translations of the Bible, the most popular printed version used in Scotland being the Geneva Bible, produced in that Swiss city by English Protestant exiles. A vernacular Bible and its associations of literacy are often considered key to the early formation of any language. The Geneva Bible was supplanted by another English translation, the familiar Authorised Version of 1611. The authoriser himself was James VI and I who ruled as King of Scotland until the union of the Scottish and English crowns in 1603. After 1603 the kingdoms of Scotland and England remained discrete sovereign states with their separate parliaments, judiciary and laws, but the court moved to England where the 'polite' language conventions of southern English held sway. The growth of printing and especially the output of English printers in the late 16th century also led to some anglicisation in Scotland. Although many Scottish printers still published in Scots at the time, they too began to shift towards English, presumably to reach a bigger market. It should be remembered, though, that printing was a marginal activity at this time, being expensive and painstakingly slow to produce. Texts offer only very incomplete clues to the vernacular language used during this period.

While acknowledging the three anglicising factors above, Aitken made a more subtle point. Even when Scots was still regarded as the national language, there were signs that it began to be perceived as inferior to southern English; as one contemporary author put it, more 'braid and plane'.[10] English prose and poetry by Chaucer, Milton, Dryden and others had circulated

10 Aitken 1985, 2015:5

and long been admired in Scotland, and some Scottish writers affected English written styling. The increasing social interactions between the two nations through religion, court and commerce would expose differences in speech too and would soon deepen bourgeois Scots' deteriorating perception of their own tongue. The Union may have only exacerbated rather than initiated pressure on Scots, but it certainly fostered and eventually formalised prejudice against the language, first among the elites of society and later among mainstream Scottish institutions.

From a sociolinguistic perspective, the Union had three consequences that played out over the following centuries. To begin with, Scots was cut off from any official apparatus that would have allowed it to evolve as a normal national language. Secondly, unionism provided a powerful ideological framework that enabled Scots to be devalued, marginalised and almost completely erased from public discourse. Thirdly, the gradual elimination of Scots from everyday upper- and, later, middle-class speech aggravated class division. The burgeoning and increasingly anglophone middle class of the time ran all the Scottish civil institutions such as education, publishing and the press (later broadcasting). As a result, the 'lower class' Scots language began to be suppressed in education, governance and the law.

No Scots! No Scots!

In his remarkable history of the Scottish Enlightenment, *How the Scots Invented the Modern World* published in 2001, US historian Arthur Herman describes the linguistic tension immediately following the Union. Scottish people with ability and ambition were eager to taste success in London and this touched on a 'thorny issue' of the time, 'whether educated Scotsmen should adopt English, instead of Scots, as their primary written and spoken tongue'.[11] The author considered the social and cultural pressures to adopt English to be 'immense'. Yet assimilation was no easy task; 'for most Scots, learning to converse and write in English was a difficult as learning a new language'.

Scotland had the misfortune of entering the English political and linguistic sphere of influence just as the English language itself was struggling for an identity. South of the border, some social critics demanded an English version of the French *Académie française*, founded in 1634. Seven years after the Union, Jonathan Swift published *Proposal for correcting, improving, and ascertaining the English Tongue* aiming to establish a standard for polite speech and writing. The Scottish elites enthusiastically imported the so-called

11 Herman 2001:115

Augustan culture of 'propriety' that was fashionable in 1720s England. Provincial and vulgar speech would soon be met with open derision, ultimately to be remedied by *prescriptivism*, ie rules for prestigious use.

Scottish intellectuals and the middle classes felt painfully self-conscious about their defective language, and anxiously sought to eradicate traces of Scots vocabulary and syntax from their writing and, if possible, their speech. Philosopher David Hume compiled a list of 'Scotticisms' to be expelled from his texts. Hume was a native Scots speaker and confessed to an English correspondent that, despite all his efforts at writing good English, 'As to my Tongue, you have seen, that I regard it as totally desperate and irreclaimable'.[12] The Scots-speaking lawyer and writer James Boswell was equally ingratiating when he first met lexicographer Samuel Johnson; 'I do indeed come from Scotland, but I cannot help it'. Johnson retorted, 'That, Sir, I find, is what a very great many of your countrymen cannot help'.[13] To be fair on Boswell, virulent anti-Scottish prejudice was not uncommon at the time. He reports attending a play in London's Covent Garden where the audience, on seeing two kilted army officers, chanted, 'No Scots! No Scots! Out with them!'.[14]

Back in Scotland, there was money to be made exploiting a nascent cultural cringe. From 1748, a veritable troop of elocution experts declared war on Scots diction, providing inspirational lectures, books and yet more lists for diligent anglophiles to memorise. In one of the more celebrated linguistic interventions, the Irish actor Thomas Sheridan, father of the English playwright Richard Sheridan, organised a series of lectures in 1761 on English elocution that attracted 300 high-ranking gentlemen. He even ran a separate series for the ladies. So successful was the venture, a grateful Edinburgh town council made the linguistic evangelist a freeman of the city.

Much of the activity was just the clever marketing of provincial social anxieties, but according to University of Edinburgh scholar Charles Jones, assimilation was encouraged by a highly organised and influential group of grammarians and linguistic commentators who were seeking what can only be described as 'language death'. The clique considered all Scottish forms of speech, 'not merely a social inconvenience, but as a barbaric relic of a backward society and, as such, to be supressed'. Behind the emollient rhetoric of 'improvement' of Scots speech lay the harsher political ideology of unionism. This local form of British nationalism asserted that the cultural and linguistic homogeneity of Britain was an essential part of its identity and

12 Quoted in Kaul 2009:119

13 Boswell 1791,1907:243

14 Jones 1995:1–5

maybe survival. Jones quotes one contemporary writer:

> [I]f the same language were spoken on both sides of the Tweed, some small diversity of our laws and ecclesiastical establishment excepted, no striking mark of distinction would remain between the sons of England and Caledonia.

In case this influential assimilationist dogma appears deterministic, just a 'natural' development of post-Union Scotland, Jones also reminds us at the time, 'there was also a substantial group who found this "linguistic cleansing" profoundly distasteful and even un-patriotic'. They promoted the continued use and improvement of Scots, often with a romantic appeal to its historic provenance and place in contemporary Scottish culture. Some advocated a more practical approach, for example the development of a new standardised Scots orthography and the consolidation of a prestigious form of written and spoken Scots to counterbalance English norms. Others, including Boswell, suggested the production of a Scots dictionary. A common refrain began to emerge by the end of the 18th century as follows.

> [I]f the Scots, remaining a separate nation, with a King and a court residing among them, had continued to improve and embellish their own dialect instead of servilely aping the English, they would at present be possessed of a language in many points superior to the English.[15]

Note that during those times the labels dialect, tongue and language seemed to be used more-or-less arbitrarily. Douglas, writing in 1800, agrees, 'had we retained a Court and Parliament of our own, the tongue of the two sister kingdoms would, indeed, have differed like the Castilian and the Portuguese'.[16] However, by that time the powerful tides of political unionism, metropolitan fashion and commercial expediency were flowing against the language, at least among the Scottish elites. James Adams, an English Jesuit with a strong interest in the Scots language, wrote in 1792, just 40 years since the start of anti-Scots language campaigns, 'the Scotch accent yields in the Capital, and the Universities, to refined English'.[17]

15 Alexander Geddes 1782, quoted in Jones 1995:14

16 Quoted in Jones 1995:14

17 Quoted in Jones 1995:18

The Eclipse of Scottish Culture?

The long-term social and political consequences of this turbulent time in Scottish history have since sparked passionate debate. Did the early anglicisation of the Scottish elites block the 'normal' European-style manifestation of nationalism of the late 19th century? Scottish Marxist historian Tom Nairn thinks not, and in *The Break-up of Britain*[18] sketches out a materialist explanation for what he calls 'Scottish belatedness', avoiding the necessity for a culture-based interpretation. In his well-accepted model, industrialisation and the rapid modernisation of the large, older core states of Europe such as England and France triggered a reactive wave of national movements in the less developed peripheries. Fearing political domination, cultural assimilation or merely to protect their own status, the provincial bourgeoisies were forced to resist. Many developed their own 'alternative' national identities, turning to the local intelligencia to construct a romantic narrative to unite them with the populace they would need in order to gain and consolidate power. According to Nairn's model:

> [T]he national or would-be national middle class is always compelled to 'turn to the people'. It is this compulsion that really determines the new political complex ('nationalism') that comes forth.[19]

Scotland at the time had a dynamic middle class and a remarkable range of distinguished Enlightenment intellectuals to hand, so, where did it all go wrong? According to Nairn, it was the economy. Scotland had industrialised early on and, via the Union, now had access to international markets. The 1840 edition of *Black's Tourist Guide to Scotland* commented that Scottish commerce had, 'increased with astonishing rapidity, especially within a comparatively recent period', and a 'vast' trade had been established particularly with America and the West Indies.[20] As a consequence, the guidebook continues:

> [T]he Scotch have advanced more rapidly than the English or Irish, in wealth, and the command of the necessities and conveniences of life. Their progress in this respect has been quite astonishing.

18 Nairn 1977, 2015

19 Nairn 1977, 2015:79

20 Black and Black 1840:10

Nairn confirms, 'there was no real, material dilemma of under-development'[21] and therefore, as 'the Scottish petty bourgeoisie had little reason to be discontented', it had no need to develop a 'populist' nationalism to protect its interests.

In Nairn's Marxist paradigm, materialistic abundance is a sufficient explanation for the non-appearance of nationalism in the 19th century, but as an aside concedes that; 'True, the Scots did not have a really separate majority language'.[22] As language identity is often regarded as a crucial component of any nascent nationalism, Nairn may have felt compelled to downplay its relevance to Scotland by adding:

> [H]owever important language becomes as a distinguishing mark in the subsequent advance of nationalism, it is rarely of primary importance in precipitating the movement. It is heavy artillery, but not the cause of battle.

That may be so, but after a century of intense and intentional self-anglicisation, it was only the Scottish bourgeoisie and intelligencia who 'did not have a really separate majority language'; the rest of the Scottish populace most certainly did.

An alternate interpretation is that at a pivotal point in European history, Scottish society's leaders were not only endeavouring to speak a different language from the populace but went out of their way to re-frame the vernacular of their fellow citizens as inferior. From this sociolinguistic perspective, it may have been impossible for the Scottish middle class to 'turn to the people' in Nairn's terms, as they had already rejected their linguistic identity. It should be acknowledged that Nairn ridicules what he called the 'old nationalist theory of the Fall', lampooning it as follows:

> It can be compressed into one word: treachery! The old Edinburgh elite was guilty of the (Romantic) original sin: cutting themselves off from the people.[23]

Nairn is correct to criticise the daft perception of 'treachery', but his mockery misses the point. Anglicisation of the key levers of Scottish society had preceded the age of European nationalist movements by a century. It may not therefore be sufficient just to declare that the intellectuals and bourgeoisie

21 Nairn 1977, 2015:94
22 Nairn 1977, 2015:84
23 Nairn 1977, 2015:96

had no material motivation to 'turn to the people'. The linguistic dynamics of 18th- and 19th-century Scotland suggests they were no longer culturally or indeed psychologically capable of it. Unfortunately, Scotland, in common with all other peripheral areas of Europe, could not escape the new fast-solidifying world of the nation state, where, again in Nairn's words, 'it had either to evolve its own nationalist-type culture, or succumb to someone else's (becoming thereby "provincialized")'.

Although dismissive of cultural causes for Scottish nationalism's failure to launch, Nairn is forthright about the country's subsequent cultural and psychological trauma.

> The Scottish bourgeoisie was not compelled to frame its own pseudo-organic 'community' of culture, in order to channel popular energies behind its separate interests. Hence there was no serious romanticism as a continuing 'tradition', and the indigenous intellectual class became in a curious sense 'unemployed' or functionless in its own terrain. The new Scottish working class, in its turn, was deprived of the normal type of 19th century cultural 'nationalisation': that is, such popular-national culture as there was (vulgar Scottishism or tartanry) was necessarily unrelated to a higher romantic-national and intellectual culture.[24]

The historic shortcoming apparently spawned 'vulgar' Kailyardism, later to be shunned by the Scottish intelligencia, including Nairn himself, as 'a sub-cultural creature rather than a performer in the elevated spheres we are concerned with'.

We will return to the myth of Kailyardism shortly, but what was the psychological impact of the 'collapse into provinciality' for the newly useless Scottish intelligencia? They had few options. Nairn described the 'forced emigration of the sort of intellectual that who elsewhere in Europe was forging a national or nationalist culture', usually to London where Scots played a large role in forging the Empire. Some turned from social sciences to build Scotland's still enviable reputation in the natural sciences, engineering and medicine. Those who did neither were compelled to rationalise their own provincialism.

In *The Eclipse of Scottish Culture* published in 1989, Craig Beveridge and Ronald Turnbull claimed that the provincialised bourgeoisie succumbed to what they term *inferiorisation*. The authors built on the work of post-colonial writer and activist Frantz Fanon. Fanon had written extensively

24 Nairn 2015:100

about the psycho-cultural effects of colonisation in the Third World, and it was provocative, to say the least, to apply this type of analysis to Scotland. Beveridge and Turnbull pugnaciously described the 'cultural oppression' of Scotland through systematic 'inferiorisation'. By this they meant the scholarly habit of contrasting the alleged civilising role of unionism and anglicisation with the barbarousness that came before. Fanon had argued that the culture of any colonised people is usually belittled as barbaric, primitive and uncivilised, to morally justify the process of colonisation itself. However, the 'natives' then begin to internalise the message, accepting, or being forced to accept, that local customs and cultures are inferior to that of their metropolitan colonisers. Continual disparagement damages the confidence and self-respect of the people, and so undermines resistance to foreign rule. The mantra is reinforced by local *évolués*, natives 'who try to escape from their backwardness by desperate identification with the culture of the metropolis'.[25]

From this perspective, Beveridge and Turnbull developed the notion of *inferiorist discourse* as a set of binary oppositions contrasting Scotland negatively against England (eg violent versus decent, parochial versus cosmopolitan, primitive versus sophisticated). The obvious opposition of Scotland (Scots-speaking) versus England (English-speaking) is not listed but fits neatly into their inferiorist framework. The writers, however, emphasised the oft-repeated 'theory of Scottish inarticulacy', quoting James Young who criticised 'the enthusiasm of the Scottish elite in aping their superiors', especially their adoption of the English language, leaving the working and rural classes to struggle with what was in practice a foreign tongue. Even though Beveridge and Turnbull stressed the significance of the 'linguistic-literary consequences of the Union', language itself was not really their focus. Whether you engage with Beveridge and Turnbull's postcolonial discourse or not, it seems hard to disagree with their view that, in a linguistic sense at least,

> [I]n replicating and enlarging the metropolitan images of native retardation, the Scottish intelligencia has fulfilled the same historic function as the colonial *évolués* whose sad condition was analysed by Frantz Fanon.[26]

Over a generation later, is hard to read their account of Scotland's 'loss of self-belief and acceptance of the superiority of metropolitan mores' without recalling the current discourse around both Scotland's languages and Scottish independence itself.

---

25 Beveridge and Turnbull 1989:6

26 Beveridge and Turnbull 1989:112

The 18th century vernacular 'revival'

While Scots was being diligently erased from everyday upper- and middle-class speech throughout the 18th century, paradoxically it continued to be tolerated, even encouraged, as an artistic vehicle. Publisher John Pinkerton acknowledged this inconsistency in 1786.

> None can more sincerely wish a total extinction of the Scottish colloquial dialect than I do, for there are few modern Scotticisms which are not barbarisms [...] Yet, I believe, no man in either kingdom would wish an extinction of the Scottish dialect in poetry.[27]

Despite the general anglicisation of the Scottish printing trade, the publication of comedic and satirical poems in Scots survived and even thrived. This informal, unruly tradition served as a bridge to the 18th century revitalisation of Scots 'vernacular' poetry by Allan Ramsay and others. Marina Dossena, however, detected the origins at this time of the 'English is the language of the head and Scots is the language of the heart' trope that would bedevil discussion about the Scots language for the next 200 years.[28] The very success of Ramsay as a 'bucolic' wordsmith may have contributed to this dualistic fantasy. Even under the prescriptive regime of improvement on both sides of the border, the value of local vernaculars to add richness to verse was widely praised. Dossena quotes Ramsay writing in 1721, the year *The Gentle Shepherd* was published; 'The Scotticisms which may offend some over-nice ear, give new life and grace to the poetry'. Both Ramsay and his successor Robert Fergusson exploited the potential of mixing English and Scots in their poetry, consciously choosing one variety over the other for expressive effect. Fergusson himself was a renowned linguist and was able to emulate Augustan English for a satirical assault on Samuel Johnson's style in 1773. Fergusson also introduced an overtly patriotic element to Scots poetry in *The Ghaists*, writing; 'Black be the day that e'er to England's ground / Scotland was eikit by the UNION'S bond'.

Robert Burns embodied all these themes; the natural bilingualism, the purposeful use of Scots expressions, the acknowledgement of a partly anglophone readership, the patriotic potential of the language and, above all, the deft switching between Scots and English for poetic and semantic effect. Burns' rich depictions of rural Scottish life radically departed from decorous Augustan themes, and his use of Scots only amplified the impact.

---

27 Quoted in McClure 1995:57

28 Dossena 2005:82

His first collection, *Poems, Chiefly in the Scottish Dialect*, commonly known as the Kilmarnock Edition, was published in 1786. This was just 15 years after the French philosopher Jean-Jacques Rousseau had concocted his ideal of the Noble Savage, implying that 'natural' men were superior to those whom civilisation had corrupted. The French influence was still strong in Edinburgh's cultural elite at the time, and much was made of Burns' modest (but 'noble') background as 'the Ayrshire Ploughman'. His daring use of now-stigmatised Scots no doubt added an accessible exoticism to freshly anglicised audiences.

Burns favoured Scots for personal or local experiences and switched to English when he wanted to generalise. Like Ramsay before him, Burns was impressively bilingual in Augustan English and Scots. He was aware of the complex interplay in his work between the two languages, and the wider meanings that both referenced. Dossena quotes several pleas for Burns to tone down his Scots, such as; 'In your future compositions, I wish you would use the modern English. You have shown your powers in Scottish sufficiently', and an appeal, 'why should you write only for a part of the island, when you can command the admiration of a whole'. It is to Burns' credit that he seems to have ignored critics' protests about his 'uncouth dialect' that was 'often unintelligible to an English reader'. On the other hand, like many Scottish poets who came after him, he may have just been canny about preserving his linguistic brand.

The early 19th century: stigmatisation and Scott

The growing prejudices surrounding Scots that emerged in the immediate post-Union period solidified into dogma as the following century progressed. Scots became a class-based sociolect, increasingly disconnected from the rich and the powerful who ran Scotland. At the beginning of the 19th century the energetic campaign to extinguish vernacular Scots among the upper elites began to dissipate, largely because the mission had by then been accomplished. The renowned Edinburgh judge Lord Cockburn, himself a Scots speaker, remarked as early as 1844, 'Scotch has ceased to be the vernacular language of the upper classes'.[29] The Scottish aristocracy had been sending their sons to be educated in English public schools since the Union of the Crowns, but the socially ambitious well-to-do anglophones soon established local educational provision. In the private Edinburgh Academy, opened in 1824, Billy Kay notes, 'Scots was banned, and the English of England fostered'. Class and linguistic stratification are still a feature of the

29 Quoted in Kay 1993:112

Edinburgh education system nearly two centuries later.

Modern linguistic nationalists might reflect on the ostensibly Chinese proverb 'the fish rots from the head down', as the middle classes were soon eagerly aping the southern speech stylings of those they considered their social superiors. Through the century, such linguistic converts would become enthusiastic and self-righteous evangelisers of English, especially via their influence on the emerging system of public education. Social stigmatisation, initiated only a few generations previously in the salons of Edinburgh, now accelerated briskly aided by the possibilities of mass print. Notions of Victorian gentility, self-help and social improvement would later add further pressure on Scotland's uncouth tongue. The eradication of Scottish vernacular speech soon became a moral crusade. Prescriptive guides to polite speech and writing, cheaply produced and with snappy titles like *Scotticisms Corrected*, continued to be bestsellers throughout the century.

The popularity of such manuals was, ironically, an indirect measure of the continuing ubiquity of Scots in the 19th century linguistic landscape. But how many Scots speakers were there? Although Gaelic speakers had been counted since 1755, nobody thought to include Scots in any Census, so we can never know exactly. That said, a crude estimate can be attempted. As stated earlier, in 1707 roughly seven Scots in ten spoke Scots (ie just about everyone who was not a Gaelic speaker) and we know in 2011 about one Scot in three still spoke some Scots. If we assume a steady decline between these two data points, we can work out the rough percentages and, by adjusting with data from the Census, approximate speaker numbers. By this crude reckoning, at the beginning of the 19th century over 60 per cent of the population would have been Scots speakers, dropping to about 50 per cent at the end. However, the era was also one of profound demographic change. The Scottish population grew from 1.6 million in 1801 to 4.4 million just a century later. If the majority were Scots speakers, by the beginning of the 20th century numbers could have reached a peak of well over 2 million speakers, dropping back over the next 100 years to the roughly 1.6 million recorded speakers today.

Such a dramatic change clearly had an impact on the language. Most of the growth was in the towns and cities, and the original Scots dialects of these places were overlaid by the speech of hundreds of thousands of incomers, including Gaelic and Highland English-speaking Highlanders and migrants from Ireland. As Kay points out, the emerging urban *lingua francas* 'remained Scots' but noticeably diverged from the rural dialects praised by the Scots revival writers of the previous century.[30] The linguistic differences were probably overstated, then as now, but the myth took hold

30 Kay 1993:121

of a dichotomy between pure, rural 'Good Scots', associated with the pastoral romance of rustic noble savages, and the apparently contaminated vernacular of the emerging industrial working class.

In the world of literature, the early 19th century is associated with the literary giant Sir Walter Scott. Scott's long romantic poems *Marmion* (1808), *The Lady of the Lake* (Loch Katrine) and *The Lord of the Isles* (1815) established his international reputation, but his immensely popular and Scots-rich Waverley novels (from 1814) consolidated his global impact. Although he had a keen ear for the vernacular spoken around him, Scott's attitude to the language itself seems ambivalent. Nairn contends that Scott's historical novels, and presumably their language, are sealed in the past.[31] Unlike nationalist romanticists elsewhere in Europe at the time, Scott does not use history as a call for national (re)awakening and action – indeed, the opposite. According to Nairn, through his novels Scott 'speaks the language of Tory Unionism and "progress"', implying 'the real interests of contemporary Scotland diverge from those of the auld sang'. In this subtle reframing, Scots could never be considered a modern language worth championing, only a quaint historical relic. As an aside, Scott is also accused of having invented 'tartanry' by organising the Edinburgh reception for a plaid-clad George IV in 1822. The incongruous association of the (Lowland) Scots language with (Highland) tartanry would cast a malignant cultural shadow in later years.

The late 19th century: beyond Kailyard

Robert Louis Stevenson became a similar literary megastar for the end of the century. Achieving instant success with *Treasure Island* (1883) and then *The Strange Case of Dr Jekyll and Mr Hyde* (1886), he continued with the classic Scottish tales *Kidnapped* (1886), *The Master of Ballantrae* (1889) and the unfinished *Weir of Hermiston* (1896). Like Scott, Stevenson used his knowledge of Scots to powerful effect, bringing an authentic voice and perspective to his romances, although he wrote only one short story, *Thrawn Janet* (1881), completely in Scots. Aside from Stevenson, though, the late 19th century is still commonly associated with a much less prestigious type of Scottish writing, the 'Kailyard School', through which the Scots language became damned by association. 'Kailyard' referred originally to a small set of late 19th century novels about Scottish rural life that featured much Scots language dialogue. Their 'couthy' subject matter, sentimentalised tone and perceived popularity, however, irritated Scottish intellectuals, who later extended the term to disparage any kitsch or 'shortbread tin' representation of Scottish identity.

31 Nairn 2015:93

Kailyard turned into an extraordinary century-long obsession for the Scottish intelligencia. Nairn saw 'the great tartan monster' as a sign that Scottish culture was fundamentally defective, a consequence of Scottish nationalism's failure to properly launch at what he saw as the historically appropriate time. In *The Break-up of Britain*, Nairn wrote:

> The popular consciousness of separate identity, uncultivated by 'national' experience or culture in the usual sense, has become curiously fixed or fossilised on the level of the *image d'Epinal* and Auld Lang Syne, of the Scott Monument, Andy Stewart and the *Sunday Post* – to the point of forming a huge, virtually self-contained universe of *Kitsch*.[32]

All the icons he names are associated with the Scots language. I remember as a student in the 1980s visiting the prominent *Scotch Myths* touring exhibition, curated by Murray and Barbara Grigor when it landed in St Andrews. Just three years after the 1979 referendum failure, the display critiqued a Scotland portrayed by images of romantic kitsch, tartan and unquestioned stereotypes. The Grigors even made an amusing *Scotch Myths* film to help identify and presumably destroy this pernicious sub-identity. I recall finding the exhibition simplistic and patronising. Beveridge and Turnbull articulated my discomfort a decade later.

> Drawn to a cultural world in which Scottish traditions and practices carry little prestige, our intellectuals display a remarkable lack of sympathy for local culture.[33]

Paradoxically, just four years after *Scotch Myths*, William Donaldson started to dismantle the myth of Kailyard through two forensically evidenced reviews of late 19th century literary history; *Popular Literature in Victorian Scotland: language fiction and the press* in 1986 and *The Language of the People: Scots prose from the Victorian revival* in 1989. Donaldson's revisionist thesis has three components: firstly, Kailyard was an English and US literary phenomenon, not primarily a Scottish one. Secondly, book publishing was a tiny and insignificant part of Scottish literary output and consumption of the time, the overwhelming majority of fiction appearing in newspapers and weeklies. Finally, much of that literary output was actually in the Scots language, although 'according to the textbooks none of it ought

32 Nairn 2015:134

33 Beveridge and Turnbull 1989:12

to exist'.[34] It should be noted that Donaldson's re-evaluation of the printed presence of Scots was not especially welcomed by Scottish academia of the time, apparently more comfortable with the Scotch Myth certainties of Kailyardism. John Corbett also cautions:

> [A]n accurate assessment of its significance remains elusive, partly since the material that Donaldson champions is still largely unexplored, and partly because the source materials were not designed to be other than ephemeral, and so little found its way into book form.[35]

Donaldson identifies Kailyard as originating with two books by JM Barrie, *Auld Licht Idylls* (1888) and *A Window in Thrums* (1892), both published in London by evangelical William Robertson Nicoll. He was the editor of the British Weekly and considered by Donaldson the 'Godfather' of the Kailyard. These small-town tales, based in a fictionalised Kirriemuir, were followed in 1894 by *Beside the Bonnie Brier Bush*, by Liverpool-based Presbyterian John Watson ('Ian Maclaren'). An instant best-seller in England and the US, the tale is based on Watson's experiences as a Free Church minister in Perthshire and the book blends homespun humour and pathos with lots of pawky Scots dialogue. Donaldson pointed out the Scottish market was comparatively tiny, so the books were deliberately aimed at an English readership with the content and Scots language adjusted appropriately. Moreover, the tone was overtly sanctimonious as these were essentially works of evangelical propaganda for a religious nonconformist readership. The connection, therefore, between the Kailyard novels and mainstream Scottish popular culture of the time may have been tenuous.

According to Donaldson, Scottish people did not tend to read novels, or at least not in this format. The repeal of the Stamp Act in 1855 led to dramatic drop in prices and the almost instant creation of a popular Scottish newspaper market. Growth was driven by the rapid pace of technological innovation, such automated papermaking, mechanical typesetting, fast steam-driven rotary presses and distribution via the ever-expanding railway network. By the end of the century, Scotland had over 200 daily and weekly titles, many of them carrying serialised fiction written specifically for a Scottish audience. Donaldson emphasised that this was a Scots-owned enterprise, mostly written by and for Scots and – in contrast to the book trade – not having to dilute content or language for an English market. Scotland had achieved 'print autonomy' for the first time ever and rejoiced in it.

---

34 Donaldson 1989:1

35 Corbett 2008:22

Donaldson calculated that some 125 novel-length works were printed in this format every year between 1860 and 1900, and compares this with the half dozen or so 'Scottish interest' novels published annually in traditional book form.[36] The writing was considerably more realist than Kailyard's pious whimsy and adding to this impressive publishing tally was 'an enormous body' of short stories and autobiographical, folklore and social history writing. Donaldson suspected the reason this remarkable aspect of Scottish printed popular culture had been systematically ignored was the class of the readership. Scotland had achieved remarkable literacy rates for the era, over 80 per cent.

> [A] significant part of the literary market in Scotland during most of the 19th century was not the middle class with its subscription libraries and imported English novels, but the Scots-speaking working class and the native writers that catered for it through the medium of the popular press.[37]

The most extraordinary aspect of the story, though, is not the existence of this lost literature but the fact that so much of it was in Scots prose. Donaldson suggests that in a competitive print market, this may just have been common business sense.

> Scots was the dominant medium of spoken communication throughout the Lowlands and this was reflected in the creation of a radical new speech based vernacular prose as soon as the means of doing it became available.

Scots was no marketing tokenism, however; 'the language was immediately revealed as an expressive and wide-ranging discursive medium' that writers used to deal not just with nostalgic peculiarity but with every aspect of contemporary Scottish life.' Donaldson's 1989 collection of Scots prose from the popular press reveals an exciting and vigorous language, dialectal and sometimes mixed with English, but an all-purpose rich and expressive form nonetheless. According to Donaldson, this was the true language of the Scottish people revealed for the first time; democratic, secular, egalitarian, anti-imperialistic, against class privilege and, above all, 'utterly removed from the douce and kirk-gaun, meek mim-mou'd brainless yokelry of Barrie,

36 Donaldson 1986:148

37 Donaldson 1986:148

Maclaren and similar middle-class book novelists'.[38]

Amid this explosive, entrepreneurial working-class celebration of the Scots language, the middle-class evangelists of anglicisation were already tightening their grip on Scottish culture at what they saw as its most vulnerable point: education. In one of its last independent Acts in 1696, the Scottish Parliament had established a church-run school in every parish, thus explaining why literacy rates in Scotland were comparatively high. Although reading in English was taught well, evidence suggests in the mid-19th century 'the language of everyday communication, indeed the language of general instruction was still Scots'.[39]

The 1872 Education (Scotland) Act would soon change all that. Celebrated at its centenary as, 'the most important Act in the history of Scottish Education'[40], the Act is equally considered as the prime instrument in the official marginalisation, stigmatisation and eventual suppression of the Scots language. In a 1950 radio series, playwright Robert Kemp called the Act 'the villain of the piece in the story of the general debasement of Scots'. David Muirson, editor of *The Scottish National Dictionary*, agreed, 'the Education Act of 1872 doesn't specifically mention the language [...] it brought in the school inspectorate with violently anti-Scottish ideas'.[41] The Act was not fully superseded until 1946, by which time its ethos of anglicisation had become deeply engrained in Scottish education. Official instruction for new primary teachers in 1946 still hammered home its oppressive message: 'the first duty of the infant teacher and the continuing duty of all primary teachers is to implant and cultivate fluent speech in standard English'.[42]

Industrialisation and rapid urbanisation in the first part of the century had put additional pressure on Scotland's hitherto successful church school system. The Disruption of 1843 (the bitter schism between the Free and Established churches that distracted the Scottish intelligencia for a decade) further fragmented provision. The 1872 Act made it compulsory for every child between the ages of five and 13 to receive education and led to the establishment of a thousand regional School Boards (supervised by London, of course) and a much-needed school building programme. Scots was not 'banned' outright – impossible anyway with so many Scots-speaking teachers but, like Gaelic, marginalised by omission. Thus, the Act openly privileged what for most working-class and rural children was still an alien language.

38 Donaldson 1986:10

39 Kay 1993:114

40 Scotland 1972:121

41 Both quoted in Kemp 2018

42 HMSO, cited in Corbett and Stuart-Smith 2013:213

However, as Kay notes, 'the changes would take a long time to percolate through the system'[43], and the report of The Committee of Education in Scotland for 1878–9 admitted 'broad Scotch is employed in several parts of the of the country' to help explain lessons.[44] More enlightened teachers appreciated the power of the home language to educate and engage pupils, and Her Majesty's Inspectorate (HMI) report suggested Burns, Hogg and popular Scots language songs such as 'There's nae luck aboot the hoose' were still being taught throughout the century. Nonetheless, the increasingly powerful Inspectorate enforced conformity through, for example, *The Scotch Code* of 1878 that set standards of examination for reading and writing in English with 'particular attention' paid to spelling and grammar.

Kay quotes one Inspector's indignation in 1904 on seeing Scots language materials used in school hours, instead of in their apparently rightful place: the home.

> English must be the staple of instruction if we are to give the children the fullest possible equipment in words and thought for modern life. The rest is luxury whatever the perfervid nationalist might say.[45]

Kay's rejoinder is scornful.

> Many will recognise the contemporary ring to that statement; indeed it is so common for establishment figures in Scotland to be agents of cultural genocide, that what in fact is a barbaric negation of civilisation and culture is accepted blandly as the norm. Anyone who stands up for Scottish culture is automatically classed 'a perfervid nationalist'.

In 1894, the Scottish Home Rule Association had been established with the aim of setting up a devolved parliament in Edinburgh, so the Inspector's fear of 'perfervid' nationalists was not as surprising as it now seems. By the late 19th century, Scotland had become an increasingly bureaucratic and undemocratic statelet run by a network of boards, unelected inspectors and commissioners only responsible to London. Supervision was eventually consolidated under the Scottish Office in 1885, but this only highlighted for some nationalists how many critical decisions affecting Scotland were made externally. In the 1890s, however, there was little public or political space in

43 Kay 1993:114

44 Cited in Corbett and Stuart-Smith 2013:212

45 Kay 1993:115–116

Scotland for nationalists or other radicals to be heard, and even less prospect of getting a meaningful response.

Political powerlessness, combined with the disorientation of rapid linguistic and social change in Scotland, had a deadening effect among the remaining middle-class Scots speakers. Instead of motivating resistance to anglicisation, discourses of decay and death began to grip their spirit. According to their fatalistic reasoning, the Scots language was now locked in an irreversible process of disintegration, dilution and debasement. Dossena quotes Lord Henry Cockburn, who observed mid-century:

> [T]he sphere of the Scotch language, and the course of Scotch feelings and ideas is rapidly abridging, even in Scotland [...] the lower orders still speak Scotch, but even among them the flavour is not fresh and natural as it was fifty years ago, particularly in towns.[46]

The secondary stigmatisation of urban forms of Scots as vulgar in comparison with the idealised memories of rural dialects consolidated itself as a recurrent theme. This pervasive discourse of decline seemed to justify passivity among those who could have intervened. Kay is typically uncompromising, seeing bourgeois loyalty to their class as more crucial than loyalty to their culture.

> [W]hen the Scottish upper classes frequently state that Scots is dying, and revel in nostalgia for the generation before when all classes spoke Scots, they are distancing themselves from the fact that Scots was still spoken in an undiluted form by the vast majority of the population.[47]

One more positive outcome of this 19th century linguistic nostalgia was a growing fascination with *antiquarianism*, the lexicographic interest in Scots words and their origins. Since the days of Boswell, who had collected his own list of 800 Scots words, the need for a Scots dictionary had been recognised. The Reverend Dr John Jamieson eventually published the two-volume *Etymological Dictionary of the Scottish Language* in 1808. The dictionary, a magnificent effort that took 20 years to complete, would serve as an inspiration as well as a linguistic treasure trove for future Scots writers. Jamieson had initially held the view that Scots was merely a corrupt dialect of English but, as the title of his masterpiece shows, he soon changed his mind. Dossena notes a subtle connection between antiquarianism and nationalism:

46 Dossena 2005:122

47 Kay 1993:112

> [T]he search for antiquity implicitly meant a search for authenticity, originality and consequently higher status, almost to compensate for the disappointment that the Union had engendered.[48]

Perhaps in confirmation, the next major dictionary of Scots, Charles Mackay's *A Dictionary of Lowland Scotch* published in 1888 opened with a pugnacious claim of linguistic status; 'The Lowland Scottish language is not a mere dialect, as many English people believe; but a true language'.[49] The power of the language, according to Mackay, lay with the people who spoke it, not the writers. His dictionary aimed to celebrate the historic richness of the language, but also 'what stores of literary wealth lie comparatively unknown and unregarded in the vernacular of what are irreverently called the "common people"'. To Mackay, 'it is the "common people" who create and shape the language', authors being just its custodians, 'uncommon people', who have a simple duty to perpetuate the language 'for the pleasure and instruction of posterity'. Sound advice some of the more self-important Scots writers of the following century might have done well to heed.

Antiquarianism also stimulated an interest in *dialectology*. The documentation of spoken Scots was to come to full fruition in the first quarter of the 20th century. The first of these works was James Murray's *The Dialect of the Southern Counties of Scotland*, published in 1873. Murray was no linguistic nationalist, claiming Lowland Scotch and Northern English were part of the same dialect group; 'they are forms of the Angle, or English, as spoken by those northern members of the Angle or English race'.[50] Notions of race should rightly ring alarm bells for modern readers,[51] but Murray's book is still a remarkably detailed document on the distinctiveness of spoken Scots of the 19th century and was the first to outline the main Scots dialect zones still used today.

The early 20th century: a death greatly exaggerated

For a tongue that had, by orthodox wisdom, been in fast decline since the Union, Scots entered the 20th century with surprising vigour, still the mother language of perhaps 2 million individuals. A speaker at a Kilsyth Burgh School Board in 1902 noted, 'the class English of the School was an entirely different thing from the language used on the street' and urged tolerance

48 Dossena 2005:129

49 Mackay 1888:viii

50 Murray 1873:5

51 Eg Kidd 2003 on 'Teutonic racism'

of the pupils' language; 'let them employ English but do not neglect braid Scots'.[52] Returning to his Dundee birthplace in 1907, Sir William Alexander Craigie, Oxford University don and founder of *A Dictionary of the Older Scottish Tongue*, commented that 'the Scottish language had never ceased to be the ordinary form of speech among the greater part of the population', and moreover it 'had not changed materially in any important respect since the sixteenth century'.[53] His view was corroborated by a remarkable memorandum published by the Scotch Education Department the same year.

> The mother-tongue of most Lowland children is so like English that they can understand simple spoken English to some extent when they enter school, though they cannot use it freely. Yet Lowland Scots, being historically a national language, possessing a literature to which the children will be introduced one day, is not to be treated like a provincial dialect. The teacher should not discourage its use by children in those familiar talks through which he seeks to give them confidence, nor hesitate to use it himself when English fails as a means of communication.[54]

The Scots language press remained busy. George Douglas Brown's Scots-rich *The House with the Green Shutters*, considered a sharp retort to Kailyardism, was published in 1901. In the same year, the US exile Reverend William Wye Smith produced a readable and surprisingly informal *New Testament in Braid Scots*, so popular it was reprinted several times. In 1902, JJ Bell launched the first book in of the immensely popular *Wee Macgreegor* series, describing the family life of working-class Glaswegians using Glasgow Scots dialogue. An energetic cottage industry of Scots-language poets had also emerged, including Charles Murray, Violet Jacob, Marion Angus, Helen B Cruikshank and many others.

Nonetheless, intellectuals feared the language losing both its status and its 'purity'. In 1909, William Grant remarked,

> Abandoned by the higher classes, the old language [has] tended to become more and more the expression of the humbler portion of the community. Within the previous twenty years the process of 'substitution' has been accelerated through the spread of education.[55]

52 Kilsyth Chronicle 1902
53 Dundee Courier 1907
54 Scotch Ed Dept 1907:Para 4
55 *Dundee Courier* 1909

About the same time, John Buchan feared what Millar would later call the 'dialectisation' of Scots. The following is from his 1915 preface to Violet Jacob's *Songs of Angus*.

> The various accents remain but the old words tend to be forgotten, and we may be in sight of the time when that noble speech shall be degraded to a northern dialect.

Not everyone succumbed to such nostalgia and despondency. Some saw the existential threat to Scots as a call to document what remained. The preservation of Scots was generally seen in cultural or heritage terms with little overt connection made during this period between language and political nationalism, 'perfervid' or otherwise. Nevertheless, the intellectual effort on behalf of Scots was impressive. Alexander Warrack's *Scots Dialect Dictionary*, published in 1911, included 60,000 entries. Later renamed the Chambers *Scots Dictionary*, it remained a mainstay for Scots language scholars until nearly the end of the century. The spoken forms of Scots were not neglected either. In 1915, Sir James Wilson published the first of three significant studies of vernacular Scots dialects. *Lowland Scotch as Spoken in the Lower Strathearn District*, based on the speech of his native Dunning (where, coincidentally, I went to school), was followed by *The Dialect of Robert Burns as Spoken in Central Ayrshire* in 1923 and *The Dialects of Central Scotland* in 1926.

The First World War had a devastating effect on Scotland and its communities. It is estimated that over a quarter of all Scots who fought in the war were killed or injured. Close village networks of young men, who sociolinguists would later realise to be vital to the maintenance of nonstandard languages, were shattered forever and non-combatants, especially women, moved to the cities to work in munitions factories. Many who returned later looked for better prospects overseas. The linguistic effect of this mass demographic disruption is unknown. Miraculously, it is possible to hear the language skills that were being lost. A pioneering German sound engineer, Wilhelm Doegen, toured prisoner-of-war camps between 1915 and 1918 to record Scottish soldiers (and other British detainees) retelling Bible stories in their own words. These can be accessed free from the British Library's online archive *The Berliner Lautarchiv British & Commonwealth Recordings* and are well worth listening to. Three things strike you immediately; the quality of their Scots, their fluency in telling the stories suggesting Scots was still used for Bible study and, lastly, the striking similarity of the Scots regional dialects.

The *Manual* and MacDiarmid

The most significant work of the immediate post-war era was William Grant and J Main Dixon's magisterial *Manual of Modern Scots* first published in 1921. It was written for students of Scottish literature and language, then undergoing something of a revival in Scotland and the United States. Through meticulous scholarship, Grant and Dixon defined the fundamentals of the structure and usage of modern literary Scots. The authors recognised the prescriptive potential of this mission and were explicit in their aim of 'establishing a certain amount of uniformity in the public use of our ancient national speech'. They justified this approach by a key argument worth quoting in full.

> At the present time, Scottish dialect varies from one district to another all over the Lowland area, in pronunciation, idiom, vocabulary, and intonation. Most of our Scottish writers, however, have refused to bind themselves to any local form of dialect. Like Moliere, they take their good where they can get it. They use the Scottish tongue and address themselves to Scottish speakers everywhere. They aim to be understood by the nation and not merely by the parish or county. 'I simply wrote my Scots as I was able,' remarks Stevenson, 'not caring if it hailed from Lauderdale or Angus, Mearns or Galloway; if I had ever heard a good word, I used it without shame, and when Scots was lacking or the rhyme jibbed I was glad, like my betters, to fall back on English.' It is this ingrained consciousness of a general Scottish speech of a real 'Lingua Scottica' apart from dialect varieties that explains the almost passionate insistence of patriotic Scotsmen on the use of the term 'Scottish Language'.[56]

The *Manual* laid the foundations of future prescriptive grammars and describes what would be later implicitly recognised as Good Scots.

It could thus be said that by the mid-1920s Scots had ample high-quality literary and academic resources to consolidate it into a respectable, fully functional language, had there been any political will to do so. One of the barriers to formalisation, however, was the unsavoury issue of 'purity'. The Scots language was changing quickly, and in ways wholly novel and disturbing to cultural observers and even many speakers. Without any modern conceptions of 'normal' sociolinguistic change, commentators of the time instinctively harked back to 18th century ideas of Augustan linguistic

56 Grant and Dixon 1921:xx

purism. The new hybrid varieties emerging, especially in the cities, were met with utter horror by many commentators, Scottophobes and Scots language enthusiasts alike. The notion of 'substitution', to use Grant's 1909 term, was invariably seen as degeneration or dilution, and contributing further to the odd linguistic passivity described earlier.

Scots was certainly under pressure. Most lowland Scots were now literate in English and mass media was quick to exploit this new market. The cultural autonomy of Scottish newspapers began to erode, and Scots language content jettisoned in the process. Such a loss of mainstream Scots reading material must have had an impact on the language. One columnist in the *Aberdeen Press and Journal* in 1925 confirmed that even if Scots was not dying out quite as fast as people claimed, 'braid Scots in its purity and beauty is steadily losing ground and giving place to slang dialect half of it bad Doric and the other half worse English'. Throughout the 1920s and 1930s, campaigners called for more Scots in education and better language and literature scholarship in universities. As ever, these calls fell on wilfully deaf ears. In a rapidly modernising Scotland, Scots was already being branded as parochial or vulgar, associated with the sentimentalised tartan caricature of Scottish culture and language peddled for example by the unimaginably popular Harry (later 'Sir Harry') Lauder.

Meanwhile, the institutional anglicisation of Scottish culture proceeded at pace. On 6 March 1923, the BBC began broadcasting radio from an attic in Bath Street, Glasgow. News, current affairs, sport, religious addresses and entertainment were sent directly into homes that, at that time, would have been largely Scots-speaking. As Corbett remarks, the new technology provided 'the potential of direct access to Scottish voices, rather than to their representation in written form', but in reality, the early years of public broadcasting in the UK were 'characterised by the promotion – by a Scottish director-general, John Reith – of a homogeneous south-eastern pronunciation as the typical "BBC accent"'.[57] The BBC's ideology of language homogenisation has become so normalised it is nowadays hard, even heretical, to think of the BBC speaking with an authentic Scots voice. That said, even the BBC up in its ideological attic could not completely deny the existence of the language spoken below on its doorstep, and the first Scottish radio play broadcast in August 1923 was a version of *Rob Roy*, and Scottish accented voices occasionally featured in other genres, such as the *Scottish Children's Hour*.

In 1924, William Grant recognised the threat from popular English-language media; 'there is a strong tendency to substitute English for Scots',

57 Corbett 2008:28

and if something was not done at once, 'it will be too late to prevent the complete degradation or even loss of our ancient speech'.[58] Reading this warning almost a century later it is hard to escape the sense of another road not taken. In the early 1920s both Grant and his fellow Scots campaigner, the indefatigable William Craigie, drew up a remarkably modern manifesto for the revitalisation of Scots and its restoration as a national language. Speaking to the Workers Education Association in Aberdeen, Grant acknowledged the utility of English in education, 'but we [are] Scotsmen as well as Britons, and if we [are] to retain our nationality, we must cultivate our own language', going on to suggest several practical measures for its formal use in schools.

Appearing in Aberdeen the same year, William Craigie delivered 'a reproach to Scotland' regarding its treatment if Scots. In an early framing of Scots as a European language, he realised the connection between language and nationality across Europe was becoming 'more and more distinct'.

> What were called language movements had had a marked influence not only on the politics but on the culture and literary development of many countries in Europe. Scotland was one of the few countries which had not gone forward in this respect, but, if anything had steadily gone back.[59]

Craigie talked of the 'neglect of the national tongue, which had led to the exclusion from the whole scheme of education'. He felt that 'This was a fault common to many countries a century ago', but by that time, 'there was scarcely one, except Scotland, in which the mistake had not already been remedied'.

Had the ideas of Craigie and Grant gained any traction, the subsequent history of Scots might have been very different, but they were up against a powerful Scottish officialdom still determined to anglicise Scotland. A contemporary editorial in *The Scotsman* captures the establishment attitudes to Scots at that time.[60] Institutional negligence was forwarded by the writer as an excuse for inaction.

> [The] decay and neglect of the vernacular tongue of Lowland Scotland has gone on so long, and has proceeded so far, that it is doubtful whether anything can now be done to restore it to its old position as a living and distinct language and literature.

58 *Aberdeen Press and Journal* 1924a

59 *Aberdeen Press and Journal* 1924b

60 *The Scotsman* 1924

Although praising Scots as, 'rich as it is almost beyond any other human speech, vernacular or classic, in humour and pathos, strength and tenderness', the editor claimed most Scots felt 'torpor and indifference' about their tongue. Consequently, he was sceptical that Scots would ever regain 'a position of credit and respectability' and even doubted the desirability of Scots establishing a 'secure place in the schools and Universities of Scotland as a regular subject of study', as Craigie had persistently demanded. The editorial continued:

> [I]t is even most questionable whether any efforts to resuscitate Scots in the sense and in the manner in which Irish Gaelic is being forced into public use in Southern Ireland would be for the benefit of the nation.

The editor thus offered kind words but only conditional support for Scots, worthwhile 'so far as it can be studied and practiced without injury to wider interests'.

An underground movement was about to shake that institutional complacency. From the early 1920s on, the Scots language started to be adopted as a *cause célèbre* for a diverse group of cultural nationalists led by the maverick and divisive poet genius of 'Hugh MacDiarmid', the literary persona of Langholm-born Christopher Grieve. MacDiarmid's first poem in Scots was self-published in a literary magazine *The Scottish Chapbook* in 1922, but he was not working in isolation. In the magazine, he recognised the campaign of the London Burns Club for the literary revival of 'the Doric' and always acknowledged, if sometimes critically, the Scots language tradition he later came to dominate. He used the dialect studies of Wilson, Murray and others for inspiration, although he was often disparaging of Scots dialect poetry and especially urban Scots. Jamieson's 1808 *Etymological Dictionary of the Scottish Language* became his word trove, MacDiarmid comparing the dictionary in linguistic richness to James Joyce's modernist classic Ulysses, first published in book form in 1922.

Best known for his 1926 long-form epic poem *A Drunk Man Looks at the Thistle*, MacDiarmid became a central figure in what was labelled the Scottish Renaissance. The poet was, among other things, a Scottish nationalist and directly connected the Scots language to a political movement. In *Language, Poetry and Nationhood*, McClure evaluates MacDiarmid's significance.

> Prior to him, the association of Scots as a poetic language with Scottish patriotic feeling was, at best, a tacit assumption: now for the first time (incredibly) in Scottish history, the Scots language was

> to be a strongly-emphasised symbol of Scottish national identity, and its liberation a preliminary to, or indeed an integral part of, the liberation of Scotland. Scots in the hands of MacDiarmid and his successors was no longer simply a language, but a weapon.[61]

MacDiarmid and his Scottish Renaissance disciples re-energised Scots as a meaningful cultural expression throughout the interwar period, with the language question being belatedly raised in public debate. However, as Millar so mordantly observed:

> [It] is in many ways regrettable that the grouping most associated with the cultural and political development of Scots was connected to modernist experimentation rather than the National Romanticism of the early to mid-19th century experienced and the Nordic nations, where the speech of the *Volk* was, at least in theory, at the heart of any literary endeavour.[62]

This politicised intellectual adventure, for all its positives, was to cause problems for the Scots language during the remainder of the century. The 'weaponisation' of Scots robbed the language of any neutrality. Politicisation is a double-edged sword in a stateless nation. Once the unionist establishment recognised Scots as a potent component of a nationalist 'threat', it became a legitimate target. The easiest response was *ad hominem* critique of the poet himself. A quarrelsome and outspoken character with varied and sometimes dubious political opinions, it was easy to vilify the individual and therefore by association his cause and achievements.

A second obvious target was the variety of literary Scots that MacDiarmid and his followers created as a vehicle for their poetry. Although a native speaker of Border Scots, MacDiarmid used dictionaries to augment his repertoire. He was also open about the need to widen the range of Scots by, in his opinion, rediscovering and reusing older or dialect-specific terms. MacDiarmid thought of this as a 'synthesis', ie a creative merging of Scots usage over time and space. This linguistic fusion became known by its proponents as 'Lallans', an old label for Scots originally used by both Burns and Stevenson.

Lallans was intended as a high-register ideologically charged variety of Scots developed specifically for literary purposes. Douglas Young, one of MacDiarmid's most energetic and talented advocates, later articulated the Scottish Renaissance's pugnacious polemic.

61 McClure 2000:100

62 Millar 2018:199

> Lallans is a language of a nation. Hugh MacDiarmid and others are restoring it in full vigour for all the purposes of national self-expression, starting with poetry, the most intense and memorable form of linguistic expression [...] That is what is happening my friends. After prolonged coma, Scotland is waking up, and the Renaissance in Lallans is only one manifestation of this process. [63]

Such a provocative public stance drew many detractors. One weakness was that MacDiarmid's unfortunate coinage 'synthetic' was burdened with the secondary meaning of 'artificial'. Critics claimed that Lallans was completely fabricated and used made-up words far removed from everyday speech. From a purely artistic standpoint the charge is meaningless. Every poet has the licence for linguistic experimentation, to stretch language in whatever way she or he likes. As McClure remarked, 'it is somewhat inequitable that this charge should be brought against MacDiarmid with the air of an accusation'[64]. McClure's own linguistic analysis showed the language used was far less exotic that the critics (or even the poet himself) claimed. MacDiarmid's 1926 masterpiece *A Drunk Man Looks at the Thistle* is written in 'what is essentially a fairly common, even colloquial Scots'. One implication is that by the late 1920s the Scottish middle-class arts establishment was so alienated from the language of the streets and villages that any use of Scots was challenging for them.

Unfortunately, MacDiarmid's impact on the everyday language itself was negligible. He was not especially interested in 'colloquial Scots' and pushed the written language in a more literary direction. This explains why his modernist experiment was, according to Millar of, 'little practical use in the development of language policy and planning for the language', explaining; 'The capriciousness of lexical choice – indeed its very novelty and quantity – made it a dead letter in terms of genuine corpus planning'.[65] Herein possibly lie the roots of Millar's later observation that 'modern literature in Scots is often perceived as distant from the everyday reality of most people's language use'.[66]

Despite, or perhaps because of, the divisive arguments and controversies, the suppression of Scots in public life, and especially in education, continued unremittingly. For all its revolutionary rhetoric, the Scottish Renaissance was uninterested in fighting on the important linguistic battlegrounds that

63 Young 1946:31

64 McClure 2000

65 Millar 2008:13

66 Millar 2018:198

Craigie and Grant had long identified: the classroom and the mainstream media. Amid the controversy, the gritty Greenock novelist and playwright George Blake bravely declared at the 1931 Scottish teachers' union congress in Clydebank 'the Scottish teacher is the most potent force in the anglicisation of Scotland'.[67]

Sunset Song and the birth of *The Broons*

Other writers approached the problem of Scotland's growing linguistic divide less directly. In 1932 Lewis Grassic Gibbon, the pen name of North-East writer James Leslie Mitchell, published *Sunset Song* as the first instalment of his *Scots Quair* trilogy. Gibbon attempted to solve the Scots language conundrum by creating yet another artificial variety of Scots, moving in the opposite direction to Lallans with his diluted 'accessible' Scots. Sunset Song tried to capture the rhythms and tones of the everyday Scots speech of its Kincardineshire village setting, but to me the style is exasperatingly anglicised, neither one thing nor another.

Some were less inclined to compromise. In 1932 the novelist Eric Linklater, after dutifully praising the vernacular and 'the marvellous power and pleasure that it gave', complained it was not 'full grown' and too geographically constrained, so Scottish writers 'would be compelled to use standard English'.[68] Poet Edwin Muir intellectualised this case 1936 in an extraordinary polemic *Scott and Scotland*, making his infamous assertion that Scottish writers should abandon the Scots language altogether. Muir's rationale was that Scottish writers apparently feel in one language and think in another, an absurd but persistent trope.

The Scottish establishment position during the 1930s and early 1940s seems to have been to ignore the tiresome debates of troublesome writers and continue the slow eradication of Scots though what has been described as 'malign neglect', especially in education. Speaking in 1938, the indefatigable William Grant, now well into his 70s but still drumming up funds for the *Scots National Dictionary*, lamented that:

> [A]t least a generation passed out of the schools with little respect for our old language and literature [...] there are more middle-aged Scottish citizens of to-day than ever before who regarded our Scottish speech as a mark of ignorance or low breeding, and a bar to their material prosperity.

67 *Aberdeen Press and Journal* 1931
68 *The Scotsman* 1932

He ends with a quite reasonable plea; 'we have instances in history of languages being revived and producing new literatures', and therefore, 'can not our native Scottish writers set themselves the task of renewing and invigorating our national speech?'.[69] The education authorities, however, continued to ignore even modest ideas such as a 1935 joint proposal by the Scottish Burns Federation, the St Andrews Societies Glasgow and Edinburgh, the Scottish National Dictionary Association and even the Glasgow Ballad Club to have Scots included in the school curriculum as optional subject.[70]

Scots, however, was to find an unlikely champion in the conservative Dundee publisher DC Thomson. On Sunday 8 March 1936 two one-page comic strips, *Oor Wullie* and *The Broons* first appeared in the immensely popular newspaper *The Sunday Post*. The most distinctive feature of both comic strips, still published weekly, was the use of Scots vernacular. The strips were created by Thomson editor RD Low and cartoonist Dudley D Watkins; the latter continued to draw and write them until his death in 1969. Watkins' visual and linguistic style has been faithfully replicated by the publisher ever since. According to Brightwell, writing in 2006, the language was closely aligned with the publisher's overall editorial policy of 'realism', intended to attract the large Scottish urban audience. Brightwell continues:

> Both strips, written in broad Scots dialect, were hits; the Scottish public rapidly took them to their hearts, and there is little doubt that they played a major part in the paper's phenomenal success. In 1971, shortly after Watkins' death, *The Sunday Post* had an estimated readership of just under 3 million, an astounding 79 per cent of the adult population of Scotland.

In 1939, *The Broons* also appeared in the form of a Christmas annual. The following year an *Oor Wullie* annual collection was published and from then until 2015 the titles alternated every second year, except between 1943 and 1946. The annuals became ubiquitous Christmas gifts and nowadays both titles are published annually. The comics' widespread popularity inevitably had a significant effect on Scottish linguistic culture. For most Scots-speakers like me, the comics were the only mainstream and regularly available written representation of our spoken language. I learned to read Scots through these publications at the same time as I learned to read English at the school. The sheer volume of text is also worth mentioning. Stalin once said (allegedly), 'quantity has a quality all its own' and the two strips generate about 30,000

---

69 *Aberdeen Press and Journal* 1938

70 *Fife Free Press &Kirkcaldy Guardian* 1935

words a year, or well over 2 million words published in the over 80-year lifetime of the comics. Compared with the miniscule print runs of poetry books and the like, Watkins' overlooked, and under-appreciated, creation remains a cultural and linguistic colossus among the printed representation of Scottish language.

The strips have some documentary value, too. Given that there was a deliberate focus on authenticity, we can assume the dialogue is at least to some extent representative of the way people speak or spoke. It is surprising there has been so little interest in it from linguists. Why has this remarkable resource been so ignored? The conservative publisher DC Thomson deliberately positioned the comic to appeal to a certain class of audience. It is still widely thought among Scottish middle-class intellectuals that *The Sunday Post* itself represents a particularly conservative and sentimentalised, even 'Kailyard' vision of Scottish life. Scottish historian and intellectual Tom Nairn's harsh 1960s quip that Scotland would only be tolerable when 'the last Kirk minister has been strangled with the last copy of the *Sunday Post*', is for many still a potent trope. Some Scots language aficionados continue to view the language of *The Broons* with distain.

In one of the few academic studies of this material, German linguist Anne Hoyer investigated the process of lexical change in *Oor Wullie*. She acknowledged that the Scotticisms in the cartoons function as instruments of national identification but, through computer-based analysis, found that the vernacular elements had been eroding over the years to be replaced by Standard English.[71] As a once-avid *Broons* reader and native Scots speaker, I was not so convinced, so as part of my linguistic studies at the Open University a few years ago ran my own computer analysis of *The Broons*, using texts spanning 60 years. I discovered that, far from eroding, Scots forms were surprisingly prominent in modern texts, up to ten per cent more than in the older scripts, although the Scots itself had been 'modernised'.[72] I found identifiably 'Scots' elements often constituted half of the texts or more. Interestingly, the most common Scots terms also related to personal interaction, ie they did more communicative and emotional work than simple frequency implied.

Perhaps in response to the comics' success, in 1939 the BBC launched its own Scots-rich family comedy on the radio. *The McFlannels* serial, based on a working-class Glasgow family, was written by Helen W Pryde and starred Molly Weir. One segment gives the flavour of Pryde's representation of Glasgow Scots.

---

71 *The Scotsman* 2006

72 Young 2012

> WILLIE: Here, is there nae sign o' that coalman yet? Folk'll soon no' get intae the close, it's that bung-fu' o' oor furnicher.
> PETER: Here 'e is, daddy. Here's the coalman! Here's the coalman! Here's …
> WILLIE: Well, you come doon affa that jawbox or ye'll be fa'in through the wundy. Come on, noo, Peter, when ye're tell't.
> PETER: Can Ah get carryin' somethin'?
> WILLIE: Mebbe. We'll see. Jist you keep oot the road for a wee.[73]

Think shame: a post-war war against Scots

Trying their best to ignore the plebeian press and radio, by the 1940s the orthodoxy among the Scottish middle class was that Scots was now moribund and already fragmented to isolated dialects. But was this true? In an illuminating feature article in *The Daily Record* prior to Burns Night in 1943, writer JD Leslie reported

> [N]o one who goes about Scotland can dispute that our local dialects and there are many of them, from those of Galloway and the South-eastern Border counties to those of Fife, Angus and Buchan are still the common speech of our country people […] the teaching of English in our schoolrooms, the influence of Americanisms introduced by the talkies, and other causes may have effected changes in certain respects but *the broad basis of the old tongue still remains*. [My emphasis].

Leslie continued with a common grievance still heard today:

> [T]o all the other complaints of inadequate Scottish representation in the wireless programmes must be added the indictment that 'Braid Scots' receives about the scantiest consideration of any tongue at the hands of the BBC.

The author observed that in wartime the BBC had broadcast 'in practically every language in the world', but Scots was largely ignored. Thus, 'there are periods specially devoted to programmes in Welsh and Gaelic, but none solely to the Lowland tongue'. Lamenting that too many Scots 'think shame' of their own tongue, Leslie finished with a forceful message across the years.

> To-day, when we are busy planning a better Scotland, we may find

73 Quoted in Corbett 2008:25

> we are building without a foundation if we neglect to preserve and sustain our native tongue [...] Nor can we Scots hope to realise our own cultural and spiritual aspirations, not even our material ambitions, if we suffer ourselves to lose the asset of speech which is our very birthright.

John Orr, a correspondent to *The Scotsman* in 1942 may provide a hint as to why such sincere and reasonable entreaties were ignored by those in power. He considered any revitalisation of Scots as a 'teachable' language would fail, 'unless it were accompanied by some radical disruption of the social and political unity of this island'.

One of the tacit roles of the BBC is to prevent 'radical disruption' and promote the cohesion of the British state. Towards the end of the war, Scottish nationalism, still at the time closely associated with the Scots language, was beginning to be seen as a threat to the British state. Douglas Young, who had earlier been jailed in Saughton prison as a conscientious objector, stood as the SNP candidate in the Kirkcaldy Burghs by-election in February 1944. In a three-way contest, Young gained 42 per cent of the vote, securing a strong second place to the successful Coalition Labour candidate. To make matters worse, Young was a talented Scots writer and a vociferous advocate of MacDiarmid's Scottish Renaissance movement. The British establishment received a second scare when the SNP won its first parliamentary seat in 1945.

The following year the BBC engineered a clever and coordinated attack on Scots and linguistic nationalism. The Scots language then as now straddles the unstable fault-line of Scottish self-confidence, a source of both pride and, in Leslie's terminology, 'shame'. Unfortunately, the Renaissance activists had neglected to connect with everyday speakers. Scots was a clear target, and the BBC had the firepower to sink it. The weapon of choice was a variant of the 'Synthetic Scots' gambit mentioned earlier. In 1946 the BBC broadcast a lecture by the conservative Scottish historian James Fergusson. Fergusson aggressively condemned poetry in Scots, calling it a 'bastard language' and coined the contemptuous but catchy phrase 'plastic Scots'.[74] In a probably coordinated manoeuvre that was unusual at the time but has since become commonplace in the Scottish media, the *Glasgow Herald* followed with an editorial that drew on the authority of the state broadcaster to intensify the onslaught.

> The BBC has this week rechristened synthetic Scots, that fantastic, original language which has become the raw material of some of our

74 Royle 2011

> poets [...] the BBC prefers to call it plastic Scots, on the theory that it can be compounded of any gobbets of language which, once thrown together, can then be punched into any shape the poet likes. It is not [...] like any tongue ever spoken or written between Shetland and the Solway.[75]

Predictably, this overt assault provoked outrage in the correspondence columns of the Scottish press. Fergusson accused the poets of being motivated by 'nationalist' reasons to separate Scottish and English literary traditions. MacDiarmid, Young and others retaliated with speeches, meetings and pamphlets. Poet Edwin Morgan wrote to the *Glasgow Herald* in late 1946 suggesting that instead of holding a purist view of Scots, authors should follow spoken practice towards 'a Scots mixture' and limit themselves to enriching 'the northern variant of the standard language'.[76] Morgan would reiterate this position some 18 years later in a debate that would define the direction for Scots in the 1960s and beyond.

Beyond the niche world of correspondence columns, the post-war war on Scots speaking children in Scottish education was still proceeding briskly. Providing us with another inadvertent update on the prevalence of Scots in their domain at that time, in 1947 the Scottish Education Department (SED) published an *Advisory Report on Primary Education in Scotland*.[77] Although acknowledging Scots' historical provenance, the language was framed as a 'difficulty' for teachers.

> Today it remains the homely, natural and pithy everyday speech of country and small-town folk in Aberdeenshire and adjacent counties, and to a lesser extent in other parts outside the great industrial areas. But it is not the language of 'educated' people anywhere, and could not be described as a suitable medium of education or culture. Elsewhere, because of extraneous influences it has sadly degenerated, and become a worthless jumble of slipshod ungrammatical and vulgar forms, still further debased by the intrusion of the less desirable Americanisms of Hollywood. Against such unlovely forms of speech masquerading as Scots we recommend that the schools should wage a planned and unrelenting campaign. Any attempt at improvement by detailed criticism would in our opinion be futile. A bolder and more positive policy is needed. As we have indicated earlier in the Report

75 Nicholson 2002

76 McGonigal 2013:123

77 Scottish Education Department, 1947

> the first duty of the infant teachers, and the continuing duty of all primary teachers, is to implant and cultivate fluent speech in standard English.

Shocking as that linguistic edict may be today, Scots was not completely proscribed by the SED. Perhaps responding to a minority view opposed to outright eradication, the advice in the subsequent paragraph was more nuanced, even emollient.

> In the higher classes of the primary school – say in the last three years – we recommend that a short but definite weekly period should be set aside exclusively for Scottish traditions and language, including the reading and recital of verse and prose, telling of stories and the discussion of typically Scottish words, phrases and proverbs. Familiarity with this world of homely Scots should be a suitable introduction to the study of Scottish Literature which should have a definite place in every secondary course. The giving of a separate period in the primary school seems, however, to be necessary to give this study a dignity of its own, instead of the casual and apologetic treatment, if not neglect, from which it so often suffers.

The SED report also emphasised the importance of promoting 'good Scots'. In the same year, Young and his 'Makars' Club' of fellow poets met in an Edinburgh bar to produce the *Scots Style Sheet*, an attempt to produce a regularised orthography of the 'correct' use of the Scots language. A diarist from *The Scotsman* highlighted one key message; 'Apostrophes to be discouraged'.[78] Although the *Style Sheet*, initially entitled *Lalland Usages*, was modest, it was an overtly political act. Nonetheless there seems to have been no plan to implement this proposal beyond the clique of poets. Sixty years later it is hard not to see a yet another lost opportunity in a climate of simmering political and cultural nationalism. Between 1947 and 1949 2 million people signed the National Covenant petition for a Scottish assembly, about 60 per cent of the contemporary electorate. Responding to complaints of a lack of Scottish input in first Edinburgh International Festival in 1947, the next year saw the hugely successful adaptation of Sir David Lyndsay's 16th-century Scots play, *Ane Plesant Satyre of the Thrie Estaitis*. Nonetheless, the contrast between a high-culture festival production in Scots and the reality that children in the same city were still being humiliated and beaten for speaking the same language underlines the ultimate failure of the Lallans movement.

78 *The Scotsman* 1947

The Guid Scots Tongue

In 1950 David Muirson, the editor of the *Scottish National Dictionary*, again asked for Scots to have 'some status in our educational system' and throughout the decade persistent campaigners kept the debate about Scots use in schools just about alive.[79] In response, in March 1952 the Scottish Education Department published a significant memorandum, *English in Secondary Schools*. *The Dundee Courier* of the time headlined, 'Braid Scots is coming back into the schools', and implied the inclusion in the syllabus of Scots prose and poetry would ensure an opportunity for the speaking of Scots.[80] Aitken, writing 30 years later, considered the memorandum's long-term influence to be more malign.[81] In it, the study of English had been predictably emphasised as 'the instrument and precondition of all intellectual progress'. The booklet did not propose that 'attempts should be made to impose on pupil or teacher any one particular speech pattern or accent', but added slyly, 'few will cavil at an exemplar of English generally acceptable to educated Scots'. 'Slovenly perversions of dialect' were to be excluded, but 'local forms of speech, words and phrases of genuine dialect, whether of the Borders or of Buchan, should find a place in the class-room'. As Aitken pointed out, the discrimination was formally made between 'genuine dialect', presumably rural Good Scots, and 'slovenly perversions of dialect', no doubt urban and mixed versions. The memorandum reinforced the prevailing idea that 'bad' forms of Scots speech should be expunged. Nonetheless the memorandum recommended that pupils should be made aware of the origins of the Scots vernacular alongside standard English, and provided clear guidance.

> [C]are should be taken to see that the existence of living dialects is viewed historically and that they are not regarded by pupils with condescension or disapproval as if they were merely debased forms of the language of books.

The 1952 memorandum, like its neglected 1907 predecessor, was a well-intentioned document in that it recognised both the persistence of Scots in 1950s Scotland and its (albeit limited) value in education. But there were no standards set, no public records of progress and no training or support initiatives for the teachers. It seems rather obvious now that if the teachers

79 *The Scotsman* 1950

80 *Dundee Courier* 1952

81 Aitken 1982, 2015

themselves were increasingly unfamiliar with spoken Scots, it would be hard to ask them to distinguish between 'genuine dialect' and 'bad' Scots. By the mid-1960s Scottish teachers were, in my experience anyway, mostly middle-class anglophones. Only a handful of teachers even in the rich Scots-speaking areas where I went to school had any overt skills in, or sympathy for, the language, with predictable consequences for 'encouraging' its use in the classroom.

In the second half of the 20th century public lobbying for Scots in schools seemed to wane, possibly because the number of middle-class Scots-speaking parents with an interest in the tongue was by then dwindling. Working-class Scots-speaking bairns were left to fend for themselves in what was, for many, an environment of humiliation and violence. The link between Scots and political nationalism had been broken after the flurry of debate just after the war. The SNP slipped into political limbo for a generation, reappearing in a very different civic form in the late 1960s, having discarded much of its cultural 'baggage', including advocacy of Scots. There was no appetite among the waning Conservative and rurally based Liberal parties and especially the expanding Labour Party to support the minority language. All three were wary of any moves that would enhance the threat of Scottish nationalism to the British state that they all hoped one day to control. The Scottish media remained, as today, tightly in the grip of middle-class anglophone British nationalists.

Only when Scots was deemed to be sufficiently neutered politically was the BBC able to acknowledge its presence. In 1950, the playwright Robert Kemp wrote and produced *The Guid Scots Tongue*, a 24-part radio series. In the weekly programmes, a refined, fictional character, 'Jean', travelled around the country, learning about the history and local varieties of Scots through explanations, readings and scripted interviews with fictional characters, real speakers and various experts.[82] Although Jean is upbeat, in the last episode she questions a gloomy David Muirson who rather squashes her enthusiasm.

> JEAN: Would you say that Scots is a dying language or is it only changing as I suppose all languages change?
> DM: There's very little doubt about the answer. Scots is dying. There is no standard form. Much of the vocab has already been lost. It has no status except in sentiment. It is not taught in or out of school. Such efforts as there are to keep it going are sporadic and unmethodical.
> JEAN: I'm sorry to hear you say that, terribly sorry.
> DM: Well Jean, what do you think I am? But I don't see any other

82 Kemp 2018

> conclusion possible. The Industrial Revolution came after English was established in Scotland, and the old tongue has only partly and not very successfully adapted itself to urban life. You can't say that Scots is simply changing as other languages do – it no longer recreates from its own resources. It simply borrows from English and American, which are of course prevalent everywhere in Scotland.

Maybe earlier episodes were cheerier. One columnist in the *Fifeshire Advertiser* felt quite uplifted by the series, remarking that though it was commonly believed that radio was having the effect of levelling out individual accents and dialects, *The Guid Scots Tongue* provided plenty of evidence 'of a national pride in the individuality of real Scottish speech'.[83]

Although poets and playwrights continued to write in the Scots language, it seemed the Scottish Renaissance began to lose its momentum during the 1950s. Without any grassroots action, the promotion of Lallans began to look elitist and out-of-touch. This drift was not helped by MacDiarmid's cranky quarrels with nearly everyone in the Scottish artistic community. The majestic *Manual of Modern Scots*, the vernacular scholarship of Wilson, the excellent dictionaries and the *Scots Style Sheet* were all but forgotten and there were few left to uphold the idea of a unified Scots language. The Scots language was therefore in a weak position to face the rapid cultural and societal challenges of the 1960s and beyond.

In the 1959 general election, Labour replaced the Conservatives for the first time as the single biggest party in Scotland, the SNP only contesting five seats. However, at the West Lothian by-election just three years later the SNP candidate William Wolfe pushed the Conservatives into third place and Scottish nationalism was back. However, the nature of the SNP, whom one might think to be the natural political sponsor of the Scots language, had changed. As historian Tom Devine observed, the 'old guard of professionals, writers, academic and upper-class lawyers' had been replaced by skilled working-class and lower-middle-class activists, 'less interested in poetry than in digging out figures on the Scottish economy',[84] and perhaps inevitably less familiar with the Scots language. In this respect the SNP is quite an unusual nationalist party. Since it reinvented itself as a modernist centre-left social democratic party in the 1960s, it largely turned its back on the populist symbolism of the past, especially anything with a whiff of kilts and Kailyardism. The SNP's nationalism aims to be 'a positive socio-political force

83 *Fifeshire Advertiser* 1950

84 Devine 2013:35

or identity'[85], inclusive and the very model of civic-minded rationalism and seems to take pride in being 'the least romantic of nationalist movements'.[86] When it can, the modern SNP tends to keep a distance from traditional or populist manifestations of Scottish nationalism, demonised in different ways by both by the Scottish unionist media and the ostensibly left-leaning Labour Party, the latter for a long time its main electoral opponent.

Vernacular voices in the 1960s

SNP success nonetheless triggered a Scottish cultural upsurge, but by the 1960s 'traditional' linguistic nationalism, now politically side-lined and often represented by the ageing and reliably cantankerous Hugh MacDiarmid, was on the back foot. It faced a demotic challenge from Scottish poets such as Edwin Morgan, Ian Hamilton Finlay and especially Tom Leonard. It seems almost comical nowadays that the often-tiresome spats in the Scottish poetry community of the 1960s and 1970s were accorded such cultural weight, but there were reasons. Firstly, before devolution literature was often a seen as proxy forum for wider political and social debate.[87] Secondly, poetry had historically been a prime carrier of the Scots language and culture, and, finally, Scottish poets of the 20th century simply provided good journalistic copy. They all seemed to be especially opinionated and argumentative, engaging in ritual combat known as 'flyting' through the correspondence columns of the Scottish newspapers.

Ian Hamilton Finlay's 1961 comic poem 'Glasgow beasts, an a burd haw, an inseks, an aw, a fush', set off one such episode. The poem's style was conventional Modern Scots spelling and vocabulary laced with some Glaswegian terms like 'haw', 'wance' and 'yin', a few phonetic spellings 'honess', 'herr-do' and a single phonetic contraction 'didjye'. The language attracted praise from long-time MacDiarmid admirer Edwin Morgan, but ire from MacDiarmid himself. Morgan's intervention was later considered as 'particularly prophetic' as it foreshadowed the fashion for demotic, dialect and overtly 'anti-standard' Scots writing that would come to dominate artistic and establishment attitudes to Scots in subsequent decades.[88] Few people read poetry, of course, but lots of people in Scotland watch television and what happened next had far greater cultural impact.

In 1963 Stanley Baxter, a hugely popular Scottish comedian from the

85 Leith and Soule 2012:4

86 Keating 1996:181

87 Eg Hames 2013:205

88 Watson 2013:87

music hall tradition, was awarded the prize of a self-titled show on the BBC. Within five years *The Stanley Baxter Show* had nearly 5.5 million viewers, mostly in Scotland and especially in the Central Belt, where it was by far the most popular programme. The show was a typical showbiz format of comedy segments, drag-act dancing numbers and so on, but the part everyone in Scotland remembers is *Parliamo Glasgow*, a recurrent sketch that probably single-handedly accounts for the skewed viewer demographics.

A spoof of the traditional BBC *Parliamo Italiano* (*Let's speak Italian*), a rather dry language series broadcast at the time, the comedy features Baxter as the RP-spouting philologist, the 'Professor'. He introduces then listens to supposedly typical conversations in Glasgow Scots, then cuts away to translate the vernacular in linguistically ornate terms, showing on screen a capitalised, phonetic text representation of the speech as if it was an exotic language. The sketches are easily available online, but an extract from one of the later accompanying books gives a flavour of the approach.

> It was my good fortune to meet with a gentleman who invited me to accompany him to the sacred Hogmaniacal rites at a residence in the remote Southern terrain of the city called RASOOSIDE. When I suggested that it might be expedient to engage in a taxicab my companion mentioned a lady's name 'NORAH!' he said, 'NORAHBLIDDICHANCE'. Before I could question him as to the lady's identity, he made certain obscure references to snow and the Yukon. 'SNOWFAUR', he stated, 'YUKONHOOFIT'.[89]

Baxter had an excellent ear for the vernacular, and the sketches and books are very funny, especially if you are familiar with the language. Both capture elements of vernacular Scots at a time when such spoken Scots language was not seen on television, nor even recorded. (Apparently, there was no recording of authentic Scots speech between the 1916 *Lautarchiv* project mentioned earlier and the 1970s when Glasgow University researchers belatedly began to take an interest.) The accuracy of *Parliamo Glasgow* is therefore impossible to verify but, as with the DC Thomson comic oeuvre, its popularity suggests a significant level of audience recognition.

What was the long-term impact of the show, though? Linguistic researcher Johann Unger recorded one of his interviewees, Agnes, reflecting some 40 years later that *Parliamo Glasgow* 'really brought home to people that we weren't speaking the same language'.[90] Ridicule and exaggeration of Scottish

89 Baxter and Mitchell 1982:27

90 Unger 2013:118

speech were, and remain, a staple of British humour but Baxter stressed later that he was not mocking the speakers or the dialect. That said, I still remember as a bairn being vaguely uncomfortable about Scots being used as the target of humour, however entertaining or well intentioned. There was still a whiff of condescension and Agnes also picked up the undertone; 'we just didn't realise how we spoke English so badly'. Unger agrees that such programmes are problematic for those wishing to promote Scots as 'they encourage viewers to laugh at Scots as "bad English", rather than according it the status of an independent, versatile language'. Nonetheless the programme raised an interest and pride in Glasgow Scots. Unfortunately, many of the subsequent 'dialect' representations of Glasgow Scots in comedy and poetry parroted Baxter's comedy orthography, ignoring the well-established Modern Scots versions that more clearly underscored the literary and linguistic roots of Glaswegian as a historic Scots dialect. 'Baxterisations' of Glasgow Scots can still be bought in the city's souvenir shops over half a century after the show was first aired. In my view, *Parliamo Glasgow* may have had another side effect which cast an equally long shadow. Baxter ridiculed the very idea that Scots could be treated seriously as a linguistic subject, worthy of analysis and teaching. This was not presumably intentional – few people in the 1960s thought that vernacular Scots was worthy of any kind of language study at all. However, when such ideas eventually emerged, they were easy to mock for Scots language opponents, damned by association with a 1960s BBC light entertainment programme.

In November 1967 the SNP's Winnie Ewing won the Hamilton by-election, only the second SNP MP to reach Westminster. This was a particular shock for the Labour Party who had taken 71.2 per cent of the vote at the general election just a year earlier. It served to remind the British establishment, both right- and left-wing versions, that Scottish nationalism was still a potential threat. In this charged political climate, the socialist writer Tom Leonard published *Six Glasgow Poems* in 1969 and was immediately appointed by the Scottish cultural establishment as a new, maybe only, authentic working-class vernacular 'voice'. The inconvenient truth was that Glasgow Scots was already well represented in literature and theatre. The list included much city-based poetry, such as that of Ian Hamilton Finlay, mentioned above, the comedy of JJ Bell and *The McFlannels*. Alexander McArthur and H Kingsley Long had also found fame in 1935 with the Scots-rich *No Mean City* set in a violent Glasgow slum. Moreover, the left-wing Glasgow Unity Theatre, formed in 1941 and active for a decade, had specifically addressed working-class audiences with stagings of Robert McLeish's *The Gorbals Story* in 1946 and the powerful *Men Should Weep* by Ena Lamont Stewart a year later. However, Leonard arrived at a convenient political time and with exactly the right talent, so the existing Glasgow Scots tradition could apparently be binned.

A mere 16 lines long, 'The Good Thief', the first and most famous of Leonard's six poems is often used to illustrate Leonard's poetic and linguistic style. The protagonist is one the thieves crucified alongside Christ, here speaking in working-class Glaswegian and making multi-layered allusions between Calvary and a Celtic football game which starts at 'three a cloke', the traditional time of the crucifixion. McClure describes the language used.

> [T]he almost disjointed phrases, pronounces with a high degree of ellipsis [ie omission] of unstressed syllables characteristic of uneducated Glasgow speech: *yawright* 'are you all right', *ma right insane* 'am I right in saying ...', *yirwanny uz* 'you're one of us'.[91]

The text is peppered with distinctive West-coast speech markers, 'awright', 'gonny', 'jimmy', 'init', and words are joined, 'lookslik', 'thinoo'. Leonard rejects conventional Scots orthographical representations of speech (eg 'gaun tae') in favour of his self-constructed semi-phonetic spelling, 'gonny'. The intention of this artifice is, like the contemporary *Parliamo Glasgow,* to exoticise Glasgow working-class vernacular. In this sense, Leonard's writing can be considered as confected as MacDiarmid's. To achieve a specific artistic outcome, McClure notes, 'spellings which at first seem to be barely intelligible turn out, if read phonetically, to be sardonically precise representations of local pronunciation'. In the last of the six poems, 'Good Style', Leonard pre-emptively strikes against potential critics: 'helluva hard tay read theez innit/ stull/if ye canny unnirston thim jiss clear off then/gawn/get tae fuck ootma road/'. In this he reveals his target audience not to be working-class Scots speakers who, after decoding *Parliamo Glasgow* for years, would have no problem understanding Leonard, but middle-class anglophones.

As McClure observes, 'more than any other poet Leonard is preoccupied with language and attitudes to language' and it is some measure of Leonard's impact that three elements of his pugnacious ethos are still prevalent in debates of the Scots language half a century later. The most obvious is a rather showy rejection of traditional Scots language spelling. Leonard's idiosyncratic pseudo-phonetic orthography, 'its thi langwij a the guhtr', has been endlessly aped by many less skilled Scots writers half a century later. Secondly, as McClure, generally an admirer of the poet, puts it, 'the use of this eye-dialect of this kind is a well-recognised literary device normally

91 McClure 2000:169

used to imply that the supposed speaker is illiterate'. Where authenticity ends and stereotyping begins is always going to be a moot point. Leonard's third legacy is clearer; a quite bizarre aversion among many modern Scots writers to using dictionaries. In 'right inuff' from 1984, the poet sets out his manifesto, 'ma language is disgraceful [...] even thi introduction tay the *Scottish National Dictionary* tellt mi with the response fuck the lohta thim'. Presumably, Leonard, born in 1944, was referring to the preface of the 1936 edition of the *Scottish National Dictionary* (SND); 'owing to the influx of Irish and foreign immigrants in the industrial area near Glasgow the dialect had become increasingly corrupt'. Leonard's reasonable critique of an antiquated elitist attitude has since mutated into an absurd conviction among some Scots writers today that simply to open a Scots dictionary will taint their own 'creativity'.

The return of Scots scholarship

Far from the daft, macho world of Scottish poetry and making the self-limiting doctrine of dictionary distain even more baffling, Scots language scholarship and lexicography progressed steadily throughout the 1970s. In 1971 the Association for Scottish Literary Studies held the first conference on the Scots language. A year later The Lallans Society, later wisely renamed The Scots Language Society, was founded as a literary association for promoting poetry and prose written in the medium of Scots, in 1973 launching *Lallans*, still the only journal devoted entirely to writing in the language. In 1977 David Muirson, editor of *The Scottish National Dictionary* (SND), published *The Guid Scots Tongue*, an uncompromising defence of the language. In conclusion, he echoed his core message from the same-titled 1950 radio series, albeit in marginally less disheartening terms.

> Scots will continue to be spoken dimuendo in familiar circles, especially in the outlying areas like the Borders, Ayrshire, Angus, the Moray Firth area and in Shetland; and the Scots will continue to utter the English language in its own peculiar way. But it cannot be restored until the Scots know what it is and want it so, and that means it must be given an assured and permanent place in our schools and colleges. Certainly, no other European nation would tolerate anything less.

Like Craigie a quarter of a century previously, Muirson saw Scots as a 'normal' European minority language, a notion revisited by Billy Kay a decade later.

In 1977 William Graham published the first edition of *The Scots Word Book*, a Scots-English and more significantly English-Scots wordlist, itself derived from the *SND*. Graham deliberately decided to 'admit only those words that have been in regular conversational or literary use over the last two centuries'. Though he included some obsolete words he thought worth keeping, there is an explicit shift from the everything-in-the-dictionary-is-valid methods of the Lallanists. Moreover, to keep the list manageable he often ignored alternative spellings, 'of which there have been all too many in Scots writing'. *The Word Book* is the beginning of what might be considered the post-Lallans 'soft standardisation' of Modern Scots that would eventually find its realisation 20 years later in the *Essential Scots Dictionary*, largely built on Graham's pioneering work.[92] Graham was aware of the significance of what he was attempting, modestly admitting 'a much better-known authority should have been entrusted with the task of compiling such a work'. His answer was pointed: 'no such authority has come forward. Meanwhile, with the Scots tongue "dying before our eyes", someone had to tackle the job. Surely.'

One area where Scots was relatively vibrant in the 1950s was on the stage. The language had a long association with the modern Scottish theatre. Scots or Scots-rich plays in the post-war period included Robert McLellan's *Jamie the Saxt* (1937) and *The Flooers o Edinburgh* (1954), Robert Kemp's Let wives tak tent (1948, a translation of Molière's *L'école des femmes*) and *Laird o' Grippy* (1955, a translation of Molière's *L'avare*), and Alexander Reid's plays *The Lass wi the Muckle Mou* (1950) and *The Warld's Wonder* (1953). Despite this prestigious history, in 1968 Clive Perry, then director of the Royal Lyceum Theatre in Edinburgh, imperiously announced 'national drama with a tongue of its own is not for the future', and predicted 'Plays about contemporary Scotland will be in English with only a slight accent'.[93] Perry was proved wrong, as the 1970s saw another vernacular revival. Although successful in their day, and often revived to much acclaim, the older plays in what Edwin Morgan once dismissed as 'costume Scots' were a challenge to stage. Scots-speaking actors and (it was perhaps feared) Scots-understanding audiences were becoming ever rarer. Throughout the 1970s, therefore, a more 'naturalistic' Scottish stage idiom emerged, described by theatre scholar Dan Rebellato in 2013 as follows:

> [A] fusion of English, Scots, and a distinctively working-class Glaswegian dialect that is robust, poetic, beautifully foul-mouthed,

92 Macleod and Cairns eds 2005

93 Quoted in Stevenson 2011:76

> and capable of wicked humour, emotional eloquence, and great beauty.

Across the decade, both historical plays like Stewart Conn's *The Burning* (1971), Hector MacMillan's *The Rising* (1973), and Donald Campbell's *The Jesuit* (1976) and modern-themed works like Roddy McMillan's *The Bevellers* (1973), or Stewart Conn's *Play Donkey* and Tom McGrath's *The Hardman* (both 1977) employed this theatrical version of Scots. Not everyone adopted this language, of course. I saw John Byrne's otherwise excellent, Paisley-set *The Slab Boys* (1978) in Glasgow in the early 1980s and remember being disappointed by the anglicised dialogue. On other stages, Billy Connolly, who had emerged from the 1960s folk music revival, worked his own linguistic magic, in his early acts especially weaving Scots and Glaswegianisms into his act with enthralling effect.

The Mither Tongue

The fun ended with a bump in 1979. Under nationalist pressure, the beleaguered Labour government conceded a referendum on Scottish devolution. However, many in the Labour Party passionately opposed any kind of Scottish self-government so as a sop to them a precondition, never used before or since, was introduced. To be successful, Yes would require the support of at least 40 per cent of the electorate. Not the actual voters, but the entire electoral roll, dead or alive. The pro-devolution side gained 51.62 per cent of the vote but as this represented only 32.9 per cent of the registered electorate, devolution failed, bringing down the shambolic, deeply divided Labour government. Waiting in the right wing was the apparently unstoppable force of Margaret Thatcher. The SNP dropped nine seats and Scottish nationalism seemed to have stalled yet again.

This setback paradoxically gave a jolt to Scottish culture. Craig believed the now-blocked political energy found an outlet in cultural activity. 'Instead of political defeat leading to quiescence, it led directly into an explosion of cultural creativity'.[94] Poetry, always a minority sport anyway, faded in cultural relevance as the debates about Scots moved into its representation in more accessible forms of entertainment: television, the theatre, novels and film. Most Scottish authors, for both artistic and commercial reasons, largely avoided Scots in their works. Several important Scottish novels were published in the 1980s, including the Alasdair Gray doorstep classic *Lanark* (1981) about a dystopian Glasgow and *Knots and Crosses* (1987)

94 Quoted in Pattie 2007:147

the first of Ian Rankin's hugely popular Edinburgh-set Rebus detective series, but neither made much use of the sound landscape of their settings. Even William McIlvanney's *Laidlaw*, pioneering the 'Tartan Noir' detective genre in 1977, had employed only very light Scots local colour. *Taggart*, STV's long running Glasgow-set police show piloted in 1983, largely adopted the same tokenistic approach to Glasgow Scots. *Taggart* is far from the only culprit, and it is impossible to judge what effect this anglicised representation of Glasgow speech on mass-market television might have on real Glasgow Scots speakers. Several studies report on the powerful effect of television on speech patterns, so a quite deliberate 'linguistic cleansing' in the media may have an impact on the vernacular reality.

Evidently, though, there was still an appetite for more traditional forms of Scots. William Graham hosted a popular Scots language quiz show *Talking Scots* on STV from 1979 to 1983. The difficulty of the questions in the accompanying quiz book suggests a deep knowledge of Scots vocabulary, history and literary culture continued among a substantial proportion of the population.[95] At the same time a belated but sincere initiative by language scholars attempted to reduce the polarisation between Glasgow Scots and everything else. The 1983 publication *Scotland and the Lowland Tongue* was hailed as a 'mini-revolution'.[96] In the same year William Lorimer's translation of *New Testament in Scots*, a work of magisterial splendour, was published, giving a hint of what Lallans could have been had it be developed by proper linguists rather than improper poets. 'In the beginning o aa things the Wurd wis there ense, an the Wurd bade wi God, an the Wurd wis God'. Sadly, John's message arrived about 400 years too late to have any real impact on the Scots language. Of more influence on writers was the first edition of *The Concise Scots Dictionary* published in 1985.[97] This was a single volume, accessible distillation of the ten-part *SND*. It is an excellent Scots-English dictionary for reading Scots, but dangerous for inexperienced writers wishing to avoid Lallanisation of their texts, as many of the words are archaic and there are, as usual, too many alternative spellings. At the other end of the Scots spectrum, Michael Munro's *The Patter*, a dictionary of Glasgow Scots, was first published by Glasgow District Libraries in 1985, going on to sell 140,000 copies over the next decade. Munro for the most part shuns both Stanley Baxter's comic orthography and Tom Leonard's eye-dialect to return to more traditional representation of Glasgow speech. Stripped of its ornamental spelling, the wordlist showed how much of Glaswegian Scots is 'just' Scots.

---

95 Graham 1981

96 Hendry 1993

97 Macleod and Cairns 1985

In an unexpected concession to the resurgent interest in the Scots language, BBC Scotland commissioned the charismatic writer and broadcaster Billy Kay to write and host *Scots: The Mither Tongue*, first shown in 1986. Over 30 years had passed since the BBC had broadcast *The Guid Scots Tongue* on the radio, so the programme was something of a milestone for Scots. It was also a bold move; Kay was an Ayrshire Scots speaker (ie, not a Glaswegian) and a committed cultural nationalist. Particularly in the classic book accompanying the series, Kay had no qualms at all about linking the cause of the Scots language with the cause of Scottish independence. In the preface he writes, 'politics determines the way we view language and culture and in time that influences how we view ourselves'[98] and 'to use the native language of what I would still consider to be the majority of Scots, an indeed be regarded as making a political statement'. Kay's main task was to recount in an accessible way the 'forgotten' history of the language. He talks of cultural colonialism, particularly in education, and the lack of funded support in comparison to Gaelic. Following Muirson a decade earlier, Scots is reframed not as a linguistic or historical oddity but as a European minority language: 'the marginalisation of any culture is regrettable; when it is the culture of the vast majority of the Scottish people it becomes quite unacceptable'. Referring to the Catalans' generations-long struggle to build confidence in their language and overcome what they call a 'slave mentality', he continued, 'in public perceptions of Scots, we face similar problems, and have not even seriously begun the process of recovery'. *Scots: The Mither Tongue* still reads as a stirring call to arms, a manifesto to re-weaponise Scots.

Unfortunately, Kay's manifesto had little political or public resonance. In the late 1980s, Scottish politics was still in the tight grip of Labourism and at the 1987 election Scottish Labour gained 50 seats out of a possible 72, with over 40 per cent of the popular vote. Labour was, as ever, wary of any potential Scottish nationalist upsurge. Their fellow unionists, the Conservatives and Liberals, had 19 seats and were similarly disinclined to support any moves to heighten Scottish cultural identity. With just three seats, the SNP had largely reinvented themselves anyway as economic nationalists. There was therefore no civic body, political, cultural organisation or trade union remotely interested in responding to Kay's call to arms.

Rab, *Trainspotting* and other 'Scots'

Any potential re-politicisation of Scots was further hindered by a sequence of popular and high-profile representations of Scottish speech through the 1980s and early 1990s that muddied the linguistic waters still further. The first in

98 Kay 1993:6 (revised edition)

1988 was the TV series *Rab C. Nesbitt* and, as with *Parliamo Glasgow*, such productions provoke multiple and contradictory responses. The titular hero is a professional skiver, a drunken street philosopher in a disintegrating pinstripe suit complete with dirty sannies, a manky headband and a signature string vest. His extended family is no less dysfunctional. However, the character became something of an unlikely cult hero over the life of the series, which ran until 2014. Beyond Ian Pattison's clever, knowing scripts and Gregor Fisher's unique interpretation, its popularity was aided by an inclination, identified by one of Unger's interviewees, to treasure Scottish comedians if they represent 'our own character' and seem to speak our language.[99] The series is remembered especially for its uncompromising use of local vernacular.

In a spirited defence of the series, Colin McArthur described the language as 'working-class Glasgow, a vernacular variant of Standard English heavily laced with Scots words' such as 'jaiket', 'wean', 'merrit', 'shilpit', 'feart', 'keech' and 'glaikit'.[100] He regarded the linguistic approach as 'extremely progressive'. Although 'serious' poets and novelists had long tried to represent an authentic Scottish voice in literature, the initiative had now moved into popular television. Not surprisingly, when shown outside Scotland, reactions were robust.[101]

> Apart from the impenetrability of the Govan Glasgow accents, given the operatic levels of violence and caricature on which Rab C. Nesbitt is pitched, subtitles would be helpful for English speakers. (*The Times*)

> ... virtually incomprehensible to anyone born south of Berwick-upon-Tweed. (*The Daily Mail*)

McArthur's argument is that, though the content is not overtly political, 'in some way it becomes so by the criticism practiced on it by its form'. He observes, however, that many of the official figures in the series such as the police, social workers and social security clerks speak in more RP-based or standard Scottish English, so that anglicisation is associated with authority.

Back in Scotland, the media view of Scots soon became reduced to, 'any dialect as long as it's Rab C. Nesbitt', what McArthur amusingly dubs, '"Hey, Jimmy!" hegemony'. Linguist Katie Gallogly-Swan recently asked,

> When did being working class become the primary form of authentic,

99 Unger 2013:118

100 McArthur 1998:109

101 Quoted in McArthur 1998:107

> Scottish voicing? Was it when Thatcher crystallised the differences between the 'Us' of Scotland and 'Them' of rUK as a class war? Or when our media became saturated with Glaswegian caricatures and comedians that communicated a monolithic Scottish culture – no Doric, no Gaidhlig, no Highland or Lowland Scots, Glaswegian or nothing?[102]

Rab was only the start. Two literary and popular behemoths were about to appear on the linguistic horizon. First up was the commercial phenomenon of Irvine Welsh's Leith-set black comedy *Trainspotting*, first published in 1993. The story is now well known, concerning the addiction-fuelled misfortunes of a group of heroin users living in what was then a very poor area of Edinburgh. Its most striking feature is the language, a rich mix of Scots, Scots English and Edinburgh-specific dialect, all delivered in a Tom Leonard-style DIY orthography. Significantly, Welsh's characters do not only speak in this vernacular, but they also narrate in it too. The book begins, 'The sweat wis lashing oafay Sick Boy; he wis trembling. Ah wis just sitting thair, focusing oan the telly, tryin no tae notice the cunt. He wis bringing me doon'.

Looking past the idiosyncratic spelling, much of the language is quite recognisably mainstream Scots – 'wis', 'oan', 'tae', 'ken', 'loupin' – colloquial East Coast Scots – 'barry', 'likeasays', 'radge', 'swedge' – and some words that may be invented Welshisms – 'biscuit-ersed'. The noticeable retention of the '-ing' ending, most English working-class dialects replacing this with '-in', is probably to aid comprehension. Using too much idiosyncratic spelling in a novel can turn a pleasant puzzle for a general audience into a bore. The language mix varies cannily through the book according to the narrative, the characters sometimes switching to standard English for effect. The hero sees off students whose train seats he has taken, 'I can only suggest that you pursue your complaint with a member of the British Rail staff', before turning to his pal, 'The lager's loupin. Seems tae huv gone dead flat, ken. Tastes like fuckin pish'. The politics of language are embedded in this code switching. In a 2008 interview John Mullan notes, 'The most vividly remembered sign of cultural "oppression" that Welsh remembered from his education was a ban on the use of the word "aye" at his school'. Mullan then quotes Welsh directly; 'If you're being told that, it does have an effect on the psyche'. English professor Mullen's arch parenthesis of the word 'oppression' is telling. The novel gained a cult status, especially following the global success of the 1996 film version. However, almost all

102 Quoted in Hassan 2016

the Scots vocabulary was purged in John Hodges' screenplay and even then, the film was partially re-dubbed for the US release, removing one of the last remaining distinctive Scots words: 'ken' for 'know'.[103]

The next Scots literature 'event' was the publication in 1994 of James Kelman's Glasgow novel *How late it was, how late*. Appearing just a year after *Trainspotting*, the two books are inevitably bracketed because of their use of vernacular narrative language, but the tone and intent are quite different. While Welsh attempts to catch the rhythms and complexities of contemporary Leith speech, Kelman adopts a more deliberately writerly approach. The protagonist of this bleak stream of consciousness is underclass Sammy, who wakes up blinded after a savage beating by policemen and must make his way home through the city. Although supposedly written in dialect, the language is more a metaphorical device to show isolation rather than a representation of real Glasgow speech:

> But it couldnay get worse than this. He was really fuckt now. This was the dregs; he was at it. He had fucking reached it now man the fucking dregs man the pits, the fucking black limboland, purgatory; that's what it was like, purgatory, where all ye can do is think. Think. That's all ye can do.[104]

Through language, Kelman is trying to show Sammy alienated from English-speaking authority, from Scots and its sense of collective identity, even from language itself. The use of 'fuck' and its derivatives, while common enough in working-class Scottish and Irish speech, is amplified in frequency by Kelman to the point of repetitive meaninglessness. The likely aim was to illustrate the frustrating breakdown between thought and expression, but Kelman's estimated 4,000 uses of the 'f-word' certainly had the hardly surprising side-effect of triggering genteel middle-class critics from the South of England.

Bearing in mind McArthur's argument that *Rab C. Nesbitt* became (more) politicised 'by the criticism practiced on it by its form', huge controversy ensued when *How late it was, how late* was nominated for the 1994 Man Booker Prize. When the novel won, one of the judges, Julia Neuberger, called the decision 'a disgrace'. She added, 'I'm really unhappy. Kelman is deeply inaccessible for a lot of people. I am implacably opposed to the book'.[105] Just to cap this literary tiff, Kelman used the award ceremony to attack what he regarded as the elitism of the literary establishment. Then, in

103 Corbett 2008:28

104 Kelman 1994:171

105 Winder 1994

a possibly accidental act of recursive irony, broadcaster Channel 4 cut him off in mid-harangue to go to an advertising break. His speech was certainly confrontational.

> As Tom Leonard pointed out more than 20 years ago the gist of the [elitist] argument amounts to the following, that vernaculars, patois, slangs, dialects, gutter-languages etc etc might well have a place in the realms of comedy and the frequent [press] references to Billy Connolly or Rab C. Nesbitt substantiate this but they are inferior linguistic forms and have no place in literature. [...] This sort of prejudice, in one guise or another, has been around for a very long time and for the sake of clarity we are better employing the contemporary label, which is racism. A fine line can exist between elitism and racism and on matters concerning language the distinction can sometimes cease to exist altogether.[106]

He continues by putting his art in a political context. Although emerging from completely different conceptions of the struggle for self-determination, the parallels with 'traditional' cultural nationalist Billy Kay, writing a decade earlier, are striking.

> There is a literary tradition to which I hope my own work belongs, I see it as part of a much wider process – or movement – toward decolonization and self-determination: it is a tradition that assumes two things: 1) The validity of indigenous culture; and 2) The right to defend in the face of attack. It is a tradition premised on a rejection of the cultural values of imperial or colonial authority, offering a defence against cultural assimilation, in particular imposed assimilation.

It is tempting to think what might have happened at that time if the shared anti-colonialist analysis of Kay in the margins and Kelman in the limelight could have been discussed properly and combined, but in Scottish politics such an association is apparently unthinkable.

The 'spectacle of voice'?

Before we continue with our historical narrative, a short detour may help explain why the positions of Kay and Kelman appear incompatible. This is going to get a bit complex, but let's start with something they have in

106 Kelman 1994

common. Both authors recognise the toxic political and cultural imbalance between establishment-backed English and the everyday vernacular used in Scotland. Kay's solution to this social wrong is clear: the re-establishment of Scots as a language equivalent in status and function to Scottish English. This path is the familiar route of language revitalisation and is usually associated with cultural nationalism. Although Kelman also sees the vernacular as a potent symbol of radicalism and resistance, Kay's 'nationalist' path is blocked to him. Kelman explicitly stated, 'I cannot accept nationalism and I am not a Scottish Nationalist'.[107] His politics therefore preclude any overtly 'nationalist' approaches to the re-balancing of linguistic power. Kelman apparently did not even recognise Scots as a language, at one point declaring, 'My language is English', adding, 'In my writings the accent is in Glasgow'.[108] While it would certainly be unfair to represent Kelman's forceful linguistic position here as being, in Beveridge and Turnbull's parlance, a 'desperate identification with the culture of the metropolis'[109], loyalty to the English language is internalised. Kelman's language has thus been characterised as 'both English and un-English'.[110] Ian Brown offers an even more intriguing interpretation. Referring specifically to *How late it was, how late,* Brown writes, 'To me, it appears to be actually Scots presented on the page with intermittent spellings that are English'. He found he had trouble processing the novel; 'I thought I had a headache until I realised, at least for my own sake, to translate it back into Scots'.[111] Once he started converting the prose, Brown's pain apparently disappeared. On closer inspection, Brown discovered that Kelman had routinely anglicised the Scots language elements in his writing, probably for a mix of for artistic, ideological and commercial reasons. Interestingly, fellow left-wing author Lewis Grassic Gibbon had similarly watered down the rural and working-class Scots language elements in his classic *Sunset Song*. Of course, un-English English will always reach a wider market than un-English Scots, but it is hardly a radical position.

Deliberate anglicisation of the vernacular voice may also have had an ideological twist. Roderick Watson asks of the literature of the 1990s:

> [B]ut where is the central national consciousness? – as opposed to the class consciousness of Kelman and Leonard and (if you like)

107 *The Herald* 2012

108 Hamilton et al 1976:51

109 Beveridge and Turnbull 1989:6

110 Shanks 2010:12

111 Brown 2013:65

> the marginalised and dismally tribal consciousness of Irvine Welsh's world of drug users and football hooligans?[112]

Watson argues persuasively that the socio-political positions of writers such as Kelman, Leonard and Welsh bring into focus important issues related to the 'hegemony of monological narrative authority in our culture: ideological issues of identity, expression, class and education which are often hidden to us'. Modern Scottish literature is therefore characterised as being confrontational, anarchic and rebellious.

> [S]ince the 18th century, Scottish literary national identity has frequently been implicitly constructed from the margins – whether by class, language, belief or (sometimes) gender. And while those margins have been given a certain collective clout by being able to lay claim to a 'national' literary tradition, at the same time the polyphonic nature of that tradition has also served to destabilise the unifying and monological premises behind the very notion (at least the old fashioned notion) of what a 'nation' is in the first place.

According to Watson's thesis, language is used to deconstruct the very notion of a cohesive linguistic national identity. Brown, however, quotes Millar and Rodger observing:

> Kelman's characters and his narrators use a range of linguistic tactics in order to poach territory from those who would be in control of language – *including those who share a similar social and linguistic background*. [My emphasis.]

Poaching, then, is how some Scottish writers, 'exploit the resources of the varieties of Scottish languages and dialects', as Brown puts it. However, it is also a way for writers to cut themselves off from vernacular communities who co-created those resources in the first place. The very opposite of authenticity, a more loaded modern term for poaching might be *appropriation*.

Scott Hames agreed that using Scottish language in writing evokes a cultural heft (or, as he calls it below, *valence*), but he also contended that the vernacular also may function as a showy 'display identity' within what he calls a 'spectacle of cultural difference'.[113]

112 Watson 1998:35

113 Hames 2013:202

> The primary claim of this identity is not a traditionary heritage and idiom of belonging, but a marginal, subjected condition conceived as beyond any re-centring or 'inclusion' within a hegemonic cultural order (such as a state, or a standardised language). It licenses a radical particularism and self-fashioning (for the individual, in the name of the group), while continuing to trade on (and exploit) the romantic 'ethnic-cultural' residues of vernacular rootedness and community.

Narrative authority may thus be challenged by 'uttering the most stinging rebukes to institutional power', but behind all the radical rhetoric, the focus is always the superficial performance of individual artistic self-expression rather than a collective political threat to the status quo, linguistic or otherwise. No credible alternative is ever given to the nationalist route to language revitalisation. McClure made the same point about Tom Leonard.

> Leonard's patois could never be anything but the speech of the underclass except by the kind of total destruction of an existing social order which was, perhaps naively dreamed of in the early days of Marxist thought.[114]

Any serious form of language recovery requires a 're-centring' around a standardised variety, but Hames postulates that 'sovereignty of the self-fashioned linguistic subject' demands that for display purposes Scottish language must remain frozen in its current 'unsettled and illegible' status.

> The advent of a distinctively 'national' Scottish literature, much of it written in a language not quite Standard English and not quite 'separatist' Scots, strongly resonates with this ideological background. A vernacular language which insists on its difference and authenticity but stops short of codifying its own standard rules and norms – a literature which 'feels Scottish' without departing from the fundamental structures it shares with 'English' – acquires a special political valence in this context.

In this way, Hames reveals the deeply conservative political ideology behind a supposedly radical rejection of Scots status-building and standardisation. What is presented as a rebellious linguistic counterculture in reality colludes with the long-term goal of the British state: to channel and assimilate divergent narratives of identity so they can never challenge its hegemony. Without taking

114 McClure 2000:172

anything from the artistic skill of individual writers, I contend this type of superficial appropriation of the Scots language is far from 'authentic'. It seems steeped in an individualistic, even anarchic, linguistic ideology that mitigates against collective action to raise the status of the language and its speakers. The everyday needs of the (usually working-class) speakers are subordinated to the creative needs of the (usually middle-class) artists.

Millar drew our attention earlier to the 'dislocation' between written and spoken forms of the language. Has an over-focus on the linguistic tinkerings of superstar writers disadvantaged the community development of Scots literacy? Millar seemed to think so; 'Too great a concentration on literature in, rather than empowerment through, the language has to be recognised as aiding this dislocation'.[115] We will leave the spectacle of voice for the moment, but the tension around individual artistic expression and collective linguistic action will reappear with a vengeance in the second part of this history when we discuss attempts to revitalise Scots.

Devolution soon

In Scottish history, the 1990s were a watershed moment. During the Thatcher years, pressure mounted to reconsider the devolution question. The 1980s had seen the Conservatives returned to power in successive elections solely by their electoral popularity in England while the numbers of Scottish Conservative MPs dwindled. SNP success at the 1988 Govan by-election kept up the momentum, aided by the active campaigning of pro-devolution groups, especially the Campaign for a Scottish Assembly (CSA). The CSA issued the Claim of Right in 1988 declaring that it was the 'sovereign right of the Scottish people to determine the form of government best suited to their needs' and promptly established a National Convention to discuss the details of how a devolved body might work. A blueprint for devolution was published on St Andrew's Day 1995, eventually providing the basis of the Scottish Parliament, (re-)established in 1999. The document contained no mention of Scotland's languages. Ann Sobey, then a researcher at Aberdeen University, summarised the linguistic state of play at the time;

> [A]ll but the most trenchant unionists pay lip service to the preservation of Scots [but] the idea of the reinstatement of Scots as the institutional language of Scotland is still seen as an extremist viewpoint, even in the SNP.[116]

115 Millar 2008:14

116 Sobey 1993:7

Education is always emblematic of the official indifference regarding Scots. In 1988 Labour MP Sam Galbraith had written a positive Ministerial Foreword to a book, *The Scots Language: its place in education*;[117]

> Scots as a community language has proved remarkably resilient and continues to flourish in several modern forms [...] it is part of our cultural heritage and, if we value that heritage, we need to cherish the language and aim to see it used with respect and sensitivity.

Despite the ministerial rhetoric, practical provision for Scots in education remained pitiful. In a contemporary review for the European minority language research centre Mercator, Liz Niven found no written textbooks in which the medium of instruction is Scots and 'it is, therefore, possible for some pupils to receive no introduction to Scots literature or language throughout the duration of their school life'.[118]

> [T]here is still reported condemnation of pupils who speak Scots. Many pupils give anecdotal information of their own personal experiences in which they are asked to repeat statements in English rather than Scots, the most common being the use of 'yes' being encouraged rather than 'aye'. Generally, the use of Scots by pupils and teachers is not discussed or given consideration as an issue of importance'.

Trainee teachers were not required to study Scots and there were no courses or certificates available for trainee or in-service teachers seeking to develop their expertise on Scots. Thus, 'The language which is spoken at home by most pupils is reduced to the level of an occasional poem learned for a competition'. She concluded, 'all of this only underlines the marginal status of Scots. It remains the private – almost secret – language of most of the population of Scotland'. Robbie Robertson, one of the leaders of *The Scottish Consultative Council on the Curriculum* (SCCC) admitted that in 1996 Scottish education was still 'an alien place for our native languages'. He believed that the lack of attention to Scots and Gaelic in most Scottish schools 'should be read as intention rather than neglect or accident'.[119]

In 1993, the European Bureau for Lesser Used Languages, a scholarly, non-governmental organisation promoting linguistic diversity and languages, became the first official body to recognise Scots as a minority European

117 McClure 1998

118 Niven 2001:13

119 Ross 1997

language and at last things seemed to start moving. In 1993 Scots Tung and the Glesca Scots Speikers' Curn were established as campaigning Scots language groups, joined by the Aiberdeen Univairsitie Scots Leid Quorum (AUSLQ) a year later. Even more surprisingly, these were soon complemented by an 'official' service, The Scots Language Centre (then named The Scots Language Resource Centre) founded in Perth in 1993. The initial role of the Centre, mooted for a decade or more, was to help schoolteachers and writers to find and use Scots language resources. The Centre is not a campaigning organisation but has become the primary source of information in Scotland and beyond, along the way providing a model for Modern Scots writing. As an early project, the Centre distributed a Scots learning pack developed in 1988 called *Gleg* (Scots for quick on the uptake, nimble) comprising poems, riddles, songs and stories, with an accompanying audio cassette.

The *Concise English-Scots Dictionary* (*CESD*) published in 1993 formed another important step to 'soft' spelling standardisation although lingering anti-dictionary prejudice blunted its impact. Aimed at, 'all who want to use the Scots language, from writers to schoolchildren, for creative work or just for pleasure', the 300-page dictionary recognised that the 1976 *Scottish National Dictionary* and to a lesser extent the 1985 *Concise Scots Dictionary* offered far too many variants which were 'historical, regional, accidental, idiosyncratic'. In the *CESD*, usually only one spelling was given, with an occasional regional variant.

In the few years immediately before the devolution referendum in 1997, Scots language activists tried to get a question on Scots in the 2001 Census. Steve Murdoch of the AUSLQ cited the European recognition as motivator.

> I discovered that Scots was the only language listed by the Bureau for which no data exists. I resolved then, with friends in Aberdeen to try to get a question relating to the Scots language built into the national census and thus put on equal terms with Scotland's other languages.[120]

In 1996 the General Register Office for Scotland, GRO(S), carried out a survey to investigate the feasibility of including such a question. The investigation explored popular perceptions of Scots and, for the first time, estimated the number of Scots speakers, quite accurately as it turned out.

The survey identified 'a continuum of speech type in the Scottish population ranging from clearly English to clearly Scots',[121] but also confirmed that the Scottish vernacular, 'retains a lot of traditional speech forms'. The main

120 Murdoch 1996: Preface

121 Máté 1996

problem the researchers found was that after years of suppression, and with no objective standards, people were poor at defining their own abilities as Scots speakers. Thus in the survey report, GRO(S) concluded that the responses to a Census question would be 'a self-assessment of a concept which is poorly defined by the public' and therefore would measure 'the prevalence of a speech tradition derived from Scots rather than a particular ability in the Scots language'. They felt, therefore, the results would 'probably be of limited use to those seeking to meet educational needs'. The report however recognised that 'the inclusion of a census question would undoubtedly raise the profile of Scots', but suggested that surveys using some (undeveloped) linguistic test/ index would be more useful and appropriate.

Even given the caveats above, the survey found about 30 per cent of the population of Scotland would respond 'Yes' to a question of the form 'Can you speak Scots or a dialect of Scots?'. This corresponded to about 1.5 million individuals affirming they speak Scots, a figure that later became widely quoted. There were some regional variances, but no data from Orkney and Shetland. Given the strong influence of attitudinal factors, the researchers considered that some of the regional variation may have been due to local differences in the status of Scots. For example, Doric has always had a reasonably high status in the North East and people might be more ready to confess to speaking it. As an aside, the researchers noted that although the idea that Scots dialects are strongly differentiated was, by the 1990s, very prevalent, older respondents who had spoken with people from all over Scotland during the war, 'denied the existence of dialect differences strong enough to hinder communication'. In other words, the post-war education and media suppression of Scots had weakened the idea of a common 'Lingua Scottica' and fostered dialectisation and fragmentation. The survey confirmed the belief that abilities in Scots were related to age and class. Younger age groups were less inclined to say that they spoke Scots and people in lower socio-economic groups were marginally more likely to say they did. Considering the mixing in Scottish spoken language, the researchers concluded that 'Pure Scots' definitely existed at one end of a continuum to English. Observing that 'many people's speech could clearly be placed as predominantly stemming from one or the other of the two languages', they also found 'much maintenance of traditional speech forms and vocabulary'.

Many attitudinal views about Scots were expressed in the survey, and the researchers suspected this might interfere with respondents' willingness to answer the questions. 'In Britain – where accent, dialect and class effect language – language ability is very difficult to assess'. Moreover, as we know from the Labov's studies in Chapter Two, in any formal assessment situation, 'language readily changes'. While many respondents thought Scots should be encouraged more in schools, English was commonly viewed as the prestige language of communication. 'Good spoken English was related to improved employment opportunities', indicating a continuing perceived or real prejudice against the language. There was much support for learning more about Scots history and literature, some backing for Scots medium teaching, but also for teaching Gaelic as what some held to be the 'true and prestigious language of Scotland'. However, while recognising the existence of the Scots language as one end of a linguistic continuum, the report warned that for survey purposes 'Scots' could at that time only be a broad concept. The linguistic diversity within the Scottish population was compounded by the lack of general education and information on what 'the Scots Language' actually was. These issues resurfaced almost unchanged in the analysis of the 2011 census some 17 years later.

So Scots, for all its complications, was at least recognised as a living entity, although politicians were still disinclined to support it. Murdoch noted at the time,

> The Scottish National Party is the only party so far to have the word 'Scots' (relating to language) in any policy document although even they have only tagged it on as a supplement to their document on Gaelic. That policy stated that it was the intention of the SNP to develop Gaelic 'as a compliment to, and not an alternative to, the Scots language'.[122]

Despite this muted interest, educational resources gradually improved. Two significant publications arrived in 1996, *The Kist/A'Chiste* developed by the Scottish Consultative Council on the Curriculum (SCCC) and the *Scots School Dictionary* by the Scottish National Dictionary Association. These were followed in 1997 by David Purves' *A Scots Grammar*. The three publications, all aimed at learners, symbolise the formidable challenges of trying to introduce Scots into the education system in a piecemeal fashion. One of the issues Sobey identified in 1993 was that most teachers have very little training in the Scots language, probably did not speak it themselves and may not even come from the area where they were teaching. *The Kist* was thus produced, 'to help with the problem of inadequate training provision' by taking a polynomic approach based on respect for the language children brings to school, meaning the children should be taught the local variety,

122 Murdoch 1996:13

while introduced to others.[123] Embedded in the strategy is what film theorists call a *structuring absence*, a vital missing element that, precisely because it disregarded, makes that type of discourse possible. The elephant in the room for Scottish education was, and remains, standard Scots.

Yet there was no need for a structuring absence at all. On the shelf next to *The Kist* was *The Scots School Dictionary*. I remember in 1996 waiting impatiently for my copy to arrive in the post. Here, I thought, was the step forward Scots needed, an attempt to reduce the chaos of spelling and dialectal variation to a manageable list. The dictionary was later described by *The Herald* in surprisingly radical terms.

> [A] wonderful victory over an education system which, when William McIlvanney's Docherty was a schoolboy, was in cultural denial, so stymied by ingrained and colonially inculcated feelings of inferiority, that dictionaries were for other mother tongues.[124]

The aim of the dictionary, a version of the *CESD* published a few years before, was to help pupils in upper primary and lower secondary classes to use the Scots language, 'whether in reading, writing or in talking to their friends'. The emphasis was on 'words which pupils are likely to meet in a modern, largely urban environment'. Most importantly, 'there has of course been no space for more than a few different spellings. You will find only the commonest Scots spellings'. The acknowledgements were a veritable 'Who's Who' of Scots scholars and the lineage unmistakably traced back to William Graham's *Word Lists*. What was this, if not a standard? An imperfect one maybe and not complete either, but still, as David Purves would say in his *A Scots Grammar* the following year, 'bannocks is better nor nae breid'. Two years later, the dictionary would appear in an electronic version called *CannieSpell* offering spellchecks on 20,000 Scots words and integration with word processors. According to *The Herald*, ambitions were high as it was also designed to help those who might need specialist professional vocabulary. 'With half an eye on the setting up of a Parliament, *CannieSpell*'s compilers have furnished the capital's lawyers with a veritable treasure trove of Lallans legalese'.

Purves' 1997 *Grammar* was well overdue, the previous grammar being Main and Dixon's *Manual of Modern Scots* from 1921. The author did not actually explain where the grammar rules came from (as Main and Dixon explicitly did), but it was undoubtedly derived from their classic work, adding some later linguistic research. The scholarly approach of

123 Judge 2007:206

124 *The Herald* 1998b

Philip Robinson's *Ulster-Scots: A Grammar of the Traditional Written and Spoken Language* published the same year made his grammar more useable. Unfortunately, the spelling system was not aligned to the new *Scots School Dictionary*, another missed opportunity. Those grumbles apart, Purves' aim was admirable – to set standards, and that he did. He was robust in his condemnation of what he called 'DIY Scots'.

> Good Scots certainly cannot be written by anyone who decides to invent his own orthography and grammar off the cuff because it is too much effort to discover the standards inherent in speech and the substantial corpus of literature which already exists.

He went further in the extended edition from 2002.

> Properly, 'Good Scots' ought to be seen as Scots which is internally consistent in which traditional linguistic features have not been seriously ignored by the writer.

The Scottish National Dictionary Association's own dictionary-aligned *Grammar Broonie* for bairns appeared in 1999. Lest such initiatives seem rather banal, discourse analyst Johann Unger spotted a covert radicalism inherent in a simple Scots grammar textbook, 'an attempt by Scots activists to map a challenge to dominant ideology onto an existing hegemonic power structure'.[125] As we shall see, the existing hegemonic power structure remained unmoved.

Following the general election of May 1997, Labour took power under Tony Blair. The SNP had once again gained seats and the long-promised devolution referendum was put to the Scottish electorate that September. A resounding 74 per cent vote in favour of a Scottish Parliament boosted optimism among Scots language enthusiasts. The linguistic features of Scots were now well documented and easily accessible, with good dictionaries and grammars, learner materials and a growing interest in the use of Scots in education. The Government's 1997 Higher Still programme of assessment for English and Communication, for example, encouraged 'substantial emphasis on Scottish texts and the languages in which they are expressed'.[126] It was genuinely felt the fate of Scots was now in the hands of the Scottish people. Thanks to the scholarship and persistence of academics and activists, Scotland now had more than adequate tools to build Scots into any shape it wanted.

125 Unger 2013:124

126 Quoted in Niven 2001:14

Realism kicked in with a *Herald* headline in June 1998: 'Claim of Scots tongue silenced'. A £40,000 Government report recommending that teachers should use the Scots language in the classroom would not be published, 'because of fears it could be a propaganda gift to the SNP'.[127] A Review of Scottish Culture working group of the Scottish Consultative Council on the Curriculum or SCCC had just spent two years producing a review, *Scottish Culture and the Curriculum*. Intended as a supposedly apolitical pre-devolution review of the role of Scottish culture in education, questionnaires had been sent to 1,100 education institutions. The overwhelming demand was (not surprisingly) the normalisation of Scottish culture in every aspect of curriculum, as Council chairman Labour MP Sam Galbraith stated in the preface.

> [T]he Group is agreed that indigenous Scottish culture, including the changes it has undergone and continues to undergo, should be studied in our schools as a pervasive feature of the whole curriculum in schools.

The review emphasised that Scotland was a multi-lingual country in which Gaelic, Scots and English were 'indigenous languages each with its distinctive history and profile of current use', and acknowledged the marginalisation of Scots.

> [F]or generations the use of Scots was discouraged in schools on the grounds that it interfered with the learning of correct English. Over the last 25 years there has been increased but spasmodic attention to the potential contribution of Scots language and literature to the curriculum. It remains true however that Scots in its varieties has never won the coherent practical support which the Group believes it merits.

The group made specific recommendations to redress this injustice.

> [F]rom the earliest stages and starting with the language forms of their local area students should investigate, use, and enjoy the diversity of Scots speech and writing. This should proceed as a balanced part of their English programme. There is a need to support and encourage schools in exploiting the opportunities that already exist in 5–14 planning and SQA syllabuses.

However, the unionist-dominated management group of the Scottish

127 *The Herald* 1998a

SCCC dramatically vetoed these tentative steps to reversing centuries of discrimination. Robbie Robertson, former assistant director of the SCCC and closely associated with the project, said the group was 'incandescent' as he could not remember a Council document not being published. Robertson was convinced the decision not to publish was 'ultimately political', and added,

> I suspect quite strongly that there was a political anxiety about this document because, quite clearly, it could be used by the SNP in ways that may be unwelcome by the present [Labour] Government and other parties.

Galbraith denied the decision was politically motivated, but a real chance for a national debate on the role of Scots had effectively been suppressed. A weakened version of the report, *The School Curriculum and the Culture of Scotland*, focusing on politics, business and values of good citizenship was published in 1999 and immediately condemned by 15 of the original 18-member group in the strongest of terms; 'the real issues surrounding Scottish culture are not being presented to the profession and indeed to the nation'.[128]

With this ominous portent, power was transferred to the new Parliament in 1999, the inaugural session taking place on 12 May 1999, and evidently bringing intact into it many of the prejudices against the Scots language that had, if anything, hardened since the old parliament dissolved in 1707.

128 *The Scotsman* 1999

CHAPTER FOUR

After Devolution

Scots 'buried alive'

IT ALL STARTED so well. On the first day of July 1999 the Scottish Parliament was officially opened on Edinburgh's historic Mound and received its full law-making powers. During the ceremony, Ian Crichton Smith's poem 'Let our three-voiced country sing in a new world' was read out and Sheena Wellington sang a stirring rendition of Burns' Scots language anthem of equality and social justice, 'A Man's A Man for A' That'. After a long, long silencing, Scots looked to be making a comeback. But 17 years later, Scots writer Matthew Fitt, visiting the Parliament in its new home at Holyrood, contrasted that sense of optimism with the nearly complete absence of the Scots language in the Parliament building itself.

> There's bonnie pamphlets tae weelcome visitors in their ain languages fae Berlin, Lyon or New Delhi, but nae weelcome for you in your Mither Tongue if ye're veesitin yer ain Pairlament fae Buckie, Lochgelly or New Cumnock. Gang ben the Pairlament foyer, dauner through the gairden loabby, jink up and doon the public sterrs, gawp in awe at the vaultit ceilin in the debatin chaumer. Ony Scots language visible tae the human ee? John Rebus couldnae find it.[1]

In fact, I found some Scots at the Parliament building the last time I was there. In in the gift shop, on the tea towels; *Wha's like us?* Wha, indeed? One of Scotland's native languages reduced to a mildly amusing low-cost heritage curio. Where did it all go wrong? Although the centuries-long discrimination against Scots had now been acknowledged, it was clear from the very outset that the first Scottish Executive, a unionist coalition

1 Fitt 2016d

of Labour and the Liberal Democrats, had no intention of doing anything about it. The suppression of the *Review* just the year before had indeed been a forewarning.

Nonetheless, one of the new Executive's first commitments was to develop a 'national cultural strategy' for Scotland. In August 1999, a consultation document was launched followed by meetings around the country. The consultation report confirmed that the public wanted Scottish culture to have a far bigger profile, and to fight negative attitudes about it. People appeared to be ahead of politicians, expressing a wide and inclusive view of Scottish culture and emphasising that 'culture should be at the heart of people's lives'. In education, broadcasting and publishing, the need to formally validate and support both Gaelic and Scots was clear.

The million dollar question – or rather the 11.8 million pound question – was even raised; should Scots be accorded the same status as Gaelic? (£11.8m was the annual spend on Gaelic that year). Although there were dissenters, the report concluded, 'the weight of opinion was that these languages are an important asset and should inform the Strategy'. Predictably, this populist enthusiasm was redacted from the published strategy, *Creating Our Future; Minding Our Past*, when it was eventually released.[2] Popular and working-class cultural expressions were, as usual, shunned in favour of well-established sectors preferred by the middle classes, such as theatre, orchestras, museums, opera, film, the Edinburgh Festival and the emerging creative industries.

'The Scots language continues to be widely spoken today and has a long and important history', the Strategy acknowledged reluctantly. It was a 'living language' but was only offered minimal official measures to support it, including an evaluation for a proposal for a language centre. In contrast, the enthusiasm for Gaelic was effusive, with the government pledging to fund 'a vigorous programme to encourage the use of the language and its transmission to the next generation' through funding for Gaelic medium education, Gaelic cultural organisations and Gaelic radio. The topic of whether Scots should be accorded the same status as Gaelic, which had been posed by the public during the consultation, was therefore officially answered by the British nationalist politicians. No.

One explanation for the contrast in treatment between Gaelic and Scots was that Gaelic activity was significantly more established at the time, thanks in part to 20 years of government support funding prior to devolution. Scots simply lacked an equivalent campaign from persistent and savvy middle-class lobbyists, allowing the Executive to disregard it. Hence Robert Millar

2 Scottish Executive 2000

titled his 2006 review of the official treatment of Scots in the early days of devolution as *Burying Alive: unfocussed governmental language policy and Scots*. He remarked, 'there is certainly little evidence that these bodies have taken the issue of language policy seriously',[3] adding that Scots language policy at the time was, 'half-hearted, ill thought-out and buried in a swathe of other "cultural" issues'. In the early days of the parliament the majority of MSPs were political unionists and likely to be ambivalent at best to any expression of autonomous Scottish culture and identity. Hence in 2001 unionist MSPs even voted down the modest proposal for Scots language signage in the Parliament.

Nonetheless, the Scottish Executive undertook a few tokenistic steps to promote the Scots language. A short-lived Cross-Party Group on Scots was established, and speeches were permitted in Scots (providing they were accompanied by an English translation), but the long campaign for a question about Scots language in the 2001 Census exposed the political divide. Jackson and Niven summarise the rationale of the time.

> The Scottish Executive knows that until it can be demonstrated that a significant number of people speak Scots, it can be treated as a subject of trivial importance – a non-issue.[4]

Thus in 2000, Labour, Conservative and Liberal Democrat MSPs voted not to include a question on Scots in the 2001 Census while pro-independence MSPs voted in favour.

> No quantification of Scots speakers was to take place; Scots speakers were not to know that their being so was of some importance; some Scots speakers may even have been denied the knowledge that such a language existed.[5]

For the first time since MacDiarmid's heyday, the Scots language had become a contentious political issue, and any promotion of Scots was viewed as part of a Scottish nationalist agenda. Growing partisanship began to inhibit open, reasoned debate on the language's future, block constructive proposals and shunt the issue ever further into political sidings.

---

3 Millar 2006:82

4 Jackson and Niven 2000:3

5 Millar 2011:6

To see oursels as ithers see us

By the turn of the century, the long-term marginalisation and mistreatment of the Scots language had become so ingrained in Scottish culture that it was almost shocking to see the institutionalised discrimination described and exposed by an external expert. Perhaps less surprising was how quickly it was supressed.

As part of the 2001 European Year of Languages, Professor 'Jo' Lo Bianco, an internationally recognised authority on language, culture and literacy education, was asked to cast his expert eye on the linguistic situation in Scotland and report back to the Executive. His detailed research, *Language and Literacy Policy in Scotland*, described 'a history of neglect, misrepresentation and even hostility' towards Scots. The unionist resistance at the time to a Census question on Scots was characterised as, 'the very denial of its existence as a distinctive code'. The expert also observed that, 'in the absence of statistical information about Scots positive moves in policy are continually challenged, delayed and frustrated'. He called for more research into the language, its use in education, especially, but also wider issues; 'What Scots is called, how it is named and spoken about by the nation's leaders and intellectuals, how "ordinary people" think about it'.

Viewing Scots as a normal minority language, Lo Bianco believed it 'warrants a prominent place in policy' and should be considered not simply as a linguistic and cultural resource, but as an integral part of the national social inclusion and adult literacy agendas. He called for 'sophisticated socio-linguistic planning' but emphasised this needed to be preceded by 'a kind of prestige-allocation process'. He reasoned, 'once prestige and regard are achieved the functional range, and place, of Scots will come to reflect more fully its demographic presence in the population'. Lo Bianco even suggested a process aiming to 'generate and recycle a "conversation" about the role and place of the languages in Scottish public life'.

The report concluded; 'the actions required to reverse the erosion of the linguistic heritage of Scotland are urgent and considerable development is required'. Several recommendations were listed. The first was that Scots should be included in the Census (as indeed transpired a decade later) and that a language research centre be established (that never happened). Secondly, Scotland needed a National Languages Act to provide legal support for both Scottish Gaelic and Scots.

> This legislation ought to acknowledge the unique cultural position of these two languages and it is appropriate and necessary that it

> also accords recognition to a wider right of public communication, personal enjoyment and use of any language in the community.

The Gaelic Language (Scotland) Act arrived within four years, but over two decades later Scots was still awaiting equivalent legal protection. Lo Bianco believed there was 'an unchallengeable case' for a representative and authoritative body to be commissioned to produce a report on the 'role of the Scots language in contemporary Scottish society', and as part of its remit consider 'how this major national resource should be supported in order to enable it to fulfil this role'. Such a group was eventually constituted eight years later, resulting in the *Scots language: Ministerial Working Group report* of 2010. Most significantly, Lo Bianco envisaged an official agency to cover education and public use, including place names, corpus planning activities and dictionary preparation work, style guide preparation committees and guidelines on public use and social inclusion.

As an external expert, the author simply viewed Scots as a normal minority language that could be revitalised using by then well-established methods. In line with earlier consultations, *Language and Literacy Policy in Scotland* had almost no impact on the public or the public debate on Scots. However, it is worth reminding ourselves that at the outset of the Parliament over 20 years ago there was a perfectly useable and authoritative blueprint to initiate a real debate into the public use of Scots and that it was ignored by Scottish politicians.

The ECRML: Lang looked for's come at last

Around the time of the Lo Bianco report in early 2001, language activists were excited about the consequences of the UK government signing up to the *European Charter for Regional or Minority Languages* (ECRML). This was a treaty developed nine years earlier by the Council of Europe (COE), the continent's main human rights organisation. There are currently 25 full signatories of ECRML. Seven languages are listed by the UK Government; Welsh, Scottish Gaelic, Irish, Scots, Ulster Scots and (since 2003) Cornish and Manx Gaelic, but not all are treated the same way. Signatories commit to providing periodic reports to the COE, the latest (fifth) being in 2018. The reports are examined by a committee of experts who evaluate progress and make proposals and recommendations. In 2021 Westminster provided the supplementary feedback on recommendations; so for the time being, the reporting process seems to have survived Brexit.[6]

6 *ECRML 2021*

The Charter clearly states, 'the right to use a regional or minority language in private and public life is an inalienable right' and ratifies the principle that the recognition of the regional or minority languages is 'an expression of cultural wealth'. It underlines 'the need for resolute action to promote regional or minority languages in order to safeguard them'. Actions are listed in two parts, labelled II and III, but there are no sanctions provided for non-compliance as the Charter is a voluntary ethical commitment.

Part II of the Charter sets out general principles that signatories should adopt to protect their minority languages, such as the proactive use of the languages in public and private life and support for their teaching and study. Any unjustified distinction, exclusion, restriction or preference relating to the use of the minority language should be eliminated, and respect, understanding and tolerance promoted. Part III is more directive and lists specific provisions for the use of languages in education, law, public services, the media, cultural activities, economic life and transnational exchanges. As Part III is quite demanding, signatory states can choose which languages they want it to be applied to. Clearly if a state wished to avoid responsibilities under the ECRML, it could simply leave some languages off the Part III list. In the UK, only three languages have been awarded Part III status, Welsh, Scottish Gaelic and Irish; four are not: Scots, Ulster Scots, Cornish and Manx Gaelic. From the outset, therefore, Scots was officially deemed 'second class' despite, as the Census later confirmed, having more speakers than all other listed UK minority languages combined.

Scots language activists at the time committed to try to get the Government to give Scots Part III recognition, but this was always in the gift of Westminster, suspicious then as now of any move that could stoke Scottish nationalism. Three criteria have been suggested to decide whether Part III could be applied: the language must have a sufficient number of speakers, it must have at least one territory in which speakers are sufficiently concentrated and speakers of the language must be active in their determination to promote the language.[7] Scots more than qualifies in the first two categories and it is only in the third the Scots language community falls dawn. This is not due to lack of public backing – consultations and surveys repeatedly show high levels of support for Scots – but lack of official support for lobby and grassroots activities. Comunn na Gàidhlig (CnaG), for example, was founded as far back 1984 by the Scottish Office to co-ordinate such developments for the Gaelic community, but no equivalent facility has ever been provided for Scots.

As Lo Bianco had identified, the Scots language urgently needed central

7 Woehrling 2006

coordination in the form of an authoritative overarching official agency integrated with Scotland's wider language interests. This would bring all the key players, stakeholders and organisations together. What was missing, therefore, was a body like the Gaelic Language Board (Bòrd na Gàidhlig), launched in 2005 to work closely with the Scottish Government and local authorities across Scotland to promote Gaelic. Very modest central funding could have established an equivalent Scots Language Board and enabled the development of a collective voice. This in turn would have petitioned for better support for Scots, provided the 'active determination' and lobbying required to raise the status of the language and the planning context for the 'urgent and considerable development' Lo Bianco felt that Scots needed. In the absence of a coordinating body, several smaller, fragmented initiatives emerged over the next five years, each significant in a way but never achieving the cohesive progress and momentum that was required.

One of the tasks such a centralised organisation would undoubtedly have set itself was corpus planning, ie the standardisation and elaboration of Scots. In the absence of a centralised official effort, what occurred was a 'free market' flurry of publications that set a 'soft' style and standard. For example, in 2002 The Scots Language Society's *Lallans* magazine published its final spelling committee report, but there was no resource to support or to promote it as a written standard. In the same year, Itchy Coo was founded to publish books in Scots for children and young people, led by authors James Robertson and Matthew Fitt. Initially funded from the National Lottery with an annual grant from the Scottish Arts Council, Itchy Coo subsequently published the best part of 40 titles and sold almost a quarter of a million books. Itchy Coo's stated aim was 'to encourage better understanding and greater acceptance of the Scots Language in education and in all aspects of Scottish life'. The imprint became an education and language promotion initiative, with Fitt working with pupils and teachers to develop their Scots reading and writing skills. He made countless visits to schools and libraries, and delivered hundreds of in-service training sessions in almost every area of Scotland. Two other innovative publications in Scots that year were Matthew Fitt's own novel *But N Ben A-Go-Go*, the first science fiction novel to be written in Scots, and L Colin Wilson's ground-breaking *Luath Scots Language Learner*, the first published book-length language course in Scots. The latter largely adopted the 'soft' spelling standard of *Concise English-Scots Dictionary* (CESD), published in 1993.

In stark contrast, Edinburgh English Language professor Charles Jones caused something of a stushie in 2002 with his provocatively-titled *The English Language in Scotland: An introduction to Scots*. He declared

Modern Scots to be merely 'the daily spoken and written form of the English language peculiar to Scotland'.[8] Much bemusement was generated by his erroneous statement on the very first page that the Scots Language Resource Centre and the Scots Language Society 'proselytised' Lallans, described as 'the largely artificial and reconstructed version of the English spoken in the sixteenth and seventeenth centuries'. Scots, we learn from Professor Jones, was just 'the variety of English which has been used in face-to-face and written communications in Scotland for the past fourteen hundred years'. To be fair, he conceded, 'Scots remains distinctive and identifiable', though adding 'in much the same way that the Englishes spoken in New Zealand and Australia do'.[9] Perhaps recognising the 'distinctive and identifiable nature' of Scots, in late 2003 the BBC drew up a list of about 100 Scots words which presenters should feel 'comfortable' about using on air. The list included 'steamin', 'glaikit', 'haar', 'puckle', 'dreich' and 'crabbit', but was definitely 'not compulsory'.[10] Scots language campaigners dismissed the approach as tokenistic at the time, and two decades later, it is long forgotten.

A Statement of Principles

Meanwhile, campaigners in The Scots Pairlament Cross Pairty Group on the Scots Language felt a more robust statement in support of Scots was needed, and in 2003 drew up a *Statement o Principles* inspired by the Universal Declaration of Linguistic Rights, sending it to all 129 MSPs.[11]

1. Scots is a language
2. Action maun be taen tae pit an end tae aw prejudice an discrimination agin the Scots language
3. The Scots language is integral an essential tae cultural an personal identity in Scotland
4. A knowledge o Scots is vital tae a knowledge o Scotland
5. Action maun be taen tae gie the Scots language whitiver means is needit tae mak siccar its transmission an continuity
6. Scots shuid be an essential pairt o the educational curriculum in Scotland at aw levels
7. Naebody shuid be penalised or pitten doun for speakin Scots
8. Scots proper names an place names shuid be valued an safegairdit

8 Jones 2002:vii

9 Jones 2002:5

10 *The Herald* 2003

11 Donati et al 2003

9. Speakers an writers o Scots shuid hae scowth tae develop an active role an presence for the Scots language in aw pairts o the communications media
10. Ongaun study an documentation o the language maun be gien ful resourcin
11. Initiatives shuid be stertit tae mainteen an uphaud Scots terms an uisage specific tae sindry trades an occupations
12. The Scots language shuid be uised in adverts, in signs, in signpostin, an in the presentation o an accurate image o Scotland
13. The people o Scotland has the ability an responsibility tae uphaud the Scots language an gar Pairlament uise its pouer an authority tae realise thir foregaun principles an statements o intent

A general problem with such initiatives is that, worthy though they may be, they never seemed to be accompanied by any coherent implementation plan. Principles like this need to be agreed, and preferably 'owned', by the government and community, then actioned though specific, measurable and time-determined policies. The Principles simply faded away, as did the lobbying to promote Scots to Part III ECRML status. Overall, too much confidence was given to the ECRML as a change mechanism. The 2005 ECRML report comprised answers from the Scottish Executive that the contemporary campaigning newsletter *Scots Tung* labelled 'embarrassing'. Perhaps with a nod to the Jones model, the report described Scots as 'Scottish English (Scots)' and avoided answering all questions put to the UK regarding Scots, stating that it would be dealt with later in the National Languages Strategy, which was working on curriculum reform.

There was little pressure on the government to support Scots from the Scottish press either, indeed quite the opposite. When in 2004 the Scottish Parliament worked up the nerve to produce a leaflet in Scots about inclusivity, *Makkin yer voice heard in the Scottish Pairlament*, the columnist Allan Massie channelled establishment derision. In his *Scotsman* column, he described the leaflet as follows

> [A] truly wretched and dismal little document, though published, I've no doubt, with the very best intentions. What it shows, sadly, is the debility of the Scots language today [...] It does nothing for the Scots language, other than expose it to ridicule and bring it into contempt. It is frankly embarrassing.[12]

12 Massie 2004

Demonstrating no awareness of modern Scots spelling practices, Massie sounded like a fuming 1950s dominie, aching to thrash the unfortunate copywriter with his tawse.

> One might begin with that title, Makkin may be permissible as an attempt at phonetic transcription, to show that the word is to be pronounced with a short 'a'; nevertheless the Scots word for 'poet' was 'makar' with only one 'k', 'Yer' is vile. 'Scottish' itself is questionable [...] The better form here would be 'Scots' or 'Scottis'.

Massie concluded; 'I have the impression that whoever wrote this booklet knows very little about the history of the language'. Massie had every right to parade his knowledge (or lack thereof) concerning contemporary Scots writing conventions, and indeed any modern Scots writer might query the actual spellings and vocabulary used, but that was not the point. Instead of standing up for itself and its right to employ the language of many of its voters, the Parliament seemed to skulk away like a beaten bairn, vowing never to make such a humiliating error again in front of their self-styled betters. Fifteen years after the Massie attack, as Matthew Fitt found, the Scottish Parliament still seemed terrified of using any Scots in a public capacity.

One of Massie's attacks echoes Jones' Lallans jibe, that 'purists would insist on using a language that, however rich, hasn't been in common use for a couple of hundred years at least'. The only way to counter this type of dismissive myth was via actual data and a question on the Scots language for the 2011 census. And that is where the tiny group of Scots activists wisely focused their campaign. However, they also asked for the publication of a national language strategy, promised by the Scottish Executive since 2003. A strategy of sorts eventually appeared in consultation form in January 2007.[13] Astute activists noted the document was suspiciously like a 1995 pre-devolution *Scots Language Factsheet*, endorsed by Michael Forsyth, then Conservative Secretary of State for Scotland. The implication was that devolution had provided almost no meaningful advance for Scots. In the strategy, Gaelic was to be 'protected and promoted' in line with the provisions of the Gaelic Language (Scotland) Act 2005 but Scots had to make do with being 'treated with respect and pride' and a vague promise that 'public bodies will also be encouraged to explore opportunities to promote and develop the Scots language'. The strategy claimed that 'Scots is not an endangered language', reasoning that, 'unlike Gaelic, Scots [...] has considerable overlap with Scottish Standard English'. Only one support

13 Scottish Executive 2007

initiative was listed, the non-prescriptive *National Guidelines on English Language 5–14*, already in force for 12 years. As one activist group put it, the document could not accurately be described as a strategy as it did not set targets, goals or aims, 'and contributes nothing to assist the development or protection of the Scots language'. Bob Fairnie writing in *Scots Tung Wittins* concluded gloomily:

> There can be nae doot noo that baith the Scottish Executive, gaun aw the wey back tae 1999 as weel as the Scottish Office afore that, haes haed nae intentions o daein onythin ither nor juist giein lip service tae the cause o the Scots language an they've never haed ony plans tae dae onythin positive tae sauf Scots. If the language survives it will be in spite o the Executive an certainly no because o it.[14]

The Strategy was almost immediately forgotten as campaigning started for the 2007 Scottish Parliament Elections. Encouragingly, most parties referred to Scots in their manifestos: Scottish Green Party (support measures), Labour (need to think about it), Lib-Dems (improve support given to projects recognising Scots), SSP (equal status with other languages) and of course the SNP (Scots in the Census, European Charter obligations, improve Scots in education, arts and broadcasting). Only the Conservative Party manifesto somehow managed to overlook Scots completely.

New government, new hope

The SNP emerged from the elections as the largest party with 47 seats, one more than the incumbent Scottish Labour Party, and was able to form a minority government. Scots language activists were again optimistic. Surely after the early disappointments of devolution we would soon be entering a new golden age for Scots.

> The Scots language can tak howp frae the SNP promises, includin a question on Scots in the 2011 Census an cairryin oot aw the obligations laid doon in Pairt II o the European Chairter for Regional or Minority Languages [...] active encouragement for the yuiss o Scots in education, braidcastin an the airts [...] At the stert o this new pairlament lat us aw seek tae win aw that is best for Scotland an tae mak Scotland a bi-lingual, tri-lingual or e'en a multi-lingual nation.[15]

14 Fairnie 2007a

15 Fairnie 2007b

A way forward certainly seemed open. At the first meeting of the Cross-Party Group at Holyrood it was clear the amateurish languages strategy of the previous administration was dead. But what would come next? Any minority government is constrained in power, and the SNP leadership had many other pressing issues and priorities. Furthermore, they still had to deal with the almost universally hostile UK and Scottish press, historically and sometimes hysterically ill-disposed to the Scots language. To give a flavour of this type of attack, in November 2009 *The Scottish Daily Mail* splashed an article entitled 'Walcome tae the Scottish Pairlament wabsite: The internet guide to Holyrood translated into *Rab C. Nesbitt* dialect':

> To a handful of proud Scots, it is a valuable guide to Scottish politics, using the language of their forefathers before the country was taken over by Sassenachs who forced them to speak the Queen's English. But to English sceptics it may sound as though *Rab C. Nesbitt* actor Gregor Fisher, who played the shambolic Glaswegian alcoholic in the Nineties television sitcom, has been given a taxpayers' grant to write his own political manifesto. A row erupted last night over public funds spent on the new internet handbook produced by the Scottish Parliament which uses the little-used Scots dialect. Scholars disagree whether Scots is a genuine dialect or a language – and some claim only a 'few thousand' Scots speak it properly.[16]

The piece quotes the website verbatim, assuming the very sight of written Scots would be sufficiently hilarious for its conservative, mostly middle-class readership. The last line was provided by the Scottish Conservative education spokeswoman and MSP Liz Smith who said, 'this is a language spoken by a few thousand people at most'. Sixteen hundred thousand, as it turned out, but at least she recognised Scots as a language, more than some of her Holyrood colleagues.

Despite this media hostility, the first SNP government tried to address the chronic lack of information on Scots speaker activity and demographics that Lo Bianco had criticised a few years earlier. Three instruments were chosen by the re-named Scottish Government, an Audit (2009), an Attitudes Survey (2010) and a question on Scots in the 2011 Census.

In 2008 an external consultant, Rhys Evans, was commissioned to undertake the baseline audit of Scots language provision to find what existed and if/how it could be enhanced. The aim was significant.

16 Walters 2009

> The Scottish Government recognises that it has a duty to protect and promote the Scots language, and the audit is the necessary first stage in the process to develop a competent and coordinated policy for the Scots language for the first time.

At last Scots was officially treated as a minority language and the audit used the ECRML framework as a reference point to categorise provision into seven public spheres: education; judicial authorities; administrative authorities and public services; media; cultural activities and facilities; economic and social life; and trans-frontier exchanges. Evans admitted he 'began the task cautiously prepared to discover a language in danger of extinction or under threat',[17] but soon realised:

> [B]oth the extent and types of provision, and the comments of informants made it clear that the situation of the Scots language within Scotland is different. It is one of growth, change and growing respect [...] Scots is a living language.

He was impressed by 'the keenness and enthusiasm on the part of all those who are currently involved in Scots language provision'. The centrality of the Scots language to a sense of identity he felt was shown by 'the passion of the respondents and the positive responses they report when providing services'. The audit was concluded by Evans as follows:

> This study discovered a healthy, vital and diverse community of passionate providers interacting with a Scots-speaking public who appeared to value the provision highly. The audit found many acts of provision across the range of COE ECRML categories of public life.[18]

One of the constants through various surveys on Scottish language and culture over the last 20 years is just how much ordinary people value Scots and wish to see it supported adequately. This is a completely non-controversial position, backed by ample evidence. It is perhaps a sign of the continuing linguistic disconnect of the establishment elites in Scotland that these reasonable and modest aspirations are rarely discussed, let alone addressed. Despite the varied grassroots engagement with Scots, Evans reported provision was patchy especially in 'official' areas, such as education, public administration and broadcasting. These are typically areas where

17 Scottish Government/Evans 2009:36

18 Scottish Government/Evans 2009:41

institutional funding is needed to sustain initiatives, and where a still-missing Scots Board would operate.

The audit identified one thought-provoking area of under-provision, namely economic and social life. Evans was surprised at the lack of recognition of the Scots language as a potential asset for economic development, as an 'intangible' asset.

> The use of regional or minority language empowers its speakers to interact with each other, reinforcing identities, and validating them within national economic and social life. It is also more specifically about economic development both within the language community and in terms of its participation in the wider economy.[19]

Evans could find 'no evidence of any Government economic development programme for Scots language-based activities, products or services', the one notable exception to this being the small Robert Burns industry. Given the substantial impact of tourism in Scotland's economy, the lack of wider promotion of the Scots language's heritage may seem unimaginative, even self-sabotaging. Opportunities suggested by the author were language teaching, festivals, music, stories and other cultural activities. He compared Scotland with Ireland where Irish language and cultural practices 'underpin a growing tourism and music/literature economy which caters to an international market'. The Doric Festival, initiated in 1994, might be another model for this, but overall the lack of institutional interest in the economic value of Scots remains puzzling to this day.

Not surprisingly, Evans found grassroots provision to be heavily reliant on voluntary activity. Voluntarism may be a strength in terms of self-motivation and energy, but also renders the network fragile and less sustainable. The activists lacked the recognition and backing to maintain long-term engagement and development, both of the participants themselves and the communities they were serving. The lack of grassroots support was exacerbated by the lack of national leadership and strategic direction.

> The audit found that there is currently no single lead organisation or person positioned with an overall and general responsibility for Scots language provision. Nor is there any overarching policy concerning the language. Rather, there are a number of individuals and organisations who, in pursuing their own agendas, operate as a loose collective with the Scots language as their major concern. This

19 Scottish Government/Evans 2009:31

has consequences for strength of provision across the COE ECRML's seven categories of public life.[20]

The suspect survey

The *Public Attitudes Towards the Scots Language* was the second information-gathering exercise by the Scottish Government, undertaken in late 2009 and published the following year. Unfortunately, the shoddy design of this survey managed to cancel the positivity of the audit and cast a dark shadow over later Government activities in the area. The aim was reasonable enough: to provide a broad overview of perceptions of the Scots language and attitudes towards it, and also to measure behaviours and expectations of its use. Lo Bianco was right to point out the need to develop an academic, political and popular agreement on how to use the term 'Scots', but he intended this exercise to be part of a wider national conversation to build awareness of the language and raise its prestige. For some reason, this vital preparatory debate was skipped, and a crudely designed public survey turned out not to be the best way to initiate this type of nuanced discourse. The dubious outcomes themselves and the clumsy way they were handled on release deeply damaged the Scots language cause for a decade.

A commercial public research agency, TNS-BMRB, was commissioned to undertake the survey, who in turn used the Scottish Opinion Survey (SOS), an interview-based research service. A series of questions in four areas were included in the survey, covering perceptions of Scots as a language, attitudes towards the Scots language, expectations of the current use of Scots and the Scots language in education. In line with previous public consultations, a sizeable majority (67 per cent) regarded it as important that Scots was used in contemporary Scotland and for a significant minority (29 per cent) this view was expressed with conviction.

> [T]he vast majority of adults agree that Scots is an important part of the history/heritage and the culture of Scotland (88% and 86% respectively), with in each instance more than half the sample indicating that these views are strongly held.[21]

Although there were dissenting voices, overall the investigators found a solid consensus that Scots had an important role in terms of the identity, culture and heritage of Scotland, 'even amongst those not considering it important,

20 Scottish Government/Evans 2009:46

21 Scottish Government/TNS-BMRB 2010:2

or not using it themselves'.

This affirmative message was not, however, what made the headlines in the ever-antagonistic Scottish media. Participants were also asked to agree or disagree with several statements, one being, 'I don't really think of Scots as a language, it's more just a way of speaking'. Most adults in the sample (64 per cent) agreed, with around half of this group holding this view with conviction (34 per cent of the total sample). The commentariat in the Scottish press gleefully pounced on this result, ridiculing Scots in order make a proxy attack the SNP government in headlines such as, 'Blow to SNP as two-thirds say Scots is not a real language'.[22] That particular article quoted MSP Ted Brocklebank, then culture spokesman for the Scottish Conservatives:

> It is no surprise that 64 per cent of the Scottish public do not believe that Scots is a language. This is because we already have a Scots language – it is called Gaelic. The Scots language that the SNP government continues to try to promote is not a separate language, but a collection of regional dialects of the English language. The SNP must stop wasting taxpayers' money trying to invent something that doesn't exist, in a futile attempt to promote the narrow Nationalist agenda.

The fragile confidence of Scots language champions inside and outside the Government was certainly dented as everybody seemed to take the results at face value. The survey's context, design and interpretation drew no critique at the time.

Was there anything specific about the structure of the survey that could have led to this not-a-language result? The first warning bell should have rung when it was reported that 85 per cent of respondents said they used Scots. The 1996 GRO(S) survey and the later Census figures from 2011 both put the percentage of Scots speakers in the population at around a more plausible (and generally accepted at the time) 30 per cent. The 55 per cent discrepancy should have suggested there was something unusually vague about the respondents' concept of 'Scots' in this survey. The questions on Scots, bearing in mind this was part of a larger survey, were introduced as follows:

> Scots uses words, phrases and expressions that are different from standard English and it also varies across different parts of Scotland.

22 *The Scotsman* 2010

> Scots spoken in the North East, for example, the Doric, is very different from the Scots used in the South West of Scotland, or the East of Scotland or Lallans, the Scots used in Lowland and Central Scotland.[23]

The survey firm argued that 'the term "language" was deliberately avoided in the opening introduction so as not to influence the respondents' views', but the introduction quoted is replete with cues and biases that worked in the opposite direction. Scots was portrayed in terms of difference from standard English and dialectal variation was exaggerated. Doric was described as 'very different', and the long list of geographical regions unsubtly hints at fragmentation and a lack of linguistic cohesion. The interviewees were then asked to comply with a clumsily worded negative, 'I don't really think of Scots as a language, it's more just a way of speaking'. Dodgy wording aside, the research professionals surely knew that agree/disagree questions in polls notoriously suffer from *acquiescence bias*, the tendency for respondents to comply with questions like that. Furthermore, immediately prior to asking the questions the interviewer played a recording of some examples of contemporary Scots. The contents are not listed anywhere, but the nature of the recordings would have been critical in shaping perceptions. Overall, the 85 per cent speaker figure suggests a very weak notion of Scots had been prompted, inadvertently or not, and this would certainly impact on respondents' thoughts of the linguistic status of Scots. Over a decade later, this sloppily designed survey is still proclaimed by zealots as absolute proof that 'Scots is not a language'.

One curiosity, though, is the 30 per cent who resisted the TNS-BMRB cues and disagreed with the 'not a language' question, over half of those doing so strongly (16 per cent in total). It would be tempting to conclude these were just hard-core nationalists, but fortunately this time TNS-BMRB dug a little deeper and found a curious and, I believe, significant phenomenon.

> [V]iews on whether or not Scots is a language differ significantly according to how frequently it is spoken: the most frequent speakers are least likely to agree that it is not a language and those never speaking Scots most likely to do so.

Remember that the 1996 GRO(S) survey estimated that 30 per cent of the population spoke Scots, a figure later confirmed by the 2011 Census. If anything can be drawn from the Survey at all, it suggests habitual Scots

23 Scottish Government/TNS-BMRB 2010:34

speakers tend to believe they are speaking a *bona fide* language and non-speakers think they do not.

The implication, if true, is grim. Power is always in the hands of a majority who are convinced Scots 'doesn't exist', so discrimination against the Scots-speaking minority is almost guaranteed. Coincidentally, in February 2009, Lesley Riddoch in her radio programme *Aftermath* debated the issue of Scots linguistic discrimination with Billy Kay. She pointed out that Gaelic at the time received £27 million a year (ie more than double the budget of a decade previously), Ulster Scots £3 million a year, while Scots received just £250,000. 'What's going on there?' Kay asked. Riddoch asserted that the 'chattering classes' at the BBC decide what is normal and like to pretend Scots doesn't exist. Opinions are then likely to be amplified by political positioning. As the less loaded questions of the survey made quite clear, 'there is particularly widespread agreement [73 per cent] that learning Scots can contribute to a sense of national cultural identity', and no self-respecting British nationalist obviously wants that. The editorial in *The Scotsman* on the day the report was published articulated the uncompromising establishment line.

> Scots is not a separate language but a collection of regional dialects of the English language. Take away the words, syntax and grammatical structure of the English language, and could Scots stand on its own? Many words are commonly used by Scots. That may make it a potent dialect, but not a language. Supporters may argue that it may not yet be a fully established language in the conventional sense but would become so were it to receive official recognition. But is there in Scotland a majority in favour of such status and the financial and educational implications such status would carry? The poll would seem to indicate: no.[24]

That question was not actually asked in the survey, but following a familiar path, *The Scotsman* journalist, deliberately or unconsciously, misrepresented the robust pro-Scots mood of the survey's respondents.

'One of the most important documents about Scots'

Behind the scenes, in 2009 the Scottish Government commissioned a group of experts to devise 'a radical vision' for the development of the language, presented as the *Scots Language: Ministerial Working Group Report* on St Andrew's Day 2010. Its ethos was profoundly at odds with *The Scotsman*'s

24 *The Scotsman* 2010

anglophone establishment opinion, and far more aligned to the public support for Scots.

> Negative attitudes towards Scots are no longer tenable, and [media organisations] must be seen to be active in promoting the mother tongue of a large proportion of the Scottish population. Scots is recognised as a language by the Scottish, European and UK governments and is seen by the Scottish people themselves as a major badge of their identity.

Chaired by respected language expert J Derrick McClure, the group comprised a gamut of activists, academics and writers. Although the core findings had been previously aired by Lo Bianco and others, the assembly consolidated modern expert thinking on the language for a government then still committed to promoting Scots. In the context of the neglect of Scots by officialdom over three centuries and the post-devolution 'burying alive' of the language question, the report was hailed later as, 'undoubtedly one of the most important documents ever to be produced about the Scots language'.[25] Its legitimacy stemmed from the fact that, despite a 'predictably vigorous and wide-ranging' debate, a consensus was eventually reached in an area typified by acrimonious individual opinion.

The group reaffirmed Scots as an indigenous language of Scotland, along with Gaelic and English. As such, Scots should, 'as a matter of right' enjoy 'an established, institutionalised and formally recognised place in all aspects of the national life', comparable to that of Gaelic. It was recognised that any change in status may take time, as the 'unsatisfactory' state of Scots at the time was the outcome of, 'long-term social and cultural developments of which the effects cannot be easily or quickly countered'.

The report listed recommendations in six areas: education, broadcasting, literature and the arts, international contacts, public awareness and dialects, the last providing an 'official' modern definition of Scots.

> The long-term socio-historical development of Scots has given it, at present, a distinctive nature as a language with a number of different dialects but – at present – no standard form. Much of the widespread ignorance and confusion surrounding Scots, already often referred to, inheres in a failure to understand that the term 'Scots' includes Buchan, Border, Fife, Ayrshire, Galloway, Shetland and all other dialects, and that there is no form (or certainly, at least, no spoken

25 Hance 2011

> form) which can be taken to be simply 'Scots' (as, for example, what is commonly and naively taken to be simply 'French' is the Île de France dialect spoken with an educated middle-class Parisian accent). This situation is by no means unique to Scots and is well understood by sociolinguists: also well recognised is the fact that a standard form to be used for governmental and other official purposes could readily be devised, and would be if a government directive to this effect were issued

Three clear positions can be inferred from this statement.

- Scots is a typical minority language, with dialectal variants like any other, so refuting the often-heard assertion that Scots is uniquely incapable of linguistic coherence.
- The 'no standard' claim is here specifically applied to the spoken language only, and some level of existing standardisation in writing is recognised but in the discussion on education the group acknowledged, 'the lack of a generally-understood relationship between spoken and written Scots'.
- An official standard could 'readily be devised', again portrayed by some critics as a near-impossible task.

The group discussed the older distinction sometimes made between 'good' rural dialects and 'bad' urban dialects, and concluded that all regional and social dialects of Scots should be recognised as worthy of respect. Central initiatives in support of Scots should therefore take into account local diversity, especially in strong dialect areas. This would of course require quite a lot of sensitivity.

> The need to preserve the individual dialects and respect their distinctive identities, while at the same time developing the language as a whole, will require careful planning: in particular, the necessity of developing a standard form of Scots for official purposes must be presented so as to avoid any appearance of a threat to the dialects.

The Government was advised to show its goodwill and commitment via the development of a Scots Language Policy aligned to ECRML. As part of this, media organisations and cultural agencies receiving Government funding 'should be actively encouraged to develop specific Scots language policies'. As advocated by Lo Bianco in 2001 and in the 2009 Audit, existing bodies ought to be consolidated, strengthened and adequately funded.

The report made several practical recommendations, but realised 'the general level of understanding of matters relating to language and its use is low in Scotland'. The group criticised 'the unsatisfactory level of public awareness on Scots' and a lack of a consistent, visible policy on Scots among public bodies.

> [A] serious handicap to the development of Scots is the widespread uncertainty, even among fluent speakers, of the actual nature and status of the language; and a key factor in the task of promoting the language is that of eradicating the deep-rooted effects of the old educational tradition of denigrating it as 'slang', 'bad English' or the like.

One way to address this was via education, but, 'due to the traditional and still deep-seated prejudice against the language and the historically inadequate resourcing of it', only a small number of children in Scotland were benefitting from Scots language provision. A key recommendation was that a Scots Language/Scottish Literature Bureau should be created and funded 'to meet the growing demand from Scotland's teachers for high-quality training, information, and resources', especially online. This would be supported by a nationwide network of Coordinators able to deliver Scots language training and advice. The report noted that while financial plans were in place for the other languages of Scotland, the government had made no provision for the future funding of Scots in schools, declaring it 'must act to restore to hundreds of thousands of young Scots the fundamental *human right* of children to be taught in their mother tongue' (my italics). As a direct result, four Scots Language Coordinators were seconded to Education Scotland for a two-year period from 2014–2016, but at the time of writing only one remains to serve the whole country.

Reflecting over a decade later, the 2010 report may now be seen as the high-water mark so far of the Scottish Government's recognition of Scots as a normal minority language. The report directly influenced Government direction in subsequent years; a Scots Language Policy eventually materialised, and several focused policy initiatives were also started quite quickly, especially in education. Nevertheless, it could be argued that central initiatives over the subsequent decade subtly de-emphasised the *Report*'s minority language ethos and reframed Scots as a cultural curio, a process I later call *heritisation*. If we are looking for a single reason, the astonishing 'success' of the 2011 Census may be the key factor.

Census and censorship

Although the results would not appear until 2013, the inclusion of a question on the Scots language in the 2011 Census was a significant achievement, and the result of decades of lobbying by determined activists. The lack of data on Scots speakers had frequently been given as an excuse for government inaction. A Census question campaign had started back in 1994 and an early success was to persuade the General Register Office for Scotland (GROS) to research the possibility, resulting in the still significant 1996 survey. Post-devolution, the new Parliament debated whether to include a Scots question in the 2001 census, but unionist MSPs blocked it. The succeeding minority SNP government was committed to a Scots Census question and the UK Government had since recognised the language under ECRML, making denial harder to defend. Now was the time to find out whether Scots was spoken by a just a few thousand souls or, as the 1996 GRO(S) survey had implied, more than a million. GRO(S) started to reconsider a Scots language question and, with the Scots Language Centre (SLC), eventually agreed on the wording; 'Can you understand, speak, read or write Scots?'.

In March 2010, MSPs agreed unanimously that Scots should be included, but the 2009 Attitudes survey had cautioned that people 'experienced difficulty in understanding the term Scots, and that people interpreted the questions on the Scots language in different ways'. The Ministerial Working Group on the Scots Language had also recommended, 'in preparation for the census the public is made aware of the meaning and implications of the questions', echoing Lo Bianco's earlier suggestion for preparatory discussion.

In response, the website Aye Can was launched in 2010 by the SLC to help the public understand the Census question on Scots language ability. The site presented examples of both spoken and written Scots and attracted significant traffic. The SLC reported later that prior to the Census at least 200,000 saw the material, and the audio clips had been downloaded 300,000 times. Moreover, about 105,000 users were reached on Facebook and 80,000 on Twitter,[26] showing public interest in Scots was as high as earlier surveys had implied. Aye Can used the spoken or 'dialectal' definition of Scots, like the 2009 survey, but this time adding a specific reference to 'language':

> Scots is the collective name for Scottish dialects such as 'Glaswegian', 'Doric', 'Buchan', 'Dundonian', or 'Shetland'. Taken altogether, Scottish dialects are called the Scots language. Sometimes Scots is

26 Scots Language Centre 2011

> known by the names 'Scotch', 'broad or braid Scots', 'Doric' and 'Lallans'.

The Census took place on 27 March 2011. Question 16 asked, 'Which of these can you do? Tick all that apply'. A little table of 12 tick boxes had been given with the choices 'English', 'Scottish Gaelic', and 'Scots' along the top, and down the side the options 'Understand', 'Speak', 'Read' and 'Write', with an additional box for 'None of these'. Scotland had to wait nearly two and a half years to hear the outcome. The results were staggering. 1,541,693 people self-identified as Scots speakers, one of the most significant and surprising cultural manifestations of national distinctiveness in Scottish history. The survey suggested Scots was by far the most spoken indigenous minority tongue in the UK, with double the number of speakers of Welsh. In any normal country this would be a newsworthy cultural event, maybe even prompting a celebration of the vitality of Scottish popular culture, but this was Scotland. The reaction in the media was so muted, many activists suspected that once again any 'good news' about Scots was being deliberately suppressed.

The figures were released via a press conference and online on the morning of 26 September 2013. Language activists flocked to the NRS (National Records of Scotland) website.

> In 2011, the proportion of the population aged 3 and over in Scotland who reported they could speak, read, write or understand Scots was 38 per cent (1.9 million). For Scotland as a whole, 30 per cent (1.5 million) of the population aged 3 and over reported they were able to speak Scots. The council areas with the highest proportions able to speak Scots were Aberdeenshire and Shetland Islands (49 per cent each), Moray (45 per cent) and Orkney Islands (41 per cent). The lowest proportions reported were in Eilean Siar (7 per cent), City of Edinburgh (21 per cent), Highland and Argyll & Bute (22 per cent each).

Was this at last the magic data Scots language advocates had long been waiting for? The very next paragraph was ominous.

> The census data on language skills in Scots needs to be carefully qualified. The question on language skills in the census questionnaire was relatively poorly answered. For example, a significant number of respondents provided information on their skills in Scots but did not

> indicate any corresponding abilities in relation to English, perhaps suggesting they considered Scots and English as inter-changeable in this context. Research carried out prior to the census also suggests that people vary considerably in their interpretation of what is meant by 'Scots' as a language, resulting in the potential for inconsistencies in the data collected.

The research mentioned was a 2009 Ipsos Mori survey to test the impact of including Scots as a language question in the Census. The survey found, as one might expect, 'understanding of what is meant by "Scots" is very varied and there is considerable confusion about the meaning of the term', the very issue Aye Can had been established to address. NRS had taken the caveat, however, not as a starting point for much-needed public debate, but as an excuse to unilaterally disown its own data. Given that civil servants knew the Census results and potential impact weeks or even months before the release date, it seems unlikely that the positioning by the NRS on such a culturally (and politically) sensitive data set was unconsidered. The deliberate downplaying of the Scots data from the NRS news release had the result that the astonishing story of Scots' vitality was almost completely overlooked by the Scottish and UK media.

Author L Colin Wilson commented on the news coverage that day.

> *Reporting Scotland* the nicht hid a nae bad piece aboot the figures for Gaelic, even a cuttie interview wi an activist, bit said naething avaw aboot Scots, nae even that the figures hid been gaither't for the first time.[27]

The only BBC News story, 'Census shows decline in Gaelic speakers "slowed"', indicates the low-key media approach. An excerpt of this story illustrates how the astounding news about Scots was yet again 'buried alive':

> A decline in the overall number of Gaelic speakers in Scotland has 'slowed', according to the latest results from the 2011 Census. The previous Census results recorded an 11% drop in speakers, while the new figures suggest a 1.2% fall from 59,000 to 58,000. The latest results also show a 0.1% increase in Gaelic speakers aged under 20. The Scottish government said the results were encouraging. The results also include detail on what languages are used in Scottish

27 Quoted in Young 2013

> homes. They suggest that 93% of people aged three and over reported that they used only English at home. About 1.5 million people reported that they regularly spoke Scots. The figures also show 1% of the population – 54,000 people – used Polish at home, while 13,000 people reported using British Sign Language. Alasdair Allan, minister for Scotland's languages, said: 'While the census shows a slight fall overall, we can take real encouragement from the growth in Gaelic speakers under the age of 20'.[28]

The important news was therefore deemed to be all about Gaelic, the 'only English' data (to be discussed later) was used as a spoiler for the subsequent Scots data, and Polish and Sign Language were given equal status to Scots. Throughout the referendum campaign of the following year, accusations of manipulation and suppression of pro-Scottish news stories by the BBC and the Scottish press would become commonplace, but for many activists at the time this censorship from hitherto trusted news sources was genuinely new and unsettling.

On the SLC Facebook group, Michael Hance summed up the treatment of Scots in despair.

> Aye weel, that wis Scots speakers cleansed fae the telly the streen an near on naethin on the radio bar a report on Radio Shetland. I did get a e-mail tho fae a quine I'm workin wi on anither project. In it she tellt me she'd heard on the news – dinna ken whit station – that jist 1% o fowk spoke Scots.[29]

In quite an astonishing feat of collective media manipulation, Scots and its one and a half million speakers were once again simply erased from the public debate.

The spiking of Scots: sense and censuses

Was the NRS right to 'spike' the good news story of Scots? Nobody denies that Scots is a disputed language entity, with diverse meanings for different people. Was that fact sufficient for the NRS subvert, even sabotage, their own findings? The release of the Census statistics, following the Working Party report, was clearly an opportunity to open the debate and propel the discussion of Scots into the public arena, but it was not to be, with long-term

28 BBC News Services 2013

29 Quoted in Young 2013

consequences for the language. There is no such thing as a perfect Census survey. Language revitalisation experts Grenoble and Whaley explained why:

> [M]ost language surveys rely on self-assessment, which is notoriously unreliable because speakers may not have an accurate idea of how well they speak the language. Moreover, because language is such an important part of identity, speakers may claim to know more or less of a particular language because that claim reinforces their sense of identity.[30]

As mentioned earlier, there is little field data to validate any position definitively, but Johann Unger reported that his focus group 'uses the term *Scots* consciously and confidently, self-identifying as Scots speakers, and distinguishing clearly between *Scots* and *English* on numerous occasions'.[31] Grenoble and Whaley also comment;

> Survey data are typically much more reliable than the intuitions of the designers themselves, who can easily mistake their own perceptions as being typical of the community as a whole.

Designers should always try to avoid retrofitting their perhaps unconscious biases onto the data, and let it speak for itself.

The preconceptions of the NRS were revealed in their comment, 'the question on language skills in the census questionnaire was relatively poorly answered'. This seems to refer to the inconsistency between answers to Question 16 'Which of these can you do? [language skills]' and Question 18 'Do you use a language other than English at home?'. Respondents had to write in an answer. Question 17 was 'How well can you speak English?'. There were 1,537,626 speakers recorded for Question 18 but only 55,817 wrote 'Scots' for Question 18. So, did the respondents really consider 'Scots and English as inter-changeable', as the NRS infer? On the same day, SLC provided a plausible alternative explanation, arguing that the question itself predisposes people 'to think in terms of the English language on one hand, and perhaps a foreign (non-Scottish) language on the other'. The choices had been English only, Sign Language and other, which required the respondent to write in the alternative. Given they had just been asked about Scots, people might have assumed what was being asked was use of

30 Grenoble and Whaley 2006:164

31 Unger 2013:135

another 'foreign' language. As was evident in the 2009 Attitudes survey, how a question is framed has a substantial impact on the response.

The NRS assertion that people 'vary considerably in their interpretation of what is meant by "Scots" as a language, resulting in the potential for inconsistencies in the data collected' was also robustly disputed by SLC.

> This claim reveals that because the NRS is itself unfamiliar with the language it makes the assumption that speakers must also be unfamiliar with it and don't understand. We cannot see that this is based on any scientific rationale and, in fact, linguistic prejudices are being allowed to cloud the interpretation of data that could not be more consistent and clear.

In preparation for the census, the SLC had run what they considered to be a successful information and promotional campaign to raise awareness of what Scots is and the SLC later made an official complaint to the NRS about its handling and biased interpretation of the Scots census figures.

Ambiguity about how people perceive Scots is no reason to suppress data. At the time I made the following comment:

> I think therefore we can say with quite a lot of confidence that 1.5 million people self-identify with the Scots language. What their interpretation of Scots is another question but to imply all these people are just a bit confused, as the NRS effectively does, was in my view simply inexcusable.[32]

In 2016 the SLC asked Scots language expert Caroline Macafee to evaluate the reliability of the Census as an academic researcher. A common challenge to the Census result was that most people who claim to speak Scots don't, ie they just have a Scottish accent and use a few dozen of the most common Scots words. We know that self-assessment of language ability is problematic, even for languages with established standards, but that imprecision applied to all languages in the Census, including Gaelic, where the figures were taken at face value. Although under- and over-reporting of other languages seem to be assumed to even out, Scots was singled out for specific critique. Certainly, Scots has complicating elements and Macafee reminded us the criteria for identifying Scots 'are not taught, or anywhere laid down', so while superficially everyone answered the same questions about Scots, 'in their own minds individuals would have been relating it to

32 Young 2013

different concepts'. While it is improbable that respondents would not be able to tell Scots from English in a word list, Scots is generally spoken in a mixture with Scottish English. Consequently:

> [T]here is no objective boundary between Scots and English, and no consensus about where the boundary should be placed. Respondents who would be judged by at least some listeners to be Scots speakers might identify their own speech as falling short of their conception of Scots.

This last reference relates to the 'Good Scots' impossible-to-reach ideal against which urban dialects are sometimes judged. In contrast, urban speakers, especially Glaswegians, may think of their own Scots-based mixtures as 'slang', and so distance it from 'old fashioned' Good Scots. Generally, the identification with a local variant such as the Doric, might have caused further under-reporting, but there is no way of telling to what extent.

Despite all these caveats, Macafee concluded: 'perhaps surprisingly, given the many validity issues, the results appear reliable'. She found the figures to be internally consistent, for example the way speaker numbers map for age and geographical spread across the different councils. Importantly, the overall Census figures (around 30 per cent) align with the 1996 GRO(S) survey that used quite different data collection methods. GRO(S) estimated 1.5 million people spoke Scots; the Census count was 1,541,693. The correspondence between the two data sets is remarkable by any standards. As a researcher, Macafee determined that 'we have here an extremely valuable set of data' as, despite all the caveats, there appeared to be a solid linguistic basis for the results.

If the Census information on Scots was as sound as any other part of Census data, the question arises as to why its value was disparaged. My own view is that prejudice against Scots and its speakers is so normalised in Scottish culture that for some monolinguals it was inconceivable that so many Scots could make a reasoned and nuanced judgement about their own linguistic ability. The timing was also unfortunate. The results were released in September 2013, about mid-way between the Edinburgh Agreement of October 2012, paving the way for the Scottish independence referendum, and the referendum itself in September 2014. Naturally, unionist politicians and British nationalist critics would not want such a (potentially) powerful symbol of Scottish distinctiveness to be recognised, let alone celebrated. A cornerstone of British nationalism is that Scotland and England are near identical in cultural terms, so any inconvenient diversity must be downplayed.

Arguing against independence at a university debate in 2013 the Labour peer Lord George Robertson pronounced, 'Catalonia and Flanders have language and culture. We don't have any of that'.[33] The politics of Scots will be explored later, but Jackson and Niven neatly captured the problematic circumstances of Scots in post-devolution Scotland.

> As the Scots language is inextricably bound up with considerations of national identity, and as the only political party wanting to see Scots adopted as an official language also seeks independence, there is a political problem. Whilst some members of the 'unionist' parties may be sympathetic to the case argued by supporters of the Scots language, they are unlikely to sanction any measures which they believe may fuel the aspirations for separate nationhood and the consequent fragmentation of the United Kingdom.[34]

Besides, in 2013 the SNP were put in an impossible position. The decision had already been made to run the independence campaign on a modernist theme around civic inclusiveness and economic efficiency. Explicit calls to 'traditional' issues of identity-based nationalism were avoided. In the Scottish Government's 2013 White Paper, a 650-page tome describing plans for Scotland's independence, Scots merited only a few dozen words and no specific commitments. The writers may already have been aware of the Census figures and wished to avoid awkward questions of how to fund any increased support for Scots. If the Scots language was to receive official status on a par with Gaelic, for example, Jackson and Niven had already issued a warning.

> [W]hen resources are scarce and there are difficulties in maintaining existing financial commitments to health, education and social services, it is unlikely that any government – unionist or nationalist – would agree to the allocation of public money to introduce, support and monitor the kind of extensive changes required, even if they were to be phased in over a number of years.

Well before the Census, Millar had prophesised the political challenge of supporting Scots properly; 'This may be a cost which no government (or population) in Scotland would be willing (or able) to foot'.[35]

---

33 Robertson 2013

34 Jackson and Niven 2001:1

35 Millar 2005:196

The Referendum

Any further lobbying for Scots would soon be overshadowed by the heated campaigning of the independence referendum that took place in September 2014. Scots was again most noticeable by its absence, at least in the formal campaigns. There was no real attempt to connect with Scots speakers apart from a few badges from the Yes campaign with the 'Aye' slogan. Without any official use of the language by either side, it was left to London-based unionist maverick George Galloway to spot the 'authentic' marketing value of Scots with his 'Just say naw!' speaking tour.

One of the features of the whole campaign, though, was the surge in social media activity, especially on Twitter and Facebook. Edinburgh University researchers found when online 'Yes users generally express a stronger Scottish linguistic identity than No users'.[36] In general, though, there was no real correlation between speaking Scots and voting Yes. Mapping the frequency of Scots speakers from the 2011 census with the regional results of the referendum, both Young[37] and Leask[38] discovered that, if anything, speaking Scots made voters less likely to support independence. Leask comments, 'all four areas with the highest levels of Scots-speaking residents had below average support for independence'. Two possible explanations spring to mind, the most plausible being that Scots tends to be spoken more by older people.[39] According to immediate post-referendum polling, older voters were the group most decisively opposed to independence.[40] Leask however hints at another intriguing possibility; Scots' purported – and officially promoted – 'strong regional variations' (ie the various dialects) often accentuate local rather than national identity.

Although the failure of the referendum may have dispirited Yes-minded Scots language activists, a realism emerged that independence *per se* was not a magic wand to revive the Scots language. Official progress under devolution could be seen as positive but only when contrasted with the historical record of exclusion and prohibition. During the referendum itself, deliberations around Scots felt isolated from the wider arguments about the nation's future. Nonetheless, one of the encouraging and well-recognised outcomes of the referendum was the opening of a wider debate, at least among political activists, as to what a future Scotland could look,

---

36 Shoemark et al 2017

37 Young 2015a

38 Leask 2015

39 Macafee 2016

40 Ashcroft 2014

feel and even sound like. The failure of the 1979 Devolution referendum had prompted a similar cultural re-evaluation, but this time a promisingly wider range of voices were heard.

As a result, a more informed and occasionally enlightened reflection on Scots' role was sparked. This is not to claim the Scots language question was transformed into a hot mainstream cultural and political concern, but it became a little more visible and legitimised as an area of discussion. In the habitual absence of interest from the mainstream media or academia, bloggers formed the vanguard, particularly the sites *Wee Ginger Dug* and *Bella Caledonia*. A guest post on *Wee Ginger Dug* captured this new tone.[41] The poster asks why the independence-minded people should support Scots.

> I'll get the atavistic nationalist thing, red in tooth and claw out the way now – Scots is ours, and if we don't cherish it and look after it, nobody else is going to. It's part of what makes us who we are. But, blood and soil nationalist hat off, one thing we often heard during the referendum debate from the Yes camp was 'I want to live in a normal country.' Implicit in that statement is the recognition that Scotland is not a normal nation, that we suffer from some kind of psychological wound due to our lack of independence. Heal and whole come from the same (Germanic) root and the way to heal this wound is to integrate (Latin root, to make whole) the national psyche. One very practical way to do that is to integrate Scots mentally so we don't see it as a second-class form of speech or mere identity marker, the sort of thing you learn by heart at school then promptly forget, but rather as a part of us that we feel entirely at home with, without embarrassment or reservation.

Others began to recognise the link between anglicisation and class identity. In the same year, Alistair Davidson wrote 'the working class voted Yes, a divided middle class voted No, and the upper class voted No as a block' and concluded that the latter see their interests as depending on the structure of the British state.

> The further down the social hierarchy you look, the weaker this interest is, and as a result it is Scotland's poorest people who have the strongest attachment to Scotland as a nation. The working and middle classes are the most likely to speak Scots or broad Scots English, rather than 'talking properly' like the upper-middle

41 Clear Contrair Spirit 2014

> and upper class. Since the days of David Hume, Scots have taken elocution lessons in order to participate in the British imperial project. We have surely all known someone with a 'restaurant voice'... Classism is hardly unique to Scotland, but it has a particular national character, where rejection of Scottish culture and language is often an elite trait. To Scotland's reactionaries, the very Scottishness of the working class is one of the things that marks it as uneducated and unfit to rule, which only makes the recent upsurge all the more terrifying to them.[42]

Davidson concludes that the 'repression of Scottish identity and language is a central feature of class rule in Scotland', reminiscent of Beveridge and Turnbull's position in their 1989 polemic *The Eclipse of Scottish Culture*.

Paradoxically, just as modest grassroots recognition of Scots as a real political issue began to emerge, the Scottish Government began to recast the Scots 'language question' as a cultural rather than a political or 'minority language' concern. Millar claimed there has long been a 'vital fault line' in the Scots language movement that he described as a struggle between what he calls *governmental* and *cultural* parties.[43] The first group considers Scots a normal ECRML-style minority language that should morally and politically be accorded the same institutional rights and resources of any equivalent tongue, with Gaelic being the Scottish reference point. The second faction sees that Scots is an unstructured and uniquely unstructurable artistic 'resource'. For the latter camp, Scots could not be treated as a conventional minority language at all, especially in relation to standardisation, for fear of undermining its creative potential. We will return to this strange but impassioned debate later.

Scots Leid Policie

In June 2015 Creative Scotland (CS), the public body that supports Scottish arts, screen and creative industries, published its first *Scots Leid Policie/Scots Language Policy*, 'underlining the organisation's commitment to supporting the language' across its activities. CS already supported a range of individual artists and projects working with Scots, including the *Scots Language Centre, Scots Hoose* (an online resource on the language for children and teachers) and the lively podcast *Scots Language Radio*. A key policy element was the creation of the role of 'Scots Scriever'. This joint initiative between

42 Davidson 2014

43 Millar 2005, 2018

CS and the National Library of Scotland, funded a two-year residency to 'produce original creative work in Scots, its variants and dialects, across any art-form', as well as raising awareness, appreciation and use of Scots. Other parts of the strategy focused on developing a Scots awareness and training programme for CS staff and for organisations that they support and partner with. They also planned to increase the use of Scots in their communications, promotions and events, and on their website and social media.

The Scots writer and publisher James Robertson welcomed the initiative with a speech entitled 'Lang looked for's come at last!', a phrase from the poet Robert Fergusson and which seemed to straddle Millar's governmental/cultural perspective:

> It has been a lang time comin. I think it's fair tae say it isna a fully-fledged burd as yet. It sits alangside Creative Scotland's Gaelic policy, and it has some growin tae dae tae match thon. But when those o us that hae been engaged in Scots language activism for years luik at whit oor Gaelic freens hae achieved, we shouldna feel envious or disappointit: we should feel energised and ambitious. This policy for Scots is a statement o intent: aye, it's aboot past and present, but even mair it's a promise tae the future. Much has been achieved already, but an awfie lot mair remains tae be done.[44]

Robertson emphasised the political significance of the policy.

> Creative Scotland is sayin that it recognises Scots, it values Scots, and it is committit tae pittin actions ahint its braw wurds [...] This policy says that the Scots language maitters and that it has a legitimate and valuable role tae play in aw oor lives.

He remarked that the policy was not just about literature, but film, theatre, visual arts, music, dance, song and oral culture. At the same event Fiona Hyslop, then Cabinet Secretary for Culture, confirmed the Government's ambition 'for the Scots language to be recognised, valued and used in Scottish public and community life', adding that the Scots language was an essential part of Scotland's distinctive culture and heritage, and 'the Scottish Government takes seriously the promotion of the Scots language throughout Scotland in all its regional and local variants'.[45]

The initiative was generally welcomed across the Scots language

44 Robertson 2015
45 Creative Scotland 2015b

community as a muckle lowp forrit for the tongue. David Officer, an artist and writer based in Aberdeenshire, captured the expectations of the initiative from an artist's perspective in a post on *Bella Caledonia*.

> Through our national arts agency we have an organisation who could enable great change in the national perception of Scots. [...] If Creative Scotland can encourage our artists and cultural organisations to advocate Scots as a form of expression and communication then we might just save this wonderfully poetic and expressive language from being a historical curiosity, and reclaim a bit of ourselves in the process.[46]

Optimists hoped it foreshadowed a more vigorous Scottish Government policy to promote the language like the 2011 Gaelic Plan. Others, such as the influential blogger Paul Kavanagh (aka Wee Ginger Dug), were less impressed.

> The measures are mild, and the Government has specifically stated that no extra funding is being made available. In a normal country they'd attract criticism on the grounds that they go nowhere near far enough and are a ridiculous tokenism for a language which has a million and a half speakers in Scotland and which is understood by many more. But this isn't a normal country, this is Scotland... [47]

In stark contrast to Robertson's elegant speech, the Scots language version of the Policy was a hapless mishmash of DIY spellings, claiming to be Central Scots, but ignoring most of its written tradition. No dictionaries were apparently opened in the making of the document, nor awareness displayed of the orthographical conventions used, for example, on the Scots Language Centre's website. While there is always sensitivity around 'correcting' Scots, this was an official, publicly funded document which should have acted as a model of good practice. In a peevish blog post, I listed over 30 spelling issues on the first page of the policy alone.[48] Most of these could have been solved easily and surely uncontroversially by checking a dictionary or web resource, so I felt the approach must have been in some way deliberate.

> Nobody wants to be the language 'polis'; Scots has already been cursed by pedants aplenty. Although the language has no equivalent

46 Officer 2015

47 Kavanagh 2015

48 Young 2015b

> of the *Académie française*, as the Scots Language Society wisely cautions, 'ye canna juist set doun whitiver ye like'. Unfortunately, a high-profile opportunity to model modern official Scots and begin to put the 'no standards' argument to rest was squandered. [...] Grammar books and dictionaries may seem somewhat antithetical to a body with 'creative' in its title. However, the surprising emergence of the standards we have, *especially* in the absence of any Académie-style guidance, is in itself a remarkable cultural achievement and one that Creative Scotland could perhaps celebrate.[49]

I was not the only one to notice. When Hamish MacDonald, the former artistic director of Inverness-based Dogstar Theatre, took up the first post of Scriever the *Financial Times* commented, 'with no standard version, many argue it is a collection of dialects, not a language' and noted,

> Creative Scotland itself acknowledges that the 'Central Scots' it used for its policy statement is far from universal. Many in Scotland see nothing familiar in spelling 'Scotland' without a 'd'.[50]

Nonetheless, instead of 'trying to force standardisation', MacDonald was reported as preferring to 'celebrate diversity, hoping to encourage people to make fuller use of their own types of Scots and to enjoy others too'. The notion of 'diversity' being used to disempower a minoritised language is ironic, to say the least.

While the eye-catching Creative Scotland initiative raised the profile of the language, it was limited to the heritage use of Scots in the arts. Three months later in September 2015, and with far less fanfare or press coverage, the Scottish Government together with Education Scotland launched the *Scots Language Policy*. The document set out the Government's position on the Scots language, its aims and objectives for Scots and the practical steps it intended to take. The Policy, however, was a disappointingly brief document of just four widely spaced pages. At the launch, Jane Renton, Assistant Director at Education Scotland, commented: 'This is a significant moment for the Scots language. It is a living modern language which children in their tens of thousands bring to school every day.' It is worth noting the report uses the phrase 'the Scots language' throughout. The document, with a regular, if 'thin', Scots version, opens with a typically bland heritage and culture statement.

49 Young 2015c
50 Dickie 2015

> The Scots language is an essential element o the culture an heritage o Scotland. For mony o us, it is a weel-kent aspect o oor sang, poetry and literature and a kenspeckle feature o the wey we express wirsels in oor community life.

Nevertheless, the three generic policy aims could (just about) be read as support for Scots as a normalised ECRML-style minority language:

1. tae enhance the status o Scots in Scottish public an community life
2. tae promote the acquisition, yiss an development o Scots in education, media, publishin an the airts
3. tae encourage the increased yiss o Scots as a valid an visible means o communication in aw aspects o Scottish life.

While the actions, including an *Education Scotland Action Plan*, are not particularly ambitious, they seem to represent a clearer focus than the mid-2000s 'buried alive' documents Millar had critiqued. The Plan implied the implementation of a minority language strategy of the type common across Europe. Although the heritage and cultural aspects of Scots were foregrounded, there were promising statements on awareness-raising and education, that Scots should be 'be affordit equal respect' with Gaelic and English and the Government would, 'encourage aw stakehauder groups tae develop an implement Scots language policies'. Although somewhat feeble, the Policy seemed to signal a historic move from nonspecific statements of government support to actionable steps, though as usual these did not come with extra finance. Moreover, as Eagle had observed a few years before, those who may be involved in developing and implementing such a strategy for Scots 'will likely have limited knowledge and experience of such endeavours'.[51] Despite its modest aims, the policy triggered a backlash from Scottish Tory MSP Alex Johnstone; 'This a predictable stunt from a Scottish Government more interested in pandering to patriots than improving education'.[52]

The 'Year of Scots'

In January 2016 *The National* newspaper published an edition with some Scots in it and the outrage that ensued was described in Chapter Two. Leask asked, 'Why do so many Scots cringe when they see the language of their neighbours written down?'.

51 Eagle 2011:256

52 Peterkin 2015

> [W]e have people who declare that, say, Scots is a dialect and not a language as if they had never heard the old linguists' joke that a dialect was just 'a language without a navy'. Such critics seem to think they are saying something meaningful.[53]

Kavanagh agreed.

> People whose knowledge of the science of linguistics fills a dictionary from A to Aa all of a sudden turn into Noam Chomsky when the subject is Scots. It's just a nationalist attempt to manufacture a language to have a grievance about, they sniff, dismissing centuries of Scots literature with an airy wave of contempt.[54]

Furthermore, he suspected such ignorance may be deliberate.

> Scotland's home-grown languages, Scots and Gaelic, are routinely dismissed, disparaged and disdained by a large segment of the Scottish population, a segment which has been educated in ignorance and taught that a lack of knowledge and awareness is something to be proud of. Scotland's languages are Ground Zero of the Cringe.

Edinburgh linguist Pavel Iosad also reminded us that 'criticism of language rarely has to do with language itself: it acts, most of time, as a proxy for social attitudes'.[55] Kavanagh expands on this point, 'we allow our language and cultural policies to be determined by arrogant ignoramuses who believe that a dose of middle-class prejudice counts as erudition', concluding:

> [I]f we want to get rid of the Cringe, we need to start treating our languages with the same respect other modern European countries grant to theirs.

In his new column in *The National*, Fitt summarised the events of January 2016:

> At the stert o this year, a puckle o folk that dinnae like the Scots language tried tae bully this newspaper. They failed. Insteid they succeedit in settin in motion a rammy aboot Scots that's got folk

53 Leask 2016a

54 Kavanagh 2016

55 Iosad 2016

> thinkin, talkin and flytin aboot the leid in weys they've no done for years, if ever. And by gode, this country wis needin it.[56]

Any raising of the profile of Scots risks accusations that the language is being 'politicised'. Columnist Dani Garavelli reported that the discussion had spread to the use of Scots in schools.

> Last year, Education Scotland urged teachers to increase the use of Scots language in the classroom. Now, the inevitable backlash that call provoked resurfaced, with one commentator, tweeting: 'What kind of school system takes on a f***ing invented language and teaches it? We'd be as well teaching Wookie or Klingon'.[57]

Garavelli was relaxed about her children learning a 'smattering' of Scots words, but was concerned that 'pupils must LEARN SCOTS [sic] in some kind of grander, declamatory way', apparently assuming a covert political purpose rather than a pedagogical benefit. She felt 'in polarised, post-referendum Scotland, pupils are just pawns in an ideological war' and looked forward to the depoliticised day 'when Scottish culture and education is once again valued for its own sake, not viewed through the prism of the independence debate'. In my view, Scots is still only minimally politicised, and that 'depoliticisation' of Scots is itself an ideological, even a class-based position.

Fitt often underlines the connection between low school attainment of children in poorer, often Scots-speaking, communities and a lack of self-belief. He asks, 'What is the impact on self-belief when we criticise the Scots language o young Scots speakers?', concluding, 'dinnae be shocked when, in an English-speakin education environment, weans fae Scots-speakin backgroonds hae lower attainment than weans fae English-speakin backgroonds'.[58] Whether children from poorer backgrounds in Scotland are being linguistically discriminated against or not, it is a serious question that in many countries would be systematically investigated and addressed. In this sense Garavelli was correct; in Scotland such an open-minded, functional approach to the Scots language 'for its own sake' seems remote.

The vitriol against Scots is not limited to random Tweeters. In March a glitch occurred in the Scottish Government's Scots language web page. For a short time, the site included baffling phrases like, 'Scots us aaaroon us in wirhameowerdaeinsan, it is a furthie, feckfupairt o Scottish culture the day'.

56 Fitt 2016c

57 Garivelli 2016

58 Fitt 2016c

Clearly some words had been jumbled in editing process and had not been checked properly before publication. As soon as the formatting errors were spotted the Scottish Government fixed the problem. It is hard to think of a story of less journalistic interest, but remember the words of Wee Ginger Dug: 'this isn't a normal country, this is Scotland'.[59] A minor technical hiccup was enough to get some Scots-deniers in a frenzy. Graham Grant, the Home Affairs Editor of the right-wing *Scottish Daily Mail* penned a full-page splash entitled 'Made-up words on a "wabsite" betray the lunacy of promoting the Scots language'. Grant was tickled by the similarity of some of the jumbled words to the comedy patois 'Izatamarraonyerbarra, Clara?' of Stanley Baxter's *Parliamo Glasgow*, but turned a mildly amusing visual gag into an ideological rant.

> The joke underlying Baxter's 1960s sketches was that Glaswegian is not a distinct language as the BBC presenter contends, with its own unique system of rules and grammar: it is a dialect. But in modern-day Scotland, that joke has taken a surreal twist that Baxter could never have predicted, as the SNP continues its madcap mission to promote 'Scots language'. There is, of course, no such thing – no more than there is a foreign language unique to Glasgow. What we call 'Scots' is in fact a rag-bag collection of words and phrases tracing their history back hundreds of years.[60]

Warming to his theme, Grant read a whole ideology behind a few 'formatting errors'.

> With an entirely synthetic language, where experts are making up words for approved usage as they go along, there is plentiful scope for such 'formatting errors'. In reality, beyond the obsessives who present themselves as 'experts' in this non-existent tongue, there is no one in the real world who would have the slightest clue as to what any of this meant, even if there were no 'formatting' errors.

Amongst the familiar criticism of the utility of Scots, Grant makes a telling comparison with the established formality of Gaelic.

> [W]hy does the Scottish Government indulge the 'experts' who tell us, for example, that the Scots for television is 'televeision' [sic] while

59 Kavanagh 2015
60 Grant 2016

> for radio it is – more predictably – 'radio'? Gaelic has had similar problems – 'eadar-lion' was coined for 'internet'. But there can be no serious comparison between Scots and Gaelic, which is indeed *a separate language with its own agreed vocabulary* and whose use in the classroom has been linked to educational benefits [my italics].

Michael Hance, then Director of the Scots Language Centre, responded,

> Being made-up is the key charge that those hostile to Scots often level at the language and clearly they were thrilled to find evidence of it. The not so subtle sub text to this charge is that Scots itself is not real, it's a figment of some rabid and politically motivated imagination.[61]

Hance pointed out that most modern Scots prose writers tend to avoid neologisms and usually rework and mix words, with various degrees of stylistic success, from normal Scots dictionaries and the daily spoken language. They must create a formal register (style) 'from scratch', lacking the stock phrases and everyday expressions we use in English. Although Hance admitted, 'it can and usually does look clumsy, awkward, gauche', especially to readers unfamiliar with this style of writing, he wondered at the presumed harm of, 'encountering a few unusual words now and again'. A seemingly trivial language issue exposed a deeper pattern of power and privilege; 'the underlying problem isn't the words it's the challenge to linguistic and cultural orthodoxies that their appearance on a website presents'. Fitt also was frank about why people feel the need to attack (*flyte*) Scots.

> We need tae be mair honest. It's aboot class. Onybody that thinks the Scottish middle classes in general dinnae hae a problem wi the wey the Scottish workin class speak doesnae ken Scotland. The lood articulate flytin o Scots is born o twinty generations haein it battered intae them that the proper language o Scotland is English. Scots in a newspaper, a book or on TV threatens that. It's why the folk that tak it upon themsels tae polis language in Scotland try tae hirple ony confident use o Scots and keep the language in the ghettoes o comedy and sentimentality they made tae thirl it in.[62]

Later in the year Creative Scotland was to publish *Cur an Aithne Cànanan na h-Alba/An Innins tae Scotlan's Leids/An Introduction to Scotland's*

61 Hance 2016

62 Fitt 2016e

Languages. Despite the multilingual titling, the document was mostly in English, with the minimal Scots included again rather eccentric. For example, 'innins' is not the normal dictionary equivalent of 'introduction', it is simply 'innin'. The use of 'Scotlan' without a final 'd' is also atypical. However, the real issue was in the English text. Although acknowledging Gaelic and Scots are the ECRML-recognised indigenous languages of Scotland, and 'the literature of both languages dates back hundreds of years', the heritage aspect was noticeably foregrounded; 'both languages are part of our history and culture with rich oral traditions still very much alive in song, drama and storytelling'. The document proclaimed a fundamental linguistic distinction between Gaelic and Scots. 'Gaelic is a Celtic language, providing Scotland with strong linguistic and cultural links to other European countries, particularly Ireland', but in contrast 'Scots is the official name for the dialects of Scotland (such as Glaswegian, Doric, Ayrshire, Shetland and Lallans)'. In other words, 'Scots' as a linguistic entity distinct from the 'dialects' was summarily expunged, as was its European connections. The inconvenient centuries-old tradition of pan-dialectal Scots literature described was also erased from CS's discourse. Maybe 'Lallans' was supposed to cover writing, but as the label is has long since been deprecated, that interpretation seems generous. In the same discriminatory messaging, although Scots' 'use today is widespread', this positive facet is framed oddly by 'oral traditional storytelling and songs'. The discourse is of course negative, of Scots 'decline' in contrast with Gaelic, where 'use is growing'.

In this light CS's taste for non-traditional Scots orthographies is logical, not based on ignorance but ideology. Although they may concede Scots is 'a language in its own right', the CS definition of Scots is not the same as that of those Scots language champions who seek normalisation of their tongue. 'Language' for Creative Scotland is used here as a term of convenience. Both the way they write about it and in the manner they write it, Scots is presented as linguistic chaos, with no standards and no grammar – essentially, an anarchic non-entity apart from its fragmented, apparently fast dwindling, dialects. The implication of the discriminatory ideology from Scotland's foremost cultural body is simple. In the final reckoning Scots can never aspire to anything beyond the couthy and the colloquial. Nobody can normalise a non-entity.

Even so, such was the growing profile of Scots that even the Scottish Labour Party, which habitually ignores Scots, included an intriguing reference to it in their manifesto for the 2016 Holyrood elections; 'We recognise Scotland's rich cultural heritage, including Gaelic, Scots and Nordic'.[63] A step forward,

63 Scottish Labour Party 2016

perhaps, but some questioned the depth of Labour's understanding of the language issue. In a bemused *Herald* article Leask reminds everyone, 'there is no such language as Nordic'.[64] It is likely the Labour manifesto writers may have been confused by Norn, a western Scandinavian tongue spoken in the Orkney and Shetland islands until the late 18th century before it was replaced by the Insular dialect of Scots. For politicians, a little linguistic knowledge can be a dangerous thing.

Fitt was disappointed in the overall lack of political interest in 2016.

> The pairties' manifestos say it aw, which is no verra much. Thir pawkie, judicious, faur-sichtit documents mak commitments tae deliver on the Scots language somewhaur on a scale atween Apologetic Wee Bittie and Absolute Hee Haw.[65]

He noted neither the Conservatives nor the Scottish Liberal Democrats mentioned Scots in their manifestos, despite representing Scots speaking rural areas. The Scottish Green Party at least supported 'cultural ventures' for Scots but couldn't quite bring itself to call the language a language. Scottish Labour was bewildered, but even the SNP seemed more interested in promoting Gaelic, mentioning only in passing, 'We will also provide support for the Scots language'. Noting the absence of any commitment to a Scots Language Bill, Fitt commented:

> Efter a strang 2011–2016 programme wi gey positive ootcomes for the leid, the subtext o this latest wersh promise o 'support' could easy read, 'Ye'll hiv had yer Scots then'.

The debate initiated by *The National* bubbled across social media, feeding back to subsequent columns and posts on *Bella Caledonia* and elsewhere. Reflecting on the disruptive role of the *Bella Caledonia* site, Matthew Fitt even declared 2016 'A year of Scots'.

> Certes, juist aboot ilka Scots piece publisht on Bella brocht oot the trowies that hate the Scots language. If the cringers and hoodies and the Scots language skelpers lowp ontae their keyboards tae batter oot 'Scots is NOT a language' aboot a Scots piece ye've juist had publisht on Bella, ye ken ye're daein somethin richt.[66]

64 Leask 2016b

65 Fitt 2016g

66 Fitt 2016h

From an academic viewpoint, Hames also welcomed the sudden progress.

> It's great that we're having debates about Scots in newspapers rather than specialist journals or thinly populated seminar rooms. The whole conversation feels more accessible and democratic, actually plugged into some of the vernacular energies it tends to champion.[67]

As might be expected, the outburst of long bottled-up discussion was often chaotic, leading Fitt to complain:

> [I]t is gey clear gettin that we as a nation or region or whitever we hope tae be cannae agree aboot the Scots language or even on whit it is or whit it's supposed tae look like.[68]

It felt like the early stages of Tuckman's well-known *forming-storming-norming-performing* model of group development. *The National* and social media had initiated a debate, and now the collective was simply 'storming', setting out differing opinions and arguing, sometimes quite aggressively.

The corresponding position of the anti-Scots faction also crystallised, as articulated by Alex Massie in *The Times*.

> This is a country that loves lying to itself. The manufacturing of comfortable myths is our biggest growth business. One of the most fashionable current myths is that 'Scots', as commonly spoken or understood by the vast majority of Scottish citizens, is a language distinct from standard English. Most of what passes for 'Scots' is patois rather than a distinct language. There is nothing objectionable about this and there's a punchy robustness about the modern Scots demotic that does differentiate it from standard English. Nevertheless, the phonetic spelling of a Scots accent does not a language make any more than the phonetic spelling of Scouse or Geordie makes those accents languages. Almost none of the people credited with writing in 'Scots', such as James Kelman or Irvine Welsh, actually do so. They write standard English flecked with a Scots vernacular.[69]

To Massie the only 'Scots' worthy of the name was the language of Barbour, Dunbar and Henryson, and even poor Burns only produced 'lighter' Scots.

67 Hames 2016

68 Fitt 2016f

69 Massie 2016

'Good Scots' apparently ceased evolving more than a century ago, so no modern coinages such as 'televeision' could be countenanced. Tiresomely, but surely deliberately, Massie misinterpreted MacDiarmid's coinage of synthetic Scots as 'artificial' rather than 'combined'. Trilingual signage and the educational work of the Scots Language coordinators are subject to particular scorn and the website glitch described earlier again ridiculed. Aware of the likely social media reaction, Massie appropriates Tom Leonard's method of predictive retaliation.

> These are treacherous waters, however, not least because questioning these shibboleths guarantees that some Tartan Commissar will accuse you of being 'ashamed' of, or 'uncomfortable' with, Scottish history, language and culture. Havering tosh, of course, but there you have it.

Massie was revealingly sensitive to potential accusations that he was just reheating the Scottish 'cringe'.

> 'Trilingual' Scotland will not permit such teasing, however. It is easier to avoid our English-speaking reality and, instead, kid ourselves that we are something we are not. A more confident culture would have no need to fool itself, but this fooling is the new Scottish cringe.

Massie's condescending attack lines against Scots provided a model for and maybe legitimised other less accomplished and more abusive critics.

In tandem with conservative Massie, a supposedly socialist anti-Scots and anti-Gaelic position was disinterred. In early 2016 Trevor Davies articulated a general leftish position on the blog *Labour Hame* (sic). He starts with the mandatory left wing mantra, that 'nationalism is seriously bad'. (Only Scottish nationalism, of course, as British nationalism has been an unexamined essential of Labour dogma since the party's foundation during the 1900s, the days of 'peak' British imperialism.)

> Only a nationalist government – strengthened by their belief that distinctiveness of language enhances national prestige and feeling would introduce, at great cost, invented Gaelic station names in places where that language has never been spoken.[70]

Davies may have forgotten it was a Labour administration that had introduced the Gaelic Language (Scotland) Act 2005. A left-wing correspondent to *The*

70 Davies 2016

National complained that the undefined 'national cultural intelligentsia' dismissed 'principled' objections to promoting Scots,[71]

> For them it's just the Scots' cringe intit? Well when I read articles like Matthew Fitt's that exactly what I do. I cringe because I'm reading a bookish Hen Broon writing in a made-up language who's trying to convince me that I should write in as well. Walloper! Why is it made up? Because nobody talks like that. Really they don't. And that's what a language is; first and foremost, it's something that people speak.

Although the denial of language rights was a serious political issue, Scots was again somehow 'synthetic', so deserved no such rights or even basic respect.

> There are radical language activists throughout the world facing persecution, torture, impoverishment, imprisonment and death for having the courage to write, speak and create art in their own tongue, to whom we should offer whatever solidarity and support we can. Then there's conceited, affected creatures like Matthew Fitt.

The second part of this argument is shrewder, building on the idea that in Scotland the vernacular language is the identifier not of nation or even locality, but class. Class is the fundamental power relationship in Scottish society and any improvement in the status of Scots will not change that fact. Thus status-building of Scots will still discriminate against working-class varieties, it is claimed, albeit in a different way. The author then reaches for the long outdated Good Scots/Bad Scots trope.

> Linguistic codes will still be used to make children who haven't grown up in a household where good language isn't spoken feel inferior. Although if current developments continue, the barometer of appropriateness will no longer be RP English, but RP Scots. This is how nationalism works.

In Chapter Three, I made the case that this position, expressed by Leonard, Kelman and others, is considerably less 'radical' than its proponents believe it to be. Nevertheless, the myth of 'standardisation by diktat' persists in debates about the Scots language, even among those who claim to be in favour of the tongue.

71 Woods 2016

Message in a box

Early in 2017 the Scottish Government piloted a scheme to send a box of clothes and babycare essentials to all new parents, the cardboard 'baby box' itself acting as a crib for the newborn child. The concept had been established in Finland and considered an uncontroversial initiative well worth exploring and evaluating. However, in Scotland the scheme attracted quite an astonishing level of spite from British nationalist politicians and media. For many, what seemed to trigger their fury was a 14-line poem in Scots, 'Welcome wee one', written by the then Scots Makar Jackie Kay. Journalist Kenny Farquharson described what happened next.

> [T]he reaction was extraordinary. A small number of people were worried that the poem's upbeat optimism might upset mums with postnatal depression. But a majority of the objections focused on the fact that it was written in Scots. 'Ridiculous nationalist bullshit,' wrote one commenter on Mumsnet. 'They didn't need to decide to write it in Scots. But they have, for political reasons.' [...] 'That poem is shite. It's too Scottish for the sake of being Scottish.' Another wrote: 'They do know that hardly anyone in Scotland actually speaks like that?'[72]

Farquharson recognised this to be the unexpected (to him, anyway) reappearance of the Scottish Cringe. He defined the cringe as follows:

> [A]n involuntary shudder at the sound of a glottal stop; an onset of the vapours when confronted with a fluttering Saltire; a pursing of the lips at any manifestation of Scottish working-class culture.

The journalist concluded:

> [T]he Scottish cringe is a cancer in the political, cultural and social life of the nation. Its influence is pernicious. It is a wet blanket thrown over the lives of young working-class Scots. Death to the cringe.

Ironically, the way the appearance or sounds of Scots can still generate such deep revulsion among parts of the Scottish population is a testament to its continuing social power and sociocultural meaning. It also says something deeply unpleasant about fossilised prejudices remaining in many parts of Scottish society.

72 Farquharson 2017

Meanwhile *The National* continued its regular Thursday column in Scots, still receiving unremitting scorn from social media warriors. David Leask, Chief Reporter for *The Herald*, *The National*'s sister paper, was eventually driven to reply.

> Usually the responses are embarrassingly ignorant, declaring words to be fake because they are cognates of English. Obviously, academics or working linguists explaining dialect continuums to people with powerful prejudices has had no impact. But, for avoidance of doubt, calling Scots in any of its forms 'fake' is not a credible stance, it's just linguistic ignorance.[73]

Not all criticism of *The National*'s Scots content came from the usual opponents, though. Reviewing several columns in 2018, prominent Scots authority J Derrick McClure praised the 'wide individual range of approaches, resulting in an exuberant variety of styles', but saw a downside.

> What is entirely lacking, however, is any kind of consistency. Even within a given essay, variant spellings of the same word, inconsistencies of dialect [...] use of English vocabulary items where Scots ones are readily available and use of obtrusive Anglicisms of phrasing or idiom.[74]

Ian Parsley, an expert on Ulster Scots, was even more direct.

> Scots is not just makey-uppy English; it is a linguistic system in its own right and, despite the lack of an absolute standard, that system has rules [...] its own etymological, literary and orthographical heritage [...] Like anything else, it must be learned properly before it is used – otherwise the result just looks like scunnersom haivers.[75]

Rab Wilson, one of *The National*'s regular columnists, responded.

> Ah wis claucht up in a Facebook discussion anent a favourite threip o some o thaim wha write in the leid; whether we need a strict orthography fir Scots or no. Nou aince, a lang time syne, ah wis keen oan the idea o a Scots orthography; ie a defined system that set oot,

73 Leask 2017

74 McClure 2018

75 Parsley 2017

> if nae exactly in stane but in 'guid black prent', the wey that Scots shuid be spelt oan the page. Fir masel, ah abandoned that idea. Ah cam roond tae the idea that there is sic a rich diversity o dialects in Scotland that fowk in aa airts hae thair ain wey o spellin (an pronunciation) fir whit can be verra seemilar wirds. It seem't wrang tae me tae try an dae awa wi hunners o years o hou fowk scrievit/ spak a wird, an lik Orwell's 'thought police' dictated tae thaim thair wis anely yin wey tae spell a wird in Scots. It's a richt personal view, but ah like this linguistic diversity an 'elasticity' in Scots. In his series o poems *Unrelated Incidents* at ae pynt the poet Tom Leonard hus a BBC type newsreader tell us 'thirza right way ti spell ana right way ti tok it. This is me tokn yir right way a spellin' – a great bit o satire that hilariously pricks the bubble o thae language thought police![76]

Again, whether Leonard-style spelling anarchy is seen as a liberation or a liability is a matter of linguistic and artistic aims, but at least Scots was being discussed on its own terms.

Meanwhile in July a depressing report was published on the state of Scots in education via *Mercator*, the European research centre on multilingualism and language learning. The author, Liz Niven, also touched on the standardisation issue.

> There is frequent debate, amongst language interest groups, about standardisation of the language. There are variations in the spelling of a great part of the Scots vocabulary from region to region. Currently, the SLD present the most common spelling as the headword in an entry, followed by other less common variations. Many Scots users, particularly creative writers, prefer to retain all the variations in Scots orthography. There is, however, another body of Scots speakers and writers who would like to see some form of standardisation. Within this group there is debate about which form of Scots should become the standard.

More heartening, and attracting unprecedentedly positive editorials from *The Herald*, was the Curriculum for Excellence (CfE) report[77] that identified good practice in using Scots in schools. The role Scots can play in developing literacy skills, encouraging learner engagement and increasing confidence and self-esteem was recognised. Not everyone was impressed; under the

---

76 Wilson 2017

77 Education Scotland 2017

headline, 'Weans talkin' lik' Rab? Naw Ta', The Daily Mail columnist Stephen Daisley proclaimed, 'Children should be learning real languages in school – not slang English'[78], adding,

> The advantages of bilingualism are well-known. That's why resources should be spent on useful tongues such as Mandarin or Spanish instead of teaching children English with a Glaswegian accent and calling it a modern language. 'Parlez-vous Rab C. Nesbitt?' is unlikely to come up in a job interview.

Not surprisingly the social media reaction was vigorous, including blogger Wee Ginger Dug, who noticed that Daisley expressed incredulity at the pedagogical usefulness of translating English language texts into Scots, one of the practices the report mentioned.

> However the point of this exercise is to get children to think about how they use language, about how different forms of language are considered proper to different circumstance. It was about getting children to open the bonnet of the language car and to start to examine the engine instead of driving them with prejudice, snobbery, and an ignorant arrogance masquerading as erudition.[79]

Kevin McKenna wrote in *The Guardian* later in the year responding to another apparently impertinent public use of Scots, this time on the radio. He urged people to try to conquer their 'fear of Scots'.

> That fear still seems to exist among those of the revitalised Scottish hard right. Any manifestations of this rough and untutored language are often greeted with howls of outrage, and entire opinion and comment articles are penned disdaining and ridiculing those who seek to promote the Scots language. They politicise it and regard it as a tool of Scottish nationalism, though quite how it could be deployed as such and for what purpose is never explained.[80]

There was a sense at the time that maybe the tide was turning. *The Sunday Post* newspaper, hitherto not known for its forward thinking on Scots despite carrying the iconic Scots-rich comics *Oor Wullie* and *The Broons*, seemed

78 Daisley 2017
79 Kavanagh 2017
80 McKenna 2017

to have a sort of epiphany when covering the publication of a new edition of the *Concise Scots Dictionary*; 'Our big slang theory? Well, for a start, Scots isn't slang'.[81]

The year 2017 turned into something of a watershed for emblematic titles. Apart from the aforementioned dictionary, the first Harry Potter book was translated into Scots by the ubiquitous Matthew Fitt and again the publication was well received by the press. *The Little Prince*, an older iconic text was belatedly published in Scots in not one but two different translations. The first Scots Manga comic *Jock Dhu* appeared,[82] and in in keeping with the modernising trend smartphone users found they could download a specially developed app to enable predictive texting in Scots.

Towards the end of the year, researchers at Abertay University discovered that the brains of people who speak two dialects seem to work in the same way as those who speak two languages. The data, confirmed by parallel research in Germany, indicated the often-claimed cognitive benefits of Scots, the 'bilingual bonus', is the same whether you consider Scots a dialect or a language.[83] The outdated notion, held in Scottish education since Victorian times, that using Scots was harmful to learning English was shown to be completely wrong.

Despite such positivity, it is hard to throw off engrained linguistic prejudice. One example was an episode of *Scot Squad*, a spoof police comedy from BBC One Scotland, made in a fly-on-the-wall style. A skit in the 2017 season was 'The Bam Whisperer', the gag being one of the characters acts as a translator for the 'neds'. The 'bam talk' was invented but clearly based on Glasgow Scots. Some thought it hilarious and according to *The Sun*, one fan tweeted: '@scotsquad Brilliant start to the new series. Best Scottish comedy show in years. Congrats to all involved. The "bam talk" scene was superb!'. Others on Facebook were less amused:

> It's the BBC middle class feeding class divisions within Scottish society and promoting self-internalised oppression. [...] If you shame people about the way they speak, they learn to shut up and the rest of society learns not to listen to them. I'm a Glaswegian and worked for years as a community development worker all over Scotland. Time and time again, I saw local people who spoke Scots afraid to speak up in mixed groups of people, ashamed of their 'accent' and afraid of humiliation and not being heard. Comedy at the expense of the

81 Smith 2017

82 Dempster 2017

83 Eg Macdonald 2017

> most marginalised in our society isn't funny, it's just another layer of oppression or justifying their conditions.[84]

At the end of 2017 the UK government's 90-page ECRML submission (revised later) included information on Scots, Scottish Gaelic, Welsh, Manx and Cornish, but not Irish and Ulster Scots, due to the then political stalemate at Stormont.[85] The devolved governments in Edinburgh and Cardiff completed the forms, as did the Isle of Man government and the UK government in respect to Cornwall. More than 60 per cent of the report focused on the Welsh language. The Scots sections mentioned the Census, the 2015 Scots Language Policy, the Creative Scotland Policy, the Scots Scriever, the now pared-back Scots language coordinators initiative and the new SQA Qualifications we will cover later. Not surprisingly the comparisons in activities around Gaelic were stark. While these are always disheartening, the actions on Scots seem feeble even when compared to Cornish, claiming just 464 local speakers, all learners, and currently with no separate funding at all. Cornwall Council leads the Cornish language programme and has developed a three-year Cornish Language Plan, including signage and increasing Cornish in publications. Learning resources are also provided on their Cornish Language Office website. A voluntary Cornish Language Board (Kesva an Taves Kernewek) has endorsed the Standard Written Form or Furv Skrifys Savonek for use in official documentation, public life and education. According to the Report, the standard had enabled collaborative work with schools and public bodies such as the National Trust and the Environment Agency, 'something which was formerly more difficult'. The Board also delivers examinations in Cornish from entry level to above A-Level equivalent, though they are not nationally recognised.

If the ECRML report reveals the treatment of Scots to be rather pitiful compared even with other UK minority languages, it is in comparison with other European languages recognised by ECRML that the neglect of Scots becomes truly shocking. An ECRML Committee of Experts fed back on the UK report with evaluation and recommendations in 2018.[86] The Scots section made grim reading. The Committee found no change since 2014 in the recognition of Scots as an expression of cultural wealth and noted a lack of 'resolute' action to promote Scots. The provision of teaching and study of Scots 'at all appropriate stages' and facilities enabling non-speakers of Scots (including adults) to learn it remained only partially fulfilled. The

84 Quoted in Young 2017

85 UK Government 2018

86 ECRML 2018

experts recommended 'immediate action' around the teaching and study of Scots at all levels. The group detected a deterioration in the facilitation and encouragement of the use of Scots in public life and reported a lack of promotion of study and research on Scots at universities. The 'needs and wishes expressed by the group which uses Scots' had failed to be considered. Finally, the report yet again highlighted the lack of a body for the purpose of advising the authorities on all matters pertaining to Scots. Was the flurry of interest around Scots in the late 2010s just another false dawn?

Optimism versus inertia

In 2018 the media reported a boost for Scots from an unexpected source. The time-jumping television romance, *Outlander*, set in Scotland and employing some Scots language dialogue, had charmed a global audience. Aberdeen University ethnologist Irene Watt regarded the show as part of a 'vanguard' in the revival of Scots in the media and part of its 'rehabilitation'. The programme was 'putting Scots back on the lips of our ancestors where it belongs, in its central place in Scottish identity and heritage.'[87] She acknowledged the Scots spoken in Outlander, may not be the language spoken today in Scotland, 'but rather a stage-Scots – essentially English dressed in tartan and cockade – yet it is still to be cheered'. The reason was emblematic rather than linguistic, 'a sign of how far an historically repressed language has come in just a few decades'.[88] She argued that Scots was 'reappearing in places it has been absent for generations', was due also to a mini boom in Scots language publishing. The best-selling Scots translations of *Harry Potter* and *Gruffalo* books were reaching a new audience, and the language was also finding itself 'back in favour in academia', with researchers studying Scots' effect on the brain. She concluded, 'The past for Scots may have been bleak, but the present is improving and the future is starting to look optimistic'.

Behind the optimism, though, the politics of Scots appeared to be entering a state of limbo. In a powerful article in April 2018, writer Kathleen Jamie said disagreements over the language, 'increasing political connotations', and 'problems of legitimacy, as well as readability' meant she could not write in Scots anymore. Her core argument concerned authenticity. She recognised some writers prefer their Scots 'unfixed, unteachable, like a sparrowhawk' but she herself took words 'from hither and yon', from people, books and dictionaries. The problem is that some complained her language was

87 Quoted in Dick 2018

88 Watt 2018

'synthetic', 'which is wrong, apparently'. The poet argued that if such Scots is judged to be illegitimate, then 'we're all reduced to the language we half-learned as a wean/bairn/child.'[89]

Blogger Wee Ginger Dug also noted when Scots writers produce a literary variety of Scots, they're still charged with creating an artificial plastic Scots that is not 'real'.

> They're accused of politicising Scots. Yet what is really politicising Scots is to deny it the same means of enriching and developing itself which have been used by every other literary language. By denying Scots these avenues of enrichment, opponents of the language are seeking to diminish its use and confine it to a dialectal ghetto. Scots, they say, isn't a proper language, and they're going to do whatever it takes to ensure that it can't act or be used as a proper language.[90]

Chronic lack of funding, whether a cause or consequence, exacerbates the challenge of 'language building'.

> But when ye compare the amount o funding Scots gets in Scotland compared wi the funding gien tae Ulster Scots in Northern Ireland or Gaelic here at hame, then the disparity is undeemous! Aa indigenous leids shuid be supportit bi public siller – but it shuid be a level playin field, an aa indigenous leids shuid be financially supportit wi equal funding tae the samen tune. Scots is, an aye hus bin in this respeck, verra much the puir relation! (leeterally!).[91]

Contining this theme in *Bella Caledonia*, Clark reminded us that while the Catalan Government's annual budget for the Catalan language is £13.50 per speaker, the Scottish Government spends 17p per speaker.[92] In other words, 'Ilka year, the Scottish Pairliament gangs roond every Scots speaker in Scotland an doles thaim oot a wan-aff peyment o hauf a Freddo bar'.[93]

> In 2018–19, the total budget for the Scots leid will be £270k – aboot 1% o whit we're spendin on Gaelic, 2% o whit we're coughin up for the Royal Botanic Gairdens, an skimmins fae oor ootlay on netbaw,

89 Quoted in Miller 2018

90 Kavanagh 2018a

91 Wilson 2018

92 Clark 2018a

93 A small chocolate bar.

> curlin, or snawsports. Ither kintraes dinnae jist spend mair siller on their ain leids than we dae – they spend mair siller on OOR leids than we dae. Northern Ireland, year on year, spends mair money on Scots than Scotland daes.

Perhaps in frustration with official inaction, and especially the ongoing absence of the long-demanded Scots Language Board, a new body the North-East Scots Language Board (NESLB) was launched in the spring of 2018. It was renamed The Doric Board the following year. As part of the growth in interest in North-East Scots, Aberdeen University's Elphinstone Institute launched a series of ten workshops in Doric, to help both locals and newcomers to the region learn to speak – and more importantly – write in the 'mither leid'. The Institute's Alistair Heather remarked that whilst north-east Scots 'can be heard throughout the region', and can often been seen in signage and adverts, 'people seldom get the chance to learn it as a written language'.[94]

Heather made headlines again in late 2018 after a short video he posted on BBC Social 'Whit's Scots Language?' was shared and viewed tens of thousands of times. In the short clip he (re)introduced the idea of Scots in an especially engaging way.

> Weegies, Fifers, Borderers, Doric speakers and Angus folk like masel, we aa grew up wi Scots voices roon aboot us. But we were never encouraged to speak it, an we certainly dinae get tae stydy it like we did English or mibbie French at school. How no? Cultural colonisation? Lack of confudence in wir ain culture? Mibbie. Nae sure.[95]

Heather reminded the audience 2019 would be the United Nations Year of Indigenous Languages so 'It's a great time to start takkin tent o Scots'.

As readers might now expect, the video triggered a backlash. Heather believed that the animosity toward the video and Scots in general stems from misunderstandings about it.

> Once it is realised that Scots is a language – a 2010 Scottish Government study found that 64% of Scots do not see it as such – people may start to embrace the idea that they are bilingual.[96]

94 University of Aberdeen 2018

95 Heather and Bircham 2018

96 Quoted in Cairns 2018

Lesley Riddoch had told him that when *Radio Nan Gaidheal* was founded Gaelic speakers still did not think of Gaelic as a 'proper language'. Heather explained:

> [Gaelic] was considered to be like Scots is noo. People on the east coast wid think 'Och, thit's no a language, it's jist a dialect ae, it's nae a real thing'. And so people in Uist nivir even kent thit people in Strathnaver spoke Gaelic. And people in Argyll and Stornoway thought thit Gaelic wis essentially Irish.

But that all changed when they started listening tae *Radio Nan Gaidheal*, and could hear all the different dialects of Gaelic, 'they realised thit it wis actually part of the linguistic family it jist hudnae been aware of itself fir 50 years, a hunner years'.

Clark summed up 2018 by writing it 'wisnae a bad wee year for Scots', adding, 'the gatekeepers micht still in place, but the back door's lyin aff its hinges, an there's wan hell o a hoolie gaun on inby'.[97]

A year of firsts

The United Nations Year of Indigenous Languages in 2019 was led by UNESCO to raise awareness of the important contribution such languages make 'to our world's rich cultural diversity'. Michael Dempster, the Scots Scriever, later described 2019 as a year of 'firsts' for the Scots language.[98]

Scots Radio director Frieda Morrison launched The Doric Film Festival[99] 'to celebrate the Doric language and its cultural identity'.[100] It featured three prize categories of five-minute films in North-East Scots; schools, community groups and individuals. The Scots Gaitherin seminar held in September covered issues such as the Scots language's role in broadcasting, women's voices and the use of Scots language in artistic work.[101] It ran in conjunction with the high-profile Scots Language Awards. Awards co-host Alistair Heather said the ceremony symbolised the 'Scots language renaissance'.

> Thir awards are designed tae heize up the grassroots activity, the scrievers, the sculs lairnin the leid tae bairns, the fowk wha've tyaved awa at

97 Clark 2018b

98 Dempster 2019

99 Doric Film Festival 2019

100 Robertson 2019

101 Creative Scotland 2019

> their lanesome dreils fir lang years keepin the leid visible an pairt – just – o the national conversation. On Friday we breenge oot, confident an vibrant, ontae a muckle platform. New energy is biggin up.[102]

He compared this progress with the recent past.

> Yet it wisnae lang I wis oot the village that I found Scots derided as 'slang', 'ned speak', aa that. Fowk sayin that ye soondit like a 'scummy Dundonian' gin ye said 'ken' insteid o 'I know'. I wis shamed oot o usin ma ain leid. It's been a lang gait back tae it.

Towards the end of the year, the Open University in Scotland launched the first part of *Scots Language and Culture* with Education Scotland. The free ten-part course was aimed at a broad audience, 'ranging from Scots speakers, to people who want to find out about and learn some Scots, as well as teachers and other educators'. Two years in the making, it highlighted the role of the language in Lowland culture and society of the past and present. Topics included the use and recognition of Scots in Scotland, the history and linguistic development of Scots, the links of Scots with other European languages and the use of Scots in different literary genres and other art forms. Michael Dempster, now the Director of the Scots Language Centre, called the course 'a significant step forward in the continued recognition and understanding of our language'.[103] The second part, covering additional topics, was released in 2020.

In the world of Scots language politics, delegates at the SNP conference in October voted to investigate the possibility of establishing a Scots Language Board – or 'Board fir the Scots Leid' – like the Bòrd na Gàidhlig promoting Gaelic. They agreed Scots should be more widely taught, learned and promoted as part of Scottish public life, and noted the 'years of linguistic prejudice' it has suffered. SNP MSP Emma Harper repeated the familiar refrain, 'We need to treat the Scots language equally. We need a Board fir the Scots leid'.[104]

In his column in *The National*, Rab Wilson suggested the stars were at last aligning for Scots, quoting Harper.

> Fae gingin tae the first Scots Language Awards ben the Mitchell Library in Glesga, tae then supportin an spikkin fir the Scots

102 Heather 2019

103 Quoted in BBC 2019a

104 Quoted in Grant 2019

> Language motion, owerwhelminly backit aff o SNP memmers at pairty conference at Aiberdeen, cryin fir the Scottish Government fir tae stert a Scots Language Buird, sib tae the Bòrd na Gàidhlig – it's aa gingin brawly.[105]

In 2022 Harper re-convened the Scottish Parliament's short-lived Cross-Party Group on Scots that had vanished around the time the Census results came out.[106] In a letter to *The National*, it was reported that the group originators also believed a new Scots Language Board was essential to carry out the following tasks.

> [T]o meet the needs of Scots in every area: to integrate and support the Scots language in the way of resources; to develop the many local initiatives in Scots in education; to encourage the use of Scots, spoken and written, by example, eg in Parliament, public notices, information leaflets etc; and to support the publication of written Scots which can bring back the status of Scots as a national language capable of all registers and able to deal with all topics.[107]

Findin oor vyce?

The beginning of the new decade was dominated, inevitably, by the Covid pandemic as live events were curtailed. The Doric Film Festival had to be postponed, but the 2020 Scots Language Awards proceeded successfully in a digital format. The award for Scots Speaker o the Year went to comedian Janey Godley, whose humorous Glasgow Scots overdubbing of First Minister's Covid briefings were a welcome relief in miserable times. Godley told the audience she was honoured to win an award, 'for something that I was told to be ashamed of for so long, my ain Scots tongue'.[108]

The BBC has been justly criticised for ignoring Scots. Billy Kay's groundbreaking television series *Scots: The Mither Tongue* dates back to 1986, although it was updated and rebroadcast in radio format as *The Scots Tongue* in 2016. In early 2020 the BBC produced a new one-hour special *The Rebel Tongue*, hosted by the charismatic Alistair Heather, whose short BBC Social video on Scots had gone viral in 2018. The writer set out on a mission to 'reclaim' the Scots language. 'For decades, his fellow Scots speakers

105 Wilson 2019
106 Harper 2022
107 Forde 2019
108 Quoted in *Hands Up For Trad* 2020

have been mocked, their language oppressed by educators, politicians and broadcasters'.[109] Prior to lockdown, Heather had visited activists, speakers and writers and discovered 'an increasing boldness shared across many areas, with working-class or rural folk committing themselves to real action'. But he encountered a problem.

> What we found to be missing on our travels for the documentary was any support from officialdom. There were no programmes in government to help connect and encourage these grassroots activities. The BBC were not part of this cultural renaissance. Schools, even with the best will in the world, don't have the ability to teach Scots at the highest level because there is no Scots Language Higher. We discovered a terrible disconnect between the people and the structures meant to empower them.

Heather arrived at the following conclusion.

> Scots is the partially submerged national tongue of a partially submerged nation. And as we continue our journey towards being a normal country again, we need to start having a more normal attitude to one of our indigenous ways of speaking.

In his 2018 article cited above, Rab Wilson linked the poor funding of Scots to the difficulty of attracting young people to the cause.

> First, whit fir shuid Scots hae tae rely oan unpeyed labour whan the promotion o comparable European leids is rin oan a professional basis wi salaried posts? […] Scots in Scotland haes tae scrape by at best and haud annual bashes in dreich Kirk Ha's, the whilk are chaip but they're no gaun tae attract young fowk are they?

In 2020 the Doric Board made several financial awards to various individuals and groups across the North-East ranging from £250 to £1000 to encourage Scots language based projects, but generally Scots initiatives are run by an army of unpaid workers. Over a decade previously, the audit of Scots language provision had found that grassroots initiatives were heavily reliant on voluntary activity. Volunteerism provides commendable self-motivation and energy, but its limits were exposed in the summer of 2020 when the international media spotlight fell on Scots Wikipedia.

109 Heather 2020

Scots Wikipedia, the Scots language version of Wikipedia, had been running since 2005. By 2020 it hosted over 40,000 articles. Any casual Scots speaker might have noticed the quality was poor, but for most people the volunteer-based and collective authoring process behind Wikipedia remained a mystery. This was to change abruptly when a social media user noticed the site contained an unusually high number of articles written by a single contributor. Almost half the articles had been produced by an American teenager who was not a native Scots speaker. With apparently no knowledge of Scots grammar or idioms he had been using online dictionaries to create crude translations of English Wikipedia topics. The news soon reached the UK and international media. *The Guardian* put it succinctly:

> The entries in question do little more than substitute occasional, and often wrongly spelled, Scots words into English grammatical constructions. As a result, the project often inadvertently ends up being used to bolster arguments that Scots is not a language in its own right.[110]

The discoverer of the anomaly called it 'cultural vandalism on a hitherto unprecedented scale'. To be fair, the anonymous author expressed contrition and the press commentary was less scornful than might be imagined. Instead of shutting down the whole site, 'it was soon discovered that there is a strong desire by many in the Scots-speaking community to come forward and help in a constructive way'.[111] Wikipedia was supportive and scores of individuals, many of them native Scots speakers, came forward to rewrite the entries in a series of editing sprints that continue to run. The need to regularise writing on such a scale using a language that does not currently enjoy official standards obviously poses something of a problem.

A little before the Wikipedia stushie broke, a new political campaign was launched demanding official recognition for the Scots Language. Oor Vyce[112] brought together entertainers, writers, academics and political campaigners who wanted the Scottish Parliament to pass a law for Scots similar to the 2005 Gaelic Language Act. Like the Cross-Party Group, they demanded an official body, like Bòrd na Gàidhlig, to raise the status and profile of Scots. Campaigning was hampered by lockdown, but the group ran a series of online webinars including a lively discussion on St Andrews Day titled 'Do we need a Scots Standard?'.

110 Brooks and Hern 2020

111 Scots Language Centre 2020

112 Oor Vyce 2020

Scholarly interest in the language also seemed to have been rekindled. Robert McColl Millar published his wide-ranging *A Sociolinguistic History of Scotland*, covering Scots, Gaelic, Scottish English and other languages in detail.[113] Millar's Aberdeen University also launched a 15-credit undergraduate course in Doric (North-East Scots).[114] Two more small steps were taken in the 'soft standardisation' of Scots. The Scots Language Centre published *Recommendations for Names of Countries, Nations, Regions & States in Scots* compiled by Dauvit Horsbroch[115] and the popular *Scots-Online* dictionary released an Android app providing definitions of Scots words and some short phrases in English or possible Scots translations of English words.[116] The app also includes a Scots pronunciation and spelling guide. A mobile web version is also available.

Towards the end of the year Iona Fyfe, an Aberdeenshire singer and winner of the 2020 Scots Language Awards, took the bold step of confronting Spotify, the world's largest music streaming platform. When she tried to upload one of her songs to the service, she realised that there was no language option for Scots, making it the sole British minority language missing from the platform.[117] Clare Adamson, an SNP MSP, raised the issue in the Scottish Parliament, writing to Spotify to demand a response. The media giant finally caved in a few months later, by confirming that 'Scots language is now available as a category for artists to select when submitting music to Spotify, alongside Scottish Gaelic'.[118] The satisfying ending was somewhat tarnished, however. Novelist and Scots enthusiast Val McDermid picks up the story,

> My heart rejoiced recently at the news that Scots singer and poet Iona Fyfe persuaded Spotify to recognise Scots as a language. And then I was cast down almost immediately when she revealed that though her singing in Scots provoked no noticeable hostility, when she posted on social media in her natural speech, she was the victim of a troll pile-on. She was called ignorant, a whore and a bitch for using the language.[119]

The abuse of a young female Scots language artist was sadly not an isolated incident that year. In October a 21-year-old student Len Pennie

113 Millar 2020
114 Campsie 2020
115 Horsbroch 2020b
116 Scots Online 2020
117 Richards 2020
118 Ferguson 2021a
119 McDermid 2021

performed her mostly Scots poem 'I'm no havin children' on social media. Despite the perhaps provocative title, the author explained, 'what the poem is about really, it's about passing on your mither's tongue, staying proud of it, and keeping family together through language'. The video went viral, and initially Pennie was overawed by the response, 'They went absolutely mad for it'.[120] However, the mood soon darkened, and by December she reported on Twitter she had been subjected to a torrent of internet abuse, being called 'trollop', 'harlot' and 'pompous little minx'.[121] The relentless insults continued into the new year when she spoke out again, 'You think your attacks don't hurt me, but they do'.[122] Scots Language Award winner Janey Godley, recording a video message of support, speculated that Iona Fyfe and Len Pennie might have been particularly targeted because they were women[123], but there was a political undercurrent too. Pennie revealed that apart from 'making Scottish people sound stupid', she had been accused of 'perpetuating a faux identity and culture in order to assert Scottish exceptionalism' and being a 'propagandist for independence'. Fyfe observed;

> The usual suspects that pile on Scots language are often unionists, they're often folk with a British flag on their logo, instead of a picture of themselves, or a Rangers logo.[124]

Referring to Fyfe and Pennie, Godley believed, 'They must really frighten them'. Pennie herself retorted on Twitter, 'It's so demoralisin' tae be a lassie oan here, some ae yous need tae shut the mooth and open the lugs mair'.[125]

Scots: to be continued

Media reports in early 2021 that the number of pupils learning Scots had 'quadrupled' were seen as an indicator that calcified anti-Scots attitudes may just be beginning to crack. Numbers were still small, but as teacher Simon Hall observed, young people in Scotland were now able to gain official accreditation for their learning in Scots from a national awards body. He felt this 'surely speaks volumes about changes in attitudes towards Scots'.[126]

Unfortunately, much of the Scottish media still does not seem to 'get'

120 Hay 2020a
121 Hay 2020b
122 Mackie 2021
123 Ferguson 2021b
124 Learmonth 2021
125 Wynne 2021
126 Hall 2019:3.4

Scots with any degree of consistency. *The Scotsman*, for example, remains inordinately fond of labelling any Scots language as 'slang' and classifies its infrequent articles on the subject as 'Heritage and Retro'. A BBC Travel article in 2021 seemed to think that the Doric (ie North East Scots) was 'Scotland's little-known fourth "language" after English, Gaelic and Scots'.[127] What effect misinformation has on public attitudes to Scots is hard to tell, but it probably does little to moderate the ongoing anti-Scots attacks on social media or the 'accent discrimination' a Shetland poet reported (ironically, in *The Scotsman*) that she experiences when she leaves her home islands.[128]

The discourse of discrimination leads us back into the field of language politics. Earlier I mentioned a fundamental dichotomy in how Scots is regarded by both the Scottish establishment and the activist community. Some see Scots as a minority language to be developed and normalised, but others frame it as a heritage or creative asset to be preserved in its supposedly 'untamed' state. In response to the threats and online abuse of young Scots artists in 2020, University of Edinburgh linguist Pavel Iosad reflected that there was, 'so much personal politics around Scots and so little serious institutional politics'.[129] He remarked; 'Most pro-Scots policy is run in arts and education, where it is essentially a vehicle of personal identity and creativity'. Consequently, 'we don't get any serious policy for language planning and no unified front'. The absence of a single organisation to defend and develop the tongue presents a problem for individual artists. As Iosad puts it, 'anti-Scots sentiment, having no actual institutional target, just devolves into attacks on anything that smells of difference'. Not surprisingly, Fyfe hoped institutional politics would take Scots 'a little more seriously'. Believing legislation is now required to protect and promote the language, the singer became active in Oor Vyce.

Oor Vyce was active in the run up to the Scottish Parliament elections in May 2021. They ran a campaign to encourage candidates to endorse '#ScotsPledge', a set of three principles in support of the Scots language as follows.

> Gin electit, Ah pledge tae:
>
> - Recognise Scots an aa its varieties (sic as Doric, Shaetlan, Orcadian etc) as a legitimate leivin leid an tak tent o the needs o its spikkers.
> - Heize up the profile o Scots in ma constituency, the chaummer, ma pairlamentary office an ayont.

127 MacEacheran 2021

128 Hay 2021

129 Quoted in Learmonth 2021

- Gie ma support, in principle, tae the idea o legislative action fir tae proteck, empooer an promuive Scots.

The manifestos of the main parties presented the usual mixed levels of commitment to Scots. The Scottish Conservatives, Alex Salmond's start-up Alba, Scottish Liberal Democrats and Labour all omitted to mention Scots. Labour had dropped its odd 2016 commitment to 'Nordic', but in an 'additional statement' prompted by the Scots Language Centre promised it 'will recognise and support the sharing and learning of the Scots language'.[130] Only the SNP and the Scottish Greens included Scots in their manifestos. The SNP pledged to bring forward a new Scottish Languages Bill, 'which takes further steps to support Gaelic, acts on the Scots language and recognises that Scotland is a multilingual society'. The SNP additional statement provided to the Scots Language Centre was also surprisingly detailed.

> That the Pairlament gies its support tae futur government muives fir tae promuive the uiss o the Scots leid in Scotland's public an private airts, baith in spaken an screivit forum, forbye in primary, seicontary an tertiary education, televeision an print media an in this pairlament; recognises that the uiss o Scots in the media is a muckle driver o a sense o inclusion for Scots spikkers; taks tent o the value o Scots lairnin initiatives sic as the Scots Language Award in shrinkin the attainment gap; encourages memmers o the neist pairlament tae recognise o Scots an aw its byleids as a legitimate leivin leid an tak tent o the needs o its spikkers; forbye encourages futur MSPs tae ettle at heizin up the leid's profile in their constituencies, the chaummer, pairlamentary offices an ayont, an gies its support in principle tae the idea o looking at legislative muives fir tae protect an promuive it mair.

Later in the summer, the SNP and the Greens would announce a 'cooperation agreement', so creating a majority in the Scottish Parliament. Their 'Draft Shared Policy Programme' did not, however, mention Scots (or Gaelic) measures.

Oor Vyce declared its pledge campaign to be successful.

> The new Scots Pairliament is a Scots-supportin ane, wi 35 oot o the 129 electit MSPs haein taen oor #Scotspledge! Here's luikin forrit tae seein MSPs staanin up fir the leid an supportin the pairty o Government's pledge tae introduce a Bill tae protect an promuive it!

130 Scots Language Centre 2021b

Making a point about Scotland's multilingualism, when the new parliament met many MSPs avoided English when making their vows, using Scots and its variants Orcadian and Doric, Gaelic of course, but also Urdu, Canadian French, Welsh, Arabic and Punjabi.[131]

I first drafted these paragraphs on Sunday 20 March 2022, Census Day. This was Scotland's biggest population survey, normally a once-in-a-decade event, but delayed a year due to the pandemic. The previous census in 2011 surveyed Scots for the first time. People were being asked again to say if they could understand Scots, speak Scots, read Scots and write Scots. The 2011 Aye Can website supporting this part of the census had been polished up, expanded and widely promoted. The site used the same definition of Scots as in 2011, presumably to allow a direct comparison with the earlier data. However this time the site itself uses the word 'language' more prominently than in 2011, and the video introduction opens with 'Scots is yin o Scotland's three indigenous languages alang wi Gaelic an Scottish Standard English'. In addition to Question 14, the straightforward skills assessment, the site was careful to highlight Question 16, asking what the respondent's main language was. As mentioned earlier, in 2011 the low figures for this question caused some muddying of the data and false reporting of the speaker numbers. This time the instructions, at least on Aye Can, were clearer; 'if your main language is Scots tick "other" and write "Scots" in the space provided', deliberately making the point that,

> If you have decided you can speak Scots, and that it is the most common way you communicate in day-to-day life, then Scots is your main language.

With Twitter open beside me on Census Day, I saw the usual anti-Scots trolling; 'Who speaks this so-called language? It's an invention', '"Scots" or to put it another way, Scottish slang', 'basically English pronounced and spelt incorrectly', 'There is only one language in Scotland and that's English and often with local pronunciation', and the classic 'No one remember *Parliamo Glasgow*?'. But their heart did not seem quite in it any more, the abundant pro-Scots tweets are mostly polite and informed, more despairing than disdainful; 'It's amazing how little conditioning it takes for someone to deny their own heritage, culture and even language', 'Having a tantrum over being asked if you can speak a recognised language, first world problems, eh?'.

The 2022 Scottish Census results, released in early 2024, revealed a significant increase in the number of people reporting some level of skill in

131 Nutt 2021

the Scots language compared to 2011.[132] In 2011, around 1.9 million people, 37.7% of the population, reported having some Scots language skills. By 2022, that figure had risen to 2.4 million, or 46.2% of the population. This overall rise not only suggests a growing recognition and appreciation of Scots, but also verifies the reliability of the 2011 data.

However, while passive knowledge of the language appears to be increasing, active use may be in decline. The number of individuals who reported being able to speak Scots fell slightly, from 1.54 million in 2011 to 1.51 million in 2022. This trend highlights the need for initiatives that encourage not just awareness of Scots, but also its active use in everyday life.

The release of the Census data coincided with discussions around the Scottish Languages Bill, which proposed granting official status to both Gaelic and Scots. Language advocates saw the findings as a call to action for greater support and recognition – especially in education and public life. Scots language author and activist Emma Grae noted the Scots language budget for 2023–24 was still just £553,500, less than 50p for each respondent who identified as having skills in Scots. She commented: 'A language that is understood by so many people in Scotland cannot flourish with so little investment.'[133]

In *A Sociolinguistic History of Scotland*, published in 2020, Robert McColl Millar made a gloomy prediction.[134] He recognised Scots was still spoken by 'a considerable part of the population' and that in terms of government support, at last 'something is being done'. Yet he feared by the end of the century Scots could become 'entirely dialectised' as a form of colloquial English, 'where pronunciation will be the primary distinguishing factor'. But this fate could be avoided if Scots finally began to be treated as an integral part of national life. It would need support by a government agency (ie a Scots Board) that 'would coordinate linguistic activities and norms in the education system and beyond'. (Scottish) English would remain the lingua franca but 'what would be encouraged instead would be a fruitful and beneficial bilingualism or by bidialectism'. We will look at the benefits of bilingualism (and bidialectism) in the next chapter.

A major milestone came in 2023 with the introduction of the Scottish Languages Bill.[135] Introduced on St. Andrews Day, the Bill sought to give both Gaelic and Scots 'official status'. Despite its title, though, the Bill offered no integrated strategy. Rather, it treated Gaelic and Scots to independent

132 The Scottish Parliament Information Centre (2024)

133 Grae (2024)

134 Millar 2020:207

135 The Scottish Parliament 2023a

sociolinguistic and policy matters, with no shared approaches or terminology. The bulk of the Bill updated the Gaelic Language (Scotland) Act of 2005 with yet more detailed proposals for Gaelic, while the commitment to Scots was limited to preparing a 'strategy', something Lo Bianco had seen as urgent two decades previously. Nonetheless, the Bill marked the first time Scots had been referenced in any Scottish Government legislation and acknowledged 'the negative views that are at times attached to Scots and the stigma and discrimination that Scots speakers often refer to'.

The tragedy for Scots is that the plan the Bill cautiously suggested developing had been readily available since the early days of devolution and had been well within the Scottish Government's devolved powers to implement. Lo Bianco documented the injustice of widespread maltreatment of Scots 20 years ago, and the clear steps required to stabilise and eventually invigorate the language. Models of language revitalisation are widely employed all around the world. In poll after poll, the Scottish people, and not only Scots speakers, have expressed support for initiatives to boost Scots' standing and provision. When I first wrote these words on Census Day many of these people would have been self-identifying as Scots speakers, defying years of cultural oppression and declaring themselves proud to speak their native tongue. These are the individuals who will save Scots. Millar fittingly concluded in 2020 that 'without active connection with the speaker population outside the activist', the revival of Scots would be 'wishful thinking'. Turning wishful thinking into concrete community action must be the next stage in the continuing story of our defiant tongue.

CHAPTER FIVE

Scots and Education

The pedagogy of shame

> The history of the Scots Language within Scottish education has, until relatively recently, been a rather sad story of ignorance, neglect, or downright hostility. Historic socio-linguistic prejudices have meant that many thousands of youngsters have endured some deeply negative experiences whilst using their home language at school – for the simple reason that the language of their communities was deemed unsuitable for formal or academic purposes...For much of the 140-year history of universal education in Scotland, the Scots language has been completely absent.[1]

SCHOOLS ARE THE front line of the linguistic and cultural campaign against the Scots language. As a parent and an educator myself, I find it disturbing that the rich language of my childhood was, and still is, suppressed. I had always held the Scottish education system in high regard. Was I wrong? Former English teacher John Hodgart thinks so.

> Surely ane o the great paradoxes o Scottish culture is the fact that mony Scots still hae a deep-ruitit faith in the merits o an educational system that historically has duin a great deal tae unnermine their ain identity, leain them ignorant aboot, or even leukin doon on, the history an culture o their ain land an often makin them ashamed o the wey they talk.[2]

A Facebook poster recently related what coercion felt like as a bairn.

1 Hall 2019a:3.1
2 Hodgart 2016

> I remember as an excited kid in school putting my hand up and saying, 'Miss I ken'. The old bag walloped my thumb with one of those long pointers they used. 70 years later I still have the scar, and her words were, 'we speak English in this school', as if the Scots tongue was second class.

How could such a psychologically toxic pedagogy ever have gained acceptance among Scottish teachers? 'It may seem bizarre that early educationalists drawing up nineteenth century curricula would deliberately exclude local language from the classroom', wrote Simon Hall. He wondered, 'whether or not the early educationalists had any awareness of Scots Language', concluding, 'we can only guess'. Sadly, very little guesswork is needed. According to official papers and accounts, Scottish education officials were well aware of the Scots language as a linguistic rival to English, and purposely sought to stifle it. The questionable pedagogic rationale for suppression will be examined later in this chapter, but the prime motive appears to have been ideological. Universal Scottish education was, for most of its 140 years, under the tight control of middle-class anglophones. With almost no democratic oversight or accountability, this unrepresentative group had over a century to try to re-engineer Scottish culture in their own linguistic and ideological image. It is no coincidence that the educational value of the Scots language only began to be reconsidered after devolution.

Scots' current educational status is therefore not 'natural', but the outcome of decades of policies and practices hostile to the language. If we are to put coercion behind us and achieve a more equitable balance, we must understand the long history of this injustice and its ongoing impacts. As we have already seen, raising the Scots Language Question is disturbing for many people and seen as a threat to the linguistic and cultural status quo. Attempts to elevate the position of Scots to any kind of normality, therefore, risks being labelled 'politicisation'. Reviewing a few of the educational themes discussed in the previous two chapters might explain the roots of such misconceptions. The various education reports of over the last century or so provide a unique insight into the stubborn persistence of Scots in classrooms but also conflicting official and establishment attitudes to the language over this period.

By the late 19th century, Scottish literacy rates were comparatively high. English was taught, as Hall put it, 'with zealous enthusiasm', but 'the language of everyday communication, indeed the language of general instruction was still Scots'.[3] The 1872 Education (Scotland) Act is often blamed for proscribing such bilingualism, but in practice Scots could not be banned immediately as teachers still needed to use it to explain lessons. A Scotch Education Department memorandum from the beginning of the 20th century acknowledged that most Lowland children were not able to use English 'freely' when they entered school, and recognised Scots was 'historically, a national language' and not a 'provincial dialect'.[4] Throughout the 1920s and 1930s tireless campaigners called for more use of Scots in education, and produced practical recommendations.[5] Had such ideas gained traction, the status of Scots in our schools might look very different today. But they were up against an equally determined and powerful Scottish education establishment, so even modest suggestions for reform were quashed.

By the Second World War a gloomy orthodoxy seemed to grip the increasingly anglophone Scottish middle class. Scots, they believed, was moribund or had already fragmented to isolated dialects. Contemporary accounts suggest this was far from true, but the authoritarian 1940s Scottish classroom still could not find room for the linguistic richness on its very doorstep. While praising 'the homely, natural and pithy everyday speech of country and small-town folk', we saw how a Scottish Education Department (SED) report in 1947 cautioned teachers that urban Scots was, 'not the language of "educated" people anywhere and could not be described as a suitable medium of education or culture'.[6] Therefore, 'against such unlovely forms of speech masquerading as Scots we recommend that the schools should wage a planned and unrelenting campaign'. That said, Scots was still recognised as a significant part of the childrens' linguistic and cultural landscape. Five years later, SED offered more nuanced advice: that Scottish children's language should be viewed 'historically' and not regarded 'with condescension or disapproval as if they were merely debased forms of the language of books'. Unfortunately, the view that 'bad' forms of Scots speech should be expunged was restated, and untrained teachers were given the near-impossible task of discriminating between 'slovenly perversions of dialect' and 'genuine dialect'.

In the second half of the 20th century public lobbying for Scots in schools seemed to wane, maybe as the number of Scots speaking parents with an interest in the tongue declined. Some books in Scots, including

---

3 Kay 1993:114

4 Cited in Corbett and Stuart-Smith 2013:212

5 *Aberdeen Press and Journal* 1924

6 Scottish Education Department 1947:181

readings, poems and songs, continued to be produced for schools, but by the early 1960s Scottish teachers were, in many areas, mostly middle-class anglophones. Only a handful of teachers, even in the rich Scots-speaking areas of my schooldays, had any overt skills in, or showed sympathy for, the language. The consequences were predictable and Caroline Macafee describes the 1970s as 'probably the nadir of education in Scots'.[7] Scots speakers who went to school from the 1980s onwards seem barely aware that Scots literature and literacy ever existed. By the 1990s one observer described Scottish education as 'an alien place for our native languages', and this 'should be read as intention rather than neglect or accident'.[8] But all was not (quite) lost. Following a long campaign, the Scots Language Resource Centre (now The Scots Language Centre) opened in 1993 to help schoolteachers and writers. Various Scottish language resources began to appear, including the breakthrough *Scots School Dictionary*.[9] Official guidelines in the early 1990s began to include some promotion of Scots literature and Scots dialects, but a Scotland-wide consultation exercise just before devolution still painted a gloomy picture.

> Over the last 25 years there has been increased but spasmodic attention to the potential contribution of Scots language and literature to the curriculum. It remains true however that Scots in its varieties has never won the coherent practical support which [...] it merits.[10]

The democratic changes in the early 21st century saw Scots begin to reappear on the official curriculum, albeit tentatively, but Millar recognised the challenges of revitalising Scots, now a minority language, after generations of being absent from schools.

> [O]ver a century of mass education in English has led many people to see not only that the path to advancement leads through Standard English, but also that Scots itself is merely a corrupt dialect of the standard. A view held by Scots speakers as much as by those who do not speak the variety, this prejudice is extremely difficult to break through.[11]

7 Commentary on Aitken 1981, 2015

8 Ross 1997

9 Renamed *The Essential Scots Dictionary* in 2005

10 Review of Scottish Culture Group 1998

11 Millar 2005:195

Eject it with violence

Even when Scots was still a majority language in many communities, the practical challenges of teaching Scots as a mainstream subject were acknowledged. During a 1924 address to the Workers Education Association in Aberdeen, William Grant, a relentless advocate for Scots in schools, made a speech that sounds rather familiar almost a century later.

> Many teachers seemed to think that the use of Scots the schools distracted the pupils in their efforts acquire standard English. They preferred therefore to ignore the vernacular, even if they did not go so far as to denounce it as barbarous and vulgar. Others urged the weary wail of the overburdened curriculum and inadvisability of adding to it yet another subject. The question at issue, however, was not that of additional subject, but the proper way of tackling what was a real difficulty in the Scottish school – the presence of two different types of speech in the experience of the average pupil. The old way was to ignore Scots, to frown it down or eject it with violence, and no attempt was made to set it in its proper relation to standard English.[12]

My own experience of Scots in primary schools in East Lothian, Fife and Perthshire almost 50 years after Grant's speech was not particularly violent and could be better described as 'benign neglect'.[13] Teachers accepted the language of the playground, and as far as I recall nobody was berated or beaten for using Scots in the classroom. We memorised Burns poems dutifully every January, and on Friday afternoons one maverick Fife teacher would read us the Scots-rich stories of JJ Bell's *Wee McGreegor*. She would ask us to list the Scots words we knew (lots!) and asked us to memorise the MC Smith's evocative Fife-set poem 'Boy in the Train'.

> I'll sune be ringin' ma Gran'ma's bell,
> She'll cry, 'Come ben, ma laddie.'
> For I ken masel' by thre queer-like smell
> That the next stop's Kirkaddy![14]

We were told by our teacher that we were 'bilingual', a talent we should all be proud of. Maybe that fleeting positive reinforcement is why I am writing

---

12 *Aberdeen Press and Journal* 1924

13 Wright 2016:231

14 Smith 1913

this book and not frothing about Scots being 'slang' on Twitter.

Unfortunately, such laissez-faire lenience was not the experience of many of my contemporaries. Mainstream thinking about Scots in education until quite recently held that, 'the Mither Tongue, a child's first language, stays in the playground and stops at the classroom door'.[15] When older Scots speakers are interviewed about their schooling, many can describe being chastised, humiliated or, pre-1987, physically beaten for speaking Scots in class. Janice Macfarlane provided an example.

> One literacies practitioner told me that 'Miss Taylor' belted him as a boy of seven or eight for saying his goldfish was deid, insisting it was dead. Yet she had given him a gold star for reciting Burns' 'Tae a Moose'. Scots from the Bard was permissible but 'speaking slang' was not.

The well-known passage in William McIlvanney's 1975 novel *Docherty* fictionalised the banal brutality. A teacher asks the young hero Conn, 'What's wrong with your face, Docherty?'. Conn replies,

> 'Skint ma nose, sur.'
> 'How?'
> 'Ah fell an bumped ma heid in the sheuch, sur.'
> 'I beg your pardon?'

Conn receives a sharp blow to the head for his linguistic insolence. Author Matthew Fitt drew on McIlvanney's portrayal 40 years later to reflect on the effect of language suppression on his own attitudes to the tongue.

> I went through the same as a lot o ma generation at the schule – the confusion, the beltin, the anxiety. It led me at first tae hate masel for speakin Scots and then tae reject that sel-loathin by stertin tae write in it. I suppose I wis tryin tae find a wey tae mak ma language real tae me. Folk telt me at ivry step whit I wis daein wis wrang, a waste o time. It didnae seem tae maitter tae them when I said it wis richt for me. But it wis.[16]

The psychological and physical abuse of children in Scottish schools for speaking their native language appears to have been widespread, even

15 Macfarlane 2012
16 Fitt 2016b

institutionalised, across decades. But where is the research on the scope of this coercion, or studies on its long-term consequences for educational attainment and mental health? Victims of such violent childhood incidents often internalise what happened to them, so why are their voices not heard? The radical Brazilian educator Paulo Freire, mentioned earlier, offers a reason. Unjust social structures can produce a 'culture of silence' that instils such a damaging self-image into the victims they can't even talk about it, let alone find the will to resist it.[17]

In his 1968 classic *Pedagogy of the Oppressed*, Friere argued that education can never be neutral. It is always a political process reflecting and reinforcing the power relationships in a society. Traditional education, he claimed, has little interest in empowering students, linguistically or socially. Rather it aims to mould or forcibly 'adapt' children to the economic and social needs of the political elites. Thus, 'the educated individual is the adapted person, because he or she is better "fit" for the world'. In Scottish education this 'fit' was never just the practical matter of learning standard English, that was easy, but the submission of Scottish cultural identity to the dominant norms of the British Empire.

Schools are one of society's main 'socialising instruments', in the terms of Oxford sociolinguist Susanne Romaine, and as such they play 'a powerful role in exerting control over its pupils, endorsing mainstream and largely middle-class values and language'.[18] Children who do not come to school equipped with appropriate linguistic and learning behaviours are likely to experience stress and conflict, either externalised or bottled-up. Fluency in standard English was, and remains, an inarguably desirable educational aim. By the 19th century, English was already the *lingua franca* of Empire and was fast becoming the global language of modernity. Everybody wanted to learn standard English and most residents of lowland Scotland were, one might think, fortunate in using a local language close enough to English to make that task straightforward. The Dutch and most Scandinavians have a similar linguistic advantage. Their local tongues are also English-like, and their language skills are universally admired. So, why is this not true for Scottish people?

Ironically, it may be that Scots was just a little too close a relative to English. This linguistic proximity, coupled with the tendency of spoken Scottish language to mix the two tongues, enabled it to be stigmatised and considered unworthy or even incapable of being taught. As the sociolinguist Jenny Cheshire laments, 'Stereotypes about "incorrect", "careless" and

17 Freire 1968/70

18 Romaine 2000:205

"ugly" speech persist, despite 40 years of sociolinguistic work demonstrating that dialects and creoles are well-formed language systems'.[19] Teachers are not immune to this prejudice; 'English' English relates to notions of power, authority, high social status, cosmopolitanism, learning, ambition and career advancement. It is understandable that teachers felt they were doing the right thing for their charges by enabling them to 'fit' and compete in that environment. Miller suggests other, more personal, motivations.

> For many teachers in Scottish schools getting a degree and going into teaching represented the jettisoning of unwanted social baggage, including the language. In religion converts are usually the most enthusiastic practitioners of their new religion, and the same holds for linguistic converts.[20]

The persecution of Scots and Gaelic was bolstered by the harsh pedagogic theories of the time. Throughout the 19th and most of the 20th centuries, educators considered a second dialect or language to be a cognitive interference that would delay a child's scholastic and intellectual development. One Cambridge University professor in 1890 famously claimed,

> If it were possible for a child or boy to live in two languages at once equally well, so much the worse. His intellectual and spiritual growth would not thereby be doubled but halved. Unity of mind and character would have great difficulty in asserting itself in such circumstances.[21]

Generations later, in 1952 the Director of Education in Orkney was still repeating the same misguided mantra.

> The use of dialect along with Standard English imposes on our young people the handicap of bilingualism that they habitually use two languages. This is a real impediment to progress.[22]

Robert Phillipson in his book *Linguistic Imperialism* argues monolingual pedagogy was linked to the ideology of the British Empire. Most colonialists were raised as monolinguals but many of the colonised peoples spoke several languages, especially those in Africa and India. To the imperial mindset native

19 Cheshire 2005:2341
20 Miller 1998:55
21 Laurie 1890:15
22 Quoted in Hall 2019a:3.2

multilingualism could not possibly be countenanced as having any social or cognitive value. Phillipson describes this as 'the monolingual Western norm'. This pernicious ethos 'has falsely claimed that monolingualism is a necessary condition for modernisation, and that a multiplicity of languages is a nuisance'.[23] Middle-class multilingualism especially in prestigious languages like Latin of French, and gained through formal education was, and remains, a different matter.

> In education, the valuation of multilingual resources is strongly linked to social-class differences. On one hand, the acquisition of foreign languages is encouraged, but on the other hand the home linguistic resources of many lower-class and migrant students are valued negatively.[24]

This linguistic value hierarchy can still be seen today. Apart from in Gaelic medium schools, in Scotland Scottish English is always 'L1', the language of instruction. Scotland's current '1+2' schools policy for language learning advocates that a second language (L2) should be taught from Primary One onwards, and a third language (L3) should be introduced from Primary Five onwards. Scots at best could only be studied as an L3 and is bracketed alongside community languages and included only where an individual teacher has the interest and skills to introduce it.[25]

A bilingual bonus?

The deficit model of bilingualism (or even bidialectism) has been thoroughly debunked, as has the notion of 'interference' between two languages/varieties spoken. Speaking and using different languages is now considered by many to be beneficial for the brain. This is why in *A Sociolinguistic History of Scotland*, published in 2020, Robert McColl Millar could imagine a future Scotland with 'fruitful and advantageous bilingualism' between Scots and Scottish English. Positive attitudes to linguistic diversity in education have arisen partly through studies into other stigmatised English or English-like vernaculars such as African American Vernacular English and Jamaican patois, but also explorations of working-class vernaculars in general. Reviewing the considerable research literature in 1999, Michael Siegal found that prejudice had all too often overridden pedagogy.

---

23 Phillipson 1992:32

24 Weber 2015:79

25 Education Scotland 2020

> [T]here is no basis for claims that using a stigmatised variety in the classroom increases interference or gets in the way of acquisition of the standard. On the contrary, research findings indicate that appropriate teaching methodology incorporating students' vernaculars may actually help them acquire the standard.[26]

Siegel cited one paper from as far back as 1947 that suggested 'the aim of establishing standard English can actually best be accomplished by a more complete understanding and appreciation of the local dialect'. Pedagogies that respect linguistic diversity have thus been available to teachers for a long time. As we saw in previous chapters, enlightened pro-Scots campaigners had been calling for a positive approach to Scots in the classroom for at least a generation before that.

It was not until the 1960s, however, that formal research really began to challenge the apparently immovable misconception of 'cognitive deficit'. In 1962, Peal and Lambert discovered that English-French bilingual children in Montreal performed better than monolinguals on many cognitive tests. Subsequent studies, especially with children, have suggested bilingualism may also improve cognitive skills not directly related to language. These include:

- Better focus on mentally demanding tasks
- Problem solving and creative thinking
- Using knowledge about how the languages they speak work
- Working memory.[27]

However, bilingualism research is still relatively new. As influences are nuanced and culturally contextualised, debate about the magnitude of such effects and their impact on various age groups continues. The most obvious benefits of bilingualism seem to be expressed in school-aged children, with the impact fading in adulthood. According to some studies, the 'bilingual advantage' may reappear as we age and protect us from dementia. To be fair, not all bilingual effects are beneficial in all settings. One review claimed 'a large body of evidence' demonstrated that the verbal skills of bilinguals in each of their languages were generally weaker than those of monolingual speakers of those languages.[28]

Studies into Scots-Scottish English bilingualism (or bidialectism) are predictably patchy, but lessons can be drawn from related studies. In 2012,

26 Siegel 1999:721

27 Lauchlan et al 2012

28 Bialystok et al 2012

research by Fraser Lauchlan and colleagues into the cognitive benefits of bilingualism in children in Sardinia (Sardinian/Italian) and Scotland (Gaelic/English) showed both sets of bilinguals outperformed the monolingual children. However, the Gaelic children accomplished significantly more than the Sardinian group. Was this a 'language-difference' effect, Sardinian and Italian being more closely related linguistically than Gaelic and English? The researchers argued that the Scottish children's performance was far more likely due to their formal education in Gaelic. Sardinian, like Scots, is generally acquired casually in the domestic environment. Thus, linguistic distance between the two languages spoken was thought not to be a major factor and 'bidialectalism' may have similar benefits to 'true' bilingualism, especially in education. There may also be a critical threshold of language ability that has to be reached before the positive effects come into play.

Further evidence of the bilingual bonus comes from the Norwegian language which has two written variations, Bokmål and Nynorsk. Both varieties are taught in schools, depending on the locality. Most Norwegians use a local dialect when speaking, close to one or other of the two written forms. Norwegian children who use Nynorsk in school (about ten per cent of the population) also learn Bokmål but the reverse is not always true. Nynorsk users therefore can be described as bidialectal. Researchers found that school results where Nynorsk was used were better than those where only Bokmål is taught, even when other social and economic differences were considered. The researchers suggested that Nynorsk 'triggers a type of cognitive training which in turn provides a more measurable positive effect on learning in general'.[29]

Nynorsk is a standardised variety, though, but what about more informal vernaculars like Scots? One intriguing study tested primary school children speaking both standard Greek and the linguistically close local variety, Cypriot Greek.[30] These bidialectals were compared with monolinguals and 'classic' bilinguals who spoke English alongside Greek in international schools on the mainland. As expected, the 'true' bilinguals performed better in cognitive tests than the two other groups, but bidialectals also performed better than monolinguals.

> What is exciting and encouraging about our findings is that we were able to replicate the advantages of bilingualism in children who speak two varieties of the same language. [...] Systematically switching between any two forms of language, even quite similar ones, seems

29 Reported in Bazilchuk 2015

30 Antoniou et al 2016

> to provide the mind with the extra stimulation that leads to higher cognitive performance.[31]

The investigators related the findings specifically to the linguistics of Scotland.

> To date, bi-dialectalism can be found in Lowland Scotland (in speakers of Scots and Standard Scottish English), in parts of Northern Ireland and elsewhere. However, the criteria for classifying two varieties as dialects rather than independent languages are not strictly objective and it could be debated whether these are cases of bilingualism instead.[32]

We can already see from a cognitive perspective there is a blurring between 'dialect' and 'language'. Back in Scotland, scientists at Abertay University found that the brain treats language and 'dialects' in much the same way. Dundonians who used Dundee Scots were asked to complete a *dialect-switching task*, timing how long participants took to change between dialects. Parallel research was undertaken with native German speakers who could speak a local German dialect. The results demonstrated that 'bidialectals' displayed the same cognitive pattern as bilinguals, suggesting that different dialects or close language varieties were stored in the brain in similar ways as formally differentiated languages. According to the lead researcher, most studies would classify people who spoke both languages as 'monolingual' since language background surveys seldom inquired about dialect usage; 'Yet the results of our study show that some monolinguals and bilinguals are cognitively not that different'.[33]

> Speakers of Scots and Standard Scottish English also do a lot of switching, like bilinguals. They have to 'monitor continuously who can or cannot be addressed in Scots', and must choose the right pronunciations and vocabulary, and inhibit the 'competing' variants – theoretically, their mental representations of 'hoose' and 'house' are both activated in their brains, and one or the other will be inhibited at any one time […] So it's reasonable to ask if switching between dialects might be anything like switching between languages.[34]

31 Reported in Woollaston 2016

32 University of Cambridge 2016

33 *Neuroscience News* 2017

34 Erard 2016

The conclusion is that 'our brains don't care' whether Scots is arbitrarily classed as a language as a dialect.

Scots and self-esteem

The idea that bilingualism can enhance core brain function is still being debated, but the Nynorsk research suggested another factor that may also enhance performance – improved self-esteem. Learning and using Nynorsk may give its speakers a certain academic pride in their mastery of the dialect, raising confidence that in turn could translate into better general test scores. If true, the impact of teaching Scots formally in Scotland could be significant, and observers of Scottish education often make quite similar points.

> [A]t a national level the child's language is a continuation of that language through which for centuries people living in Scotland have expressed their awareness of their own individuality and their sense of inhabiting this place, Scotland. At a personal level it is the child's own language through which he carries on the business of living in a community and must be worthy of respect.[35]

> It is hardly surprising that many Scots children in turn reject an education system which is seen to value only 'posh' English.[36]

> Apart from the suppression of the child's natural voice and any subsequent loss of expression, another barrier emerges when the language of the school is different from the home. For some pupils the sense of failure beds in early if they feel their language and possibly culture are not acceptable in school.[37]

> What is the impact on self-belief when we criticise the Scots language o young Scots speakers? [...] dinnae be shocked when, in an English-speakin education environment, weans fae Scots-speakin backgroonds hae lower attainment than weans fae English-speakin backgroonds.[38]

> More teachers than ever are committed to the view that Scots plays a crucial role for many pupils in raising levels of attainment and

35 Scottish Consultative Committee on the Curriculum 1980, quoted in Kay 1993:25

36 Miller 1998

37 Niven and Jackson eds 1998:61

38 Fitt 2016c

> confidence, improving behaviour and literacy skills and supporting social inclusion and Scottish identity.[39]

To achieve the kind of educational self-esteem claimed for Nynorsk, the pedagogical role of Scots would have to be both recognised and formalised. Nearly a quarter of a century ago Lo Bianco's 1998 R*eview of Scottish Culture in the Curriculum*, recommended that, starting with the dialects spoken in their local area, students should 'investigate, use and enjoy the diversity of Scots speech and writing'. The author, while acknowledging the educational importance of standard English, believed that especially for children born into Scots-speaking families and communities, a major aim of their primary school education should be to help them become, 'literate as well as orate in both languages as a platform for all of their subsequent language learning'.[40] This seems to imply Scots being taught and used as a minority language.

The role of Scots to help students' self-esteem and engagement is at last beginning to be acknowledged officially. The *3–18 Literacy and English Review* published by Education Scotland published in 2015 explains why.

> Learning Scots can often improve learners' engagement in learning and their development of wider literacy skills. Through Scots, learners can explore language in more depth, making connections and comparisons with the linguistic structures and vocabularies of other languages. Scots as a context for learning can also provide an engaging platform for children and young people to explore language, register and audience. It can encourage reluctant readers and writers to become involved as texts in Scots can capture the imagination and speak to them in a familiar voice.[41]

Back on the curriculum

As the quote above suggests, support for Scots in education is now stronger than ever, and occasionally hints at a minority language approach. Consider the extract below from a 2016 official briefing document for teachers.

> Many learners bring Scots language to the classroom. When Scots is presented as a valid medium for communication in educational

39 Scottish Government 2010a:11

40 Lo Bianco 2001

41 Education Scotland 2015a

> settings, practitioners may discover that their learners already have a wealth of knowledge about the language. Many pupils can already speak Scots. There is evidence from across the country that developing the place of Scots in learning settings can motivate those who are less engaged, and that many learners can become effective contributors.[42]

This attitudinal change was the result of a continuing cultural struggle at the very heart of Scottish education. The main driver was the Curriculum for Excellence (CfE), since 2005 the Scottish Government's official guidelines for the education of learners with ages 3–18. Behind that, though, was a political determination to address a Scottish cultural deficit in education. Scots is mentioned throughout the CfE documentation and the guidance produced by Education Scotland (ES) who administer it. For example, the 2015 CfE *Literacy and English: principles and practice* includes the following statement.

> The languages, dialects and literature of Scotland provide a rich resource for children and young people to learn about Scotland's culture, identity and language. Through engaging with a wide range of texts they will develop an appreciation of Scotland's vibrant literary and linguistic heritage and its indigenous languages and dialects. This principle suffuses the experiences and outcomes and it is expected that practitioners will build upon the diversity of language represented within the communities of Scotland, valuing the languages which children and young people bring to school.[43]

Hall noted: 'It is unfortunate that the writers of this document did not go as far as to identify the "languages" of Scotland as English, Scots and Gaelic'.[44] He felt the inclusion of the word 'dialect' with all its connotations muddies the waters.

> If Scots can be considered a 'language' with parity to English or Gaelic, it is much more likely to be taken seriously; even to refer to it as 'language', if not as "a language", helps to raise the status of Scots.

John Hodgart, a former English teacher, felt that, in any case, the lack of obligation (and resourcing) of 'such braw words' blunted their impact and

42 Education Scotland 2016a:4

43 Education Scotland 2015b:4

44 Hall 2019a:3.3

'faur owre many excellent recommendations have either yet to be implementit or hae buin ignored aw thegither'.[45] That said, the *Scots Language Policy* in 2015 and *3–18 Literacy and English Review* was considered significant in that it 'provided early evidence of the extent to which Scots was featuring in the Literacy and English curriculum', but also 'its impact on learners' experiences and achievements'.[46] This led to a ground-breaking second report published a few years later, as described below.

'A way with words is a wonderful thing'

In 2017 Liz Niven produced a dossier on the still patchy state of Scots in education to Mercator, a leading European research centre on multilingualism and language learning.[47] The Scots Language Centre (SLC) updated and expanded some of her findings in 2021, providing a valuable snapshot of the state (and status) of Scots in schools today.[48]

Starting with pre-school provision, Niven wrote that there was no Scots language equivalent of the Gaelic nurseries now being promoted throughout Scotland. Scots will undoubtedly be used by some nursery staff, but there is no statutory guidance. She was concerned that the Scottish Government's initiative to improve early learning provision for three- and four-year-olds could put more pressure on the Scots language. Without Scots speakers in the nurseries and Scots learning resources such as stories, songs and nursery rhymes readily available, there was a real risk that 'the anglicisation of children's speech starts at an even earlier age than previously'. SLC added, though, that Scots materials were now available via, for example, the Scottish Book Trust's Bookbug initiative. The lack of parental pressure to increase Scots early years provision, compared again with Gaelic, is conspicuous. Niven's explanation of parental indifference reminds us of the persistence of those discredited models of interference and deficit that were never corrected during that generation's own time at school.

> [M]any families wish to encourage adequate English proficiency in their offspring, presuming that their broad Scots is not compatible with this aim. This opinion still exists because young parents continue to believe that their own school experience, wherein they were taught not to value Scots, is correct. Many parents view Scots as a hindrance

45 Hodgart 2016

46 Education Scotland 2017

47 Niven 2017

48 Scots Language Centre 2021a

> to their children's future educational and vocational aims even though the families continue to speak it fluently.

When Scots-speaking bairns reach primary education, they will find their language is almost never used as a language of instruction, unless the teacher happens to speak it, and is rarely treated as a study topic outside the traditional celebrations of Burns Nicht and St Andrews Day. ES's 2015 *3–18 Literacy and English Review* quoted above suggests the 'next step' beyond one-off events could be 'to plan opportunities for children and young people to use Scots language, and Scots and Scottish texts' and provides a list of practical ideas, including to:

- Audit current practice and provision for Scots language and text
- Create a coherent progression of skills plan for Scots language
- Develop a specific Scots language and literature policy.

SLC added that Scots may be taught as part of interdisciplinary learning, ie 'as part of work on Scottish culture, music or geography, or as part of literacy work', but recognised 'the provision of languages that a school teaches is not dictated by national policy and is a matter for schools and local authorities to decide'. Although there are now many examples of good practice, especially from the primary sector described in the ES document and elsewhere, Niven noted that the presence of Scots varied greatly across the system, 'with interested individuals teaching pupils about Scots (though not necessarily in Scots), and non-interested teachers omitting it almost entirely from the curriculum'.

Niven uncovered a climate in secondary education still hostile to Scots.

> Scots is rarely the language of instruction and if the teacher is Scottish then instruction may occur somewhere on the Scottish-English continuum. Scots-language teaching is mainly, but no longer exclusively, subsumed into the English departments of Scottish secondary schools. There is no discrete department for Scots, and it is not taught as a language.

She added that although Scots may sometimes be heard in the classroom, the practical steps suggested by the *3–18 Literacy and English Review* are largely ignored and, 'generally the use of Scots by pupils is not discussed or even given consideration as an area of importance'.

At secondary school, if the Scots language is studied at all, it is mostly treated as a heritage topic through the medium of literature and as part of the Literacy and English curriculum. The study of Scottish literature, ie a Scottish writer or text from an approved list, has been a compulsory part of the National 5 and Higher English syllabus since 2014–15, though the texts do not have to be written in Scots. Literature is not the only route, though. Scots can also be delivered through courses leading to the Scottish Qualifications Authority's Scottish Studies and Scots Language Awards. Scottish Studies was launched in 2013 to provide an opportunity for learners to develop their knowledge and understanding of Scotland, its people, languages (including Scots and Gaelic), society, culture, natural environment and heritage, and to make connections across the curriculum.[49] Novelist James Robertson observed at the time, 'the opposition in some quarters of the education sector to any specific Scottish Studies has been quite strong'[50], with one Labour MSP even dismissing the whole notion of Scots being used in Scottish schools as 'brainwashing'.[51]

The SQA Scots Language Award, initiated in 2014[52], described by John Hodgart as 'a truly historic step for the Scots language'[53], gives learners the opportunity to study the history and development of the Scots language. It is intended to help them develop their ability to understand, and communicate in Scots, which involves listening to or reading texts in Scots, and creating and producing written or oral communications in Scots. It is still only offered by a few schools. Hodgart provided an explanation. Although the curriculum is accessible for any moderately competent Scots speaker,

> Yet again this depends on an haein an interestit English dept / teacher (tho it could be duin in ither subjects) an I wid guess that no owre mony are confident aboot teachin Scottish literature written in Scots, never mind qualified tae teach the Scots language itsel.

He also adds a note of caution about the standing of the qualification.

> However, as wi the Scottish Studies Award, whit is on offer here is jist an optional internally assessed award, no a national exam course, so the doots owre status an value crop up again. Yet it is a furst step in the richt direction an mibbie a national exam course is somethin that

49 Scottish Qualifications Authority 2013
50 Denholm 2014
51 BBC News Services 2011
52 Scottish Qualifications Authority 2014
53 Hodgart 2016

will eventually come, tho again we'll hae tae fecht for it, an fecht for it gey hard.

Students studying National 5 or Higher English, both externally assessed by examination, may also choose to study a Scottish text written in Scots. The choice of text is left to the discretion of schools and local authorities. Learners who complete these qualifications must additionally submit a written portfolio which can be in either English or Scots.

Thanks to these initiatives, there is now a sense that Scots in education may have turned a corner in recognition and acceptance, if not yet in provision on the ground. This cautious optimism is corroborated by a quite remarkable follow-up report to the 2015 *3–18 Literacy and English Review*. The 2017 report, *Scots Language in Curriculum for Excellence*, published by Education Scotland, identified good practice in using Scots in schools as part of CfE. It emphasised the role Scots can play in developing literacy skills, encouraging learner engagement, and increasing confidence and self-esteem.[54] A wide range of activities were described in selected primary and secondary schools; Scots used in group discussion, analysis of speakers' use of Scots, working with Scots in texts and some translation and creative writing. Teachers spoke to the class mostly in Scottish Standard English, using only occasional Scots phrases, but the report noted that a small number of teachers spoke Scots to the class. In these cases, most children and young people responded in Scots, 'demonstrating their understanding of the teacher's use of Scots and their own proficiency in using the language'. Frequent use of Scots words helped learners increase their vocabulary and confidence in the language. They also believed it raised the status of the language, encouraged them to use it themselves and generally improved relationships in the classroom 'as a result of learners feeling their language was valued'. Back in 1991 Janet Menzies, working with young speakers of Glasgow Scots, had found just a simple introduction to 'the facts relating to the Scots language' had a substantial impact on linguistic self-confidence. A brief discussion had been 'sufficient to cure the habit of equating all non-standard variables with slang'. Instead the students began to describe those words as 'my dialect' or 'the Scots language'.[55]

What caught the eye of the press in the 2017 report, though, was not enhanced self-confidence in the language itself, but how studying Scots positively impacted on other areas. Scots seemed to be able to help learners develop the skills required for success in national qualifications in English.

54 Education Scotland 2017

55 Menzies 1991

Most teachers agreed that the use of Scots could help to engage reluctant learners and the use of Scots 'gave some lower-attaining children the confidence to take on leadership roles for the first time'.[56] Teachers in one secondary school felt that allowing pupils to use Scots 'removed the barriers to learning experiences for some and created opportunities for them to access the curriculum'. The report found that the use of Scots resulted in improvements in the writing skills, motivation and behaviour of some lower-attaining pupils.

> There is clear evidence to confirm the educational benefits of including Scots in Curriculum for Excellence. Scots can support children and young people to develop a range of important skills in literacy, including advanced reading and writing skills required for success in national qualifications. Scots as part of Curriculum for Excellence can support young people in developing their confidence and a sense of their own identity. It can help to engage learners whose mither tongue is Scots by making them feel more valued and included, and therefore more motivated to take part in lessons, to lead learning, and to achieve more highly.

An effusive editorial in *The Herald* inspired by the report is worth reproducing in full for its surprising public praise for an oft-maligned language.

> A way with words is a wonderful thing. It allows for confident expression and easy interacting with one's peers. Alas, for years, if the words were Scots, they were frowned upon and the speaker ridiculed. Now it transpires children speaking Scots at school are not only happier and more inclined to get involved, but they improve their chances of attaining English qualifications.
>
> Education Scotland found evidence that including Scots in the curriculum increases the confidence of reluctant learners and encourages them to take leading roles. Speaking the leid persuaded them to participate in class discussions and led them to perform well in English.
>
> From what we already know of the benefits of bilingual education, this comes as no surprise. Studies have shown high levels of attainment in Gaelic-speaking schools. Whether one sees Scots as a variant of English or a distinct language, it certainly has a different way with words. That is valuable for making comparisons, detecting

56 Denholm 2017

> connotations and widening rhythm and cadence.
>
> Shunning Scots was to shut the doors on a child's perception and make them feel they were doing wrong. Thankfully, such attitudes no longer prevail. Today, the rights and wrongs of language concern pronunciation, not discrimination. That speaking Scots improves English is braw, just as a good command of English makes for better blethering in Scots.[57]

Scots after school: 'Ah've goat ma speech back'

Beyond compulsory education, Niven found that Scots was not taught as a general subject in any Further Education colleges, although there is limited Scots training and options in performance studies, namely acting and traditional music. Otherwise, teachers mostly speak Scottish Standard English in classes using only occasional Scots phrases, though some will certainly be native Scots speakers. There is still no official policy on the use of Scots in FE. Adult education is in much the same position. In 2010 the Scottish Government launched a strategy for adult literacies: *Strategic Guidance for Adult Literacies in Scotland 2020* (*ALIS* 2020).[58] The vision of *ALIS 2020* was for every citizen in Scotland

> [T]o have the literacies capabilities necessary to bridge the poverty gap, to understand and shape the world they live in, and to enjoy the rich knowledge and benefits that being able to read, write and use numbers can bring.

Scots was not even mentioned. Although for many adult learners Scots will very likely infuse the language of their home and community, literacies provision is usually delivered in standard (Scottish) English, sometimes by tutors with limited knowledge of Scots. As Lyn Tett commented, 'if this issue is not addressed then oral traditions and speech patterns are presented as somehow separate from literacy'.[59] When no connection is made between spoken Scots and written English, 'negative views about language are internalised, and this has consequences for how people see themselves and thus functions to undermine their own self-esteem'. She quotes one participant, 'I don't like the way I speak'. Thus, despite promoting a 'learner-centred

57 *The Herald* 2017

58 Scottish Government 2010b

59 Tett 2000:125

approach', the discourse implicitly marginalises community literacies.[60]

Literacy is a complex issue, as entrance to the workplace usually needs skills in both oral and written (Scottish) English.[61] Although fluency in a standard form of spoken and written English is a key component of communication skills, Tett argues that it should not be the exclusive goal of literacy education. Marginalising or undervaluing existing oral skills (and these are real skills, too) is poor pedagogy and practice. Janice Macfarlane believed 'adult literacies practitioners adhering to Scotland's social practice model ought to be acknowledging and working with the learners' language'. She suggested a version of critical literacy that validates the learners' own language and combats the sense of stigma that makes some Scots feel inferior about how they speak. Learners can feel empowered hearing tutors speak Scots in class and feel the language they use is validated. Macfarlane quoted one learner: 'Ah've goat ma speech back'. The Scots language becomes a talking point and 'can help learners from other countries to integrate and communicate'.

Tett proposed a wider interpretation of critical literacy.

> [T]he social practices of institutions, and the language and literacy they reinforce, have to be made visible to show that they represent a selection from a wider range of possibilities – none of which are neutral. These practices then become a critical resource for learning and literacy.

Attractive as this might sound in theory, Macfarlane's 2011 survey of Scottish practitioners found 'much ambivalence' around the role of Scots in adult literacies. Most viewed it positively, but others were more hostile, claiming it was 'pointless, unhelpful, unacceptable in the workplace'. Macfarlane understood that championing Scots may conflict with demands to prioritise learning for employability but nevertheless felt these tutors were 'arguably turning their backs on the biggest resource learners bring to class – their own tongue'.

Possibly in recognition of these pragmatic and attitudinal constraints, in reviewing adult literacy policies in 2016, Education Scotland added Scotland's native languages almost as a postscript. Scots (and Gaelic) speakers may 'struggle to read the languages and to write them with confidence' due to the fact 'they have never had the opportunity to learn spelling and grammar

60 Macfarlane 2012

61 Eg Eustace 2012

rules'.[62] It is no doubt true that 'many of these people would welcome the chance to improve their literacy, rather than their linguistic skills', but this seems to be regarded as a separate topic and not fully integrated in the way Tett and Macfarlane both recommend.

While Scots and Gaelic can often be considered together, in terms of skills this is less than helpful as they present very different literacy challenges. The Education Scotland statement that learning, teaching and assessment of Scots or Gaelic literacy 'would not differ in terms of teaching methods and approaches from those used in English literacy' is neither accurate nor useful. Nonetheless, Education Scotland here seems to align with Tett and Macfarlane in saying that tutors need to become skilled and literate in Scots with access to high quality, adult-appropriate resources. Practitioner negativity may mask a perceived lack of personal proficiency and confidence. Macfarlane stressed the importance of getting this balance right as she felt Scots speakers were still being excluded:

> As long as people remain voiceless with their experience interpreted on their behalf by others, then their own meanings are rendered illegitimate and disqualified.

Scotland's higher education has long been entirely anglicised. That said, it is harder to justify our universities' historic disinterest in the Scots language and Lowland culture that surrounds them. There is still no Scots equivalent of Gaelic Studies, with the language and its culture as a cohesive focus of study and research. Aberdeen University's Elphinstone Institute provides a model of what could be achieved in this field. The institute researches the vernacular culture of the North-East and North of Scotland and recently launched a new credit-bearing undergraduate module, *Doric and Scots Language: Introduction to North East Scots*. As the 2021 SLC report notes, provision elsewhere is more fragmented.

> Scots texts and linguistics continue to be taught as part of the undergraduate and postgraduate Language & Linguistics, English literature, Scottish Literature, Ethnographic and History programmes of Scotland's universities.

The University of the Highlands and Islands also offers modules covering minority languages, including Scots, with particular focus on the Orkney and Shetland dialects.

62 Education Scotland 2016b

The Open University in Scotland released their two-part *Scots Language and Culture* course in 2019, written for a broad audience 'ranging from Scots speakers to people who want to find out about and learn some Scots, as well as teachers and other educators'. The Higher Education level course represents an exceptional collection of contemporary thought about Scots language and its cultural context. Even if it is not credit bearing and does not 'teach' much of the language itself, the joint OU/Education Scotland initiative proves the rich academic potential of this still mostly untaught 'lost curriculum'.

Teacher training is also part of the Scottish HE system and delivered through eight Teacher Education Institutions, the largest being at the University of Strathclyde. Back in 1924 William Grant outlined what was required to maintain Scots as a working language in our schools.

> The Education Department and the Authorities must take measures to ensure that every student who was to be accepted an elementary teacher, or a teacher English in a secondary school, had an adequate knowledge of Scottish literature, ancient and modern; an adequate knowledge the history of our language, of its grammar and modern variations; and an adequate knowledge the sounds in Standard English and Scottish.[63]

Sadly, despite a century of lobbying, multiple report recommendations and a census report nearly a decade ago suggesting a third of bairns might be bilingual, there is still no requirement for student teachers to study the Scots language. Nonetheless, Scots is slowly becoming integrated into teacher training at degree level via the Elphinstone Institute and lectures by Education Scotland's Scots Language Co-ordinator. Teachers with an interest in Scots, or inspired by the language awards, can also focus on the language as part of dissertation studies. At the time of writing, The Open University in Scotland is also piloting a teacher CPD course to develop skills in the delivery of the SQA awards.

Even if formal provision is still disappointingly disjointed, there is now an impressive array of materials available for the informal study and development of Scots. Remembering Max Weinreich's famous adage, 'A language is a dialect with an army and navy', it may be argued that Scots has survived over the years as a coherent linguistic variety thanks in large part to its own irregular army of enthusiasts, writers, researchers and teachers. The Scottish government has begun to fund initiatives over the last decade,

63 *Aberdeen Press and Journal* 1924a

but the support is still minimal. The whole strategy still has the sense of a fragmented linguistic insurgency rather than a cohesive operation, to stretch Weinreich's 'army and navy' metaphor a little further.

Such initiatives include The Scots Language Centre and Creative Scotland's support for the language through arts and cultural projects, including the Scots Scriever residency, The Scots Language Awards, Scots Radio, the Doric Board grants and various cultural events and smaller projects. The government-funded *Dictionaries of the Scots Language* has a pivotal role in the formalisation of Scots. Itchy Coo, Scotland's only dedicated Scots publisher, has produced a wide catalogue of original and translated titles. Scots Hoose provides online resources for Scots speaking children and young people. The Scottish Book Trust more broadly promotes children's literacy and runs an annual Scots language publication grant 'to increase the incidence and quantity of Scots language publications'. The Scots Language Society/Scots Leid Associe was formed in 1973 to promote and preserve the use of Scots in all forms and provides an independent voice. The main educational activities of the Society include the publication of the *Lallans* magazine, a writing competition and an annual collogue. Since its establishment in 2019 The Doric Board is becoming an influential focus for support of Scots' north-east dialect and culture. Scots in Northern Ireland has a completely different (and far less miserly) funding arrangement as will be outlined in the next chapter.

Scots and accessibility: a double discrimination?

Gaelic is not the only language now protected by legislation in Scotland. The British Sign Language (Scotland) Act 2015, passed a decade after the Gaelic Language (Scotland) Act, formally recognised the status of BSL in Scotland, making Scotland the first nation in the UK to do so. The main motivation was to ensure that the Scottish BSL community, numbering around 12,500 individuals, had equitable access to information and services. However, according to Maartje De Meulder,[64] the debate over the Act was more nuanced. BSL users were already protected to some level under existing disability discrimination legislation, primarily the Equality Act 2010, requiring employers and service providers to make reasonable adjustments. The new Act, however, reframed BSL as a minority language, so 'the main motives for the Act were a desire to put BSL on a similar footing with Gaelic'. She quotes a 2009 Scottish Government paper explaining the reasons.

64 De Meulder 2017

> Deaf BSL users consider themselves a distinct language group and not disabled. They have a unique culture, history and life experience as a language minority and feel that action to improve their inclusion in society should be based on exactly the same language approach to other groups, such as speakers of Gaelic or Welsh.

Once the Act had been passed, Scottish Ministers published a BSL National Plan and, as with the Gaelic Act, public authorities must publish their own plans. While BSL and Scots are quite different, the Scottish legislature has recently progressed and passed complex and, in some respects, contentious legislation to recognise a minority language other than Gaelic.

In this context, another facet of the 2010 Equality Act and accessibility legislation should have a more direct influence on Scots in education. Public sector organisations in Scotland now have a legal obligation to make their online information accessible to everyone, including individuals with disabilities. In this context, accessibility refers to providing online resources 'perceivable, operable, understandable, and robust', particularly for people with low vision or hearing. The regulations' impact on educational services is still being determined, but one typical accessibility test is whether content is compatible with a screen reader. This is a type of assistive technology that enables users to hear online texts read out to them by the computer. Text-to-speech is invaluable for blind or partially sighted users, but it can also help dyslexic learners and others. Automatic subtitling is the converse process and uses speech-to-text technology. Real-time transcriptions are now offered in mainstream video communication tools such as Zoom and Microsoft Teams. Both methods rely entirely on a standardised version of the language. As we consider the pros and cons of standardising Scots later, bear in mind that if Scots remains unstandardised, Scots texts can never be made inclusive in this way, violating at least a moral, if not a legal, duty to provide equal access. At the end of the book, we will look at broader legal rights to prevent discrimination against Scots speakers, but accessibility is one area where a response may be required sooner rather than later.

The future of Scots in education?

At the end of the Education section of the OU *Scots Language and Culture* course, Hall concludes on a positive note.

> [I]t can be said that Scots language has survived into the twenty first century with no official support, and its growing presence in

> modern Scottish classrooms, and the backing it is now enjoying from the Scottish Government and Education Scotland is cause for both wonder and celebration.

The change in tone over the last decade has indeed been astonishing, remembering that, prior to devolution, Scots not only suffered 'no official support' but was still actively suppressed in schools, with a history of being 'ejected with violence'.[65] The route back into the curriculum has been largely though literature and cultural heritage, perhaps seen as the line of least resistance. It is a step forward, undoubtedly, but Millar is concerned that narrow heritage pigeonholing is almost inevitably backward-looking and so students 'may even consider Scots to be irrelevant in the modern age'.[66]

Such risks are compounded by the fact, in Hall's words, that:

> [T]he young people of the twenty first century are subject to a greater range of linguistic influence than ever before. The language of their community or family vies with the language being used by their peers across the world, listenable via the internet. Other media also play a role.

Alan Gillespie, a teacher of English, made a bleak assessment in the *Times Educational Supplement* (*TES*) recently.

> I've taught in various rural and inner-city schools, both in the Highlands and the Central Belt, and have yet to work with a group of children who speak confidently or fluently in Scots, rather than standard English, in their daily lives. More often, their linguistic influences come from America or online trends. When they do use Scots, it is often intended to be comedic, banter, something of a parody; not to be taken seriously.[67]

Gillespie is generally sympathetic to Scots but here he expresses a widely held belief that the Scots element of Scottish vernacular has eroded as to be possibly unsalvageable. While the fatalistic 'discourse of death' trope has been around for at least a century, it is true that basic knowledge of Scots is now weak in many areas of the country. A naturalised acceptance of a trajectory of decline, though, only prolongs the social injustice of too many Scots-speaking bairns

65 *Aberdeen Press and Journal* 1924a

66 Millar 2008:8

67 Gillespie 2022

still being denied access to their own linguistic heritage. The irony is that, as we saw earlier, with a relatively light-touch intervention, ingrained negative attitudes may be reversed, linguistic awareness and acceptance heightened, and language abilities strengthened.

We shall look at various alternatives to improve the use of Scots in education in Chapter Seven. These range from maximalist viewpoints such as Scots Medium Education (SME) through Scots-as-a-subject to more limited tweaks and upgrades to present approaches. However, only with the cooperation of the whole Scottish society, particularly funders, teachers, parents and students, can any gains be achieved. One of Gaelic Medium Education's (GME) successes is its purposeful positioning of Gaelic as a 'public good' for the whole nation. As the survival of Gaelic is seen by most of the electorate nowadays as a worthwhile aim that enhances Scottish society and culture, it attracts high levels of support and funding. Scots is still a long way from that position, even though poll after poll has shown widespread support for the language, even among non-speakers. Progress is hampered, however, by several unresolved stushies or controversies that will have to be faced and addressed before Scots can enjoy the same degree of public and governmental support as Gaelic. These are the issues we will explore in the next chapter before moving on to possible educational and community initiatives to save the Scots language.

CHAPTER SIX

Stushies

We need to talk about Scots

RARELY DISCUSSED SERIOUSLY outwith education, most Scottish governmental legislation and guidelines routinely overlook Scots. The limited academic interest in Scottish minority language issues tends to focus on Gaelic, with Scots, it seems, at best a 'confounding factor in relation to the national status of Gaelic'.[1] When the Gaelic Language (Scotland) Act was passed in 2005, negligible public discussion was heard about the equity of passing legislation for one Scottish minority language but not the other. By the time the third Gaelic Plan was debated in 2018, the huge numbers of Scots speakers had been known for five years. The notion that initiatives to support Scots are unrelated to Gaelic legislation is an ideology so deeply entrenched it seems just common sense. This explains why no one bothers to justify the startling disparities in the support of Scotland's two minority languages over several ECRML submissions, the most recent in 2021. The Scottish civil servants who produced the reports, and the politicians who signed them off, seemed to be unaware that such a glaring inequity was even worthy of an explanation.

Language policy expert Johann Unger used the powerful method of critical discourse analysis (CDA), mentioned earlier, to try to better understand how the way we talk about the Scots language influences how we approach it. In his 2013 book *The discursive construction of the Scots language*, Unger wrote, 'discourse analysis is crucial to understanding how these language attitudes, beliefs and ideologies are developed, maintained and possibly changed'.[2] He stated his own position; 'I regard the low status of Scots as partly constitutive of a social wrong, and the plight of its speakers a struggle against hegemony'. Unger examined Scottish Executive education policies and language strategies,

1 McLeod 2019:148

2 Unger 2013:155

transcripts of debates and official websites during the early years of devolution. He traced how the concept of Scots was constructed at the time, and what impact this had on everyday attitudes as revealed through his focus groups. Unger discovered that although strategies often stated that Scots was 'a language', they were undermined by 'under-specification and vagueness of definition and reference'. In what he called 'the repressive climate towards Scots before the late 1990s', clear official statements on the status of the Scots were avoided. Vagueness allowed 'many potential interpretations of what Scots should be defined as, and in turn also of what constitutes Scots'. By this he meant 'whether a given utterance might be regarded as Scots or not'. In his book and an accompanying paper pointedly titled 'Legitimating Inaction', Unger criticised the reimagining of Scots as part of cultural heritage rather than as a minority language. The official discourse was 'unhelpful or potentially even damaging in the process of changing public attitude'.[3] Heritage-based approaches 'obscure issues that are more important to the *contemporary* use [author's italics] and even survival of the language'. He defined contemporary use as, 'the use of Scots as a functional communicative medium for living Scottish people' and the protection of Scots-speakers from, 'discrimination in schools, in the job market and in other areas of public life'. Here Unger made the distinction between what I call *normalisation*, that is treating Scots as a normal minority language, and *heritisation*, its reformulation as a politically neutered cultural resource. Unger implied that the narrow heritage-bound framing had blocked politically challenging initiatives such as status building, real minority language revitalisation and language rights.

The ambiguity and heritage focus of official narratives trickle down to attitudes among the Scots artistic and speaker communities. Tammas Clark's *A Scots Manifesto* published on the blog site *Bella Caledonia* at the end of 2016 (the 'Year of Scots') provided a useful snapshot of debates among Scots authors and activists at that time. Occurring at a critical juncture in the cautious re-emergence of the Scots language question as a legitimate political concern, his manifesto provided a valuable starting point to delve further into some of the stushies still surrounding the language.

Clark felt attempts to 'fix' Scots risk isolating the language from its speakers: 'ah'm no wantin ma language stuck in a museum, no while ah'm still uisin it'. Thus he saw any politicisation as a threat.

> [G]in we leave the meanin o Scots in the weaponisin hauns o the politeecians, the leid is liable tae become naething mair than a Scout badge.

---

3 Unger 2010

His manifesto contained five declarations.

1. Scots is a language.
2. Gin Scots is a language, it's the language that we're speakin nou.
3. Dialects first. Scots leid second.
4. Scots belongs tae naebody.
5. Scots belongs tae aabody.

The first declaration is the Prime Directive of any Scots language advocate, but the author then seemed to challenge the idea of Scots' languageness. He proposed reasonably that, 'the meisure o its wirth is no in hou mony linguists or politeecians concur that it's a leid' but in how it is used. However, he added, 'ower mony o the things Scots is used for are aboot pittin doon fowk wha dinnae scrieve Scots accordin tae the rules, which is tae say everybody wha wis never taucht it formally, which is tae say everybody. An that's nae guid'. Clark here reflected both the familiar anti-standards rhetoric among some Scots writers such as Leonard, McIlvanney and Kelman, but also the broader postmodernist trend in academic language studies against 'prescriptivism', the making and following of language rules. As we saw earlier, the assumption that said rules would be enforced by some sort of Scots language police remains a disconcertingly common trope. The second declaration captured the modern ideology that spoken language should always be privileged over written forms.

> Fae here on in, Scots is whit happens when A) Somebody self-identifies as a speaker o Scots, an B) They open their yap. It's no perfect, but ken whit, at least it'll gie us a language that stems fae people, no fae dictionaries.

There are a few recurrent opinions embedded here that we will return to later: an anything-goes approach to Scots, language as a 'performance', that spoken and written language are unconnected, that spoken language is privileged, dictionaries are *ipso facto* bad, and that irregularity should be celebrated.

In recent Scots language activism, the third proclamation regarding dialects has become something of an orthodoxy. It implies that regional dialects, such as the Doric, Border Scots and urban dialects should take precedence over the notion of a cohesive national tongue. Nobody would argue that the language has been kept alive in regional spoken varieties since the 'official' shift to English centuries ago.

So whit kept it alive fae then tae nou? Naethin but the spoken dialects

> o the wirkin classes. Borders Scots, Glesga Scots, Dundonian an Doric an Orkney Scots; these were the life-support machines that saved the tongue fae oblivion. These are the reasons wiv a language left tae talk aboot.

In my view, though, the Scots literary legacy, and familiarity with it, played an equally key role in the language's survival. Moreover, I'll make the case later that dialects were only recently deemed distinct from 'Scots'. Clark concedes, though, that 'sae lang as oor dialects are mutually intelligible, which they are, ah ween we'll get alang juist fine'. He thus acknowledges the differences are just not that substantial. A focus on dialects was again presented in direct opposition to the notion of standardisation. Clark however did acknowledge, 'there micht be plenty o guid reasons tae devise a Standart Scots, an ah'm no arguin that there shouldnae be ane' but continued, 'there willnae be mony guid reasons for a speaker o an existin dialect tae learn the standard'. The implication here was that standardisation would apply to spoken as much as written forms, something that standardisers invariably reject.

The last two declarations – 'Scots belongs tae naebody' and 'Scots belongs tae aabody' – span a range of principles. The main one is that the historic and artistic anarchy of Scots should be celebrated. Scots is 'oot in the linguistic badlands unclaimed bi governments' so 'something guid micht come o fowk explorin the boondaries o Scots – artistically, ah mean, but in ither weys as well'. This unleashed creativity is preferable to the apparently tedious alternative, an 'English-like' fully functional Scots.

> Champions o the Scots leid are ayeweys ettlin efter weys tae posit Scots as nae mair nor less than a fully viable alternative tae English. That's fine, but it ayeweys winds up brandin Scots as a sort o piggyback product, an English Lite, or Ah Cannae Believe It's No English!

Towards the end Clark reiterates his attitude to prescriptivism.

> [I]f ye're the kind o chiel that likes things tae hae a bit mair structure tae them – ye can gan richt aheid an mak it happen. Naebody will stap ye. Sae lang as ye're no kiddin yersel (or onybody else) that whit ye're daein is in some wey prescriptive, ye can knock yersel oot.

Clark's 2016 manifesto was a passionate and reasoned position statement drawing on a range of wider issues and undercurrents at that time. We will start our deep dive by looking at the general political barriers to the development of Scots and from that progress to the conflicting ideologies of normalisation and heritisation that I suggest provide a backdrop to Clark's article.

Is Scots really over-politicised?

On the rare occasions an initiative around the Scots language goes public, unionist politicians, commentators and social media warriors routinely claim it is a 'nationalist plot'. Remembering Dani Garavelli's 2016 view that 'pupils are just pawns in an ideological war', some might assume that the Scots language question is already politically loaded. In her study of the post-devolution politics of Scots, published the same year as Clark's manifesto and Garavelli's comments, Ashley Douglas found the exact opposite.

> In the context of the increasingly fraught constitutional politics of modern Scotland, in particular the relationship between cultural identity and nationalism, Scots emerges as unwanted by either side of the independence debate: naebody's bairn.[4]

The politics of language cannot just be ignored, though. Even trivial issues like Gaelic signage can trigger surprisingly emotionalised responses. Why do people feel so strongly about language? We do not need to look far for an answer. On a social level, people are drawn to others with whom they can communicate easily. Language also determines who we are in that community, or who we wish to be. Sociolinguists Carmen Llamas and Dominic Watt argue that people's choice of languages and ways of speaking do not simply reflect who they are, but 'make them who they are'. Thus, 'our very sense of who we are, where we belong to and why, and how we relate to those around us, all have language at their centre'.[5] In his classic 1973 volume *Language and Nationalism*, linguistic rights pioneer Joshua Fishman believed communities generally regard language as 'the most undeniable indicator of uniqueness'[6] and, even more importantly, a contrastive device to distinguish your community from 'others'.

Language identity, not surprisingly, played a crucial role in the wave of cultural and political nationalism that swept through Europe in the 19th century. Even so, the idea of a community defined by a shared

4 Douglas 2016:41

5 Llamas and Watt 2010:9

6 Fishman 1973:53

language is quite recent, appearing to emerge only about the time of the French revolution of 1789. Up to that point, rulers had not placed much value on linguistic uniformity. That was to change with 19th century industrialisation, demanding mass literacy and a shared linguistic code. One language or variety of language became dominant in the community, usually the vernacular of the ruling elite. According to Marxist historian Eric Hobsbawm, 'linguistic nationalism', the promotion and development of national languages, was associated largely with the lower middle classes; teachers, shopkeepers, clerks and the like.[7] These community 'norm setters' used language to self-identify as middle-class and so consolidate their social position. In Scotland's case, by the late 19th century the bourgeoisie mostly spoke Scottish English, or at least were Scots-Scottish English bilinguals. They sought public status by performing the language of the powerful elites. The middle classes would then promote these appropriated standards to the working class and rural population though their dominance in education, politics and commerce. The spread of English in the British Isles led to the geographical marginalisation of indigenous Celtic languages to the north and west of the archipelago, the stigmatisation of Scots in Scotland and the rapid decline of non-standard varieties in England. Marginalisation was therefore not just geographical, but cultural and social. Standard English can be considered an instrument of colonisation; 'English is simply another way in which a particular community can be controlled and exploited'.[8] In 19th century emerging nation states, non-dominant groups were usually faced with a stark choice: assimilate with the dominant linguistic group or resist by developing their own national identity. Using or promoting any non-standard language or variety soon became regarded as an act of defiance.

> [A] fear of divided loyalties and identities – supposedly the result of unassimilated ethnic groups – has underlain the foundation of most nation-states.[9]

Unionism, an ideology that had originally accommodated extensive Scottish distinctiveness, soon mutated into British nationalism, with its strident demands for cultural and political homogeneity. The rise of autonomous Scottish political movements in the 20th century only intensified that trend. British nationalism continues to cast a long shadow over Scottish politics and its adherents regard any form of identity based on the Scots language with

7 Eg Hobsbawm 1990

8 Trousdale 2010:101

9 Romaine 2000:224

suspicion or even outright hostility. The Conservative Party especially consider themselves the main defender of British state power in Scotland, so 'remains wary of promoting anything which may, by asserting national distinctiveness in the present, lend itself to modern political nationalism'.[10] Before devolution the Tories were possibly a little more sympathetic to Scots as a living language, even using it in campaigning slogans, 'New Labour – Nae Britain', but those days are long gone. By 2000 the Conservatives voted with the other two unionist parties to exclude Scots from the Census and to reject a proposal for Scots language signage in the Parliament. Since devolution, Douglas observes the position of the Conservatives seems to have hardened.

> Scots is no longer promoted as a living national language, but rather relegated to the realms of heritage. To the extent that Scots is acknowledged in the present, meanwhile, it is as an informal register of English, or as a disparate collection of local dialects.

Scots is treated as dead, or dialectised beyond redemption, 'a collection of disjointed regional variants'. Douglas suggests here that dialectisation is itself an ideology as, 'the emphasis on disparate regional dialects serves to portray a fractured identity, as opposed to a single national language around which nationalism may rally'.

The Labour Party in Scotland is just as wary of any manifestations of Scottish identity, but their sidelining of Scots is more nuanced. The pre-devolution suppression of the 1998 draft *Scottish Consultative Council on the Curriculum* (SCCC) report that had advocated a more 'minority language' approach foreshadowed Labour's inaction when it led the first devolved Scottish Executive. Devolution had, after all, been designed to quash separatism so, in Douglas' words, 'Labour conscientiously avoided doing anything that might raise the profile of Scots'.[11] She explained:

> Scots is treated by the Labour party as located firmly in the past, a language of literature and heritage, but not a living language of modern-day Scotland, requiring of protection and promotion on that basis.

Douglas confirmed that the UK Government's ratification of the Charter in respect of Scots in 2001 was 'not called for' by the Labour Scottish Executive and the subsequent devolution of responsibility for its implementation to

---

10 Douglas 2016:12

11 Douglas 2016:16

Holyrood was greeted with little enthusiasm.[12] As a result, Scots was largely ignored, with no official policy, few initiatives and no measures to encourage its use. Reflecting on this period, Millar commented that, despite the odd positive reference to Scots as a language in Executive publications, the effect in policy and in practice – the true marker of commitment – is 'negligible', resulting in Scots being 'buried alive'.[13] Labour politicians also regularly adopt the same rhetoric as their Tory counterparts, claiming that Scots, if existing at all, is now a series of fragmented dialects. One Labour MSP, Frank McAveety, claimed in 2002 that although 'a variety of dialects and a variety of forms of Scots language are spoken, [...] I do not think that there is a commonality'.[14] Douglas also identifies the tendency of Labour to exploit multiculturalism to neuter Scots, 'shunning the favouring of indigenous minority cultures and promoting pluralism for all'.

The Scottish National Party, as might be expected, have had a longstanding commitment to support both Scots and Gaelic. In their 1997 manifesto the party even declared that Scots and Gaelic should have equal status with English, 'both legally and in broadcasting and the arts'. In 2003, a Languages Act was pledged to secure the status of Scots and Gaelic. Douglas sums up the SNP position at that time.

> It is clear that the SNP at this point demonstrates no reservations in identifying Scots as an 'indigenous' language, and as deserving of special treatment and recognition on that basis [...] the SNP during the early years of devolution were unanimous and unambiguous in their conception of Scots as a national language, made up of different dialects, both in the past and in the present.

In government from 2007, the SNP initiated a limited range of positive actions to support Scots. However, their previous commitment to equal legal status for the Scots language in the form of an Act had already been quietly dropped from their manifesto. 'Perhaps the SNP took greater account of the likely political and financial pressures of running a government?'.[15] As a result, progress remained patchy. No Scots Act was drafted, no legal status confirmed, no coordinating organisation equivalent to the Bòrd na Gàidhlig established, no properly funded community building initiatives started, resulting in no official visibility for Scots, even on signage in the

12 Douglas 2019:5.5

13 Millar 2018:18

14 Quoted in Douglas 2016:20

15 Douglas 2019:5.5

Scottish Parliament. Millar implies some of the procrastination may have been pragmatic as the world economic crisis from 2007 onwards led to 'a severe tightening of Scottish purse strings'. Thus, 'the amount of money and attention the government could give to Scots was limited'.[16] Douglas detected another theme mitigating against Scots in the following years and during the run-up to the 2014 referendum.

> [T]he party became increasingly anxious to disassociate itself from any trappings of a more ethnic or cultural nationalism – such as the promotion of an indigenous language – this passive indifference can be seen to give way to an active distancing from Scots.[17]

The 650-page White Paper, *Scotland's Future: Your Guide to an Independent Scotland*, that the Scottish Government published the year before the independence referendum covered Scots in few dozen words. No immediate change to the status of Scots was foreseen, only a Constitutional Convention which 'could consider the position of Scotland's languages within the permanent written constitution'. As both Douglas and Millar had implied, the release in 2013 of the Census data revealing there were 25 Scots speakers for every Gaelic speaker may have brought the SNP budget experts out in a cold sweat.

In 2014, the YES camp would campaign for independence almost entirely on civic and economic grounds, with cultural identity issues downplayed. Douglas describes the ensuing disappearance of Scots as a 'staggering reversal' in the SNP's commitment to the language.

> This striking shift in both tone and commitment towards the indigenous national language of Scots lays bare the extent of the SNP's anxiety to portray its nationalist cause as unequivocally and indisputably civic, with no favourable treatment of anything culturally or ethnically 'Scottish'.

The alarming rise of a nativist form of English nationalism south of the Border associated with Brexit campaign of 2016 may have exacerbated this trend towards ultra-civic Scottish nationalism as a contrastive position.

> [A]s the Unionist parties increased their hostility to Scots post-2011, viewed as a nationalist ploy, the SNP was in actual fact distancing

16 Millar 2018:210

17 Douglas 2016:35

itself from Scots, viewed as an impediment to the progress of its civic brand of nationalism.

Scots, of course, could not just be edited out of Scottish culture. After all, it has 1.5 million speakers. The SNP adopted a different strategy, covertly shifting from supporting Scots as a minority language to 'heritisation', downgrading the language to a politically neutered cultural resource. But before unpicking that, we should look at the minority language alternative, often known as *normalisation*.

What would normal look like?

The position of the SNP, at least until 2007, was to frame Scots as a normal minority language, potentially with equivalent rights to Gaelic and English. What might 'normality' mean in practice for Scots, given the complexity of the Scots language context? J Derrick McClure addressed this problem back in 1980 with his manifesto *Developing Scots as a National Language*. To him, 'the revival of Scots and its establishment as a national language' presented 'in no way an unrealistic aim', implying:

> Nothing less than the complete regeneration of the Scots language – a process which will involve clarifying and defining its status, establishing a popular awareness of the facts relating to its historical, social and literary background, freeing it from the social stigma which is presently attached to it, and extending its range of uses both in speech and writing.

McClure's manifesto was overtly ideological. Such a revival of the Scots language would 'give a focus to Scottish patriotism that will render it irresistible as a social and political force'.[18] Sociolinguist John Edwards remarked that in many societies linguistic pride and self-confidence 'can be resurgent when groups previously oppressed, discriminated against and thought to be inferior recover a broader social strength and assertion'.[19] McClure was of the same view.

> When a self-contained group within a state uses a language different from the governmental or official language, it is *ipso facto* making a gesture of independence, in that respect if in no other, from the ruling culture.

18 McClure 1980:40

19 Edwards 2009:96

As a consequence,

> [U]se of the Scots language is automatically an assertion of identity: and if we seek to enlarge the scope of the language and increase the extent of its use, we are thereby asserting some degree, and some kind, of Scottish independence.

Later he warned, though, 'we had better be prepared, too, for intense opposition from the forces of unionism'.

Language revival is often motivated by anti-colonialism or resistance to a dominant political power. McClure lamented that, 'In Scotland, such an association hardly exists in the popular mind'. Even in the wider independence movement:

> [P]robably very few Scottish nationalists (and by that I do not, of course, mean only card-carrying members of the SNP) would regard the notion of establishing Scots as an official language with anything but incredulity or even incomprehension.

What he proposed was a strikingly radical cultural re-evaluation.

> [T]he revival of Scots as a living and all-purpose language – as something more than a set of restricted and low-prestige dialects and an artificial learned language for poets – will come in the context of a total revival of Scottish national culture, or not at all.

He cautioned, though, 'such a revival will not come automatically with political independence'.

Catalonia is often given as an example and the common Catalan term for this ambitious type of revival is *normalisació*, hence 'normalisation'.[20] The ideology of normalisation became the main model for minority language planners in Spain and elsewhere. Catalan linguist Solé i Camardons regarded normalisation as a sociocultural rather than a linguistic process, a project in which the language is standardised then 'succeeds in reaching all the social functions until then reserved for the dominant language'. Therefore, 'a language is fully normalised when it is used in all formal and informal contexts'.[21]

Success does not depend therefore simply on the numbers of speakers but

20 Aracil 1965

21 Solé i Camardons 2012:117 [my translation]

the comprehensiveness of its social use. It is a major political commitment that takes years to implement and brings long-term social ramifications. To flourish, normalisation needs a combination of official, linguistic and above all 'perception' planning to elevate the status of the language. Generations of stigmatisation require to be overturned to foster both language loyalty and social solidarity. In a modern society the state or local government are primary agents, but not everything is under direct state control. Support from the press and broadcasting media were, according to Catalans, crucial in building language awareness and positive public attitudes. The existence of a significant Catalan-speaking middle class facilitated this endeavour enormously. The British nationalist inclinations of the press and broadcast media in Scotland would make any equivalent campaign challenging. Post-Franco Spain was also comparatively sympathetic to speakers of minority languages, who were seen as having suffered under the dictatorship. Millar was wary of the Catalan comparison, though, pointing out Catalonia is the wealthiest province of Spain, and any Scottish government 'would not have anything like the financial and political clout of Catalonia for any policy, never mind language policies'.[22]

Modern theories of systematic language revival are relatively recent, dating back only to the 1964 publication of Joshua Fishman's *Language Maintenance and Language Shift as a Field of Inquiry*. However, within two years the American-Norwegian linguist Emil Haugen had outlined the main features of language planning. His hugely influential model listed two linguistic elements, *codification* and *elaboration* (or corpus planning) and two social ones, *selection* and *implementation* (or status-planning). Selection implies a choice between different linguistic varieties, followed by codification providing a standard written form with a regularised orthography, vocabulary and grammar. Implementation includes official promotion and use in education, while elaboration expands and modernises the language to keep it up to date with modern needs. How this model might work for Scots is covered in Chapter Seven.

In the earlier discussion on bidialectalism and bilingualism, the two official written forms of Norwegian, Bokmål and Nynorsk were described. These two varieties are regularly mentioned by Scots language champions as examples of language revival. Bokmål is a Norwegianised version of Danish spoken in the bigger urban areas of Norway. Some compare this to Scottish English. After Norwegian independence in 1905, Nynorsk was created by the linguist Ivar Aasen. It was constructed from the regional dialects of Western Norway and Aasen's idea was to create a more 'authentic' Norwegian language via

22 Millar 2011:4

a convoluted *Ausbau* (language-building) process.[23] Although considered a successful project in its day, Nynorsk never broke out of its rural origins and seems to be declining even in its Western heartlands. Fortunately, Scots already has an established literary language to provide a basis for revival, so an equivalent of Aasen-style *de novo* language engineering is not necessary, nor probably now possible.

The issue of dialect variants *within* Scots is a bigger issue, and here the modern standardisation of Basque may provide a more useful case study. In the 1970s the Basque Language Academy, following its own post-Franco nationalist momentum, needed to create a unified 'official' version of the language from half a dozen, and to a varying extent mutually incomprehensible, spoken dialects. The resulting Standard Basque or *euskara batua* was built around the central dialect. Initially, purists condemned it as an artificial 'Euskeranto' that would kill off genuine Basque dialects, but the 'artificial' variety has since been adopted in education at all levels, in the media and for most writing. It has become the most used variant of Basque, especially for new speakers and in those towns remote from a rural dialect heritage. Standard Basque is now generally seen as having improved communication and solidarity between the different dialect groups and stalled the erosion of the language as a whole. In this way, Basque presents a far more modern and relevant lesson for Scots than Nynorsk. Language planning expert Sue Wright summarises the Basque success as follows.

> In the classic nation building tradition Basque has been introduced into the areas where the state has some leverage for example education media and political life and is encouraged in civil society and industry and commerce. But more importantly since intergenerational transmission is held to be the key to regeneration the language it is increasingly reported as the habitual language of family interaction.[24]

In Scotland, though such language planning is routine for Gaelic, there has been no official support any Scots equivalent. Inaction, however, is far from a neutral position. As Millar notes mordantly, 'The Scots-speaking world presents a useful portrait of what *laissez-faire* attitudes and policies towards a socially disadvantaged kin tongue produces'.[25] Wright explains why neglect invariably leads to minority language decline.

---

23 Detailed, for example, in Millar 2005, Hyvik et al 2016

24 Wright 2016:266

25 Millar 2018:219

> The classic liberal response to the problem of language minorities has been to practice '*benign neglect*', that is to allow any group to organise the group life in the language that they choose. Since the language of the institutions on forums of the state results from past or present power, benign neglect must always be a reinforcement of that power. Together with the blindness to group difference it favours the majority because it encourages a default language, which is always that of the majority.[26]

Beyond the obvious political motivations opposing normalisation, Millar suggests a more subtle barrier. The post-devolution Scottish Executive may have been an unwitting inheritor of the old British tradition of language planning ignorance.

> [I]t is not, perhaps, surprising that there is little understanding of the fact that the intervention of governmental and semi-governmental organisations in language use is a norm in many places. Whilst the Executive may make warm noises about Scots in its cultural strategy, it might genuinely not occur to many of its members that Scots would be in need of status planning and the same way has Gaelic is.[27]

Moreover, planning for Scots has been problematised in ways that have served to marginalise the language further. The first of these is, bizarrely, postmodernism.

Postmodernism versus planning

It all seemed so simple back in the days of Aasen. Most nation-building projects were assumed to include some form of language planning. Although the methods and outcomes might have been contentious, the direction and utility of the mission were taken as a given. Times, however, have changed. Scots is exposed to trends and affectations in cultural, literary and linguistic theory that have had almost no equivalent impact on Gaelic. Paradoxically, this is because Scots is not the humble dialect some like to imagine but has its own distinct and dynamic literary form. Millar notes an ironic outcome; 'there is too much literary activity with too little non-literary. This warps the perception of the variety'.[28] Most modern Scots writing has been creative and literary in character, 'literature, after all, is a linguistic space where identity is affirmed, celebrated

26 Wright 2016:231
27 Millar 2005:194
28 Millar 2005:197

or challenged'.[29] Since the 1920s Scots has been appropriated, mistreated and experimented on by a motley crew of writers. The artists involved, whatever their individual merit, have shown trifling interest in Scots as a living language. Scots has been seen as a convenient blank canvas for their personal literary performance and for some, it seems, the blanker the canvas the better.

Which brings us to postmodernism, since the 1960s the most pervasive and misunderstood movement in literary theory. Pratt Paulson provides a neat summation of postmodernism's formidable complexities.

> Postmodernism opposes the universalizing of arguments and positions, rejects metanarratives or any one privileged discourse, sees disagreements over meanings as integral to its own position and welcomes diversity and variety of analysis, which can only be approached by each observer from his or her opinion.[30]

You do not need a background in literary theory to see that postmodernism is diametrically opposed to Aasen-style ideas of language planning. Postmodernism has also influenced how many professional linguists think of their own discipline.

> In scholarship there have been two divergent positions on the nature of language. The first derives from the scientific tradition that holds that there is a 'real' world 'out there' that can be understood and described objectively in language. It finds expression in positivism in the 19th century and some strands of structuralism in the 20th. The second is rooted in the belief that speakers/writers are autonomous subjects who, through free will, co-construct meaning with their interlocutors. From 19th century romanticism to late 20th post-modernism, scholars in this tradition argue that individuals create language from their own life experiences and for their own personal communicative needs. For the first group language is used to describe reality and for the second language frames that reality.[31]

Academia has thus turned away from identifying rules towards the passive description of how people speak and their fluid performance in discourse, with all its messy diversity. As Wright put it, this 'construction' of language on the fly re-frames human language as 'essentially creative, and therefore

29 Bann and Corbett 2015:140

30 Paulson 2002, cited in Wright 2016:311

31 Wright 2015:1

inevitably divergent and tending to heterogeneity'.

To the individualistic, probably monolingual and cosmopolitan mind, such multiplicity might appear to be delightfully progressive and liberating. However, any theoretical model of language that prioritises creativity and variation undermines the idea of language as a unified construct requiring standardisation or planning. According to Wright, the theoretical shift explains the reasons for scholarly scepticism of Aasen-like interventions.

> Standardisation has come to have negative connotations, in that it is at loggerheads with the current tendency to demand respect for difference. Prescriptivism seems part and parcel of a nationalist philosophy that has been questioned in an increasingly post-national era.[32]

In my view, when language is privatised as an individualised performance space, the potential for collective enterprises like planning is stifled, and the language community is politically disempowered. Gaelic language scholar Conchúr Ó Giollagáin describes such trendy academic positioning as 'a postmodernist fiddler playing on while vernacular speech goes up in flames'.[33]

Language policy and planning became deeply unfashionable and, according to Wright, had largely disappeared from international conferences and publications. Consequently, it is less common to find research-active linguists engaged in prescriptive projects such as developing rules for language use. She recognised, 'this has driven a wedge between theorists and many practitioners'. In Scotland, Corbett observed, 'Language planning is sometimes perceived, with reason, to be at the margins of linguistic study'.[34] Millar agreed that most of the recent polices of the Scottish Government towards Scots tended towards the cultural end of the continuum rather than establishing Scots as a minority language. He added, 'there is no sense that the initiative is committed to a secure position for the language in Scottish official life'.[35] The alternative pursued has been to frame the Scots language as a nebulously defined heritage resource.

The dead hand of heritisation

Heritisation and normalisation can be regarded as the extremes of yet another Scots language continuum. Normalisers demand the renaissance of Scots into an all-purpose modern language, but heritisers prefer Scots to be locked in

32 Wright 2016:64
33 Ó Giollagáin et al 2020:12
34 Corbett 2003:272
35 Millar 2018:211

its current 'heritage and retro' state of disrepair, a quaint cultural curio and artistic resource for edgy writers. Heritisation is not wholly negative, though. It at least acknowledges Scots as a vital component of Scotland's history and culture, albeit one with lamentable limitations. Furthermore, heritisation has a lengthy pedigree in Scots scholarship. Its origins may be traced back to 18th-century antiquarianism and the collection of Scots words, through Jamieson's dictionary and even Grant and Dixon's literary grammar project.

The detailed descriptions of early 20th century Scots vernacular by Sir James Wilson were certainly motivated by a sense that Scottish forms of speech were fast vanishing. In his preface to Wilson's 1915 work on Perthshire speech, James Cragie comments on the urgency of the task; 'There can be no doubt that if it is to be done at all, it should be done without delay'. It could be argued this legacy still constrains much of modern Scots language scholarship in, for example, dictionary development. For all its cultural curation positives, as an ideology heritisation is fundamentally a backward-looking and limiting ethos, conservative and disempowering both socially and politically.

How did the odd ideology of heritisation become so dominant in Scotland? We saw previously how Scots had been appropriated by a group of prominent Scottish writers in the late 20th century for specific literary purposes. Scott Hames explained that the focus of these writers was not Scots as a language, but exploited its *de facto* excluded status to depict, 'a marginal, subjected condition conceived as beyond any re-centring or "inclusion" within a hegemonic cultural order (such as a state, or a standardised language)'.[36] This ostentatious 'spectacle of voice' described earlier blocked any normal collective development of the tongue, including standardisation, revitalisation and normalisation. As the writers themselves had no real interest in addressing the social injustice of Scots linguistic marginalisation, it was to their benefit to push Scots further to the extremes to better exploit this symbolic heft.

To understand the more recent roots of this strange narrative, we may have to go back to 1994 and James Robertson's introduction to a collection of Scots short stories called *A Tongue in yer Heid*. Including tales by writers Matthew Fitt and Billy Kay, in those days the publication of any book in Scots was still a significant event. The editor was a writer and Scott scholar, later to become a significant figure in Scottish literature, co-founding of the Scots language publisher Itchy Coo. To researcher James Costa, the authoritative vision for Scots presented by Robertson was a significant ideological tipping-point.

---

36 Hames 2013:208

> Robertson develops a full sociolinguistic manifesto for Scots, dealing both with what it stands for as 'a language' and with how it should be graphically represented. In claiming to represent the full reality of Scottish speech, he is promoting a particular view on language in society, one which values diversity and representativeness of several geographic and/or social sectors of society.[37]

Costa drew particular attention to the following passage.

> There is a wide variety of approaches in these stories to problems of Scots orthography, and I have not sought to eliminate these. One argument against a standardisation of Scots spelling is that one of the language's very strengths lies in its flexibility and its less-than-respectable status: writers turn to it because it offers a refuge for linguistic individualism, anarchism, nomadism and hedonism. What has often been perceived as a fatal weakness may in fact be the secret of its resilience and survival against four hundred years of creeping Anglicisation. If there are inconsistencies – to adapt Walt Whitman – very well then, there are inconsistencies: the language contains multitudes.[38]

Robertson asserted his authority in a pre-emptive rhetorical strike.

> If on turning through these pages some readers are surprised, affronted or confused to find language which, in their view, is not 'true' or 'proper' Scots, or perhaps not even Scots at all, I make no apology for that.

Robertson's view here was not only strikingly divergent from, for example, the normalisation manifesto of McClure, written fourteen years earlier, it was unlike any mainstream minority language revitalisation ideologies anywhere. In retrospect, the individualistic, anti-collective, almost free-market formulation seems closer to the Thatcherite ethos around that time rather than a cohesive vision for a language under threat. There is a case to be made, of course, for Roberson's thesis that the malleability of Scots has helped its survival. However, the reference to Scots' allegedly 'less-than-respectable status' offering 'a refuge for linguistic individualism, anarchism, nomadism and hedonism' is less defensible. Robertson seems

---

37 Costa 2010

38 Robertson 1994:viii and xiv

to appeal to, and appease, the very regressive cultural stereotypes of the Scots language that destroyed its status in the first place. The implication seemed to be that the tongue's disreputable state was a cultural resource only worth preserving as a go-to rebellious register for writers, rather than a marginalised community vernacular. To be fair on Robertson, he was not the only prominent author at the time articulating this idea. The deliberately positioned 'unEnglish' of James Kelman was discussed earlier, and in 2002 another lion of Scottish literature, William McIlvanney, expressed horror at the notion of status enhancement for Scots.

> [A]ny serious rehabilitation of the Scots language? Forget it. A language lives on the streets and, when its ability to be creatively subversive dies there, so does the language.[39]

In a riposte to the Robertson text, former Shetland language activist John Tait identified other ideological nuances. He saw Roberson's reluctance to *define* Scots in order 'not to [...] classify Scots as a minority in its own country' as an overt denial of Scots' status as a minority language.[40] The non-definition of the language, according to Tait, helped Robertson inculcate a sense of optimism when he declared:

> [I]f we start from the premise that Scots is alive and well and in a majority, then a very different message replaces the mixture of pessimism and nostalgia which is contained in the usual well-worn farewell.

Tait implied that with a bit of canny redefinition, the language question just disappears and there is no need to revitalise Scots at all.

Acknowledging some activists might still prefer normalisation, Roberson again resorted to deterrence.

> [T]he influence on Scots writing of a few individuals who are obsessional about standardised spelling systems or determined somehow to keep 'bad' language out of their representation of vernacular speech, should not be overestimated.

Regardless of whether or not that was true the time, Costa discovered the exact reverse situation sixteen years later. The ethos of Robertsonian heritisation had apparently triumphed.

39 McIlvanney 2002

40 Tait 2017

Scots activists opposed to standardisation are now powerful enough to make their arguments visible, giving the ideological debate a very unusual turn.[41]

Dialects and dialectisation

To a 21st-century reader, the Roberson manifesto of 1994 has one glaring omission. There is no mention of Scottish dialects, now an obligatory part of any discussion of Scots. Although dialects have always been an important and valued part of the Scots language ecology, it is only over the last 30 years or so that dialect diversity has become something of a shibboleth among Scots language proponents. As Clark proclaimed in 2016, 'Dialects first. Scots leid second'. The linguistic cohesion of the spoken varieties of Scots was explored earlier, remembering in the early 20th century, when Scots was still the majority vernacular, the leading field researcher at the time wrote, 'the Lowland dialects are not sharply divided from each other'.[42]

People's loyalty to local speech forms is both understandable and commendable, but as we have seen there is a political twist to any 'Dialects first' tenet, making the idea less liberating than it initially seems. Wright reminded us that, in the political context, 'a unified language is held to promote cohesion, allowing the nation to develop a shared culture. There is a symbolic dimension to this'.[43] British nationalist politicians and commentators press their claim at every opportunity that Scots has long since degenerated into a string of scrappy, slangy local vernaculars. The 2016 Creative Scotland claim that 'Scots is the official name for the dialects of Scotland' could be regarded in that political context, or at least a response to a weakening of the public concept of Scots. The Ministerial Working Group on Scots had reported six years earlier that much of the 'widespread ignorance and confusion surrounding Scots' stemmed from 'a failure to understand that the term Scots includes Buchan, Border, Fife, Ayrshire, Galloway, Shetland and all other dialects'.[44] While the Group agreed, 'there is no form (or certainly, at least, no spoken form) which can be taken to be simply Scots', even this progressive report emphased the divergence and apparent 'striking differences' between the dialects. Andy Eagle thought this position may 'run the risk of causing Scots-speakers to assume their dialect is specific to their locality', and therefore might have 'little in common with the dialects

41 Costa 2010:7
42 Wilson 1915:Foreword
43 Wright 2016:47
44 Scottish Government, 2010a:19

spoken elsewhere in Lowland Scotland'. Such localism could inadvertently 'foster a feeling among Scots-speakers that their dialect is marginal and of little relevance or use elsewhere'.[45] On a personal note, while researching this book I visited Shetland. Shetland dialect is sometimes claimed to be so distinct from Scots as to be a separate tongue. What I heard was an almost wholly comprehensible, though distinctive, variant of the same Scots I had learned in East Lothian, Fife and Perthshire. It was a joy to hear Shetlanders speak, but to my lugs they were speaking Scots, no more and no less.

In the context of the dialect-or-language debate earlier, Millar was quoted as saying Scots was a 'near-perfect example' of a dialectised language.[46] He was referring to the gradual erosion of distinctive Scots components in the Scottish language mix, making it ever easier to make trite comparisons with genuine English dialects such as Geordie and Australian English. However, we can add another layer of meaning: the relatively recent view that 'Scots' is itself only a generic label for a set of disjointed dialects. The notion of the Scots language emerging from the shadows of 'Scots is a dialect' dogma at the turn of the 20th century only to be re-dialectised in this sense early in the 21st century is a little ironic. That said, in any revitalisation of Scots it is neither possible nor desirable to reverse three decades or so of 'dialects first' ideology. Local loyalties are not a problem if they form part of the solution. The 2010 Ministerial Working Group acknowledged the need to respect and preserve the individual dialects while at the same time developing the language as a whole 'will require careful planning'. We will explore the details in the next chapter, but before that, it may be useful to illustrate the very different fates of three well-known dialects of Scots: Doric, Ulster Scots (Ullans) and Glasgow Scots.

North-East Scots: Daein the Doric

Doric, often 'The' Doric, is the best-known of the 'traditional' Scots dialects and the native variety of about 15 per cent of all Scots speakers. Once the name was used to denote the whole Scots language, but it now usually refers to the distinctive speech and culture of North East Scotland, 'not simply a geographical expression' but a distinctive regional identity.[47] With little industrialisation until the mid-20th century, many inhabitants were employed in farming and fishing. Village and small-town communities remained stable far longer than in other parts of Scotland. As a result,

45 Eagle 2011:6

46 Millar 2018:2

47 McClure 2002:1

Robert McColl Millar, a leading academic expert on the variety, describes Doric as one of 'the most conservative dialects of Scots, being, at least until recently, vibrant features of the language use of almost all members of their communities'.[48]

The 2011 Census revealed the concentration of Scots speakers in the area to be 40 per cent, not a majority but still the highest speaker density on the mainland. Millar makes what may be an even more significant observation; 'dialect use has rarely been associated with a particular social class'. Minority language maintenance needs middle-class speakers to provide status and, more importantly, the time, confidence and capability to support it. Gaelic and the Doric dialect have both benefitted from a small middle-class speaker base. Underlining this point, an identifiable working-class urban variety, *Toonser*, has emerged in Aberdeen relatively recently. Without middle-class endorsement, mongrel Toonser seems to be stigmatised by Doric and Scottish English speakers alike.[49]

Should Doric be considered a separate language? When I moved to Aberdeen in the 1990s, I expected to hear a very different way of speaking from the Central Scots I had been brought up with. I was almost disappointed to discover this was not the case. Once I was used to the accent, I found the underlying grammar and most of the words to be much the same, though used more frequently. Among scholars, too, Doric is recognised a dialect of Scots and even popularisers such as *Teach Yourself Doric* author Douglas Kynoch agree. The label 'Doric' may therefore be misleading, implying a distinct entity from Scots, and it should be remembered the 18th century poet Allan Ramsay originally coined the term to refer to the whole Scots language. Classically trained Ramsay believed 'provincial' Scots had a parallel in the peasant Dorian dialects of ancient Greek. By analogy, the then-anglicised language of Edinburgh, 'the Athens of the North', was associated with the civilised language of the Greek capital. Doric just meant rural, only later implying specifically North East speech. The label only became popular towards the end of the 20th century. Before then, speakers referred to their tongue as Scots or Scotch, or used more local identifiers like 'Buchan' or 'Aberdeenshire'. So why did the term 'Doric' become so dominant?

> Many would see this emphasis on local culture as being open to regionalism, perhaps even regional particularism. Living in the North-East, I am very much aware how divisive the local term for the region's variety of Scots – the Doric – can actually be. I know that I,

48 Millar 2007:1

49 Millar 2007:118

> along with others, am quite strong on using *North-East Scots* for this variety, perhaps as an expression of ideology.[50]

Journalist David Leask claimed that the officially endorsed strong regional variations of Scots seem to accentuate (deliberately or accidentally) local rather than national identity.[51] It may be coincidence, but at the 2019 General Election it was the traditionally strong Scots dialect areas of the North-East, Orkney, Shetland and the Borders that remained most resistant to the electoral charms of the SNP.

Introducing the infamous attitudes survey of 2009, the supposedly objective statement was made that, 'Scots spoken in the North East, for example, the Doric, is very different'. It is true that North East rural speech has quite a few prominent features such as 'foo', 'fit', 'far' and 'fan', which in Central Scots would be 'hoo', 'whit', 'whaur' and 'whan'. Vowels can be different, too, such as 'een' for 'ane' and 'neen' for 'nane', 'meen' for 'muin', 'gweed' for 'guid' and, especially in Aberdeen city, 'ging' for 'gang'. North East vernacular is infectious. After living in Aberdeen for a few years, I found myself using 'nae' in more contexts such as 'A'm nae comin' for 'A'm no comin'. The Doric retains quite a few words that are particular to the area or have become obsolete in other Scots dialects, though equally many words thought by speakers be uniquely Doric are in fact commonly used elsewhere. Daniel Knox observed that although the speech of the area certainly features the characteristics above, it was not generally as 'pure' as some claim.

> [I]t would be fair to say that much of the mass of contemporary speech in the north-east is not unproblematically Doric or characteristically regional and thus *could* [author's emphasis] be classified as regional English, Scots-English or Scots.[52]

That said, in the broader form and when spoken at speed, Doric is not usually comprehensible to English monolinguals, but should be intelligible to most Scots speakers. When working in an Aberdeen college in the early 1990s, I remember overhearing two work colleagues blethering in the Doric. The ladies were discussing other members of staff, so I thought I'd better make a confession, 'Yez ken a can unnerstaun aw that ye're seyin. We spoke the same wey whan A wis a bairn doon in Pairthshire an Fife'. The blethering stopped. Both looked at me in astonishment, as if a dog had just got up on

50 Millar 2008:10

51 Leask 2015

52 Knox 2003:70

his hind legs and started talking. 'That's impossible, only Aberdeenshire folk speak the Doric'. 'No it isn't', I replied, 'you say "fit" and I'd say "whit" and stuff like that but it's much the same otherwise'. They were having none of it. It was as if I had broken their secret code. In the rest of my time in the college, they never used Doric in my company again. The ladies' misconception was quite understandable, though. With the limited exposure of any other Scots varieties in mainstream media, Doric speakers may have no idea how similar their tongue is to the dialects just down the road. Unfortunately when such myths become embedded, they are hard to rationalise away.

The idea of Doric autonomy does not only rely on supposed intelligibility. The variety enjoys a literary tradition to call its own, from Alexander Ross in the 18th century to the present-day poet, writer and storyteller Sheena Blackhall who translated *The Doric Gruffalo* in 2015. Doric still appears regularly in the local media, for example though Robbie Shepherd's dialect books and regular columns for the Aberdeen-based *Press and Journal*. A loose written standard, or at least visual identity, emerged recently, exemplified by Douglas Kynoch's 1994 *Teach Yourself Doric*. This short manual, closely modelled on an old-school language textbook, pulls off the clever trick of being serious and jokey at the same time. The notion of writing a learners' textbook for any form of Scots, however tongue in cheek, was innovative, but Kynoch took an even bolder step.

> With great temerity (and perhaps foolishness), I have abandoned the standard form of Scots spelling in favour of a style which emphasises Doric's uniqueness among Scottish dialects, as well as highlighting its idiosyncratic pronunciation.

Kynoch's consistent orthography was expanded by *A Doric Dictionary* in 1996 and, 'for advanced students', *Doric for Swots* the following year. His system has become so influential that the caveat in the original volume is worth repeating. In his reference to 'a standard form of Scots', he recognised there had been a long tradition of writing Doric Scots using traditional orthography.

> [I]t is to be hoped that any resistance to the changes on the part of the Doric-speaking reader will quickly disappear and that any inconsistencies of spelling will be forgiven. The appearance of some words seemed too familiar to change.

The flavour of Kynoch's orthography is given in this passage from *Doric for Swots* 'for translation and oral practice'.

> There cam a day, fin Arthur fun his queen, the Leddy Grimavere, sittin on her leen in her bed-chaamer, leukin rale doon-i-the moo. 'Fit like?' spiert the keeng. Grimivere niver said naething. 'Fit's the maitter' he says. 'Hiv ye tint a shullin an fun a sixpence?' Syne, Grimavere halt oot her hunkie an dabbit her een. 'Leave's aleen' she said. 'Fit wye?' says the keeng. 'Fit ails ye queen-quine? Yer face is fair trippin ye.' 'A ken,' she says. 'I canna help it. A feel aat dowie nooadays. A dinna ken fit's come ower me. A canna hud fae greetin'.

This passage is clearly a variant of Scots though Kynoch's orthography sometimes obscures the fact, and maybe encourages sporadic claims that Doric is something different. His practice of rendering English words (or, more precisely, words shared between Scots and English) in the same consistent spelling system, such as 'suppersteeshun' or 'oonprincipelt' is also unusual and nowadays rather frowned upon in Modern Scots. Nevertheless, his approach provides a visual coherence to the page and allows the easy assimilation of new English words into the system. Like any standard, however, Kynoch Doric overrode local variation, and the author admitted 'the truth is that there is not one monolithic form of Doric but a multiplicity of forms'.[53]

The North-East way of life came under pressure in the 1960s and 1970s following the discovery of North Sea oil. Economic opportunity brought wealthy English-speaking incomers as well as less affluent Scots from the Central Belt who settled in urban neighbourhoods. The modernisation of farming and the contraction of the fishing industry drastically reduced both the number of local workers and the traditional work-based speech communities associated with them. The long-term effects of this social upheaval on the language and culture of the North-East are still playing out, but over a decade ago Millar warned: 'The future of the Doric as a highly distinctive dialect is by no means assured'.[54]

One response in the early 1990s was a re-evaluation and re-imagining of local language and culture in terms of both public exhibition and academic scholarship. The Doric Festival started in 1994 and grew into a popular two-week celebration of the dialect and the traditional music, song and way of life associated with it. The University of Aberdeen founded the Elphinstone Institute the following year, also dedicated to the culture and traditions of this part of Scotland. Both of these initiatives have to some extent institutionalised 'North-Eastern-ness' and raised Doric's public profile and

53 Kynoch 1996:v

54 Millar 2007:120

status. In the continuing absence of a Scots Language Board as mentioned earlier, the North-East Scots Language Board (NESLB) was launched in 2018. With representatives from Aberdeen University, Robert Gordon University, Aberdeen City and Shire Councils, Moray Council and Angus, the new body proclaimed a clear remit.

> The Board his been foonit tae reflect an uphaud this goal by promotin an developin North-East Scots as an integral pairt o the region's heritage, identity, an cultural life. Steps maun be taen tae mak siccar that its use is normalised in education, the airts, media, an ither sectors.[55]

The following year, the Doric Board was formally constituted 'tae energise public appreciation o this heritage'. With funding from Scottish Government, since then it has been active in promoting the variety through competitions and awards.

Although this all seems very positive, and the energy put into these initiatives is impressive, not all were convinced. One blogger expressed a concern.

> This should not be seen as an advance for the Scots language movement, but rather a retreat. It is the last circling of the wagons around some notional defensible dialect 'Hertland' or 'stronghold' [...] the Scots language movement has regressed intellectually, and now seems intent on geographical retrenchment.[56]

A second problem Millar identified with this type of heritage-based initiative is the association of the dialect with a nostalgic, vanishing lifestyle.

> [K]nowledge and, in particular, use of the language is being compartmentalised, with North-East Scots no longer being the default code, but rather one being brought out on special occasions.[57]

He reported on research from the University of Aberdeen suggesting there has already been a break-down in transfer of the language from parents to children and in some areas, Doric being no longer the language of the playground. From his own experience he had found many distinctive features of the variety were now only heard from elderly speakers. If the story of

55 University of Aberdeen 2018

56 Purves 2018

57 Millar 2007:119

the Doric illustrates the limitations of a local dialect-based and heritage-focused approach to language maintenance, the next case study shows what can happen when local politics veers language building in a very different direction.

The extraordinary story of Scots in Ulster

Scots is not only spoken in Scotland. A dialect known variously as Ulster Scots, Ulster-Scots or sometimes Ullans, can be heard in rural and coastal parts of Ulster, especially the Antrim area, and just over the border in Donegal. Although it is a small community, less than one per cent of all Scots speakers, the peculiar politics of Northern Ireland have propelled Ulster Scots along a very different trajectory from what I will call in this context the 'Mither Tongue' in Scotland. The status of Ulster Scots became curiously totemic in the slow transformation from violent to cultural forms of struggle in the province.

Scots was established in the area from the early 17th century, as the language of the Protestant migrants and colonialists who displaced the Irish-speaking inhabitants during what is termed the 'Plantation'. The incomers were mostly from the Scots-speaking parts of southwest Scotland. Although considered a discrete dialect,[58] the variety is very similar to Central Scots, especially the vernacular of Galloway. Philip Robinson, author of the first grammar of Ulster Scots, acknowledged that the 'broad' spoken form was 'at times indistinguishable' from the literary form of Scots.[59]

Apart from a spate of vernacular poetry in the late 18th and early 19th centuries (the 'Rhyming Weavers'), the variety survived primarily in oral form and lacked the continuous literary tradition of the Mither Tongue. Until the end of the 20th century, the Ulster dialect seems to have been almost forgotten, even by scholars. John Hewitt's 1974 account of the Weaver poets was a notable exception, but as it was published during the bloodiest phase of the 'Troubles', 'its appeal for a lost local cultural form seemed unimportant to many since larger issues were being contested in a violent public sphere'.[60] Without institutional recognition or presence in education, the Ulster dialect predictably became stigmatised and gradually declined in speaker numbers and distinctiveness. To the educated middle classes, 'it was symbolic of a backward, premodern rural existence that

58 Eg Kirk 2011

59 Robinson 1997:2

60 Crowley 2006:25

had no place in the modern, industrialized, north-east of the island'.[61] Most inhabitants of the area gradually shifted to the distinctive spoken variety, Ulster English. Scots-rich urban varieties never developed so Scots is not habitually used in Belfast or Derry, but local language expert Ian Parsley observed, 'speech there retains a significant Scots influence'.[62] Anyone who has visited Belfast or even just watched the 2018 Channel 4 television series *Derry Girls* can confirm the frequency of Scots words and idioms. Though even in its Antrim heartland, Parsley conceded, 'most Scots speakers' speech today falls along a spectrum between traditional Scots and Standard English, with a trend towards the latter'.

The Ulster linguistic landscape is therefore as complex and nuanced as that of Scotland, but the proportion of Scots speakers is considerably lower. A recent Northern Ireland Continuous Household Survey (2017/18) found only about 14 per cent of residents had some knowledge of Ulster Scots and just five per cent used it at home or socially. Speakers are surveyed in far more detail than in Scotland and it seems even among those who knew Ulster Scots, capability was quite low. Just over one third could cope with a conversation at either a simple or complicated level; the rest could understand only simple spoken sentences, words or phrases. Speakers were likely to be older and live in rural areas and, predictably, more Protestants (20 per cent) and those with other or no religion (12 per cent) knew the variety than Catholics (7 per cent).

In the historical context of *laissez faire* neglect, researcher Tony Crowley described the success of the Ulster Scots language movement in Northern Ireland as 'remarkable by any standards'. He noted as recently as 1982 Ian Adamson's influential *The Identity of Ulster: The Land, the Language and the People* still referred to the variety as a dialect of English. Nevertheless, the publication marked 'the beginning of an ideological challenge to received notions of linguistic and cultural identity'. For the first time Ulster Scots was considered as a component of a distinctive and historical Ulster Protestant identity. In 20 years, a wide range of initiatives, institutions and practices had established Ulster Scots as 'a language with serious political support'.[63] Language politics gained currency prompted by the revival of Irish Gaelic among the Nationalist community through the 1980s and 1990s. The Irish language had become a symbol of Irish identity, a form of non-violent resistance to British rule. Small Irish-speaker communities became established in inner-city Belfast and well-funded educational and social initiatives had

61 McCall 2002:203

62 Parsley 2012:2

63 Crowley 2006:25

flourished. By the early 1990s, as ideas of a peaceful settlement began to take root among Nationalists, the focus moved to cultural identity and civil rights, signified by a call for recognition and respect for the Irish language. In this way, language recognition became part of a 'parity of esteem' and a core component of the emerging discourse of peace.

Nonetheless, for all its emblematic heft then and now, in sociolinguistic terms the Irish language remains a minority practice, even in the Nationalist community. The Continuous Household Survey, mentioned above, found about 15 per cent of residents to have some knowledge of Irish but only four per cent used it, at home or socially. The overall speaker count was little more than for Ulster Scots, but Irish speakers tend to be younger learners rather than older native speakers. Proficiency in Irish is also low; only one in four of adult Irish speakers could carry on a conversation in Irish beyond simple sentences and phrases. Reading capabilities were even lower. Not surprisingly, a higher proportion of Catholics (29 per cent) had knowledge of Irish than both those with other or no religion (9 per cent) or Protestants (2 per cent). The data showing low numbers of speakers of both tongues illustrates the largely symbolic nature of language initiatives for both Nationalist and Unionist communities.

As the peace process began to develop, the Adamson notion of language as a part of Ulster Protestant identity also solidified. Sceptics believed all this was just a spiteful Unionist reaction to the promotion of Irish, with Ulster Scots a makeweight, merely confected to provide a cultural balance. Cathal McCall quoted the Unionist politician Ian Paisley Jr, who, speaking shortly after the Agreement, believed that the Ulster Scots movement at the time was 'largely reactionary, to be honest'. Paisley had added:

> I respect those who say there is a language but I think the reality is the unionist community is neither convinced by it nor exposed to it sufficiently to underpin it.[64]

McCall illustrated this last point with an anecdote. New bilingual Ulster Scots street signs were put up in east Belfast in 1999 only to be torn down by local loyalists who thought the Ulster Scots place names were in Irish.

Despite the display of political theatre, the elevation of Ulster Scots was not without scholarly and community foundations. A grassroots Ulster Scots education network had been established by the early 1990s, though not on the scale or ambition of Irish language initiatives. The Ulster-Scots Language Society was formed in 1992, and in the first edition of its journal *Ullans* stated its aim.

64 McCall 2002:210

> [T]o promote the status of Ulster Scots as a language, and to re-establish its dignity as a language with an important part to play in our cultural heritage.[65]

Ullans Press published the first dictionary of Ulster Scots, James Fenton's *The Hamely Tongue: a personal record of Ulster-Scots in County Antrim* in 1995 and Philip Robinson's scholarly grammar just two years later. The Society also founded the Ulster-Scots Academy in 1992 as a community-based, independent body modelled of the Frisian Academy, acting primarily as 'the authoritative community and academic voice on the language, including the setting of standards for spellings and translations'.[66]

While the Mither Tongue in 1990s Scotland remained side-lined in political terms, Ulster Scots was thrust into the mainstream. The Ulster-Scots Heritage Council (Ulstèr-Scotch Hierskip Cooncil), launched in 1995, lobbied for funding for a range of marginalised cultural groups 'in some way Ulster-Scots related' including the Scottish Pipe Band Association, Robert Burns Clubs, the Royal Scottish Country Dance Society and, naturally, the Academy. The Cooncil, however, brought together Ulster Scots activists and key Unionist politicians at a pivotal moment in the formation of what was to become the 1998 Belfast or Good Friday Agreement. Peter Gardner pointed out, 'given the structural position of its personnel, the council had the capacity to wield considerable leverage in the political sphere at the time'. The timing of their involvement was also critical, the four years between the 1994 ceasefires and the 1998 Agreement. Gardner argues the 'two community' model with 'parity of esteem', both fundamental elements of the peace process, 'meant that a "Protestant" language/culture to correspond to Irish(ness) was politically expedient'.[67]

While expediency certainly played a large part, an additional factor was a perception that the 'traditional' symbolism of Unionism, at least to some, had begun to seem crude, isolated and outdated. The assertive revival of Irish had actually 'persuaded many unionists of the importance of engagement in cultural politics and the expansion of cultural resource of the unionist identity'.[68] By promoting Ulster Scots as a language (rather than a mere dialect), Unionists could participate in the identity politics debates previously dominated by Nationalists, so 'it became the medium by which identity-claims and demands for civil rights were articulated in a political realm that

65 Quoted in Crowley 2006:27

66 Ulster-Scots Academy website:About

67 Gardner 2018:148

68 McCall 2002:215

had expanded to include both'.[69]

The speaker community itself was barely involved in this top-down, politically charged and even intellectual approach to language promotion. As the Household Surveys revealed, most Ulster Protestants (and indeed Ulster Catholics) speak Ulster English and have little exposure to Scots, even in a diluted form. The result was predictable, according to Gardner.

> [O]ne need only have perused the columns and letters pages of regional and national newspapers during the negotiations that led to the Agreement to realize that, far from respect, understanding, and tolerance the Ulster-Scots issue generated much ridicule, mockery and intolerance.

Despite the public scepticism, by 1998 the variety had 'gained enough traction amongst unionist elites'[70] to be successfully put forward for inclusion in the Agreement alongside Irish. In his autobiography, Tony Blair admitted he was incredulous that the inclusion of Ulster-Scots, as he put it, 'some obscure language', could potentially have been a deal breaker.[71]

The Belfast/Good Friday Agreement outlined the post-conflict government structure for power sharing between Unionists and Nationalists. The co-signers were the British and Irish governments and political parties in Northern Ireland. Part of the text committed signatories as follows.

> [To] recognise the importance of respect, understanding and tolerance in relation to linguistic diversity, including in Northern Ireland, the Irish language, Ulster-Scots and the languages of the various ethnic minorities, all of which are part of the cultural wealth of the island or Ireland.

Although the Agreement did not state that Ulster-Scots (note the hyphen) was a 'language', it was now formally legitimised and would soon be integrated into the governmental structures. The Agreement included actions replicated from the as-yet-unsigned European Charter for Regional or Minority Languages, forcing the UK Government to finally sign the Charter in 2000 and ratify it the following year. Both Ulster-Scots and Scots had to be included among the original five languages listed, but the pair were excluded from the higher 'Part III' status awarded to Welsh, Scottish Gaelic and Irish. Adherence was to be monitored by the Northern Ireland

69 Crowley 2006:31

70 Gardner 2018:149

71 Blair 2010:166

Human Rights Commission (NIHRC).

The Agreement and the ECRML propelled Ulster Scots well away from the 'hamely' roots of its remaining Ulster heartlands and the Mither Tongue in Scotland. The most significant step was the establishment in 1999 of the Ulster-Scots Agency (Tha Boord o Ulstèr-Scotch), alongside Foras na Gaeilge with parallel responsibility for the development of the Irish language. The Agency would become the official voice of the 'new' Ulster-Scots language. Gardner underlined the extraordinary nature of this initiative in which 'a fledgling ethnic "revivalist" movement without a widespread base of popular support was apportioned considerable political and economic power', reminding us that at the time, 'vocal opposition to the idea of Ulster-Scots was widespread, even among its target population'.[72]

Initially there was little shared idea of what 'Ulster-Scots' was, either as a specific language variety or as a broader component of a (mainly) Protestant cultural identity. The aim of the Agency was twofold; to stimulate the use of Ulster-Scots as a 'living language' and to propagate that wider understanding of Ulster-Scots history and culture. In its latter remit it supports a range of non-language activities associated with the Protestant tradition. Historic and cultural connections between Northern Ireland and Scotland were emphasised on its website; 'the Ulster-Scots story is of massive significance to both countries, and to people on both sides of the slim stretch of water'. For anyone with experience of the miserly funding of the Mither Tongue in Scotland, the budget of the Agency, around £3 million a year, was staggering, though it should be said Foras na Gaeilge received more than five times that. Given the significant sums involved, the effectiveness of the spend remains hotly debated, and confidence in the Agency was dented by various financial scandals throughout its early years. The Agency seems to have had most real impact in education, where the generous funding of initiatives over the last decade such as the Ulster-Scots Flagship Schools Award has motivated teachers and learners. A 2010 survey by the Department of Culture, Arts and Leisure found similar proportions of Protestant and Catholic respondents believing that studying the Ulster Scots language at school should be an option: 23 per cent and 21 per cent respectively.

The integration of Ulster Scots into post-1998 government structures forced it to become a language of record with translations of some official documents. This demanded a rapid process of *Ausbau* language-building, the expansion of what was still essentially a colloquial spoken tongue into a formal written variety capable of high register officialese. Early attempts were often impenetrable, attracting much derision. The new artificial form

72 Gardner 2018:149

sometimes dubbed 'Ullans' seemed far removed from the hamely tongue of Fenton's Antrim speakers. John Kirk analysed an early document from 2010, the *Hannlin Rede* (Business Plan) of the *Männystrie o Fairms an Kintra Fordèrin* (Department of Agriculture and Rural Development), full of phrases such as 'Wi tha sillerie haudin tae tha fore thenoo it's weel seen thar's a wheen o sillerie kittles we'll rin agane in tha towmond tae cum' (In the current economic climate there are obviously a number of financial challenges to be faced in the year ahead).[73] The documents were apparently written by a small group of writers and language planners, who adopted a strategy of maximum differentiation from English and with little regard for authentic speech or, maybe worse, existing literary Scots. Vocabulary derived from French or Latin was avoided, obsolescent words and colloquialisms re-purposed, and ad hoc eye-dialect spellings applied, producing a text which felt so 'artificial and counter-intuitive' it was barely decipherable. Kirk argued that a 'proper' version in Ulster Scots at this register would be a minimally modified English version with limited use of Scots words, expressions and grammar. More recent translations, however, seem to adopt a style better aligned to spoken usages. As an example, the 2017 *Ulster Scots Policy* of the Mid Ulster District Council is certainly more readable, for example in stating its aim.

> Operatin waein tha spirit o tha Euraip Chairtèr fur Kintrie-Pairt or Unnèr-Docht Leids, an haein due regard tae tha status afforded tae Ullans waein that Chairtèr, Mid Ulstèr Airt Cooncil aims tae tak positive hannlin tae promote tha uise o Ullans leid in tha Airt an waein tha Cooncil.

Nonetheless, the NIHRC monitoring body, reported that by May 2018 Mid Ulster District Council was one of only four of the 11 Northern Ireland Councils to have policies for Ulster-Scots and Irish, with one having an Irish policy only.

If actual implementation is patchy, language remains a potent symbol and cultural marker. The 2006 St Andrews Agreement promised an Irish Language Act analogous to the Gaelic Language (Scotland) Act 2005. This would in theory give Irish parity with English in Northern Ireland. Apart from challenging the cost, Unionists regard an Irish Language Act as an erosion of British identity. The issue contributed to the collapse of the NI Assembly in 2017. After a three-year hiatus, the impasse was resolved in 2020 via the New Decade, New Approach agreement. This promised an

73 Kirk 2013

amendment to the Northern Ireland Act 1998 to grant official status to both the Irish language and Ulster Scots in Northern Ireland with Commissioners appointed to oversee both. Unionists then objected to the term, 'Ulster-Scots commissioner', preferring 'Ulster-British commissioner'. The draft Identity and Language (Northern Ireland) Bill, refers to new 'Ulster Scots/Ulster British Commissioner'. The recognition for Ulster Scots however would extend to giving it status as a National Minority under the Framework Convention for the Protection of National Minorities. The NIHRC expressed concerns over the new reference to 'Ulster British', 'not a term, or a linguistic/national minority group presently recognised by human rights treaty bodies'. As it was not a term used within the Ulster Scots community either, they feared that Ulster Scots culture was at risk of being conflated with a specific political identity.[74] It recommended that Ulster Britishness should be promoted though the new Office of Identity and Cultural Expression (also part of the Bill) with the Commissioner focusing on the language.

The story of Ulster Scots since the turn of the century is so divergent from the main historical trajectory for the Mither Tongue it could be dismissed as a curious localised anomaly; a half-forgotten rural dialect promoted way above its capacities by a set of unique political circumstances. This is fair but would overlook some serious sociolinguistic lessons. As minority language experts Grenoble and Whaley put it, 'Local politics can be divisive, but used properly can be a powerful advocacy force for revitalization'.[75] The first thing to note is that cultural politics are real politics with real meaning; Irish Gaelic advocates showed that in the context of linguistic rights, speaker numbers and even public opinion are immaterial. In contrast, Scots language policy in Scotland was, and still is, in the thrall of often reactionary public opinion, fuelled by a largely antagonistic British nationalist press. Ulster Scots certainly had the huge advantage over the Mither Tongue of not threatening the Union. Moreover, Ulster Scots had to be promoted to be a normal minority language and not 'just' a dialect of Scots (or English) to provide parity of esteem. Parity of esteem is a useful concept, even if parity of funding is not achieved, though the Northern Ireland experience shows money is not the whole answer either. Language planning needs careful preparation and the early attempts at 'hothousing' language development seem poorly conceived. When the Mither Tongue gets to this stage, some lessons will hopefully be learned. Finally, the Ulster Scots story also highlights the weakness of Scots dialectisation; a dialect is just a badge of local difference, but a language represents a unifying culture and can acquire real rights.

74 NI Human Rights Commission 2020:2.13

75 Grenoble and Whaley 2006:178

Glasgow Scots: the power of the patter

Due to its size, location and sheer gallusness, Glasgow asserts a significant influence on Scottish culture. Over a quarter of all Scots speakers live in the Greater Glasgow area. The distinctive way its inhabitants speak, and to what extent their variety can be considered 'Scots', has been integral to the modern self-definition of the Scots language. Since the 1960s a series of skirmishes about the artistic representation of Glasgow speech has distorted the debate and public perception about Scots. The story of 'Glaswegian', sometimes affectionately known as 'The Patter' and (more dubiously) 'Glasgow Slang' illustrates some of the challenges facing the Scots language today. So, what relation does Glaswegian have to Scots anyway? Annette Hagen provided a useful starting point.

> Underlying Glaswegian is the West Central dialect of Scots. However this traditional variety has been greatly modified in the course of the last two centuries with the result that Glaswegian now forms a hybrid variety which, although it has retained features of West Central Scots, is characterised by the varied influences exerted on it by other varieties and indeed languages.[76]

Those influences trace back to the Industrial Revolution and 18th century immigration from Ireland, the Gaelic Highlands and elsewhere. With no taught standardised Scots to stabilise it, working-class Glasgow became a linguistic melting pot. Over the next century a distinctive and, to some ears, disagreeable urban variety began to emerge. In 1863 an English writer, Cuthbert Bede, described Glasgow's Saltmarket as follows:

> While the nose is assailed with countless stinks, the ear is stormed by a babel of bastard Scotch and bad English, mixed with fragments of genuine Gaelic, and the rolling periods and rough brogue that mark the Irish Celt.[77]

McClure claimed the 'virtual obliteration of the native dialects' had occurred by the 20th century[78] and Aitken quotes a turn-of-the-century tirade by a middle-class writer about the prevalence among the young of 'Glasgow-Irish', described as 'a certain wonderful gibberish which now

76 Hagen 2002:87

77 Bede 1863:50

78 McClure 1995:11

passes currently for Scots'.[79] As with many aspects of the Scots story, the linguistic impact of the newcomers may have been exaggerated. After a century and half of alleged debasement, the 1934 Glasgow Local Association of the Educational Institute of Scotland reported that Scots was still a significant part of the Glasgow linguistic environment.

> In most cases Glasgow pupils enter the schools with one language only, the Central Scottish Dialect, and they proceed to learn to write Standard English. As the result of education the vernacular is gradually eliminated from written work, but it persists in colloquial use [...]. In the playground children who try to speak Standard English are generally laughed at, whilst in the class-room a lapse into the mother-tongue is greeted with hilarity [...]. Children usually hear little else than a Scots dialect and so they come to regard Standard English as artificial.[80]

Given the popular reading material of the time, this should come as no surprise. The rich Scots dialogue of JJ Bell's hugely popular *Wee Macgreegor* stories of working-class Glasgow first appeared in the *Evening Times* in 1901 and over subsequent decades was republished as a series of best-selling books. Writing about the same time, *Para Handy* author Neil Munro used everyday Scots forms to represent Glasgow speech, as did the popular *Evening Times* cartoons of Bud Neil appearing from the late 1940s on. Although originating in Dundee, the Scots-rich newspaper cartoon strips *The Broons* and *Oor Wullie* were often appropriated by Glaswegians as representing the voice of their city. Scots is therefore inseparable from Glaswegian and vice versa.

Fast forward 50 years and Michael Munro, author of the very successful 1985 mini-dictionary of Glaswegian, *The Patter*, insisted that his subject was, 'a valid and creative dialect of Scots, not, as some would have it, a slovenly corruption of standard English'.[81] Indeed, a glance at a few pages of his book reveals that a hefty proportion of the 'Glaswegian' terms are 'just' mainstream Scots, eg 'bauchle', 'backie', 'baggie', 'bahookie', 'bampot', 'baries', 'barra', 'baw', 'bawhair', 'bawheid', 'beamer', 'beardie', 'beelin', 'beezer'... Whether these are Scots words in Glaswegian or Glaswegian words in Scots hardly matters. Munro reminds us:

79 Aitken 1982, 2015:3

80 Quoted in Horsbroch 2020a

81 Munro 1996:v (compendium edition)

> [T]he Glasgow region has often been at the forefront of innovation, coining many new Scots words and phrases that reflect changes in modern society [...] what is spoken in the Glasgow area today is not spoken in isolation but forms a wider entity which is the Scots language.[82]

Unfortunately, linguistic creativity is not always appreciated. It was clear the Glasgow variety of Scots was doubly stigmatised from its very birth by comparison against both Standard English and sentimentalised 'Good' Scots. Working-class and urban speech came to be noticed after the Industrial Revolution and was soon characterised as 'Bad Scots', 'in origin a feature of slum life'.[83] The prejudice against this variety proved remarkably persistent, as this quote from a university lecturer a century later shows.

> The accent of the lowest state of Glaswegians is the ugliest accent one can encounter, but that is partly because it is associated with the unwashed and the violent.[84]

Negativity trickles down, and question testing for the 1996 Census showed many urban speakers of Scots identified their own speech as 'slang'.[85] The double-strength linguistic insecurity may explain why 'traditional' Scots elements may have eroded more quickly from Glasgow speech than other Scots dialects.[86]

> The education authorities had succeeded in conditioning Glasgow people to self-censure their own language in favour of English and to self-denigrate Scots generally. As part of this process, speakers in Glasgow have discarded certain key markers of Scots. For example, no Glaswegian born and bred today would use the Scots words 'awa', 'ken', 'nicht' or 'twa' but rather the English forms – away, know, night and two'.[87]

A further disruption between traditional Scots written language and the Glasgow vernacular occurred in the 1960s through the Stanley Baxter's low-brow *Parliamo Glasgow* and the high-brow eye-dialect poetry of Tom Leonard and subsequent imitators. Both sought to exoticise and alienate the written

82 Scots Language Centre undated, b
83 Aitken 1982, 2015
84 University lecturer quoted in Macaulay 1997:52
85 Macafee 2015
86 Eg Macafee 1983
87 Scots Language Centre undated, b

representations of Glasgow speech for different artistic reasons. They attempted to break the link between 'traditional' (and more accessible) methods of writing Scots by turning to deliberately obscure, bespoke systems fixated on phonetics.

Modern academic research into Glasgow speech still tends to focus on phonetics rather than vocabulary or structure.[88] Over two decades, The University of Glasgow undertook extensive research on change in Glasgow speech.[89] While this work is fascinating, especially the impact of TV on speech practice, a phonetic focus tends to condense the complexities of Glaswegian speech patterns into 'the Glasgow accent'. Glasgow Scots is all too often benchmarked for academic purposes against standard English, so reduced to 'Glasgow English'.

This is not the only scholarly approach available, however. In 1991 Janet Menzies applied a distinctive speaker-centred and historically informed view in her remarkable study of attitudes to Scots and Glaswegian in secondary schools. She thought it 'unfortunate that in Scotland, spoken dialects are often termed "English" when their historical origin shows that they are not this'. She considered this important, as speakers of 'dialect' tend to 'view their speech negatively when told that they are speaking a form of English, but one which does not sound like the prestigious standard'. Speakers then concude 'that their mode of communication is sub-standard'.[90] Her research found disapproval and overall poor knowledge of Scots forms among her subjects. '[E]ven though feelings of national and regional (Scottish and Glasgow) identity are strong, these young people held underlying negative attitudes to their spoken vernacular'. However, instead of passively recording her findings as is the academic norm in Scotland, she decided to intervene.

> I feel it to be significant that the informants have a very poor knowledge of Scottish literary figures and their work (whether in Scots or English). In my opinion, a vital factor in cultivating a healthy attitude towards a language within the language community is that it must be perceived as having enough status to be an acceptable medium for creative art. Scots literature must be a contributory factor towards the survival of the Scots language. In addition, if schools took a little time to highlight the history, status and use of Scots, the effects could only be beneficial. Perhaps the result would be a greater confidence in the use both of the vernacular and of English.

88 Eg Lawson 2014

89 Eg Stuart-Smith et al 2007

90 Menzies 1991:unnumbered

To test this thesis, she discussed the results of the first (negative) attitudinal surveys with her participants and provided a basic introduction to, 'the facts relating to the Scots language'. This minimal intervention she found to be 'sufficient to cure the habit of equating all non-standard variables with slang'.

> Instead they now described those words as 'my dialect' or 'the Scots language'. The abolition of that quintessentially negative term 'slang', which taints attitudes towards any speech form to which it is applied or misapplied, might contribute to the saving of Lowland Scots.

The 2017 Education Scotland report quoted earlier found that working with the language can help young people, especially learners whose mother tongue is Scots, develop their language confidence, their own identity and make them feel more valued and engaged. Janet Menzies' study suggests two things; that attitudes to Scots dialects and attitudes to Scots are closely linked, and that a little intervention goes a long way.

The 'three-voiced country'

When the first Scottish Parliament in almost three centuries was convened in July 1999, Iain Crichton Smith's moving poem 'The Beginning of a New Song' was read out. It starts, 'Let our three-voiced country, sing in a new world', and ends with; 'Then without shame we can esteem ourselves'. After two decades of devolution, Gaelic has gained esteem far beyond its vernacular base, and Scottish English remains the strident and dominant 'L1' in the life and governance of Scotland. Before we look at revitalising Scots, the still-unesteemed member of Crichton Smith's vocal triptych, it is worth turning our attention to the other two Scottish languages with which it shares a linguistic, social and political space.

Gaelic: your other national tongue

Like most Scottish people, I have great affection for Gaelic. It was the first language I tried to learn on my own, back in the 1980s, rising early on Sunday mornings to watch the BBC beginners' series *Can Seo*. Since then, I have attended countless evening classes from St Andrews/Cill Rìmhinn to London/Lunnainn and (just) managed to pass *An Cùrsa Inntrigidh* from Skye's Sabhal Mòr Ostaig. Like thousands of others, I am now working though Duolingo's online Gaelic course. Alas, despite an elapsed learning time of some 40 years, my proficiency in the language remains frustratingly basic. I mention this in case my critique of Scotland's Gaelic language policy below is interpreted as hostility toward the language itself, its advocates or its speakers. That is not the case; I believe in our 'three-voiced country' too.

From a straightforward minority language viewpoint, Scots has much in common with Gaelic. Both have suffered a long history of stigmatisation and marginalisation. Both are endangered and both require support to survive and thrive. There would appear to be plenty of scope for collaboration, practice sharing and the opportunity to work together to make Scotland genuinely the multilingual nation that Crichton Smith imagined. For a variety of reasons, such solidarity has never emerged. Since the 1980s Gaelic has enjoyed the status of a favoured child in comparison to Scots. The Scottish Government's annual spend on support for Gaelic in 2019 was £12.8m for broadcasting, £6.5m on education and £5.2m for the Bòrd na Gàidhlig. The annual spend on Scots over the same period was a paltry £270,000.[91] Although Scots has over 25 times the number of speakers, the budget for Scots was just over one per cent of the budget for Gaelic. To underline the comparison, in that year, Gaelic was funded at £500 per speaker and Scots at 17.5p per speaker.

Is there any justification for this staggering disparity? To some extent, yes. In its heartlands, Gaelic faces an immediate existential threat. The 2011 Census found only 57,375 self-declared Gaelic speakers. Worse, the report of sociolinguistic survey of Gaelic speakers in its Western Isles published nine years later bore the gloomy title *The Gaelic crisis in the vernacular community*. Working with both census data since the 1980s and more recent speaker questionnaires, the researchers' findings were grim.

> The picture emerging from this research is that the threat to the Gaelic vernacular is so severe that under current circumstances even marginal vestiges of Gaelic's communal presence will be soon lost [...] there is almost no cross-generational communal practice of Gaelic within the younger generations in the remaining indigenous community.[92]

No advocate of minority language rights would question that Gaelic should be saved if possible. Gaelic has a symbolic place in Scottish culture. The MacPherson Taskforce, first identifying the risk to the language a generation ago, included a statement stating that Gaelic was 'fundamental' to Scotland's distinctive sense of self, a 'public good' worth preserving.

91 Scottish Government 2018

92 Ó Giollagáin et al 2020:362

> Gaelic is a precious jewel in the heart and soul of Scotland. It is not constrained within strict boundaries or herded into tight corners. Gaelic is national, European and international. It is fundamental to Scotland; it is not on the periphery or on the fringes. It must be normalised, and its rights must be secured.[93]

I have never come across any genuine advocate of the Scots language who disputes the support given to Gaelic. On the contrary, important lessons may be learned, both positive and negative, from the case of Gaelic. Gaelic policy has pioneered a Scottish pathway towards language revitalisation, shown the power of dedicated advocacy and has put a financial value on local preservation. Unfortunately, it has also exposed how high-profile and expensive polices may not necessarily benefit the native speaker community.

The funding gulf between the two languages stems from very different forms of discussion around Scots and Gaelic, as mentioned earlier. These biases long predate devolution and are not necessarily intentional, and it is worth highlighting the simple sociolinguistic advantages Gaelic has over Scots.

- Gaelic is an *Abstand* (linguistically distinctive) language, very different from English. Although close to Irish, its 'languageness' is not in doubt.
- The Welsh and Irish models provided a readymade template for Gaelic. However, Ó Giollagáin criticised the 'derivative thinking' that failed to adapt such frameworks to Scotland's linguistic context,[94] and a (surely?) obvious point was that neither Ireland nor Wales have a second minority language to accommodate.
- Gaelic provides little threat to the political status quo.
- The speaker base is small, so funding can be capped.
- Long-term Gaelic funding has enabled the emergence articulate cadre of middle-class professionals and activists, intermediaries and lobbyists who fight hard for their linguistic corner.

The outcome is that the discourses around Gaelic and Scots are disconnected. To most of the Scottish population, Scots is just as much 'a precious jewel in the heart and soul of Scotland', but the two languages are rarely spoken of in the same breath. Gaelic language proponents rarely acknowledge Scots and, if they do so, tend to dismiss it as dialectal English. The sheer size of the spend on Gaelic is also problematic for Scots. With 25 times the number of speakers, Millar had already warned that, 'This may be a cost which no

93 Scottish Executive 2000

94 Ó Giollagáin et al 2020:396

government (or population) in Scotland would be willing (or able) to foot'.[95] Scots could never attract or require Gaelic's high level of per capita funding, but affordable models for the revitalisation of Scots have never been budgeted or even discussed; the aim being not equality but equity. In any case, the cultural worth of Scots as a 'precious jewel' remains seriously undervalued.

Some degree of rivalry is understandable; there is 'history' between the two languages. In the early Middle Ages, Gaelic expanded across most of Scotland but then lost out to Scots, by the 13th century beginning its slow retreat to the Highlands. Although once as stigmatised as Scots, recognition of Gaelic's cultural value has grown since the 19th century. A question relating to Gaelic was included in the Census as early as 1881, while Scots speakers had to wait another 130 years to be counted. By the end of the 19th century, An Comunn Gàidhealach (The Gaelic Association) and the Royal National Mòd had been established. In 1984, after years of lobbying, the Scottish Office established Comunn na Gàidhlig (CnaG) to promote Gaelic language and culture, and coordinate language policy. CnaG became a pivotal pressure group at Westminster, lobbying politicians for legislative change. As a visible example, Gaelic road signs were soon introduced. The National Heritage (Scotland) Act of 1985 enabled financial support for organisations promoting Gaelic language, culture and Gaelic medium education, again with funding attached. CnaG also promoted Gaelic broadcasting, leading to the 1992 Gaelic Television Fund. Linked to the 1990 Broadcasting Act, the fund provided the foundations for a secure Gaelic broadcasting service. Even before devolution, an active Gaelic 'industry' had already formed.

The establishment of the Scottish Parliament in 1999 provided a further impetus and instrument to promote Gaelic legislation. A draft Gaelic Language Act, again driven by CnaG, was drawn up quickly, eventually to become The Gaelic Language (Scotland) Act 2005. Meanwhile Gaelic was granted the privileged Part III status in 2001 when the UK government signed up to the European Charter for Regional or Minority Languages (ECRML), while Scots had to make do with the inferior Part II status.

Despite Labour's avowed aversion to cultural nationalism, the Executive of the time openly privileged Gaelic over Scots.

> Labour's inequity of approach towards the two languages permeates every official document and statement on Scotland's languages and culture; is glaringly apparent in the complete lack of Scots in the Parliament building alongside English and Gaelic, and was most strikingly realised in the legal

95 Millar 2005:196

> protection afforded Gaelic through the Gaelic Language (Scotland) Act 2005, whilst Scots received no equivalent.[96]

According to Douglas the indefensibility of this inequality was quietly acknowledged. She quotes a Scottish Executive memo admitting, 'there is little in linguistic grounds to defend a different approach to Scots'. Political grounds, though, are different; the 2005 Act was modeled on legislation for other Celtic languages, the Welsh Language Act 1993 and the Official Language Act 2003 in Ireland. Not to follow suit could have been seen as discriminatory. Scots and its speakers were again excluded from any such rights-based discourse.

Gaelic is also less associated with political nationalism, or at least the 'dangerous' kind in the Central Belt. The speaker base is remote and endangered so is, 'relatively straightforward to be ignored by the great part of the population, except in highly formulaic and token circumstances'.[97] Douglas has another explanation.

> The evocative associations of Gaelic with the Highland Clearances, as well as the attempted suppression of Gaelic culture in the aftermath of the Jacobite uprisings, furthermore means that any national commitment to Gaelic can be seen as rooted more in national atonement than in nationalism.

Scots, by contrast, is still widely spoken by the working classes in the country's heavily populated, once-industrial heartlands, and unlike Gaelic is readily accessible and learnable. For these reasons Douglas considers Scots, 'considerably more of a living, national, language, and consequently holds greater potential for nationalist exploitation'. It may be no accident that 20 years after devolution there is still no Scots equivalent to the CnaG pressure group nor a Scots version of the 2005 Act. Scottish politicians, both unionist and nationalist, know fine well where that sort of thing leads. The Gaelic Act set up the Bòrd na Gàidhlig as an official language agency, with a view to securing the status of the Gaelic language as an official language of Scotland commanding equal respect to English. The main instrument was the National Gaelic Language Plan with its guidance to local authorities with regards for example to Gaelic medium education (GME) and public signage. The Act promotes Gaelic as a 'public good', owned not only by the remaining speaker communities, but the whole of Scotland.

Scots language advocates have long campaigned for equivalent Scots

96 Douglas 2016:23

97 Millar 2005:196

legislation. This type of national status-building project would undoubtedly boost Scots given its substantial speaker base. However, the 2020 *Crisis* report suggested the Gaelic Act had achieved little for the language's fragile speaker base.

> The national plans for Gaelic, with their primary focus on status planning, meet a symbolic need to assert the civic presence of Gaelic in Scotland without creating the official capacity or mechanisms to influence behavioural change at the vernacular level.[98]

Worse, the report implied that the Scotland-wide emphasis of the policy pulled resources and energy from areas of real need. An example is investment in GME provision for 'new speakers' (ie second language learners) in Glasgow and Edinburgh where there is negligible speaker density. The report suggests such flagship initiatives create the illusion of action while distracting from the plight of the vernacular community. Ó Giollagáin was concerned here about a subtle discourse shift to ideas of 'post-vernacular' Gaelic. In a disturbing parallel to discussion of the 'heritisation' of Scots earlier in this chapter, the author believed emerging policy was now 'progressing towards a primary focus on Gaelic as a heritage language'.[99]

That said, the Act has undoubtedly increased the general visibility and symbolic usage of Gaelic across Scotland, through bilingual signs and aspects of official corporate identity. As one journalist put it, a casual visitor to Scotland 'might assume that the Gaelic language is thriving, with every police car carrying the word *poileas* and every ambulance *ambaileans*'.[100] Ironically, a higher profile has made Gaelic a target for language bigotry, and in terms Scots activists well recognise. The costs of Gaelic promotion and SME are frequently challenged in the Scottish press and social media, often presented in terms of lack of utility. Emily McEwan-Fujita, a researcher into media discourses, highlighted the way the way the Scottish and British media habitually use stereotypically negative 'discourses of death' when discussing Gaelic. She created 'Anti-Gaelic Bingo',[101] a game listing typically-used words and phrases such as 'ancient', 'declining', 'poetic', 'obsolete', 'has no written form', 'guttural', 'artificial', 'primitive', 'backward' and the ever popular 'has no word for helicopter'. This type of derision is regularly heaped on Scots, too. Not surprisingly, an Anti-Scots Bingo card soon appeared on social media adding 'no-one talks like that',

98 Ó Giollagáin et al 2020:378
99 Ó Giollagáin et al 2020:397
100 Carrell 2020
101 McEwan-Fujita 2015

'dialect of English', 'cringe', 'no standard form', 'slang' and so on.[102]

From this perspective of prejudice, we can return to what Gaelic and Scots have in common. The current differences in status and funding could simply be due to Gaelic having had a long head start on Scots in the promotion game, and so being at a more advanced stage of political and social acceptance. Neither community should assume language diversity is a zero-sum game, ie that promotion of Scots will inevitably result in fewer resources for Gaelic or vice versa. Raising awareness of language diversity across Scotland would surely benefit both, and Gaelic's more developed stage in policy, promotion and standardisation may provide a useful guide for Scots. This can only work, though, if there is recognition that Scotland is a genuinely trilingual nation. Currently, this is not the case. The Scottish Government has a national policy to encourage very visible Gaelic medium education and 'bilingual' (ie Gaelic/English) public signage. This occurs even in areas of high Scots-speaker density. Just one example is the Gaelic signage of South Ayrshire where the 2011 Census figures showed 35,000 Scots speakers (a third of its population) but fewer than 400 people speaking Gaelic. The very visible erasure of the linguistic heritage of a substantial minority may partially explain a sometimes crudely expressed 'anti-Gaelic' backlash in such places, and that is good for neither language.

Whether or not the Gaelic Act has had any real impact on the linguistic health of the remaining vernacular community remains a moot point for some, but the 2005 legislation and especially the Gaelic Plan have at least set a precedent for concerted government action around language revitalisation in Scotland. Any Scots Plan resulting from the Scottish Languages Act would do well to parallel some of these principles. The Gaelic legislation, for example, officially validates four key concepts (usage, status, acquisition and corpus) that are often regarded as fundamental to the protection and revitalisation of minority tongues.

Scottish English: your other, other national tongue.

Let us also cast a glance at Scotland's linguistic juggernaut. Despite its dominance and power, in my view Scottish English needs a little linguistic love too. The Scottish form of English may not have been in Scotland for anything like as long as Scots or Gaelic, but over three centuries its spoken form, the Scottish 'accent', has become a significant carrier of Scottish identity. It is easy to paint English as the villain in Scotland's linguistic story, but the truth is that Scots and Gaelic are merely in bed with an English

102 McEwan-Fujita 2018

elephant. English is the majority language of our closest neighbours, England and Ireland, and is the global *lingua franca* of unimaginable scale that everybody wants to learn.

In his 1980 revitalisation manifesto *Developing Scots as a National Language* McClure was pragmatic regarding the role of (Scottish) English:

> Even after Scots is established, English will retain the accepted status which it has had for three hundred years, as one of the spoken and written languages of Scotland. A large and distinguished body of Scottish literature is written in English; and we have made of Scottish English a highly individual form of the international language. If these facts have been ignored in the course of this paper, this is simply because the existence and survival of English are not in question. We are discussing the development of Scots as *a* national language, not *the* national language: probably nobody, and certainly not I, would advocate monolingualism in Scots as the goal for a language planning project.[103]

We can take it that full Catalan-style normalisation is not on the cards. How, then, can we find an accommodation with English in Scotland that rebalances the chronic diglossia discussed in Chapter Two?

> As we all know, the present sociolinguistic state of non-Gaelic Scotland is one of fundamental inequality between Scots and English. English, the High variety, is considered, at least under most circumstances, to be the more prestigious variety, the language which will 'get you places'.[104]

In other words, English is here to stay. While Scots and the Scottish language mix remain potent identity markers, the spoken, accented forms of Scottish English are too, so we may need to think about its maintenance as another cultural 'jewel'. The survival of international English is never threatened, but our highly distinct spoken form could well be. Should we standardise Scottish English, or at least define it better? In the same counterintuitive way that a more standardised Scots would boost its dialects, a properly standardised Scottish English might strengthen Scots. As any advocacy of Scottish English is so unusual, some clarification might be necessary.

Scottish Standard English (SSE) is defined in *World Englishes* as, 'Standard

103 McClure 1980:40
104 Millar 2011:8

English pronounced with a Scottish accent and with a few Scotticisms in grammar and vocabulary'.[105] This variety has been the official language of Scotland for at least three centuries, but Scottish English has never been codified in a dictionary. The *World Englishes* definition is useful, but remember in the academic literature the terminology is far from consistent. Jane Stuart-Smith, for example, provides below a definition of 'Scottish English' that explicitly includes Scots.

> [A] range of varieties forming a sociolinguistic continuum between two poles, broad vernacular Scots spoken by working-class speakers at one end [...] and Standard Scottish English (SSE), spoken by middle-class speakers at the other.[106]

In Chapter One, I noted that other scholars have applied the term 'Scots' to what is here defined by Stuart-Smith as 'Scottish English'. This suggests neither term is adequate enough to describe a linguistic complex that both in fact and definition spans two distinct linguistic varieties.

To be fair, there has always been ambiguity in the use of national and regional labels for varieties of English in linguistic descriptions. 'Irish English', for example, could refer to all forms of English in Ireland, or only the standard forms. Tom McArthur, like many modern writers on the subject tends to refer to English in the plural. In his influential 1998 review *The English Languages*, he recognised pluralist models accommodating multiple standards have gradually replaced 'the "straightforward" monolithic model' of one indivisible English.[107] This framework is now widely used, for example by the core student text, *Global Englishes*.[108] These pluralistic models include American English, Australian English, Irish English, Indian English, and Scottish English but also recognise hard-to-categorise 'sub varieties' such as Singlish (Singapore English), African American Vernacular English, various creoles and Scots. Whether Scots is treated as 'an English' or 'a language' in this context really depends on the ideology and purposes of the writer.

SSE arose from the long anglicisation of lowland Scottish language that predates the Union. As Millar and colleagues note, by the end of the 17th century, 'most non-Gaelic Scots continued to speak their local dialect as default code, employing, if literate, a rather uncomfortable Standard English when

105 Melchers and Shaw 2011
106 Stuart-Smith et al 2014:2
107 McArthur 1998:xiv
108 Jenkins 2015

this became necessary'.[109] Later 'dialect' poetry apart, the standard written form was established about the time of the Union. Spoken Scottish English, on the other hand, emerged more slowly over the next century. Despite all the attempts at 'correcting' Scots usages and pronunciations, the result was a linguistic hybrid. Any adult learner of a second language knows it is hard to hide their native accent and SSE bears traces of the original Scots language 'substrate' in its pronunciation. McClure claims the Scottish identity of SSE may have been deliberately preserved, due to the conscious belief of many 18th-century Scottish writers and intellectuals 'that a total Anglicisation of their speech, leaving no Scottish features whatsoever, was not a desirable aim'.[110] Scottish English became to be regarded as a separate identity marker and, McClure adds, 'like other national forms of English it is characterised by some extent by grammar, vocabulary and idiom, but most obviously in pronunciation'.

Although I was educated at all levels in Scotland, I was never taught what specific elements of grammar, vocabulary and idiom were distinctive to SSE, outwith the famous exception of 'outwith'. Should SSE include Scots words in the same way that American English or Indian English are enriched by local vocabulary? Maybe Scots could 'officially' donate this type of vocabulary to SSE. Handy lists of Scottish words already exist and are widely available. The bestselling *Collins Gem Scots Dictionary*, for example, in print for almost a quarter century, contains some 1,800 words and phrases from both literary sources and everyday language, including 'outwith'. An adapted version of that would add greatly to the lexical distinctiveness of SSE. Millar made a similar case for a formalised SSE-Scots written hybrid analogous to the Dano-Norwegian language Bokmål in Norway[111], discussed earlier. In my view, an enriched and formalised SSE to be used alongside a standardised Scots would be much more desirable and feasible.

Without official lists, the use of distinctive Scottish vocabulary is inevitably haphazard. Fiona Douglas' corpus analysis of Scots words in the otherwise SSE text of Scottish newspapers in 2009 revealed that the frequency of identifiable Scottish words was very low and largely confined to individual writers and specific contexts, especially humour and personal commentary. Interestingly the most Scots vocabulary was found in *The Scottish Sun*, considered at the time an interloper, but 'behaving as more linguistically Scottish than some of Scotland's indigenous newspapers'.[112] Douglas linked the 'authentic' language of the paper to its success in entering Scottish

109 Millar et al 2014:11
110 McClure 2008:79
111 Millar 2005:197
112 Douglas 2009:162

market, asking whether the indigenous newspapers should be 'making more of their own and essentially Scottish linguistic resources, and challenging rather than accepting the hegemonic constraints of Standard English'. Given the British nationalist leanings of most of the Scottish press, this seems unlikely, but may represent a lost commercial opportunity.

A different type of hegemony operates in the spoken version of SSE. McClure refers to 'a common phonological system, differing in several conspicuous ways from those of other accents of English'. This distinctive phonetic identity (ie accent) 'is close to being a defining feature of it'. Some local variation is introduced from underlying dialects of Scots, but generally, spoken SSE is immediately recognised as a definitive Scottish identity marker. SSE became 'the characteristic speech of the professional class and the accepted norm in schools' and, nowadays, the default accent of Scottish broadcasting. It should be noted in passing that Received Pronunciation (RP), once the voice of the BBC, has never enjoyed the prestige in Scotland it had in England, and the local RP-like variants, middle-class 'Kelvinside' and 'Morningside', have both vanished.

The phonology of SSE has been meticulously described,[113] but it is hard to determine its long-term stability. It can be assumed though that SSE will be under the same dialect attrition pressure as any other regional variety. Will linguistic loyalty keep it distinctive, or will we hear a gradual levelling to Southern English norm? It may be time to get a little more prescriptive to maintain the distinctive Scottish English forms. If you learn Gaelic, for example, much care is taken in getting the pronunciation and intonation exactly right. Does SSE not deserve the same level of care? If that notion now seems bizarre, it was not always so. In 1913 William Grant wrote a delightful phonetic manual on *The Pronunciation of English in Scotland*. It was intended for trainee teachers, English teachers, 'lawyers and ministers and all those who, in the course of their calling, have to engage in public speaking'.[114] Grant maintains, 'all students of language should be interested in the study of the Scottish variety of Standard English'. As indeed they still should.

The Standardisation of Scots

What is the Scots for 'workshop'?

Standardiation is the biggest stushie of them all. Should there be a consistent way to write and use the language? From Chapter One, I have argued that there should be, to improve the language's prestige, usefulness and literacy.

113 Eg Wells 1982

114 Grant 1913: v

Before we discuss this thorny debate in more detail, I'll provide an example if you are unfamiliar with the complications of writing normal Scots.

A new writer recently asked members of the popular Facebook group Scots Language Forum what was the Scots equivalent of the English term 'workshop'. The collective response illustrates the problem of not having a standard. For most languages there is a fairly simple answer, and a dictionary or Google Translate will provide *atelier* for French, *Werkstatt* for German, *bùth-obrach* for Gaelic and so on. Scots, however, does not yet have a complete English-to-Scots dictionary, so workshop as a word does not appear. In the *Concise English-Scots Dictionary* you can find 'wark' (a noun) and 'wirk' (a verb), and 'shop' which gives 'chop', 'shap' and a Doric variant, 'tchop'. The much bigger *Concise Scots Dictionary* lists 'shoap', usually considered a West Coast variant. The popular *Scots Online Dictionary* actually includes the complete word as 'warkshap' but someone on the Forum noted that compound neologisms such as my own creation, 'wabsteid', 'maks fowk girn'. Another complication is that in many languages the word has a traditional meaning associated with making and repairs and its extended meaning as a kind of discussion group is seen by some to be pretentious.

The Forum community offered quite a few DIY alternatives. Maybe just use the French or German equivalents, not an uncommon approach in English. Many thought the English word should just be used, 'It's jist a wird that disna need translating', although it was pointed out at least one part of the compound has a long-established traditional form. But was it 'wark' the noun or 'wirk' the verb? Dictionary validity was, as ever, challenged; 'Scottish dictionaries dinna spik on a daily basis tho. Mainly formulated by academics fae dinna spik it aa the time'. Others offered a range of novel phonetic renditions; 'wurkshoap', 'workshoap', 'wirkshope', 'wirkshoap', 'warkshoap', 'wirkshop' and 'wurkshap', presumably based on individual pronunciation. One contributor thought he always used the English term: 'Ach – that's fit I say, online or aff, it's – workshop'. Another contributor realised his own pronunciation was maybe not the best guide; 'tae ma lug A spik wark, wirk, wurk an werk jist hou a say "work" [...] dunno' and concluded, 'sax o yin hauf dozen o thethither'. A more cynical voice concluded that as there were no official standards; 'The Scots for workshop is whatever you want it to be'. And this is essentially the problem. Without standards, writing even the simplest of texts is transformed from an enjoyable communicative or stylistic task to a lexicographical, orthographical and ideological minefield.

The conversation highlights another significant issue. Scots writers are all, by necessity, self-taught.

> It has been left to the individual learner to develop more in-depth knowledge about traditional Scots spelling, grammatical forms that may not be immediately apparent to Scots speakers and learners, or how to access dictionaries and Scots language resources alongside developing ideas about best practice.[115]

Building productive writing skills in Scots remains a challenging personal journey.

> Often with Scots, one develops one's literacy on one's own. A person brings their own conscious and unconscious linguistic knowledge, and prejudices to some sort of body of written Scots and finds an expressive solution that satisfies their needs.[116]

Therefore, beliefs about the rightness of one's own solutions may be quite strong and may subvert discussions on communal strategies.

The write stuff

Many of the recent debates around Scots among writers and artists assume the superiority of the spoken tongue. Thus, 'Gin Scots is a language, it's the language that we're speakin nou.'[117] Speech in all its diversity is claimed to be more 'authentic', with the written 'literary dialect' seen as a secondary expression or ignored altogether. This dichotomy is even more widespread in academia, where everyday dialogue is considered more spontaneous and worthier of research. Florian Coulmas calls this privileging the 'dominance of vernacular speech'.[118] He argues that such a bias may have been more pertinent in the past, when early linguistic pioneers wanted to overthrow the previous 'tyranny of writing'. However, in modern highly literate societies, the binary division is not so useful.

> Humanity has moved steadily towards relying on written communication in ever more domains of life. This involves changes in communicative behaviour, in language socialization, in the ways we learn and acquire knowledge, and in the formation and maintaining of social networks.

115 Dempster 2019:20.6

116 Dempster 2019:20.1

117 Clark 2016

118 Coulmas 2013:1

The linguistic consequence is that no aspect of speech in modern Scotland can nowadays truly be considered 'authentic'. The written word influences everyone's speech behaviour and perception of language. The pragmatic reason is that writing, according to Coulmas, 'expands the range of intellectual pursuits beyond what is possible without it'.

Writing is therefore more than just a secondary mode of communication; it also serves as a tool for the creation of novel and precise linguistic abstractions. Writing lets us break out of the restricted domains of spoken dialect, always rooted in the mundane here and now.

> [W]riting invariably plays a central role in any design for changing the status hierarchy and laying claim to language status for a variety that has none.[119]

Having a written norm is an indispensable condition for a language striving for higher status. Minority language activists across the globe consider the adoption of a single written standard enabling and liberating. Usually, it's the first step towards rebalancing unfair cultural, social or political power relationships and *laissez faire* neglect. To them, a language without a written standard is intellectually decapitated.

Coulmas described a written norm as a shared asset that belongs to nobody but is accessible to all.

> The industrial age [...] brought demands for stricter regimentation. Conformity and standardization, turning the written language into a public good, that is, a means of communication that came to be recognized as a prerequisite for success in collective endeavours, notably endeavours of the nation state.

In this model, the current self-regulation of Scots spelling represents a series of privatised acts, while standardisation is the only way of realising the communal benefits of a public good. Therefore, Unger considered the nature of Scots writing 'a key ideological battleground between the Scots activists and the proponents of the status quo'.[120]

Adding to this fog of war, however, is the ambivalent attitude that some people have to seeing Scots written down. Until the latter part of the 20th century, speakers would probably see printed 'Good' Scots quite regularly.

119 Coulmas 2013:46

120 Unger 2013:103

As this literacy practice faded, especially in schools, most people's experience of written Scots became very limited. In parallel, spoken Scottish language became more fragmented and access to the 'full canon' speech of older relatives and community worthies declined. The result was sadly predictable.

> [W]hen people encounter Scots in a wide range of registers, particularly those that require an 'elevated' register (eg in the political field and in formal educational settings), it is seen as something artificial, which someone has looked up in a dictionary.[121]

For and against standards

> The ins and oots o hoo tae spell the Scots language can be yin o maist borin subjects ablow the sunless lift o bonnie Scotland. But it does seem tae fascinate a wheen o folk as weel. Some feel sae strangly aboot spellin in Scots it can whiles mak them loss the tattie awthegither.[122]

If it was just about utility, agreeing for example the Scots equivalent of 'workshop', then surely there would be no need for tatties to be lost. However, as I have suggested, the standardisation of the written language represents something far deeper: the main battleground between the heritisation and normalisation camps. Thus, 'it is the question of norms (particularly the issue of orthographic standardisation) that reveals ideological positioning'.[123] Standardisation is not, as Fitt suggests, just for geeks but goes to the heart of what people think a normal language is and should possess. Put simply, 'with no standard version, many argue it is a collection of dialects, not a language'.[124]

What makes this point of conflict especially bizarre is that the ubiquitous notion that Scots has no written standards is largely a fiction. In the opening chapter, I used Andy Eagle's 2011 definition of the Scots language as 'a number of (closely) related spoken dialects accompanied by a literary tradition employing established and *prestigious (pan-dialect) orthographic conventions*' [my italics]. But to what extent do these 'conventions' really constitute an unofficial 'soft' standard for Scots? We will start by looking at ideologies of standardisation and anti-standardisation, how these apply to Scots, the conventions that already exist for Scots, the ways in which people have tried to improve them over the last 70 years, and why people demand (and resist) an official version.

121 Unger 2013:139
122 Fitt 2016d
123 Costa 2010:2
124 Dickie 2015

Any 'language' is usually thought of in terms of 'discrete entities, defined by standard grammars, standard dictionaries, standard phonologies and the like'.[125] Scots language champion Alasdair Allan found, in the early years of the new Scottish Parliament, 'that the lack of an accepted written standard form was a brick wall that he commonly hit when arguing for official recognition for Scots'.[126] Comparison with English or Gaelic, for which standards have long been established, are unavoidable. In Scotland there exists what Costa et al called a 'double linguistic regime', with a standard for English and ostensibly none for Scots.[127] This is significant as 'minority language advocates and users cannot escape the standard language debate because of the model imposed by the dominant language'. Reporting on language revitalisation efforts globally, Grenoble and Whaley noted that standardisation is usually considered an obligatory and critical step, as 'without standardization, writing becomes idiosyncratic and cannot be interpreted by a large enough body of speakers'.[128] Costa realised Scots had the same problem.

> The absence of a publicly available standard makes the use of Scots tied to who the user is, and to where they originate – socially as well as geographically.

Without an 'authorised' or neutral version of Scots, an individual's language skills and dialectal or class origins become the symbolic focus instead of the communicative function of the text itself.

> Cosmopolitanism and decontextualisation emphasise the need for a neutral, ie purely referential medium of communication available to all for the conduct of common affairs and the government of the nation, thus, in principle, affording to all who can acquire such a medium the (at least theoretical) possibility to take part without the burdensome interference of social or geographic provenance.[129]

From a historical perspective, too, Costa and colleagues reminded us,

> [S]tandardisation remains a potent way of doing or inventing a language, of producing languages as bounded, discrete entities and

125 Fettes 1997:301
126 Macafee, 2015
127 Costa et al 2017:61
128 Grenoble and Whaley 2006:130
129 Costa et al 2017:5

as social institutions and subsequently increasing the social status of those who use them.

Official standardisation would therefore confirm the status of Scots as a language, allowing it to grow and evolve naturally. As the Japanese engineering axiom puts it, 'Without standards, there can be no improvement'.

If this sounds eminently logical, what are the ideological arguments against standardisation? The main claim is that standardisation implies a decrease in diversity.[130] The written standard, aiming to be decontextualised and neutral, could become disconnected from everyday speech practices and the gradual evolution of the language itself. Remember William McIlvanney's 2002 impassioned plea: 'A language lives on the streets and, when its ability to be creatively subversive dies there, so does the language'. The same issue applies to every spoken language, of course, even well-regulated ones like Dutch.

> What looks like 'Dutch' from the viewpoint of a non-speaker becomes a constellation of stylistic norms for the learner of the 'standard', a shifting mosaic of regional and class-based varieties, which when observed in their social context are a subtle ever-turning kaleidoscope of individual and group speech patterns of speakers going through their daily lives.[131]

The Dutch 'kaleidoscope' evokes Warren Maguire's earlier description of Scots as a multi-dimensional sociolinguistic variation space.[132] It is easy to see how an artistic respect for linguistic diversity intersects with the resistance in current language scholarship to 'prescriptivism', the making and following of language rules. Edwards worries that the result has been the emergence of a restricting orthodoxy.

> At more rarified levels, prescriptivism has become a four-letter word, with scholars arguing that its neither desirable nor feasible to attempt to intervene in the 'natural' social life of the language.[133]

While the fetishisation of 'natural' or authentic language may be comprehensible from an artistic, scholarly or heritage perspective, for a minority language such an ideology is always destructive. There is little 'natural' in the coercive power imbalances that lead to the marginalisation of minority languages. Edwards saw the blank refusal of linguistic elites to intervene, and especially the way

130 Eg Milroy and Milroy 1985, 1999

131 Fettes 1997:302

132 Maguire 2012:3

133 Edwards 2009:17

they routinely disparaged minority language standardisation, as essentially 'prescriptivism in reverse'. It this context, Edwards called for 'modified' prescriptivism, that is, for a more nuanced type of intervention that respected a wider range of perspectives.

In the specific case of Scots, the privileging of 'natural' language has another dimension. Corbett suggested that the existing literary tradition of Scots may itself be problematic, 'because this literary tradition is associated less and less with the everyday speech, the texts that result tend to be rejected as "artificial"'.[134] He recognised that, while all written standard languages are always artificial social constructs designed to various official communicative functions,

> [W]e have become socialised into considering Scottish Standard English as 'natural' for fulfilling these pragmatic functions and the use of the Braid Scots would be likely to seem 'unnatural', as well as unncecessary, to many people who are currently uninvolved with the debate.

Schrödinger's Scots standards

The debate so far has been based on the widespread belief there is no 'Standard Scots', yet James Costa observed, 'the writing of Scots is constrained by a number of covert rules, stratified through decades of academic and scholarly conversations'.[135] Like Schrödinger's poor cat, such rules exist and don't exist at the same time. Costa realises ambiguity presents a problem for writers; 'It is a game, in other words, whose rules are more complicated than the absence of a standard would have new players believe'. How did this strange situation arise?

People have been writing and reading Scots for centuries, so spelling conventions and traditions have had to emerge simply to make texts more accessible. Scots as a distinctive language dates back to the 14th century, and by the 17th century an official form was in use. According to the traditional account, what followed was 'failed standardisation'.[136] Although pre-Union Scots may have come close to achieving systematic and prescriptive regularity, from the 18th century onwards its autonomy was eroded under social, political and linguistic pressure from dominant English. Yet this familiar tale of decline is again only part of the story. Throughout the 19th, 20th and 21st centuries literary or Modern Scots remained a staple and popular feature of Scottish print culture. As any form of writing requires some form of standardisation,

134 Corbett 2003:262

135 Costa 2017:50

136 Millar 2005:89

why did the myth that Scots has 'no standards' arise?

Scots was cut free from any state apparatus over three centuries ago. As it depended on partial, ad hoc, informal and emergent stylings it is easy to believe that Scots turned linguistically feral and descended into orthographic chaos. But that is not how language works; communication requires coherence. Thus, Caroline Macafee explains, 'there is a tradeetional orthography. It gaes back tae Allan Ramsay an, mair importantly, is fameeliar fae the screivin o Burns'.[137] Andy Eagle wrote that in the 18th and 19th centuries literary Scots was remarkably regularised.[138] Eagle's thesis was confirmed by by Bann and Corbett's digital analysis of literature spanning this period. Although the researchers saw variability in texts, they also discovered 'a historical tendency for readers and writers to favour some consistency in orthographic practice', even if the written variety 'never quite solidified into a "fixed" set of orthographic forms'.[139]

Bann and Corbett quote Robert Louis Stevenson, who declared in 1887 that the Scots tongue had an 'orthography of its own', although lacking neither 'authority nor author'. Eagle's own detailed analysis confirmed that most well-read 18th and 19th century writers 'were aware of the concept of a "standard" or "pan-dialectal" Scots and the orthographic practices of which it was comprised'. This is why Grant and Dixon's 1921 grammar *Manual of Modern Scots* could draw so effectively from the Scots literature from this period. Their achievement illustrates the pan-dialectal cohesiveness of the written language at that time. The continuing notion of literary 'Good Scots' (ie prestige usage) was based at least implicitly on this model. Current Scots dictionaries and grammars draw heavily from this late 19th century regularised version of Scots. Aitken acknowledges the influence of that communal tradition.

> It seems natural to follow what I call the mainstream literary Scots tradition, what Grant and Dixon in their *Manual of Modern Scots* (1921) call Standard Scots, namely the somewhat archaistic and idealised variety of Central Scots used in much Scots literature from Allan Ramsay onwards, which also forms the main core of the Lallans of modern makars like Hugh MacDiarmid and Robert Garioch, and which is adopted without question or discussion by the magazine *Lallans*, and also by William Graham for his lessons on Scots published in that magazine.[140]

137 Macafee 2012

138 Eagle 2022

139 Bann and Corbett 2015:143

140 Aitken 1980, 2015

He adds, 'this variety already has some recognition as a national literary standard. We will do well to capitalise on this'. It should be remembered that William Graham updated the 'archaistic and idealised variety' via his 1977 *Scots Word Book*, the foundation of the current *Essential Scots Dictionary*. As Aitken mentions, the Scots language magazine *Lallans*, in continuous publication since 1973, has also contributed to the maintenance of this tradition, although is far less prescriptive than might be thought. Macafee observes, 'Lallans has ayeweys acceptit screivins in regional varieties o Scots an even, gin contributors feel strangly enough, in deefferent wad-be staundart orthographies'.[141]

The existence of such broad conventions now explains why McClure could assume, 'all of us know roughly, or have some idea, of what is meant by "Lowland Scots"'[142] as some possibly vague undocumented notion of the 'Grant-Dixon-*Lallans*-Graham norm' (as Aitken later labeled it). Nearly 40 years later Costa found this notional standard is to some extent still in place; 'there is in fact an established common way of writing, based on covert, but well entrenched, ideas about what type Scots writing should follow'. The web pages of the Scots Language Centre or the printed publications of Itchy Coo illustrate the cohesion and regularity of this type of mainstream modern Scots prose. Costa recounts the tale of a constructed orthography SSS or *Staunirt Scóts Screivin* that was developed by a conlang (constructed or artificial language) enthusiast. SSS received some press coverage in 2015 but was poorly received by the Scots language community. As Costa observed, 'when presented with a form of writing that is markedly different, writers of Scots recognise what does, or does not, fit within the standard type'. By this token 'variation is acceptable, but only if it fits the loose pattern of familiarity'. Costa concluded that even in the absence of explicit standards, Scots writing is not a free-for-all at all, but rather a 'closely monitored community undertaking'. The 2021 *Scots Warks: Support and guidance for writing* from the Scots Language Centre agreed; 'We do have well known spellings that are favoured and patterns of grammar and syntax that are uniquely ours'.[143] The disparaging reaction to 'artificial' Ullans, a type of Ulster Scots used for official documentation, only underlines the point. There is simply no need to develop a new orthography or worse some Nynorsk-style conlang from scratch. This may have been the rationale behind Kloss' 1984 description of Scots as a *Halbsprach* or 'half language'. As Millar commented, 'half' was

141 Macafee 2012

142 McClure 1980:11

143 Scots Language Centre 2021

perhaps a 'less than generous measure'.[144]

Even if Scots was only 'half-standardised', the achievement of any level of cohesion in the absence of any official diktat is extraordinary. Macafee believes, however, by the beginning of the 20th century the orthography of much traditional Scots writing was far more regular than that.

> There wis only twae real problems wi the tradeetional spellin seestem: the 'spray o apostrophes' an the ambiguous <oo> spellin. The apostrophes, as we ken, wis felt tae be apologetic, because they relatit the reduced forms o Scots tae the fu forms o Inglis, though there nae dout that thon is halpfu tae readers whase leeteracy is, an ayweys will be, primarily in Inglis, an they micht juist as weill be cried etymological spellins that relatit tae the earlier fu forms. The <oo> in wirds lik shoon an aboon led tae spellin pronunciations, but there wis nae problem ava wi its uise in wirds lik hoose.

Corbett explained the logical basis for this variation as follows.

> Those writing in the 18th and 19th centuries were well aware that a Scots-speaking readership would never pronounce the likes of 'about', 'dead', 'sleight' and 'night' as in Standard English but by the 20th century that could no longer be taken for granted and spellings such as 'aboot', 'deid', 'slicht' and 'nicht' had become more common.[145]

As widespread knowledge of older Scots literature began to fade, growing mass literacy meant that the English orthography learned at school tended to overshadow any residual knowledge of traditional conventions in spelling and pronunciation. If traditional Scots was not to be taught, Bann and Corbett explained that writers wanting to represent contemporary Scots speech had to draw to some extent on the readers' knowledge of English orthography.

> When literature in Modern Scots began to be written and read more widely, therefore, the orthographic practices were a hybrid form, partly harking back to the Older Scots period and partly adapted from the norms of standard English.[146]

Eagle, together with Bann and Corbett, argue these practices were far from

144 Millar 2005:15

145 Corbett 2003:262

146 Bann and Corbett 2015:63

unsystematic. Macafee concedes dictionaries often give the impression that 'every conceivable spelling of a given word will turn up somewhere', but she agrees, 'there is nevertheless an orthographic system'.[147]

Thus, *The Scots Spelling Comatee*, convening in 1996, found there was already a 75 per cent consensus on spellings of a very long word list.[148] Most of the remaining disagreements could be addressed by choosing from a limited range of spelling options. Scots language activist John Tait believed Scots already to be very close to an acceptable standard.

> The practical problems with the actual SLD [Scots Language Dictionaries] spellings do not effect the majority of words. It may be that as little as 10% or even 5% would need to be changed or added. However, as these are often frequently used words, they comprise a much larger proportion of a given text.[149]

So why was this standard not ratified a long time ago? Tait argued it was due to the heritage-orientated 'owners' of Scots holding a dogmatic view that Scots should be limited to what McClure's described as 'a set of restricted and low-prestige dialects and an artificial learned language for poets'. For heritisers, creating a general standard 'using a normative orthography with the aim of producing an expository written register' is deemed outrageously radical. From this perspective, the ideology of heritisation has saddled Scots with a cultural 'speed limiter' to block its revival as a 'living and all-purpose language' and to keep it dialectally fragmented and so politically neutered. Tait dubbed the covert linguistic regulator the '95% Rule'.

> In order to preserve the existing hegemony of standard English and to ring-fence its exclusive use in all prestigious domains, it is expedient to support 'dialect' or 'Scots' provided that you resist the crucial measures (possibly as little as a 5% adjustment to already well established practices) which would make it possible for it to be used for purposes outwith its allocated role in vernacular speech and literature.[150]

If Scots is so close to a standard, what are the unresolved issues? In the absence of any official guidance, earlier Scots writers had to choose practically between accessibility (anglicised spellings) or authenticity (historically

147 Macafee 1987:4
148 Scots Spellin Comatee 1998:15
149 Tait 2019
150 Tait 2018

distinctive Scots spellings). Modern writers also have the additional challenge of how much to represent the by now partially anglicised and dialectical spoken mix of vernacular Scottish language in their writing style. This tension is expressed in the standardisation debate by the occasionally charged argument between 'minimalists' and 'maximalists', according to how differently they think written Scots should be from standard English. Bann and Corbett outline the contrasting positions.

> A 'minimalist' approach is largely set on refining the corpus of familiar, adapted and traditional spellings that inform the Scots dictionary record, while a 'maximalist' position favours systematic innovations that highlight differences from English.[151]

As with many debates around the Scots language, the disparities may be exaggerated. An example is the 1998 *Report and Reccomends o the Scots Spellin Comatee*. After two years of discussion and many disagreements, the Comatee of experts eventually managed to find an acceptable consensus 'airtit maistlie at narrative an expository prose'. Predicatably, a minority contrarian view was asserted.

> [T]hare wis a somewhit contar leiterary trend amang screivers generally no sae closslie associatit wi SLS an sceptical o the Lallans project, ti uise Scots in mair naituralistic, less consciously leiterary weys, aften exploitin urban dialects an exploring workin-cless experience.[152]

Complicating matters further, *The Scots School Dictionary* (SSD) had just been published in 1996, representing what seemed to be a more prescriptive approach from the Scottish National Dictionary Association (SNDA). The SSD was recognised as 'the state of the art' but 'SNDA naiturallie sees it as its function ti record the leid the wey it's kythed ower a lang period'. The Association's dictionaries are therefore based on collecting historical usage in all its inconsistency. Even when choices are made in the SSD (based presumably on frequency of occurrence), some alternatives are also given, so it can be only prescriptive up to a point. Another obvious drawback is that the SSD was not a complete dictionary, so lists entries only where Scots usage diverges from English. Nevertheless, the *Report* 'taks as its stertin pynt the word-leet gien in SSD, wi a puckle chynges'. The 'puckle chynges' were actually quite lengthy and represent an alternative word list to the SSD

151 Bann and Corbett 2015:93

152 Scots Spellin Comatee 1998

for many of the commonest words. It was stated pointedly that 'SNDA disna accept the recommends gien in this Report'. Lexicographers and language revitalisers of course come from radically different traditions.

That said, John Law informed the group at its first meeting that of a long vocabulary list prepared previously, 'noncontentious spellings exceeded contentious by three to one, so that the task facing any committee was by no means an impossibly difficult one'. He explained why:

> [A]s everybody knew, the bulk of contentious words was made up of those tending to use ee/ei or oo/ou digraphs, much of the rest involving different default choices for the schwa [unstressed vowel].

Indeed, most of the challenges to the SSD listings seemed focused on the representation of vowels. There was particular concern about the perceived overuse of 'oo' instead of the more historic 'ou' form, and likewise 'ee' replacing 'ei'. The dialectal 'oa' sound (eg 'shoap') was problematic, as vowels are pronounced differently in different dialects. Similarly, the word 'guid' (the 'neutral' recommended form) can be pronounced as 'gyid', 'gid', 'gweed' or 'göd', and 'uise' (the recommended form) as 'yaize', 'eeze' or 'öze'. In the last case it was noted that the SSD had unfortunately only listed one West Central variant, 'yaize', which, although common enough, was not representative of more general pronunciation. This obsession with vowels may seem a little strange but the production of vowels is central in forging the phonetic identity of all Germanic languages and dialects.

Generally, the recommendations centred on consistency and recognition of well-established spellings. The Comatee took a generally 'anti-maximalist' stance. Words common with English were largely left alone unless pronounced differently, and the general advice was:

> Dinna lichtlie invent new weys o spellin at haes naither precedent nor authority. Conseider homogeneity, readabeility, aesthetics, conseistency, diaphonology. Evyte hyperphonetic spellins. Dinna mak it ower hard for the English-thirlt reader: written Scots shuid be accessible ti sic readers.

Regarding the thorny issues of dialects and creative writing, the Comatee recognised 'the primacy o screivers in recordin the leid' and did not want to discourage 'uisin dialects o Scots freely in creative screivin'. They thought that even with such writing 'haudin wi whitiver in oor recommends set oot here can aye be hauden wi, will impruve readabeility an benefit aabodie'.

The *Report* makes the interesting point that even in literary texts that use standard Scots for the main text, dialectal variants can still be featured; 'in maist written leids it's common ti uise phonetic spellins in dialogue, ti indicate local pronunciations, an a mair staundard spellin for the narrative'. A little creativity could thus accommodate both dialect and standard writing.

By any yardstick, and especially given the fractiousness of the issue, the *Report* was an impressive communal achievement. Whether you agree personally with all the recommendations or not, it showed what could be achieved with determination, leadership and compromise. Unfortunately, Costa was correct that it was not adopted subsequently in education, publishing or official usage.[153] It did, however, influence *The Online Scots Dictionary*, a popular internet English-Scots lexicon, and its innovations can be traced in many instances of modern Scots writing. Nonetheless, in common with previous attempts by language activists and reformers, the *Report* simply, 'never met with broad approval'.[154] As a contributing factor, Tait reports one of the most influential people in Scots academia and promotion at the time called the whole exercise 'totally irrelevant'.[155] Standardisers were marginalised, and even disparaged, in the Scottish academic establishment of the time. Corbett, writing a few years later, remarked,

> It is all too easy to ridicule the enthusiasts who regularly turn up with a new and 'authentic' way of spelling Scots, or the activists who disconcertingly code-switch into Lallans in the pub after a conference.[156]

Tait therefore came to a gloomy conclusion.

> Sae it disna maiter whit airguments ye uise, whit principles ye apply, or whit recommends ye mak. It's richt eneuch that onie threipin aboot orthography is feckless, cause the hale ideology o Scots in Scotland is agin it.

Standardisation: a change of heart?

Although I argue there is already significant standardisation of Scots, Fitt was correct to state in 2016 there is no 'Standard Scots'. Costa thought that the prevailing opinion among language advocates then was 'that Scots needs

153 Costa 2017:54
154 Bann and Corbett 2015:95
155 Tait 2016
156 Corbett 2003:272

no standard since it is overly diverse dialectally for a general agreement to be reached without much conflict'.[157] In that context, Fitt's message in *The National* newspaper article was significant. He asked, 'dae we need a Standard form o the guid Scots tongue?' Fitt confessed to formerly being strongly opposed to standardisation. After weighing up the pros and cons he had changed his mind.

> The lack o a Standard is simply haudin the language back when it needs tae be gangin forrit. Ower mony folk fae teachers tae weans tae new writers and people fae ither countries are lookin for guidance on Scots and juist no gettin it. And the authorities can faur ower easily clap the language on the heid or ignore it awthegither. Sae I'm sayin the day let's agree on a standard for Scots – and let's stert that process noo.[158]

The author outlined the reasons for his previous stance echoing some of the general anti-standardisation arguments covered above. Overlaying all this was the kind of performative linguistic anti-authoritarianism quite common in Scottish culture and as modeled by Leonard, McIlvanney, Kelman and many others.

> As a Scots writer, I'd hate the idea o onybody tellin me hoo tae write it. Bad enough gettin telt tae speak proper English aw the time, never mind some kind o Scots Language polis nippin ma heid for no writin in 'proper' Scots.

The irrational fear of a Scots Language polis 'pittin doon fowk wha dinnae scrieve Scots accordin tae the rules' was raised earlier. This may be based on the belief that Scots standardisation would inevitably follow the same repressive pattern as English standardisation when it was applied in schools. For some, the psychological damage of that pedagogy evidently still hurts. On a Facebook Scots language forum in 2018 a new member made a complaint.

> To a beginner, it feels like there are far too many armchair critics sitting on their porches with their guns cocked, just daring you to even *attempt* to use the language in a way they don't approve of.

While evidence for such monitoring is elusive, to say the least, it is the

157 Costa 2017:47
158 Fitt 2016i

perception that is more worrying. Fettes articulated what seems to be a general uneasiness, 'if languages are seen as "things" separate from their speakers, then the latter cease to have a sense of ownership and control'.[159] There are two responses to this. Firstly, pre-emptive defensiveness may paradoxically result from the lack of a recognised standard, the absence of linguistic authority outside the individual or the context of communication, in this case the online forum. A language needs an established, supported external standard representing 'a form of decontextualized, neutral, widely accessible and learnable language',[160] what Coulmas earlier called a 'common good'. This would allow neutral or depersonalised comments to be made and accepted but also enables the learner, at least in theory, to achieve the same level of mastery as the 'armchair critics'. Without standards there can be no impartiality. Secondly, Costa believed it would be improbable that revitalisation initiatives for Scots would ever duplicate the dominant English language ideology with all its hierarchies and inequalities. Fettes considered it was possible to find a 'dynamic balance' between the spoken and written language, 'one that allows language to continue to evolve through its use in informal situated negotiation of ways to live together'. According to Costa, in the case of Scots there is probably no choice.

> [W]here standards are rejected for a minority language but where standard language is nevertheless the norm because of the presence of a standardized dominant language such as English, not addressing the issue results in its cyclical return to the front of the scene.[161]

In other words, unless we sort this one out, we will continue Fitt's 'maist borin conversation' endlessly.

The main counter argument is still the creative and stylistic 'opportunities' unstandardised Scots orthography allegedly provides; 'Some caw that a dampt disgrace, ithers a big bourach. Still ithers caw it pure liberation'.[162] The linguistically libertarian ideas asserted in the Robertson manifesto nearly 30 years ago still have surprising currency. But maybe we should remain skeptical that a lack of standards inherently leads to freedom, hedonism and so on in terms of individual language use. Do standards 'inevitably impinge on people's right to poetic license and idiosyncrasies'? Surely constraints can equally provide focus and a creative challenge. Highly standardised English

159 Fettes 1997:303
160 Costa et al 2017:5
161 Costa 2017:59
162 Fitt 2016i

seems to be doing quite well, creatively speaking.

> The claim that Scots is a refuge for hedonists and anarchists is thus, sadly perhaps, an illusion maintained only by those who have mastered the semiotic type of written Scots, or whose intrinsic characteristic and position of authority make it possible to play around with that type – in a way not dissimilar to poetic license in standardized languages.

The anti-standards position ultimately ghettoises Scots in a restricted heritage or literary function. Anti-standardisation is diametrically opposed to mainstream models of community-oriented language revitalisation that emphasise the liberating aspects of standardising a previously stigmatised variety. Standardisation in this model is a step to rebalancing unequal cultural, status or political power relationships. Costa et al summarised the pro-standards position.

> Language advocates [...] often view standards as emancipatory and empowering, a way to promote education and other forms of civic communication through mother tongues and ensure better chances of equal achievement for minority groups.[163]

Fitt's most significant commentary on his previous anti-standards position focuses on the possible harmful effect an official standard might have on the Scots dialects; 'wale ae Scots dialect as the Standard and the ithers, awready pit doon as common or coorse, will be even mair diminished'. He was worried about a possible backlash: 'elevate Embra Scots for example tae the national standard and watch as Scots speakers in the rest o Scotland tak the collective huff at it'. Again, there are two obvious responses. The first is that Scots already has a well-established '95%' standard that with very little upgrading could be 'elevated' to Standard Scots.[164] The advantage of building on the current convention is that it is not 'Embra Scots' but a variant evolved specifically to be pan-dialectal. To be fair, it is indeed based on Central Scots, but that dialect has by far the most speakers anyway and, in my personal experience, already acts as a *lingua franca*. The second dialect-focused argument is more political; Costa et al again suggest 'standardization is always a *groupness* project', later adding, that a prescriptive standard, alongside some degree of legal recognition, 'is often the weapon of choice in struggles to resist minority status and marginalisation'. One of the principles

163 Costa et al 2017:1

164 Tait 2018

of all minority language revitalisation is that speakers recognise they belong to a wider speech community than that of their immediate locale. This is partly a 'strength in numbers' case to combine usually scarce resources, but also provides a symbolic shared space, that 'common good' again, where speakers can contribute to issues beyond the local, such as the use of Scots in countrywide education or broadcasting.

One of the functions of the standard is therefore to act as a bond between the speakers of the whole language community and unite the different dialects. Catalan is worth mentioning again as, like all once-stigmatised minority languages, it faces this spoken dialect versus written standard issue conundrum. Catalan writer Jesús Tuson is uncompromising;

> [S]ome speakers will have the responsibility to make a rather dramatic choice, especially regarding the language models for major means of communication: save the language via a standard or lose the dialects and with them the language (itself).[165]

If this sounds harsh, in Catalonia the language question has been politicised for generations and standardisation is clearly seen there as a weapon of resistance to Hispanisation. The Catalan language space is considered a site of political as well as cultural engagement, an arena for community action and not just limited to individual and localised performance. One influential voice in forming this position was Jordi Solé in a best-selling language polemic in 1988, republished in 2012 as *Sociolinguistics for young people of the 21st century* (my translation). As might be expected, Solé believed a standard provides a symbolic 'equality of prestige with other standards'. In practical terms, 'the expansion and use of a language produces a development of its internal structure', so 'vocabulary and grammar must be elaborated to enable the precise expression of abstract concepts'.[166] Like Tucson, he considered that one of the functions of the standard was 'to act as a bond between the speakers of the whole language community and unite the different dialects', but also added the important caveat that, 'the community must be engaged enough to feel responsibility and linguistic loyalty to standard to avoid localism and dialectisation'. The alternative was stark in his view; 'restrictions in use produce regression, impoverishment or atrophy', resulting in the complete disappearance of the language, 'save for a few fragments assimilated in the dominant tongue'.

But this fate can be avoided. Three years after Matthew Fitt's change of

165 Tuson 1988:109 [my translation]

166 Solé 1988, 2012:90 [my translation]

heart, Michael Dempster, Director of the Scots Language Centre, wrote the following text for the final unit of the OU's *Scots Language and Culture* course.

> The author of this unit's own preference is for a Standard Written Scots that can capture as much as is spoken today, particularly with grammatical veracity. Others want a single standard of prescriptive spelling that all can work to. Some believe ease of learning ought to be a priority when developing a standard for Scots. Others still feel that in the language shift towards a standard historical reconstruction ought to be a priority.[167]

Hopefully an open discussion of such options may now proceed, helped by the fact that, as he put it,

> [M]uch of the work to achieve a Standard Scots has already been carried out, and the knowledge attained to develop a functional Standard Written Scots that is independent of dialects.

So now in the 2020s there finally seems to be a more general understanding that a standard of some sort is vital for the survival of Scots as a cohesive language system. Dempster believed that increasing literacy would boost the normalising and de-stigmatising of Scots.

> An agreed authoritative standard for written Scots, ratified by authoritative groups, could very well support speakers, learners and teachers in further overcoming barriers to literacy. Agreement on one spelling per word, a grammatical preference and a curriculum for teaching the language are vital components in achieving this.

He concluded, 'Perhaps we are now at a time where our increasing Scots literacy is ready to accept and utilize a Standard Written Scots'. And assuming this is indeed the case, we can at last turn our attention to the question of how we as a community can go about saving Scots.

---

167 Dempster 2019:20.6

CHAPTER SEVEN

Saving Scots

The 'devitalisation' of Scots

SCOTS HAS DEFIED many predictions of its demise. The 2011 Census revealed that Scots is very much still with us in speech and spirit, albeit diminished in vitality. The simple fact it has endured at all through three centuries of neglect is an act of social solidarity and cultural resistance in itself. Nonetheless, it is difficult to envisage Scots holding out for more than another couple of generations without far more robust official backing. The odds are increasingly stacking up against Scots. Over the last century, English language cinema, radio and television were all branded as existential threats. Popular as they are, these technologies can now be regarded as mere part-time diversions. The beguiling, always-on anglophone information environment of smartphones may be more of a linguistic menace. Children in Scotland now spend far more time online, captivated by social media, than in front of the television with their families[1] and the trend will only increase. The anglicising effects of TV, radio and cinema were previously counterbalanced by the Scots-rich sound environment many bairns were brought up in. However, as traditional communities break up, children can become isolated from older relatives and the local community. Much of the Scots I learned as a bairn came from older folk in Dunbar, Burntisland and Dunning. One of Johann Unger's interviewees, Carol, made the same point.

> I think I know more words than some o my friends at my age but that's cos I spend a lot of time wi ma granny an my great gran an they were words that [...] were everyday words to them.[2]

1 Ofcom 2019

2 Unger 2013:133

Carol later tried to use words like 'driech' in her community and, 'young neighbours' kids say what's that?'. Earlier, I quoted journalist Ian Jack's lament that once common Scots terms like 'bairn', 'blate', 'breeks' and 'brig' were now for him reduced to, 'words that my parents used'.

Each wave of anglicisation has weakened the language itself and undermined the social value that has kept it afloat. Scots is now facing its own existential crisis, different in form but every bit as lethal as that of Gaelic. Unless there is intervention, Scots as a recognisable and distinctive linguistic system is going to wither away within a generation or two. Scots will simply stop being a significant part of our day-to-day oral culture and will take its dialects with it. People may remember the occasional word, but 'Scots' as a cohesive language will only serve as a symbolic curio for dilettante poets and artists to appropriate. One day, history buffs and perhaps some future revivalists will wonder why the Scottish people let something once so beautiful and vibrant just die out. Scottish English will probably survive for a few generations more and will take over the mantle of linguistic identity marker, but without care that might fade too. The longer we put off fixing the issues, the more difficult the revitalisation task will be. Those who oppose Scots, for whatever reason, have time on their side and they know it. We have already failed a whole generation of young Scots speakers since devolution. Leave it another few decades and the 300-year-long quest to eradicate Scots as a living language will have been accomplished. The longer we indulge in *laissez faire* attitudes and vague policies, and squabble over status and standardisation, the more likely Scots will perish.

Offsetting all this gloom, we now understand much better how minority languages work, their social value and how they can be revitalised. There are many examples of minority language revitalisation in countries not all that different from Scotland. Tried-and-tested methods can be adapted and localised to ensure Scots is stabilised, de-stigmatised, sustained and strengthened. In this last chapter we will look at what could be done to revitalise Scots and how to re-establish its everyday use in Scottish society. If we can somehow find the political will, the 'discourse of death'[3] can be replaced by a tale of transformation.

Let us take a moment to review how Scots was stripped of its former strength and status, how it was 'devitalised', as this may help us reverse the process. At the time of the Union, nearly all non-Gaelic Scots spoke 'full canon' Scots, normally over the full range of domains. Three centuries later this capability was reduced to a third, with the Scots component of Scottish

3 McEwan-Fujita 2006, 2011

speech weaker in vocabulary and structure. To implement this mass social engineering, Scots had to be systematically de-normalised as a linguistic practice. There was nothing 'natural' in this, so the term *minoritisation* is often used nowadays to underline the methodical social and political forces at work.[4] Tracing the history of Scots back over the past 310 years or so, we can identify five overlapping stages, each of which will have to be overturned to reverse the fortunes of the language

- *Social marginalisation*: From 1707, Scots was excluded from the evolving linguistic functions of the state. The natural development of the written language was effectively stalled. The spoken language practice became disparaged, especially in official settings, so reducing its social value. New urban varieties of Scots were doubly stigmatised when compared with older, supposedly 'purer' forms, encouraging the idea the language was divided and degraded.
- *Educational suppression*: From the Education Act of 1872 onwards, Scots was increasingly excluded from schools. Although some limited 'heritage' use of the language was permitted (songs, poetry, etc) until the 1970s, day-to-day classroom use of the language was suppressed, often violently, and vilified as 'slang'. Only recently has the language been re-evaluated as an asset to students and teachers.
- *Dialectisation*: The unity of Scots was fragmented further by (in my view) an over-emphasis on spoken dialectal variation such as the Doric and Glasgow 'patter'. Without a formal written standard to transmit status and continuity, Scots was rarely presented as a cohesive language system and the centuries-old grammatical structure allowed to erode.
- *Promotion of illiteracy*: The denunciation of the traditional pan-dialectal literary variety, as represented by dictionaries, in favour of 'eye-dialect' orthographies ensured a further disconnection with the Scots literary tradition. Written Scots became less visible, especially in education. Scots speakers were coerced into illiteracy in their own tongue.
- *Heritisation*: Shorn of functionality and with diminishing social value, 'Scots' was reduced to a heritage or literary 'resource' to be included at best as local flavour in English language or cultural studies. This is a mainly 21st century phenomenon, as the devolved administrations avoided real commitment to Scots as a living tongue.

Consequently, the language risks being reduced to a scrappy 'tea-towel' parody of its former self, a couthy or comic linguistic remnant. In this state

4 Eg Costa et al 2017

it can be even more easily dismissed as irrecoverable as a living language. It is surely time to stop, retrace those steps and look for a better route forward.

What does revitalisation mean anyway?

Any increase in the use of a minoritised language in a diglossic environment will involve significant political and social reengineering. Joshua Fishman called this wide-ranging transformation *reversing language shift*[5] to emphasise the need to address the economic and power imbalances that drove marginalisation in the first place. Minority language experts Grenoble and Whaley describe the linguistic process itself as *revitalisation*. The goal of revitalisation is to 'increase the number of speakers of a language and extend the domains in which it is used' in both speech and writing.[6] This is not the same as *revival*, where a dead language is brought back to life by enthusiasts. In the UK, Manx and Cornish are revived languages. Scots, however, is still in the fortunate position of retaining a substantial speaker base. The initial priority with Scots is stabilisation, reinforcement, and maintenance rather than reconstruction. But what is the target beyond that? The aim of Catalan 'normalisation' is the replacement of Castilian Spanish as the dominant public language that territory. Even in his pugnacious 1980 manifesto calling for the renaissance of Scots as a 'living and all-purpose language'[7], McClure did not envisage Scots replacing Scottish English in that way; 'English will retain the accepted status which it has had for three hundred years, as one of the spoken and written languages of Scotland'. The other minority language is Gaelic, and McClure's demands could now be considered compatible with Scots being raised to same status as Gaelic as benchmarked by the European Charter for Regional or Minority Languages. The more prescriptive Part III ECRML categorisation that Gaelic enjoys includes specific provisions for the use of the language in education, law, public services, the media, cultural activities, economic life and transnational exchanges.

The main policy document current at the time of writing is the Scottish Government's 2015 Scots Language Policy. On the face of it, the three aims would be recognisable to any international language revitaliser,

- tae enhance the status o Scots in Scottish public an community life
- tae promote the acquisition, yiss an development o Scots in education, media, publishin an the airts

5 Fishman 1991

6 Grenoble and Whaley 2006:13

7 McClure 1980:37

- tae encourage the increased yiss o Scots as a valid an visible means o communication in aw aspects o Scottish life.

However, the interpretation of these aims depends on how Scots is defined and, as we now know, at the moment Scots is not officially defined. The aims could certainly represent a move towards full minority language status as envisaged by McClure, even including ECRML Part III inclusion. Equally though, the Policy aims are vague enough to continue the second-class heritisation treatment of the language where children just learn a 'smattering' of Scots words at school, and it is used tokenistically elsewhere. In other words, the Policy hedges its bets, one rationale highlighting the 'richness o the Scots language as expressed in sang, poetry and literature' (heritisation focus) and another stating that 'The Scottish Government regairds Scots, in its scrievit and spoken forms, as a valid means o communication' (normalisation focus). These positions are by no means mutually exclusive, and some constructive ambiguity may be pragmatic in a still antagonistic Scottish media environment. Such haziness, however, may also validate Millar's charge that 'The elements necessary for language revitalisation and the development of a coherent policy for Scots are fragmented and misunderstood by both practitioners and end-users'.[8]

To take an example, the Policy does not distinguish between the revitalisation of written and spoken Scots, though each requires different approaches. It is reasonable to infer from the Policy an ambition to establish *written* Scots as a mainstream part of public life in official communications, public signage, education and so on. The official use of Ulster Scots in Northern Ireland sets a precedent. Even a minimal usage, for example in public signage, would require some process of standardisation, with all that entails. Producing signage and documentation is the easy part of reversing language shift, though, compared with the challenge of reinvigorating spoken Scots. As the Ulster Scots case study showed earlier, standards and official use are themselves only window dressing if there is no systematic attempt to stabilise and increase the Scots component of Scottish *spoken* language. The failure of the 2005 Gaelic Act to stem the erosion of intergenerational transmission among the remaining Gaelic-speaking communities underlines this point.

Earlier, Millar claimed that policy had been hampered by a 'lack of a strong idea of what Scots is'. The type of sociolinguistic model outlined earlier in this book at least makes effective policymaking theoretically possible. As we know, although 1.5 million people may declare themselves to be Scots speakers, they certainly will not speak braid Scots consistently but

8 Millar 2011:11

will use Scots components in a Scots-Scottish English mix. Most speakers are never going to be willing, or able, to switch cleanly to braid Scots, nor would anyone ever wish to force it upon them. Any revitalisation efforts would have to build from 'where we are', ie the current hybrid speech model. This plan assumes people will continue to use their spoken Scots dialect mixed to varying extent with Scottish English. In this significant aspect, Scots is not a 'typical' minoritised language like Gaelic. There is no off-the-shelf formula we can just adopt to reverse language shift for such a fluid translanguaging context. I sometimes draw comparisons between Scots and Catalan, but although the latter's revitalisation may provide many insights, the rhetoric there includes quite puritan views about the minority tongue that are not realistic or desirable when applied to Scots. Scotland will have to develop a bespoke model specific to the Scottish language dynamic, but here the once-disdained language mixing described earlier could act in Scots' favour.

Here is how this could work, in theory anyway. To increase the status and use of Scots as a wider medium of communication properly, the language would need be elaborated and extended. Official documents and communications would have braid(ish) Scots versions. The official visibility and prestige of Scots would rise, people would be comfortable to use it more and it is likely the spoken Scottish language mix would begin to be fortified by input from the more visible written language. At a minimum, the current drift to Scottish English would be disrupted and marginalisation may even be stalled or reversed. Speaker confidence and repertoire might naturally increase as more Scots was used by more people in more domains. Current semi-speakers with some skills could convert to more fluent, capable speakers as Scots social value and use increased. The vernacular Scottish language mix then should become more Scots-like. In spoken forms we could hear a drift 'back' to using more Scots words, phrases and structures. Whether, after over three centuries of relentless suppression, Scots can ever reach the level of everyday use that McClure dreamed of – that is the equal use of Scots in official situations, in education and in public spheres – is a question for future generations. As Grenoble and Whaley remind us, 'successfully revitalising a language is a slow, arduous process, one that will outlast those who start it'.[9] In modern language revitalisation, the journey determines the destination.

The Scots revitalisation journey

In this section I return to Grenoble and Whaley's classic 2005 formulation for language revitalisation in *Saving Languages*. I will also refer to Robert

9 Grenoble and Whaley 2006:178

McColl Millar's work, especially his 2011 paper on 'linguistic democracy' in which he outlines a pragmatic but unusually ambitious top-down approach to Scots revitalisation policy. Millar envisages what would be required to implement Part III status of the ECRML. Scots would then be brought into line with provision for Gaelic, so ending almost 20 years of officially sanctioned discrimination between the two tongues.

But first, let's ground this conversation in the here and now. There is currently no unambiguous governmental commitment or community momentum to revitalise Scots in the manner suggested by McClure, Millar or Grenoble and Whaley. As we know, there is no practical mechanism or national body to initiate and manage revitalisation anyway, despite decades of lobbying. Anti-Scots politicians know how much moral pressure groups like Comunn na Gàidhlig and Bòrd na Gàidhlig can apply and will try to block such a lobby organisation for Scots.

> There's a serious problem even before we get to the 'upgrading' of Scots in Charter terms: I think it very unlikely that any Scottish government, of whatever political kidney, would willingly carry out this action. They would marshal all kinds of arguments about lack of clarity and distinction on the part of the Scots-speaking population, and about how much they are doing already for creative and academic use and study of the language, but in the end the bottom line is financial.[10]

As Scotland enters the third decade of the 21st century, the political winds are still not blowing in Scots' favour. Brexit will begin to undermine any British commitment to the ECRML. Westminster is never going to have the slightest interest in revitalising Scots and Holyrood is likely to be preoccupied with issues around self-determination for the foreseeable future.

Since devolution, building any kind of sustained political support for Scots has proved a struggle. Discriminatory policies and practices against Scots are entrenched and normalised in UK politics, extending to the Scottish Government. Writing over a decade ago, Millar came to a stark conclusion.

> [T]hose who control institutions of this type are inclined towards the status quo with, at best, the token recognition of Scots without either the force or the funds to make genuine language policy possible.[11]

10 Millar 2011:2

11 Millar 2008:5

Despite several initiatives since then, the statement still holds broadly true. Scots-positive approaches have always been available, though. Nearly two decades ago, Lo Bianco argued that Scots deserved a more 'prominent place in policy' and far more attention than the hitherto *laissez faire* neglect, calling for 'sophisticated socio-linguistic planning'. Millar suggested the then Scottish Executive was ignorant of language planning and 'it might genuinely not occur to many of its members that Scots would be in need of status planning and the same way as Gaelic is'.[12] More recently, he wrote that policy and planning for Scots 'has never assumed, and does not ever seem likely to assume' the organisational and theoretical sophistication of equivalent organisations in Europe and beyond.

Actions of whatever sort need a framework and a plan of some kind; otherwise, it's all just talk. Many of the issues identified here have come about because Scots language activists (and speakers for that matter) have not developed a full understanding of the theoretical and practical issues associated with language policy and planning. One way to address such obstructions is to sketch out a pragmatic plan.

Sketching out a roadmap

If, as an outcome of the Scottish Languages Act, the Scottish Government committed to promoting Scots to ECRML Part III (or equivalent) status, they might be surprised to find the path forward surprisingly well signposted. Despite Wright claiming that language policy and planning was *démodé* in mainstream academia,[13] a global network of language revitalisation study and practice thrives among socially committed linguists. Beyond ensuring the basic survival of the threatened language, nowadays the focus of revitalisation is to establish a sustainable coexistence with the dominant language. Much revitalisation activity takes place in the developing world, perhaps contributing to its academic side-lining. In Europe, the ECRML exemplifies modern revitalisation ideology in its resolve that 'the right to use a regional or minority language in private and public life is an inalienable right', and in the local context we can draw from both the Gaelic and Ulster Scots experiences.

Strategies for revival and revitalisation often revolve around the need for linguistic repair and/or construction work on vocabulary, grammar and writing systems. Standardisation in the modern era requires a structured and informed approach to language planning. Although genuine community

12 Millar 2018:201

13 Wright 2016:64

engagement is essential, much still relies on 'top-down' government policies, including protective laws, funding to support the language, national language planning, education priorities and encouraging language use in official spheres. Emil Haugen's four-stage model[14] below remains the most recognised planning approach.

- *Selection*: choosing which variety to be developed.
- *Codification*: developing a standard written form with a regularised orthography, vocabulary, and grammar.
- *Elaboration* (also known as *corpus planning*): a continuous process expanding and modernising the vocabulary and keeping it up to date with modern needs.
- *Implementation*: using the new standard in government, the media and education. Education and community literacy activities are often termed *acquisition planning*.

Kloss later added *status planning* to this list, that is, raising the prestige of the standard[15], what Lo Bianco termed its 'reputation'.[16] I suggest Scots needs a sixth element, one related to status planning but preceding all the other stages: *acknowledgement*. Acknowledgement implies recognising the marginalisation of Scots and its speakers as a social wrong, addressing anti-Scots discrimination and reducing the policy inequities between Scots and Gaelic.

Acknowledgement

Any attempts to revitalise Scots face two initial obstacles as recognised by Millar. Firstly, there is the 'lack of recognition of the problem by most Scots speakers'.[17] Secondly, for a planned revitalisation to proceed, 'there would need to be meaningful government acceptance of the existence of a problem and a willingness to carry out remedial action'. Acknowledgement is therefore a political precondition. At the beginning of the book, I highlighted Johann Unger's view that the stigmatisation of Scots was a social wrong.[18] In my view, the wrongness stems from elements that seem to clash with progressive and inclusive notions of Scottish social values.

---

14 Haugen 1966

15 Kloss 1967, 1969

16 Lo Bianco 2001:31

17 Millar 2011:4

18 Unger 2013:2

Discrimination: Too little is being done to address anti-Scots prejudice. To quote Unger again, 'There has to date been a high level of discrimination against Scots speakers in all areas of Scottish society, and in many cases this is (knowingly or unknowingly) sanctioned by institutions and supported or at least allowed by official language policies'. The Scottish Government, as it should, confirms its opposition to discrimination in many areas with statements like, 'In a vibrant, modern Scotland, everyone should be treated equally'.[19] The discrimination must stop, full stop.

- *Human rights*: Why do speakers not have the positive right to use Scots? The ECRML, to which the Scottish and UK governments are both signatories, view language right as 'inalienable'. As we will see later, that pledge is moral rather than legal at the moment, but it is an obligation nonetheless.
- *Democratic voice*: 30 per cent of the population is being routinely ignored, mostly working-class and rural people. Are class, geographic or linguistic prejudices still so entrenched in Scotland?
- *Education*: Open anti-Scots discrimination may be reducing in schools, but why are we letting our bairns miss out on the benefits of bilingualism?
- *Equity*: Gaelic has established the value of one native Scottish language. Marvellous, but why is the other one deemed less deserving?
- *Civic engagement*: The revitalisation of Scots should be an inclusive national project; a positive way to remedy past wrongs and value the language skills of Scots-speakers, both young and old.
- *It's Scottish*: Why does the simple fact that a cultural practice is uniquely and defiantly Scottish consign it to the end of this list?

Recognition of Scots revitalisation as a mainstream and serious issue will also require quite a lot of political work to engage with social activists and organisations, reach out directly to the speaker community (indeed, build a 'speaker community') and lobby politicians and funders. Voluntarism by interest groups will probably have to initiate this process but eventually government support and intervention will be needed to move through the next 'official' stages.

Status planning

Lo Bianco recognised that planning would have to be preceded by 'a kind of prestige-allocation process', and only once this was achieved, 'the functional range, and place, of Scots will come to reflect more fully its demographic

19 Scottish Goverrnment 2018

presence in the population'. Revitalisation can build the generally positive attitudes to Scots revealed in surveys and consultations into a more concrete and confident view of the language itself. Eagle feared that without preparing the ground in this way any attempt to normalise Scots would be 'met with both derision and hostility'[20], although he recognised that attitudes could be changed via government intervention. This had been demonstrated by 'legislation and awareness campaigns directed against prejudice and discrimination based on race, ethnicity, gender and sexuality'. Initial antagonism against normalisation is a predictable feature in language revitalisation projects and is caused by marginalisation.

> World-wide many native communities have been proclaimed by outsiders as 'primitive' or 'backward', with the result that generations of speakers have been ashamed to speak the local language and reluctant to use it with their children. The resulting attitude in the community is that they view their own language and culture as inherently 'bad' in some way, and the language/culture of the external, dominant group as 'good'.[21]

Whether Scots speakers think of themselves as a 'native community' or not, the feeling of stigmatisation is much the same. Fettes suggested that revitalisation narratives should include, with a nod to Paulo Freire, an understanding of critical literacy that teaches people how to 'filter' the discourses to which they are exposed. This includes identifying hidden forms of manipulation and developing their own alternative narratives based more on their own experience.[22] Costa and colleagues believed such a critical, community-centred engagement processes should be framed as social action, in practice meaning:

> [T]he nature and result of language politics are co-constructed not only by politicians and recognized experts, but also inevitably by teachers, learners and everyday participants of the speech community.[23]

Lo Bianco agreed the key was 'to generate and recycle a "conversation" about the role and place of the languages in Scottish public life', implying

20 Eagle 2011
21 Grenoble and Whaley 2006:173
22 Fettes 1997:308
23 Costa et al 2017:13

a community-focused engagement that Fitt later described as a 'Muckle Conversation'.[24]

Any collaborative and inclusive approach should try to foster a genuine feeling of ownership of the revitalisation process by the community. Millar described this as *linguistic democracy*.[25] Grenoble and Whaley found that whenever people are asked, as Scots were in the 2009 Attitudes survey, if they want to preserve or revitalise their language and culture, 'the politically and emotionally correct answer' is usually 'yes'. However, behind this response may lie 'unspoken but deep doubts, fears, and anxieties about traditional language and culture may mean that people are not willing to become personally involved'. [26]

> [T]hey may believe that others can 'save' the language for them. Yet any revitalization program requires an ongoing personal commitment from at least a large percentage of community members.

The second significance of community involvement is to blunt the impact of any anti-Scots cynicism in Scottish press and social media. One lesson from Ulster Scots is that systematic ridicule by politically motivated cliques cannot be allowed to block progress. Despite initial scepticism, the Ulster-Scots Agency was eventually able to make noticeable gains in the public acceptance and social visibility of the Ulster Scots dialect.[27]

Selection

Choosing which variety to be developed and used is often problematic for minoritised languages, but this step should, in theory, be less fraught for Scots. All minority languages have spoken dialects and without the historical commonality of a standard, can often diverge quite considerably. Irish, for example, has three remaining spoken dialects, all somewhat different in their vocabulary, grammar and pronunciation. An official synthetic standard was developed, but, unlike Standard Basque mentioned earlier, native speakers still tend to shun it as inauthentic. Learners of 'Irish' must adopt the artificial version or align with a particular dialect such as Ulster Irish. Scots fortunately is underpinned by the well-documented pan-dialectal and semi-standardised prestige form, with grammars, dictionaries and language courses already

24 Fitt 2016d

25 Millar 2011

26 Grenoble and Whaley 2006:48

27 Gardner 2018:153

developed. There is simply no need to 'elevate Embra Scots for example tae the national standard', as Fitt once worried about.[28] Starting with the literary variety also underlines the idea that standardisation refers to the written language only and will not impact overtly on spoken and dialectal Scots. The latter point is worth restating. A standard variety can be seen in two ways. It can be an idealised set of abstract norms about all language (spoken and written) that should be aspired to,[29] or a mainly written variant that *could* be spoken, for example in educational and official settings,[30] but is certainly not presented as a spoken 'ideal'. Grenoble and Whaley prefer the second interpretation; 'it cannot be overemphasized that the standard does not supplant language varieties or dialects, but rather offers an additional form'.[31] Writing of his experiences with Catalan, Solé stressed the importance of *not* trying to standardise the spoken language.[32] He was adamant that speech practices should be left alone, with no attempt made to regularise them at all. A fellow Catalan writer, Carles Castellanos, described standardisation of the oral language as 'a trap', as the natural variation in spoken forms is used as a pretext to hinder standardisation of the written forms.[33] A 2014 report on standardisation in Scottish Gaelic reached the same conclusion regarding the spoken tongue.

> Language planners should be explicit from the outset about the intended restricted domain of the standard (eg for formal, written texts only), and that no-one will be required to use it outside of these contexts. The standard is intended to be used professionally by teachers, writers and broadcasters, not by ordinary people in their everyday lives.[34]

Nevertheless, a semi-standardised spoken model (dubbed Mid-Minch Gaelic) has *de facto* emerged in Gaelic Scotland for use in broadcasting and teaching. As implied earlier, both that presentational format and the written standards will probably start to influence less formal domains as people get used to them, but that can never be the primary aim.

28 Fitt 2016d

29 Milroy and Milroy 1985, 1999:22

30 Trudgill 1984:32

31 Grenoble and Whaley 2006:130

32 Solé 1988, 2012

33 Castellanos 1993:17

34 Bell et al 2014:28

Codification

Issues of codification relate to the allegedly troublesome orthography of Scots. As we know, non-dialectal written Scots has existing 'soft' standards, whether individual authors choose to adhere to them or not. An officially sanctioned orthography would, however, remove an often-cited barrier to the public and functional use of Scots. Fitt argued the lack of an officially sanctioned standard was, 'simply haudin the language back'.[35]

> And a Standard micht mak the Scottish Government tak Scots mair seriously. Although aye sayin it supports Scots, it aften stauns ahint the fact there is nae Standard as yet anither reason for no pittin adequate resources intae the language. Wi a Standard Scots in play, the Scottish Government micht still no resource Scots tae the levels they morally should but at least there wid be wan less excuse for them no tae.

Millar is likewise clear on this point; 'If Scots literacy was being taught, there would have to be a standard orthography and, at the very least, prescriptive grammars'.[36] As we shall see shortly, standardisation is also connected to language rights.

A sceptical language community will need to be persuaded of the benefits of standardisation, and the same issue have also arisen with Gaelic. A 2014 report *Dlùth is Inneach*[37] commissioned by Bòrd na Gàidhlig listed the 'real benefits' of standardisation that could be promoted to the community.

- Easier acquisition of literacy as written spellings are consistent.
- Easier communication across distance – a standard variety allows for ease of intelligibility between areas and across dialects.
- Clearer and unambiguous terms – people working in specialised areas do not constantly have to explain which terms they use to each other.
- Equality of education – teachers do not need to learn several different acceptable varieties.
- Economies of scale – publications have a better opportunity of reaching a justifiable size of market.

The standardisation process of Scots may not be quite the wicked problem

35 Fitt 2016d

36 Millar 2011:3

37 Bell et al 2014

it is often portrayed to be. In a post to the Facebook Scots Language Forum in 2017, I outlined a possible 'fast-track' process.

> Get a Scottish Govt Comattee o the great an the guid tae get thegither an mak a 5% supplement tae the current *Concise English-Scots Dictionary*. This can be by time-leemitit blether or (ma preference) by analysis o current prentit Scots. Disna maitter. Pit siller aside tae prent a new fu vairsion o CESD later. Aw Government-fundit organisations (eddication, SLC, Creative Scotland etc) hae thereaifter tae yaise this spellin as a condeetion o their siller. Mairket the new spellin tae awbodie. That's it, cud dae the hale jing bang in a year wi aboot £100k of stairt-aff fundin.

My thinking was that codification could be fast-tracked by updating the herculean effort of the 1998 *Report & Recommends o the Scots Spellin Comatee*. There is no reason why a reboot of their recommended standard would not be acceptable to Scots speakers or the wider Scottish community, based as it was on well-known literary forms. That standard was easily learnable and could have gained status at the time had there been an implementation plan, funding or any mechanism for its promotion. It is surely a long overdue task to dust off and review the *Recommends*. The review should be properly funded and, as I suggested in the post, time bound. That means not just a list of clear orthographic proposals, but a business and implementation plan. The production of a full dictionary in online and (later) print form would be a priority. The popular *Scots Online Dictionary* shows what can be achieved with focus and commitment.

Nowadays with a 'social action' ethos, we would expect public engagement from the outset. Fitt asks for 'no juist the usual worthies on a comatee decidin it aw ahint steekit doors but a Muckle Conversation wi aabody (includin bairns) contributin'.[38] Technology and social media could certainly make this type of engagement far more achievable than back in the 1990s. Any such campaign would have to have a two-way function. In the Preface I wrote that Scot is not at 'ground zero', so the first aim is to raise awareness of *existing* standards, and only then to enable people 'sharin their Scots words and ideas on orthography and giein their thochts on whit a Standard Scots should look like'. While Fitt's ethos of crowdsourcing vocabulary is stirring, unmoderated crowd codification could rapidly descend into chaos and rancour, the very last thing the beleaguered language needs. Communities can certainly be expected to decide, for example, their local place names, and focus groups can be used to 'road test' and pilot orthographic ideas, but Grenoble and Whaley have seen

38 Fitt 2016d

this sort of well-meaning initiative struggle before, and advise moderation by experts.

> Committees can be inefficient, and they do not always operate as expected, particularly when cultural taboos or powerful personalities make truly cooperative deliberation difficult or even impossible, but they still represent the best way to reach a consensus on the nature of the orthography that meets local needs. When constructed properly, they also represent the best way to legitimize an orthography within and among communities.[39]

The authors even include advice for the possibility of disagreements, always a risk in Scotland.

> Battles over orthography can become surprisingly passionate. While perhaps unavoidable to some degree, the potential for divisiveness can be lessened by encouraging people to see early decisions about orthography as tentative, and by constantly returning to the unifying vision of why the orthography is being created in the first place.

Whatever the process of codification, Fitt recognises the urgency of this task.

> I think we owe it tae the nixt generation o bairns and weans tae pit differences aside and stert [...] let's get on wi makkin a Standard Scots while there's still a leevin language cawed Scots tae mak it for.[40]

Elaboration

> Not all corpus planning activities are helpful to language revitalisation. Indeed in many cases, corpus planning has actively hindered the process. Bad corpus planning can alienate speakers and therefore accelerate language shift away from the minority language. Language planners should tread very carefully, and focus on not alienating people.[41]

If Scots is really to be used, for example, as a teaching language and for official and general purposes, elaboration or corpus planning will be required from the outset. Essentially in an on-going process of language building (*Ausbau*), the idea is to expand and modernise Scots vocabulary through

39 Grenoble and Whaley 2006:157

40 Fitt 2016i

41 Fishman 1991:349

the introduction and standardisation of loan words and to recognise or add neologisms, ie new words or expressions. As literary Scots was effectively frozen about a century ago, it lacks much of the vocabulary needed for modern life. Some new words have been coined, such as 'bidie-in' (cohabiting partner) and 'sitooterie' (conservatory), but not many. Writing extended prose in Scots is therefore quite hard. Leaving Ullans aside for a moment, most modern Scots prose writers tend to avoid neologisms and prefer words from mainstream Scots dictionaries and the daily spoken language. MacDiarmid's failed experiment with 'synthetic' Lallans still casts a long shadow. However, when authors need more technical, or specific vocabulary in texts, they must create this register from scratch. Either they use the English forms of the words, remembering the 'workshop' example previously, or Scotticise the spelling in some way, eg 'eddication', 'tradeetion', 'warkshop', where there is an established (ie dictionary) form. At this higher register a Scots text could still end up being essentially an adapted English version with the incorporation of some limited Scots words, expressions and grammar, so additional style guides would be needed.

Gaelic scholar Nancy Dorian posed the moot question of how 'dilute' a language can become 'while still remaining the linguistic entity it was, distinct from all others including (and especially) the neighbouring language of wider currency'.[42] With reference to non-standard 'Belfast Irish', Gabrielle Maguire argued that 'a language which is very much on the defensive must aim higher in order to ensure its own separateness from the dominant language'.[43] As we saw earlier, on the other side of Ulster's linguistic divide, Ulster Scots planners coined a wide range of vocabulary to fulfil its official role. They decided not to stick with largely English vocabulary and spelling conventions, ie the Mither Tongue method, but to try to diverge significantly from these. The result was an alien-looking written form, remote from what most native speakers would understand. This is not to condemn the Ulster inventions outright, as they had little time to develop or test plausible alternatives. While remaining ambivalent about linguistic separatism, Dorian herself recognises 'a sense of separate identity is a valuable sustaining feature in ethnic language revival and revitalisation efforts'. Ullans certainly has a distinctive look on the page, a visual cohesion that many standardised Mither Tongue texts may lack.

Again, we may learn from Gaelic, also struggling with elaboration for decades. The Gaelic Language (Scotland) Act 2005, while covering acquisition and status planning, said little of corpus planning. The *Dlùth is Inneach* report mentioned above recognised the phenomenon of 'unidirectional

42 Dorian 1994:492

43 Maguire 1987:88

bilingualism' where Gaelic was, like Scots, retreating into informal and domestic settings leading to the loss of both vocabulary and general speaker competence. The result is, 'there are no longer any domains which are "Gaelic-only"'.[44] Although a very different language from Scots, mixing with Scottish English also occurs.

> Gaelic language practice (of most users in most domains) is typically characterised by language mixing, where English words (sounds, idioms, etc) are inserted into Gaelic speech.

As with Scots, the reason for this is partly the limited word pool; 'it is difficult to use Gaelic in any domain without having access to domain-specific vocabulary and styles'. The report considers the coordination and management required to 'shift' any domain into Gaelic. The same issues would apply equally to any serious elaboration of Scots.

> A new Gaelic-friendly domain (or sub-domain) may require the cultivation of a new Gaelic 'register' (or sub-register), which is expressive enough to allow everything to be said that needs to be, stable enough to allow speakers to use with confidence, distinctive enough to satisfy other identity-based requirements (eg aesthetics, status, ego) of the participants, and acceptable enough to the community of speakers.[45]

Inspired by the work of Fishman, *Dlùth is Inneach* makes several suggestions on community engagement around elaboration, again as relevant to Scots as to Gaelic.

- Find out what the community wants or is willing to accept.
- Make a concerted effort to persuade people of the need for standardisation and modernisation of the language (see above).
- Consult with a wide range of speakers on both the big questions (eg on the whole standardisation process) and on the small questions too, such as 'What do you think about this particular word?'.
- Be prepared to accept that the community may not be ready to make certain kinds of decision of this type. Don't force a decision on them.
- Be prepared to wait and be flexible.

44 Bell et al 2014:16
45 Bell et al 2014:26

Covering similar ground, Catalan sociolinguist Jordi Solé adds a few words of advice.[46]

- Choices must be made between different forms, but extremes should be avoided, 'neither obscure nor colloquial, neither old-fashioned nor dialectal'.
- The implementation should not be too strict or purist, either, avoiding terms like 'wrong' and 'bad', rather encouraging writing that emphasises 'the richness of the language, clarity, precision', in other words, the authority and effectiveness of the modern form.
- The model should stress the linguistic autonomy of the language. Thus, Scots should look distinctive and cohesive.

Implementation

Implementation implies encouraging the use of Scots and its new standard in government, the media and education. Part III status would be quite demanding.

> Government and bureaucracy at all levels would have to be available in the language on demand. All forms of employment would eventually be expected to conduct business in Scots, should the need be shown. The broadcast, print and online media would be expected to give up more than a token amount of space to material in the language; this would have to be more than entertainment programming. All of this would require a considerable cadre of adult speakers and writers.[47]

Publicly funded bodies would be required to use standard Scots in their publications and transactions and avoid the Creative Scotland DIY-style approaches discussed earlier. With a better understanding of Scots, the idea of a Scots Language Act (last seen in a SNP manifesto back in 2003) might be more implementable. After half a page on advancing Gaelic provision, the latest (2021) SNP manifesto could only manage five words relating to Scots.

> We will also bring forward a new Scottish Languages Bill which takes further steps to support Gaelic, act on the Scots language and recognises that Scotland is a multilingual society.[48]

---

46 Solé 2012

47 Millar 2011:3

48 Scottish National Party 2021:66

As we know, Gaelic is already protected by the 2005 Act and the Scottish Government funds the Bòrd na Gàidhlig as an implementation and planning body. There is no linguistic and, in my view, moral reason why Scots should not be treated in a similar fashion, with a Scots statutory body, formal planning and the cascading of planning down through local authorities. Although the 2015 Scots Language Policy admirably encouraged, 'aw stakehauder groups tae develop an implement Scots language policies', without coordination and support, since then little has happened to set the heather on fire.

A Scots Language Board has, as we know, been demanded for at least a generation to act as the natural focal point and incentive for revitalisation. Currently, the official 'owner' of Scots is the Scottish Government who have taken responsibility for language planning. This leaves initiatives, however well meaning, at the whim of transient political policy and funding priorities. Back in 2010, the Ministerial Working Group on the Scots Language reported that discussions had focused on the need for a body to support and promote Scots, 'as Bòrd na Gàidhlig does for Gaelic, and receiving a comparable amount of recognition, attention, publicity and funding'. Mysteriously, the report then concluded, 'the general feeling of the Group was that the setting up of an entirely new body would be unrealistic at this time'. To put this absence in perspective, via ECRML the UK government recognises seven indigenous languages in the British Isles. Four of them have funded language boards with a statutory role to campaign, coordinate and lobby for secure status and support for their respective tongues. These are Gaelic (Bòrd na Gàidhlig), Irish (Foras na Gaeilge), Welsh (Bwrdd yr Iaith Gymraeg) and Ulster-Scots (Tha Boord o Ulster Scotch). Manx is directly supported by the Isle of Man Government and Kesva an Taves Kernewek, the Cornish language board, is a voluntary body. Scots has more speakers than all those languages combined but no equivalent language board, voluntary or otherwise. Just to underline their role, the Boards act as custodians of a language and typically coordinate a range of revitalisation initiatives.

- *Education*: Use in schools, developing learning/teaching methods and materials, teacher training, adult education, cultural use (eg song, poetry and theatre) through exhibitions, competitions etc.
- *Public Use*: Status building, cultural events, linguistic landscape (place names, signs), guidelines and training for government and media use, social inclusion.
- *Linguistics*: Corpus planning activities, dictionary preparation work, style guide spelling, grammars, sociolinguistic research, surveys, recording current use, text and audio collections, new media and publishing.

The above list, derived from 'revival linguistics' expert Ghil'ad Zuckermann's Language Revival Diamond[49], illustrates how many essential revitalisation activities are still missing for Scots.

One of the main outreach tasks of any Board would be to engage with and develop the attitudes and language practices of the speaker community itself, the awareness raising and status planning activities described earlier. Clark rightly said, 'Scots belongs tae aabody', and 'Scots belongs tae naebody'.[50] In a democratic sense, he is right. On the other hand, if Scots is 'owned' by a diverse set of individuals with very different types of interaction with and experience of the language, with wildly variable language skills, different motivations for declaring themselves 'Scots speakers' and probably strong opinions, very little will happen to revitalise the language. Given the historic lack of public discourse around Scots and the current official message emphasising dialect diversity, this community is likely to need some group-building work if it wants to achieve anything useful with its presumed ownership. Most minority language communities in the world establish activist organisations, often initiated and usually maintained by government grants or fund-raising. These would have to be initiated also for Scots to develop the organisational skills and social capital for a speaker community that has been historically disempowered and marginalised. Delegates to the 2019 SNP conference voted to review the need for a Scots Language Board with initial priorities similar to Zuckermann's list above.

> [T]he three areas o public life a Scots Language Board will need tae get tae grips wi richt oot the gate are exactly the same three whaur Gaelic has cairved oot sic an inalienable place for itsel in modern Scotland – media, education, an the airts.[51]

Revitalising Scots in education

Assuming we could get past the initial hurdles of establishing a sustainable organisational structure and media/public acceptance/engagement, most minority language communities prioritise educational programmes. Although as we saw in Chapter Five, the current provision for Scots remains sparse, at least the Scottish Qualifications Authority awards in Scottish Studies and the Scots Language are already developed and running. Moreover, the current Scots Language Policy also aims to:

49 Zuckermann 2017
50 Clark 2016
51 Clark 2019

> [P]romote a coherent approach tae the planning, lairnin, teachin an assessment o Scots within the context o relatit national policy an the national Curriculum for Excellence (CfE) implementation plan.

Grenoble and Whaley explain why a sound education policy is so important.

> When mandatory schooling occurs exclusively in a national language, the use of local languages almost inevitably declines. When local languages are part of the formal educational process, they typically maintain a higher degree of vitality, though here again the amount a specific language is used plays into the equation.[52]

The authors prefer *total immersion* programmes built on the 'common-sense' principle that 'the best way to learn a language is to create an environment in which that language, and only that language, is used constantly'.[53] In Scotland (Scottish) English is 'L1', the language of instruction with Scots rarely if ever used for that purpose. Immersion approaches may sound outlandish for Scots, but they are far from alien to Scotland. Gaelic schools in Glasgow and Edinburgh, a long way from their language's heartlands now use Gaelic in everyday teaching (Gaelic Medium Education or GME). A full 'total immersion' programme for Scots, if adopted, would require that most, if not all, school instruction would be conducted in the language, or at least in the Scottish language mix. Teachers would require training and teaching materials developed for a whole range of subjects, such as science, maths and history. Apart from the elaboration requirements we looked at earlier, immersion would demand considerable buy-in from parents. The 2009 Attitudes survey had found that although attitudes to learning Scots were generally positive, 'there was less of a consensus on its role in education, parents with children under 5 in particular showing significant opposition to encouraging children to speak Scots'. Until quite recently, Gaelic faced much the same problem, but nowadays Gaelic medium schools in Glasgow and Edinburgh are seen as a prestige option. These schools attract committed parents and students and are comparatively well resourced. It is hard to see Scots-medium education attracting quite the same level of parental support, initially at least. On the contrary, Millar feared a possible backlash.

> I would be very surprised if considerable dissent over the idea that children were going to be partly schooled in a language which parents

52 Grenoble and Whaley 2006:10

53 Grenoble and Whaley 2006:50

> themselves may have felt had acted as a handicap to their progress did not develop.[54]

He worried any discontent might be stirred by an anti-Scots political and media environment; 'it would be very unlikely that considerable and well-funded sociopolitical forces within Scotland would not organise against "misuse of funds"'. Would any Scottish Government have the political will to face down a media-led, middle-class revolt? It seems unlikely at the moment.

The only real alternative, and maybe a more palatable approach, is for Scots to be taught as a secondary subject, a method known as *partial immersion*. Millar felt integration might be achieved by enhancing the current Scottish Studies Award and making it compulsory until the age of 16.

> The curriculum would be flexible, incorporating assessment for those with native speaker abilities in Scots or Gaelic or non-native abilities in either language. All children who had lived for four or more consecutive years in Scotland would be expected to be assessed at some level in these matters. Naturally, Scottish Studies would include historical, economic, political, musical and geographical focuses as well as linguistic and literary; whenever possible, however, these would be taught in one of the national vernaculars. Every child who went through this programme would have considerable command of at least one of the national languages.[55]

The obvious objection to a supplementary approach would be that Scots would then be in timetable competition with other subjects including modern foreign languages like French or Spanish. Nonetheless, oral and written fluency in Scots could certainly be taught in this way, and given the linguistic closeness to English, probably quite quickly. In practice, most teachers are likely to have a limited command of and confidence in Scots, and retraining would be required. Teaching a language is challenging anyway, and overturning years of prejudice towards Scots, understanding the Scottish language mix and navigating the Good Scots/Bad Scots/dialect issues require considerable sensitivity and nuance. Perhaps optimistically, Millar thought retraining could be covered by a short in-service course covering the history of language in Scotland, linguistic study and dialect diversity. He recognised, though, that if teachers were immediately expected to teach *in* Scots after one short course, 'there would be great stress, uproar and quite possibly a major

54 Millar 2008:17

55 Millar 2011:16

revolt against the proposal'. The 2010 *English Excellence Group Report* suggested that local authorities could encourage schools to appoint Scots language co-ordinators and develop local Scots language policies. Millar suggested forming a group of peripatetic Scots teachers, similar perhaps to the 2014 Scots Language Coordinators programme, to support and scaffold the initiative, share good practice and help foster teacher confidence. At the time of writing, campaigners were calling for a Scots language coordinator in every region for education in Scotland.[56]

Such ventures might be supplemented by extracurricular initiatives. One well-known idea is *language nests*, started in the 1980s to revitalise Māori in New Zealand. With a focus on intergenerational transmission, fluent elders were invited to teach preschoolers to speak and 'live' the language. Apart from the language transmission gain, the principle of valuing the role and contribution of older members of the community is attractive. Closer to home, the *Gaeltacht* summer schools in Ireland take a similar immersion approach, albeit for a few weeks at a time. These subsidised courses focus on the Irish language, but sport, music and other activities are integrated into the curriculum. My wife, who is from Belfast, attended 'The Gaeltacht' in Donegal many times when younger and remains, even now, a reasonably skilled speaker of Ulster Irish.

Whatever the approaches chosen, Scottish educators would have to acknowledge the other lessons from Ireland where poor-quality pedagogy and mandatory teaching of Irish created, according to Andrew Carnie, 'widespread resentment of the language'.[57] Grenoble and Whaley consider partial immersion an option only if the community is unable or unwilling 'to commit to the time, effort, and cost necessary to make the local language a primary language of communication'. Given the initial hurdles listed, Scottish Studies may be the only practical and politically acceptable route forward. But the Irish experience also shows schools-only approaches are not enough, as Carnie explained.

> It is fairly clear that in order to revive a language, emphasis has to be placed on usage in the home and in the general community rather than isolating it in the educational system.

The 2020 Gaelic Crisis report highlighted a similar disconnect between formal education and language use in communities. It recommended that more energy should go into ensuring the language is embedded in all aspects

56 Duffy 2022

57 Carnie 1996:108

of day-to-day life, and not just at school.[58]

The role of parents, carers and the wider community is vital, not simply to endorse in-school changes above, but to participate in the longer-term goal of enhancing intergenerational transmission. Initiatives for revitalisation always try to connect with this 'middle generation', who may already be familiar with some of the language, and to gain support among those who are not native speakers. Dorian observed that when any language survives precariously, support efforts will require the following:

> [T]he mobilization of remaining speakers as well as the recruitment all new speakers; in fact, the mobilisation or at least some of the remaining speakers is typically crucial to the recruitment of new ones.[59]

Scots-speaking parents may well be capable of teaching the language to their own offspring but due to their own anti-Scots schooling might, initially at least, be likely to hold negative views of the language and even the desirability of passing it on. Parents and carers are also busy people with many other responsibilities. Even fluent Scots speakers may lack confidence in their own language (and teaching) skills or believe it not to be their responsibility.

Writing in 2011, Millar felt that few Scots speakers would be able to read or write their language. The Census, however, revealed speakers' surprising confidence in their own literacy. Eighty-eight per cent of speakers said they could read Scots, almost 80 per cent claiming they could write it too. For a marginalised language, literacy at this level is a huge advantage. The figures most probably refer to technical literacy, the basic ability to read and perhaps write the language, rather than the wider notion of cultural and creative literacy discussed earlier. Nonetheless, the immediate visual accessibility of Scots would be an important element its revitalisation, easing the production and distribution of Scots language promotional and teaching materials. Print-based (eg guides, word lists) and online methods (courses, forums, chat, etc) could be used for very wide impact. When I started visiting Catalonia in the 1980s, basic guides for Catalan learners and improvers were commonly distributed, sometimes free with newspapers. Once *The National* started printing articles in Scots in 2016, the 'shock of the new' (or was it 'shock of the old'?) seemed to overwhelm some people, but if Scots texts become more commonplace again, few will remember what all the fuss was about. Higher visibility might itself increase the status of Scots. All effort should be made

58 Quoted in Carrel 2020

59 Dorian 1994:481

to increase public signage in Scots and public bodies encouraged to use the language in documents, online sites and public transactions.

Grenoble and Whaley suggested one other partial immersion approach, the *formulaic method*, that might work well with the wider adult community. It takes advantage of the fact that in everyday speech Scots is already mixed with English (here 'the language of wider communication').

> In the first stage, individual words and one-word expressions are taught, to be used intermingled with the language of wider communication. These words should be easy to pronounce and to remember, and should carry a high functional load. Examples include not only such obvious words as 'yes' and 'no,' but also expletives and exclamations like 'terrific' or 'shame,' as well as greetings, interrogative words, and simple imperatives (eg 'come,' 'sit,' or 'go'). When these have been mastered, longer and longer expressions can be introduced (eg 'Let's go,' 'Where are we going?,' 'When are we going?,' or 'I'm going home'). Ultimately the student has a fairly large stock of formulaic expressions which can be used more or less flexibly, and the expectation is that they be used whenever possible.[60]

The formulaic model provides a method for anyone with an interest in Scots to build confidence in their own language knowledge, help parents use Scots with their children and 'give permission' for children to use their Scots in the community. Ironically, the method is precisely the opposite of those 18th century guides that identified Scots words and phrases to be eradicated from 'polite' English speech. As ever, an additive approach should be adopted, recognising and building on local dialect practices, words and expressions. There is already a substantial market for publications about Scots and its dialects, and, as we know, local newspapers frequently print lists like '20 Words Unique to our Town', which, although not entirely exclusive to the town in question, do suggest a popular interest in the language. Finally, there may be a temptation to focus Scots initiatives in areas where there is still a high percentage of Scots spoken, but that could be considered discriminatory against bairns who live elsewhere. One of the strengths of Scots is that it is spoken across Scotland. Any attempts retrench the Scots language into geographic 'heartlands' should, in my view, be strongly resisted. There seems to be similar opposition to such 'ghettoising' ideologies in Gaelic discourses, too.[61]

60 Grenoble and Whaley 2006:56

61 Ó Giollagáin et al 2020:409

Scots as a right

As we now know, the ECRML proclaims the right to use a regional or minority language in private and public life as 'an inalienable right'. The question is whether that implies a statutory right to speak or use Scots. Shortly after devolution, Niven and Jackson investigated whether language 'rights' have any legal basis at all. They looked at the *United Nations International Covenant on Civil and Political Rights* and *The European Convention on Human Rights,* both of which protect against discrimination based on language. Could the Scottish Government (or Executive as it was then) be challenged on the basis of discrimination against Scots? Back in 2000, it was concluded that to have any chance of success a litigant would not only need to cite a specific instance of discriminatory treatment, but also to be able to establish (ie prove) that Scots was a language and not a dialect. Niven and Jackson thought at the time the freshly signed Charter buttressed the case but still might not be sufficient. After nearly 20 years of documented governmental assertion of Scots language status, the situation may now be different.

The legal perspective might explain the curious reluctance of the Scottish Government so far to endorse any type of official standardisation of Scots, to accord it statutory status, or even use it in signage. All these actions would support the legal claim that Scots was a language, and the Government may fear a legal challenge, maybe on educational provision or access to services. Like Niven and Jackson, Singaporean language rights expert Lionel Wee believed that legal rights seem to imply the existence of a standardised language, so might be difficult to uphold with respect to spoken and non-standardised hybrid varieties. Wee is an expert on Singlish, an emergent post-colonial variety used in Singapore that mixes Malay, Mandarin and Tamil with English. Singlish speakers may combine elements from different varieties, consciously or otherwise, in the same way vernacular Scottish language mixes Scots and Scottish English. From a purely linguistic perspective, Wee rather approved of all this fluidity, aligning as it did with the performance-based trends in modern linguistics that spurn any prescriptivism. However, he made an important comment about rights that in my view applies especially to Scots. 'Impure' varieties and blends carry significant social value for the speakers and 'while not neatly corresponding to a coherent linguistic identity, carry ideological significance that must be accounted for'.[62] In other words, they create identity and convey different types of social positioning. As Singlish is, like Scots, still stigmatised, overt social positioning can therefore lead to discrimination.

62 Wee 2011:46

> The experience of linguistic discrimination need not always involve identifiable or established varieties, since the very act of speaking differently – as an 'other' – may be sufficient for discrimination.

Wee makes fundamental point is made here; the actual linguistic status of Singlish (or Scots) is immaterial (language, dialect or whatever), nor is the lack of community consensus on its status important; discrimination is still discrimination. Wee felt, nonetheless, that if a speaker wanted to seek formal or legal redress against discrimination, establishing the legal status of her speech would still be essential.

Back in Scotland, Niven and Jackson similarly concluded it may be difficult to address language discrimination properly until the linguistic status of Scots as a 'normal' minority language is unequivocally accepted. Wee clearly opposed 'essentialism' from an ideological standpoint. However, from the legal perspective he conceded that there may be 'good reasons why a rights discourse ought to encourage essentialism, since it aims to protect specific attributes or conditions that are considered especially significant'.[63] Wee provides a very relevant example; 'any language that is used as a medium of education [...] will have to undergo some degree of standardisation'. And through that process may well acquire rights.

What we need to do politically

I know what you are thinking; all this revitalisation will never happen. Millar was forthright on what was needed.

> Without a strong top-down approach any major policy initiative of this type would be highly unlikely to be effective; without support from below, any chance of effectiveness would be non-existent.[64]

Scots currently seems to be squeezed between a cynical politicians content for Scots to perish, and a public who have never seen the case for the revitalisation of Scots articulated by anyone, anywhere. It has taken three centuries of neglect, suppression and silencing to reduce Scots to the weakened state it is in, and such a profound harm cannot be repaired overnight. There are some green shoots poking through, though. The 2015 Scots Language Policy may be feeble, but it still aims, 'tae encourage the increased yiss o Scots as a valid an visible means o communication in aw

63 Wee 2011:37

64 Millar 2011:8

aspects o Scottish life'. The related educational policies are limited but sound, and qualifications are at last available in the language. In late 2022, the Scottish Government launched a new consultation under the banner 'Creating a Robust Future for Gaelic and Scots'. The consultation recognised that Scots had 'never benefited from formal support through legislation' and therefore, 'it may be time to consider this to help promote, strengthen and raise the profile of the language'. The consultation fed into the Scottish Languages Bill. However, despite renewed calls for a Scots Language Board, the proposal was rejected yet again, even as Bòrd na Gàidhlig was praised as a model of arms-length governance. The reluctance to create a Scots body may reflect fears of political pressure, as happened with Gaelic in the 1980s when modest funding enabled an organised lobby to emerge. Similar concerns likely underpin resistance to standardising written Scots, now widely seen as essential for public use. Though the Bill's Memorandum acknowledged this, it offered no support – perhaps wary that standardisation would require investment, invite comparisons with Gaelic funding, and raise politically awkward questions about language rights.

Both Gaelic and Scots face fundamental questions about their future. They share challenges such as English dominance and declining community transmission, but each also needs tailored solutions. The implementation of the Scottish Languages Act should spark political and public debate on speaker needs but it is undermined by a lack of an integrated national strategy. Without coordination, well-meaning measures in the Act like Gaelic-only 'areas of linguistic significance' may risk deepening local inequities for Scots provision. The Act may be a historic step, but its guarded approach to Scots shows how far Scotland still is from becoming a truly 'three-voiced country'.

What we need to do as a community

This chapter has sketched out a systematic method to revitalise the Scots language. Other approaches are available but, whatever the details, the key is to have an agreed plan. All the other languages on the UK's ECRML list, including Ulster Scots, have benefited from going through some variant of this process. It is simply now the turn of Scots. Revitalisation means we put a stop to discrimination against the language and its speakers, and begin to treat Scots like the minority language it is. Let us summarise possible actions as a few 'Scots positive' bullet points.

1. Build the Scots language community and raise awareness that, despite

cherished dialect differences, Scots is one language, and its literary tradition is as valuable as its spoken diversity.

2. Stop the erosion of spoken Scots and stabilise written Scots, to ultimately increase the number of speakers who are able and linguistically confident enough to use Scots in a wide range of everyday contexts.
3. Continue to call for a co-ordinating, planning, and monitoring body analogous to Bòrd na Gàidhlig, since little of substance will be achieved without one. Without such a provision, any Scots strategy developed under the Scottish Languages Act is likely to be ineffective.
4. Stop anti-Scots discrimination in education, one of the main causes of Scots' retreat. We must decide as a community how Scots is embedded in education. Teacher training and resources will be required.
5. Engage with parents and adults. Without their support, none of this will work. As with Gaelic, it is important to reach beyond current speakers of the language, and promote the idea of Scots as a 'common good' for all.
6. Develop a standardised written version to enable Scots to be taught, seen and used in public. There has been considerable work in this area, and we have the recommendations from 20 years ago to build on.
7. Secure language rights, both moral and legal, for speakers.
8. Build and extend the language in the same way as has been achieved for Gaelic. Elaboration may seem challenging, but we now know more about methods that can be accepted by the community. 'Lallans' was long ago.

Writing in 2011, Millar was concerned that the changes he proposed might not be supported by the majority, at least initially. Whether this is true or not, in an earlier 2008 paper he acknowledged that language initiatives can initially appear risible or irritating to members of the public, but stressed 'the work continues *because it is the right thing to do*' (his emphasis).[65] Grenoble and Whaley warn us that although the eventual results can be impressive, 'language revitalization is hard work'.

> Any success comes only with a long-term, sustained effort, involving many parties. Critically, it requires a dedicated sense of collaboration, a willingness to put aside disagreements (about goals, spelling, "correct" speech, appropriate domains for language use, etc.) so as to reach consensus and work toward achieving these goals.[66]

65 Millar 2008:16

66 Grenoble and Whaley 2006:49

The personal is still political

Now we understand better how Scots works, its history and politics. Hopefully it is clearer that, with a reasonable amount of (good)will and effort, Scots could be re-established and stabilised as a normal part of the rich linguistic landscape of Scotland. However, there is a risk that people think that someone else will sort it out it. This could not be further from what is needed. Clark was correct; despite the desperate need for workable policies and support structures, Scots fundamentally belongs to its speakers. Just as Scots was created by millions of Scottish voices, it needs millions more to make sure it survives and thrives to be enjoyed by future generations. So, what can we, as individuals, do about it with the meagre time and skills we have available?

As I was writing this section, I picked up a recent book by Andreu González Castro titled something like *A Self-Help Manual for Catalan Speakers* (my translation). At first sight, the need for such a guide was surprising. Catalan is usually thought of as the most successful example of minoritised language revitalisation in Europe, and a model for how language shift can be reversed in a modern state. Catalan now claims some 10 million speakers, but the author worries his language is not out of the woods yet. Research shows only half of speakers use it regularly and only a quarter speak it 'correctly'.[67] A third of regular speakers mix up Catalan phrases with Castilian ones (where have we heard that before?), and about half use what González terms 'budget' forms of Catalan infused with Spanish grammar, phrases and vocabulary, a disparaged variety I described earlier as Catanyol.

González makes the point that even with a language as well supported as Catalan, the pressures on individuals to 'revert' to the dominant language in social situations remain powerful and relentless. To resist assimilation, individuals and communities must develop and, more importantly, practice a healthy linguistic loyalty for their tongue. Loyalty may not come naturally. To counter the effects of long-embedded stigmatisation, some practical form of 'resistance training' may be required, essentially a conscious effort to use the language in as many circumstances and with as many people as possible. Like language itself, linguistic loyalty is something you do, and a habit (perhaps with some effort) you can acquire.

If this tactic needs to be encouraged for 'successful' Catalan, how much more is it needed for still badly stigmatised Scots? It feels, after all, more 'natural' to use Scottish English when speaking with strangers. People assume everyone speaks Scottish English in Scotland, so communication of some sort is guaranteed. That is true, but once that practice becomes

67 González 2019:13

normalised, it will also marginalise and kill off what remains of Scots in everyone's speech, not just yours. As we have seen, what we think of as 'natural' is really the result of intense suppression and marginalisation of the language. Sometimes therefore there is a need for us all to be more confident, even assertive, in the use of Scots. Not everyone is comfortable with that degree of firmness, but it is comparatively easy with Scots where you can subtly 'turn up' the language, rather than make a noticeable switch.

Speaking Scots outside a familiar environment requires constant affirmation and a fair degree of self-assurance in your own Scots skills. If it seems like an effort to think 'Scots positive', here are ten reasons why you should speak Scots, inspired by González' Catalan list. You can probably think of many others.

1. It is *your* language if you are a speaker, or even just know it passively.
2. It is a wonderful social language if you live in Scotland.
3. It is a historic language of Scotland, part of our distinctive culture.
4. It is a cool thing to be able to do; who doesn't want to be bilingual?
5. It is quite easy to learn or improve.
6. It is fun to speak and write.
7. It sharpens the mind; bilingualism is good for the brain.
8. It helps you think about how dialects and languages fit into society.
9. It adds to diversity; not everything has to be boringly monolingual.
10. It annoys the hell out of some people, but the people Scots annoys, you probably won't want to speak to anyway.

Carol, one of Johann Unger's interviewees puts it more briefly, '[M]ind and say it cos it'll be lost forever an I hink that'd be terrible […] be a tragedy to lose.'[68]

As you can probably tell, I like lists, so here is my final one, a ten-point action plan to get you started. Again, I hope you will be able to think of much better ideas, 'Acause gin ye've read this faur, an unnerstood the hauf o it (or even tried tae), Scots belangs tae you as much as tae onybody'.[69]

1. Build up your Scots skills, find out what 'good' Scots is and respect it, even if you don't use it. Honestly, dictionaries and grammars can really help you. Try to speak and write 'good'(ish) Scots, too.
2. Be proud of your local dialect, but don't fall for the myths of 'dialectism'. Dialects are different toppings on the same cake.
3. Speak Scots with people, even a few words and phrases.

68 Unger 2013:133
69 Clark 2016

4. Read stuff in Scots. If you can't find what you want, write it!
5. Be respectful of the 'rules' but be playful – language is fun.
6. Start a local group of like-minded folk to blether with.
7. Pass on your enthusiasm to your family, friends, school and workmates. Don't be discouraged or disrespectful if people don't 'get it' at first.
8. Teach Scots to bairns and learn as much as you can from older folk – ask them for words and phrases they remember.
9. When you have confidence, offer to teach Scots at schools and social groups. You are now a fluent speaker, flaunt it.
10. Campaign for Scots rights, locally and nationally.

Acause if you dinna dae it, wha wull?

References

Aberdeen Press and Journal (1924a) 'Scots language in schools: vernacular not vulgar, need for inclusion in all curricula'. 23 Feb.

Aberdeen Press and Journal (1924b) 'Reviving the Scots Tongue'. 7 Oct.

Aberdeen Press and Journal (1925) 'From a Scottish study: the future of the vernacular tongue'. 5 Sep.

Aberdeen Press and Journal (1931) 'Anglicisation of Scots language'. 31 Dec.

Aberdeen Press and Journal (1938) 'Dr W Grant's plea for Scots Language'. 28 Feb.

Aitken, AJ (1979) 'Scottish speech: a historical view with special reference to the Standard English of Scotland'. In Aitken and McArthur (eds), *Languages of Scotland*. Edinburgh: W & R Chambers, 85–118.

Aitken, AJ (1980, 2015) 'New Scots: the problems'. In AJ Aitken (ed), Caroline Macafee, *Collected Writings on the Scots Language* (2015), Scots Language Centre. [d3lmsxlb5aor5x.cloudfront.net/library/document/aitken/New_Scots_the_problems.pdf]. Originally published in J Derrick McClure (ed), *The Scots Language. Planning for Modern Usage*. Edinburgh: The Ramsay Head Press, 1980, 45–63.

Aitken, AJ (1981, 2015) 'The good old Scots tongue: does Scots have an identity?'. In AJ Aitken (ed), Caroline Macafee, *Collected Writings on the Scots Language* (2015), Scots Language Centre. [d3lmsxlb5aor5x.cloudfront.net/library/document/aitken/The_good_old_Scots_tongue.pdf]. Originally published in Einar Haugen, J Derrick McClure and Derick Thomson (eds), *Minority Languages Today*. Edinburgh: Edinburgh University Press, 72–90.

Aitken, AJ (1982, 2015) 'Bad Scots: some superstitions about Scots speech'. In AJ Aitken (ed), Caroline Macafee, *Collected Writings on the Scots Language* (2015). Scots Language Centre. [d3lmsxlb5aor5x.cloudfront.net/library/document/aitken/Bad_Scots_some_superstitions_about_Scots_speech.pdf]. Originally published in *Scottish Language*, 1 (1982), 30–44.

Aitken, AJ (1984, 2015) 'Scots and English in Scotland'. In AJ Aitken (ed), Caroline Macafee, *Collected Writings on the Scots Language* (2015), Scots Language Centre. Originally published P Trudgill (ed), *Language in the British Isles*. Cambridge: Cambridge University Press, 517–532. [d3lmsxlb5aor5x.cloudfront.net/library/document/aitken/Scots_and_English_in_Scotland.pdf]

Aitken, AJ (1985, 2015) 'A history of Scots'. In AJ Aitken (ed), C Macafee, 'Collected Writings on the Scots Language' (2015), Scots Language Centre. [medio.scotslanguage.com/library/document/aitken/A_history_of_Scots_(1985)].

Allan, D (2021) 'Drew Allan: So how does The Herald keep the heid when it comes to Scots?', *The Herald*, 6 Feb. [www.heraldscotland.com/news/19061270.drew-allan-herald-keep-heid-comes-scots/].

Anderson, J (2021) 'Burns charity convener urged to resign after appearing to criticise young Scots poet'. Deadline News Agency, 15 June. [www.deadlinenews.co.uk/2021/06/15/burns-charity-convener-urged-to-resign-after-criticising-young-scots-poet-poetry-news-scotland/].

Antoniou, K, Grohmann, KK, Kambanaros, M and Katsos, N (2016) 'The effect of childhood bilectalism and multilingualism on executive control'. *Cognition*, 149, 18–30.

Aracil, LV (1965) *Conflit linguistique et normalisation linguistique dans l'Europe nouvelle*. Nancy: Centre Universitaire Européen.

Ashcroft (2014) 'How Scotland voted, and why'. Lord Ashcroft Polls, 19 September. [lordashcroftpolls.com/2014/09/scotland-voted/].

Aye Can (2011, 2022) Scotland's Census website. Perth: Scots Language Centre. [www.ayecan.com/].

Bann, J and Corbett, J (2015) *Spelling Scots: The orthography of literary Scots, 1700-2000*. Edinburgh: Edinburgh University Press.

Bateman, E (2000) 'Attitudes to Scots'. Scots Language Centre.

Baxter, S and Mitchell, A (1982) *Stanley Baxter's Parliamo Glasgow*. Edinburgh: Paul Harris Publishing.

Bazilchuk, N (2015) 'Students who master two written dialects do better in school'. Sciencenorway.no, 28 Aug. [sciencenorway.no/education-forskningno-language/students-who-master-two-written-dialects-do-better-in-school/1421554].

BBC News Services (2011) 'Scots studies 'not brainwashing', says SNP minister'. 29 Sep. [www.bbc.co.uk/news/uk-scotland-15093213].

BBC News Services (2013) 'Census shows decline in Gaelic speakers 'slowed''. 26 Sep. [www.bbc.co.uk/news/uk-scotland-highlands-islands-24281487].

BBC News Services (2019a) ''Gie it a shot' - OU offers free Scots language course'. 5 Dec. [www.bbc.com/news/uk-scotland-50662854].

Bede, C (1863) *A tour in Tartan-land*. London: Richard Bentley. [archive.org/details/atourintartanlaoobradgoog].

Bell, JJ (1901) *Wee Macgreegor*. London: Harper and Brothers.

Bell, S, McConville, M, McLeod, W and Ó Maolalaigh, R (2014) *Dlùth is inneach: Linguistic and institutional foundations for Gaelic corpus planning*. Project report. Inverness: Bòrd na Gàidhlig. [eprints.gla.ac.uk/98132/].

Beveridge, C and Turnbull, R (1989) *The eclipse of Scottish culture*. Edinburgh: Polygon.

Bialystok, E, Craik, FIM and Luk, G (2012) 'Bilingualism: Consequences for mind and brain'. *Trends in Cognitive Sciences* 16.4, 240–250.

Black, A and Black, C (1840) *Black's picturesque tourist guide of Scotland*. Edinburgh: Adam and Charles Black. (Reprinted 2017 Glasgow: Collins).

Blair, T (2010) *Tony Blair: A journey*. London: Hutchinson. [archive.org/details/A.Journey..My.Political.Life.by.Tony.Blair].

Blanchet, P (2016) *Discriminations: combattre la glottophobie*. Paris: Éd Textuel.

Boswell, J (1791, 1907) *The life of Samuel Johnson*. London: JM Dent. [archive.org/details/lifeofsamueljohnooboswuoft].

Briggs, S (2021) 'Introduction'. In *Scots Warks: Support and guidance for writing/Uphaud an guidance for screivars*. Scots Language Centre. [d3lmsxlb5aor5x.cloudfront.net/library/document/Scots%20Warks_support%20and%20guidance%20for%20writing.pdf].

British Library (undated) *Berliner Lautarchiv British and Commonwealth recordings*. [sounds.bl.uk/Accents-and-dialects/Berliner-Lautarchiv-British-and-Commonwealth-recordings].

Brooks, L and Hern, A (2020) 'Shock an aw: US teenager wrote huge slice of Scots Wikipedia'. *The Guardian*, 26 Aug. [www.theguardian.com/uk-news/2020/aug/26/shock-an-aw-us-teenager-wrote-huge-slice-of-scots-wikipedia].

Brown, I (2013) 'Scottish theatre: diversity, language, continuity'. *SCROLL: Scottish Cultural Review of Language and Literature*, 22. Amsterdam: Rodolphi.

Buchan, J (1915) 'Preface'. In V Jacob, *Songs of Angus*. London: John Murray. [digital.nls.uk/works-by-selected-scottish-authors/archive/128693608#?c=0&m=0&s=0&cv=9&xywh=-1%2C-1161%2C2972%2C4577].

Burnett, C (2021) 'This is why there's such a stigma around the Scots language'. *The National*, 19 Oct. [www.thenational.scot/politics/19656055.stigma-around-scots-language/].

Cairns, C (2018) 'Video sees National columnist's Scots language video go viral'. *The National*, 28 Nov. [www.thenational.scot/news/17259865.video-sees-national-columnists-scots-language-video-go-viral/].

Calvet, L-J (1998) *Language wars and linguistic politics*. Oxford: Oxford University Press.

Campsie, A (2020) 'Doric to be taught at university to empower form of Scots'. *The Scotsman*, 13 Sep. [www.scotsman.com/heritage-and-retro/heritage/doric-be-taught-university-empower-form-scots-2969894].

Carnie, A (1996) 'Modern Irish: a case study in language revival failure'. *Papers on Endangered Languages, MIT Working Papers in Linguistics*, 28, 99–114. [carnie.sbs.arizona.edu/sites/carnie.sbs.arizona.edu/files/publications/Endangered.pdf].

Carrell, S (2020) 'Scots Gaelic could die out within a decade, study finds'. *The Guardian*, 2 Jul. [www.theguardian.com/uk-news/2020/jul/02/scots-gaelic-could-die-out-within-a-decade-study-finds].

Castellanos, C (1993) *Una llengua sense ordre ni concert*. Barcelona: Oikos-Tau.

Cheshire, J (2005) 'Sociolinguistics and mother-tongue education'. In U Ammon, N Dittmar, K Mattheier and P Trudgill (eds), *Sociolinguistics: an introductory handbook of the science of language and society* (2nd edition). Berlin: Mouton de Gruyter.

Clark, T (2016) 'A Scots Manifesto'. *Bella Caledonia*, 6 Dec. [bellacaledonia.org.uk/2016/12/06/a-scots-manifesto/].

Clark, T (2018a) 'Wha's Like Us? Weel, No Catalonia'. *Bella Caledonia*, 7 Jun. [www.thenational.scot/news/16274036.whas-like-us-weel-no-catalonia/].

Clark, T (2018b) 'Radge Against the Machine: Deid Wirds, Deid Warlds, an Why Scots Maitters'. *Bella Caledonia*, 27 Dec. [bellacaledonia.org.uk/2018/12/27/radge-against-the-machine-deid-wirds-deid-warlds-an-why-scots-maitters/].

Clark, T (2019) 'Aw Aboard! The fecht for the Scots language stairts the day!' *Bella Caledonia*, 14 Oct. [bellacaledonia.org.uk/2019/10/14/aw-aboard-the-fecht-for-the-scots-language-stairts-the-day/].

Clear Contrair Spirit (2014) 'The Scots tung: how to support it without tying up the Yes movement'. *Wee Ginger Dug* blog, 21 Nov. [weegingerdug.wordpress.com/2014/11/21/the-scots-tung/].

Corbett, J (2003) 'Language planning and modern Scots'. In JB Corbett, D McClure and J Stuart-Smith (eds), *The Edinburgh Companion to Scots*. Edinburgh: Edinburgh University Press, 251–273.

Corbett, J (2008) 'Scots, English and community languages in the Scottish media'. In N Blain and D Hutchison (eds), *The Media in Scotland*. Edinburgh: Edinburgh University Press, 20–34.

Corbett, J and Stuart-Smith, J (2013) 'English in Scotland'. In T Hopkins and J McKenny (eds), *World Englishes Volume I: The British Isles*. London: Bloomsbury.

Corbett, J, McClure, JD and Stuart-Smith, J (2003) 'A brief history of Scots'. In J Corbett, JD McClure and J Stuart-Smith (eds), *The Edinburgh Companion to Scots*. Edinburgh: Edinburgh University Press, 1–16.

Costa, J (2009) 'Language History as Charter Myth? Scots and the (Re)Invention of Scotland'. *Scottish Language*, 28, 1–25.

Costa, J (2010), 'Occasional Paper: Language, Ideology and the "Scottish Voice"'. *International Journal of Scottish Literature*, 7 Autumn/Winter.

Costa, J (2017) 'On the pros and cons of standardizing Scots: Notes from the North of a small island'. In P Lane, J Costa and H de Korne (eds), *Standardizing minority languages: competing ideologies of authority and authenticity in the global periphery*. New York: Routledge.

Costa, J, de Korne, H and Lane, P (2017) 'Standardising minority languages: reinventing peripheral languages in the 21st Century'. In P Lane, J Costa and H de Korne (eds), *Standardizing minority languages: competing ideologies of authority and authenticity in the global periphery*. New York: Routledge.

Coulmas, F (2013) *Writing and society: An introduction*. Cambridge: Cambridge University Press.

Craig, C (1996) *Out of history: narrative paradigms in Scottish and English culture*. Edinburgh: Polygon.

Creative Scotland (2015a) *Scots Leid Policie/ Scots Language Policy*. [www.creativescotland.com/__data/assets/pdf_file/0018/31590/Scots-Language-Policy-June-2015.pdf].

Creative Scotland (2015b) Scots Language Policy published – News release 3 Jun. [www.creativescotland.com/what-we-do/latest-news/archive/2015/06/scots-language-policy-published].

Creative Scotland (2016) *Cur an Aithne Cànanan na h-Alba/An Innins tae Scotlan's Leids/ An Introduction to Scotland's Languages*, March. [www.creativescotland.com/resources/our-publications/marketing/an-introduction-to-scotlands-languages].

Creative Scotland (2019) 'Developin forby forderin the yaise o Scots language'. News release, 27 Sep. [www.creativescotland.com/what-we-do/latest-news/archive/2019/09/scots-gaitherin-2019].

Crowley, T (2006) 'The political production of a language: The case of Ulster-Scots'. *Journal of Linguistic Anthropology*, 16.1, 23–35.

Daisley, S (2017) 'SNP foreign forays are about selling independence, not Irn-Bru to Indians'. *Daily Mail*, 4 Sept. [stephendaisley.com/2017/09/04/snp-foreign-forays-are-about-selling-independence-not-irn-bru-to-indians/].

Davidson, A (2014) 'Scotland, Class and Nation'. *Bella Caledonia* blog, 7 Dec. [bellacaledonia.org.uk/2014/12/07/scotland-class-and-nation/].

Davidson, N (2000) *The origins of Scottish nationhood*. London: Pluto Press.

Davies, T (2016) 'Why nationalism is bad for you'. *Labour Hame* blog, 15 Feb. [labourhame.com/why-nationalism-bad-for-you/].

De Meulder, M (2017) 'The influence of deaf people's dual category status on sign language planning: the British Sign Language (Scotland) Act (2015)'. *Current Issues in Language Planning*, 18.2, 215–232.

Dempster, A (2017) *Gie ma regairds tae Jock Dhu* (bi Shuho Sato owerset bi Andra Dempster).
[jockdhu.scot/].

Dempster, M (2019) 'A year o firsts fir the Scots language'. Open University Scotland.
[www.open.ac.uk/scotland/news/blogs/drmichaeldempster-scotslanguage].

Dempster, M (2020) *Scots Language An Accent*. Series of eight videos. [www.youtube.com/watch?v=43pdwJMZxOQ&list=PLmk3hiyUEgWl7Qa9pBGN3r94ahQiSXJ2U].

Denholm, A (2017) 'Scots language 'helps pupils in English exams''. *The Herald*, 2 Sep. [www.heraldscotland.com/news/15510561.scots-language-helps-pupils-in-english-exams/].

Devine, TM (2013) 'The Sixties in Scotland: A Historical Context'. In T Devine (ed), *Scottish Cultural Review of Language and Literature*, 20, 23–46.

Dick, S (2018) 'Speaking our language: Historical films give a boost to Scots tongue'. *The Herald*, 23 Aug. [www.heraldscotland.com/news/16592911.speaking-language-historical-films-give-boost-scots-tongue/].

Dickie, M (2015) 'New 'scriever' to push Scots 'amang folk an toons athort Scotlan'', *Financial Times*, 26 Aug. [www.ft.com/content/79ee7b1e-4b35-11e5-a089-1a3e2cd1819b].

Donaldson, W (1986) *Popular literature in Victorian Scotland: language fiction and the press*. Aberdeen: Aberdeen University Press.

Donaldson, W (1989) *The language of the people: Scots prose from the Victorian revival*. Aberdeen: Aberdeen University Press.

Donati, C, Hendry, J, Robertson, J and Scott, PH (2023) 'Scots: A Statement o Principles'. Edinburgh: The Scots Pairlament Cross Pairty Group on the Scots Leid. [www.dropbox.com/s/a6td2z5i702wpow/Scots%20-%20Statement%20o%20Principles%202003.pdf].

Dorian, NC (1994) 'Purism vs. compromise in language revitalization and language revival'. *Language in Society*, 23.4, 479–494.

Doric Film Festival (2019). [doricfilmfestival.com/].

Dossena, M (2005) *Scotticisms in grammar and vocabulary*. Edinburgh: John Donald Publishers.

Douglas Brown, G (1901) *House with the Green Shutters*. London: John MacQueen.

Douglas, A (2016) 'Scots, Devolution, and Nationalism 1992 – 2016'. M.Litt thesis, University of St Andrews. [d3lmsxlb5aor5x.cloudfront.net/library/document/scots-devloution-and-nationalism.pdf].

Douglas, A (2019) 'Politics, Scots language and culture – part 1' (online course). Milton Keynes: The Open University.

Douglas, FM (2009) *Scottish newspapers, language and identity*. Edinburgh: Edinburgh University Press.

Duffy, J (2022) 'Scots language needs more promotion, Rab Wilson and Michael Dempster say'. *The National Wales*, 28 Aug. [www.thenational.wales/news/20811032.scots-language-needs-promotion-rab-wilson-michael-dempster-say/].

Dundee Courier (1907) 'Preserving the Scottish language: Importance of the dialect'. 28 Oct.

Dundee Courier (1909) 'The decay of the Scottish language'. 27 Nov.

Dundee Courier (1952) 'Braid Scots is coming back into the schools'. 5 May.

Eagle, A (2011) 'A language strategy for Scots?'. In JM Kirk and DP Ó Boill (eds), *Strategies for Minority languages: Northern Ireland, the Republic of Ireland, and Scotland*. Belfast: Cló Ollscoil na Banríona, 256–266.

Eagle, A (2022) *Written Scots in Scotland and Ulster: A review of traditional spelling practice and recent recommendations for a normative orthography*. Dundee: Evertype. [www.scots-online.org/articles/contents/AwAeWey.pdf. This an earlier version *Aw Ae Wey – Written Scots in Scotland and Ulster*].

ECRML (European Charter for Regional or Minority Languages) (2018) *Fifth periodical report presented to the Secretary General of the Council of Europe in accordance with Article 15 of the Charter: United Kingdom*. 23 Jan. [rm.coe.int/ukpr5-en-revised/168077fb40].

ECRML (European Charter for Regional or Minority Languages) (2021) *Information Document on the implementation of the Recommendations for Immediate Action based on the 5th monitoring cycle. Submitted by the United Kingdom on 5 January 2021*. [rm.coe.int/ukiria5rev-en/1680a0eef6].

Education Scotland (2015a) *3–18 Literacy and English Review*. Livingston: Education Scotland. [education.gov.scot/improvement/documents/lit18-3to18-curr-review-lit-and-eng.pdf].

Education Scotland (2015b) *Curriculum for Excellence Literacy and English: Principles and practice*. Livingston: Education Scotland. [education.gov.scot/Documents/literacy-english-pp.pdf].

Education Scotland (2016a) 'Curriculum for Excellence: Scots language'. *CfE Briefing 17*. Glasgow: Education Scotland. [education.gov.scot/Documents/cfe-briefing-17.pdf].

Education Scotland (2016b) *Adult Literacies in Scotland: Survey of progress and priorities 2010-2015*. Livingston: Education Scotland.
[www.education.gov.scot/Documents/ALIS-2020-Survey-Report2016.pdf].

Education Scotland (2017) *Scots language in Curriculum for Excellence: enhancing skills in literacy, developing successful learners and confident individuals*. Livingston: Education Scotland. [education.gov.scot/improvement/Documents/ScotsLanguageinCfEAug17.pdf].

Education Scotland (2020) 'A 1+2 approach to modern languages'. *Policy support resource*. [education.gov.scot/improvement/learning-resources/a-1-plus-2-approach-to-modern-languages/].

Edwards, J (2009) *Language and identity: an introduction*. Cambridge: Cambridge University Press.

Elinguistics.net (2021) *Quantitative comparative linguistics* blog. [www.elinguistics.net/].

Erard, M (2016) 'Street talk'. *Aeon*, 26 Sep. [aeon.co/essays/do-dialect-speakers-get-the-same-benefits-as-bilinguals].

Eunson, B (2019) 'Dialect diversity, Scots language and culture – part 1' (online course). Milton Keynes: The Open University. [www.open.edu/openlearncreate/course/view.php?id=2705].

Eustace, E (2012) 'Speaking allowed? Workplace regulation of regional dialect'. *Work, Employment and Society*, 26.2, 331–348.

Fairnie, R (2007a) 'Language strategy'. *Scots Tung Wittins*, 160, Mairch.
[www.scottishcorpus.ac.uk/document/?documentid=1811].

Fairnie, R (2007b) 'The Scots language efter Mey 3rd'. *Scots Tung Wittins*, 163, Juin.
[www.scottishcorpus.ac.uk/document/?documentid=1814].

Farquharson, K (2017) 'Speak up for Scottishness and ban the cringe'. *The Sunday Times*, 6 Jan.
[www.thetimes.co.uk/article/speak-up-for-scottishness-and-ban-the-cringe-g6l5h6vc7].

Ferguson, B (2021a) 'Singer wins campaign to persuade Spotify to recognise Scots language for first time'. *The Scotsman*, 4 Mar. [www.scotsman.com/whats-on/arts-and-entertainment/singer-wins-campaign-to-persuade-spotify-to-recognise-scots-language-for-first-time-3155256].

Ferguson, B (2021b) 'Janey Godley records video message of support for Scots language campaigners abused on social media'. *The Scotsman*,12 Jan.
[www.scotsman.com/whats-on/arts-and-entertainment/janey-godley-records-video-message-support-scots-language-campaigners-abused-social-media-3093304].

Ferguson, CA (1959) 'Diglossia'. *Word*, 15, 325–340.

Fettes, M (1997) 'Stabilizing what? An ecological approach to language renewal'. In J Reyhner (ed), *Teaching Indigenous Languages*. Flagstaff: Northern Arizona University.
[files.eric.ed.gov/fulltext/ED415083.pdf].

Fife Free Press & Kirkcaldy Guardian (1935) 'The Scots vernacular'. 22 Jun.

Fifeshire Advertiser (1950). 'Scottish radio news: The guid Scots tongue'. 24 Jun.

Fishman, JA (1973) *Language and Nationalism: Two Integrative Essays*. Rowley, Mass: Newbury House Publishers.

Fishman, JA (1991) *Reversing language shift: Theoretical and empirical foundations of assistance to threatened languages*. Philadelphia: Multilingual Matters.

Fitt, M (2002) *But n ben a-go-go*. Edinburgh: Luath Press.

Fitt, M (2016a) 'Jings or whit! A spang-new column in the Mither Tongue', *The National*, 7 Jan. [www.thenational.scot/comment/14859890.Matthew_Fitt__Jings_or_whit__A_spang_new_column_in_the_Mither_Tongue/].

Fitt, M (2016b) 'Fae Mooth tae Page'. *Bella Caledonia* blog, 7 Jan. [bellacaledonia.org.uk/2016/01/07/fae-mooth-tae-page/].

Fitt, M (2016c) 'Prejudice against Scots hauds back ower mony o oor bairns', *The National*, 28 Jan. [www.thenational.scot/comment/14860843.Matthew_Fitt__Prejudice_against_Scots_hauds_back_ower_mony_o_oor_bairns/].

Fitt, M (2016d) 'Pairlament should mirror aw oor three languages'. *The National*, 4 Feb. [www.thenational.scot/news/14861179.matthew-fitt-pairlament-should-mirror-aw-oor-three-languages/].

Fitt, M (2016e) 'Flytin my Scots is aboot class, not Yes or Naw'. *The National*, 7 Apr. [www.thenational.scot/comment/14864122.Matthew_Fitt__Flytin_my_Scots_is_aboot_class__not_Yes_or_Naw/].

Fitt, M (2016f) 'Attainment o oor weans: Let me spell it oot in Scots', *The National*, 21 Apr. [www.thenational.scot/comment/14864722.Matthew_Fitt__Attainment_o_oor_weans__Let_me_spell_it_oot_in_Scots/].

Fitt, M (2016g) 'Politicians... yer bums are oot the windae!'. *The National*, 28 Apr. [www.thenational.scot/comment/14864984.Matthew_Fitt__Politicians____yer_bums_are_oot_the_windae_/].

Fitt, M (2016h) 'A Year o Scots'. *Bella Caledonia*, 16 Dec. [bellacaledonia.org.uk/2016/12/16/a-year-of-scots-in-bella/].

Fitt, M (2016i) 'We maun tak a tip fae the Klingons for futur o Scots'. *The National*, 11 Feb. [www.thenational.scot/news/14861494.matthew-fitt-we-maun-tak-a-tip-fae-the-klingons-for-futur-o-scots/].

Fitt, M (2019) 'Scots today, Scots language and culture – part 1' (online course). Milton Keynes: The Open University. [www.open.edu/openlearncreate/course/view.php?id=2705].

Forbes, E (2021) 'Hundreds more pupils take up the Scots language'. *The Times (Scotland)*, 26 Jan. [www.thetimes.co.uk/article/hundreds-more-pupils-take-up-the-scots-language-l2s07lc3l].

Forde, SFG (2019) 'Cross-party Scots group ended at exactly the wrong time' (letter). *The National*, 5 Jun. [www.thenational.scot/news/18497441.cross-party-scots-group-ended-exactly-wrong-time/].

Fotheringham, R (2021) 'A history of the independence movement'. In R Fotheringham, D Sherry and C Bryce (eds), *Breaking up the British State: Scotland, Independence and Socialism*. London: Bookmarks.

Freire, P (1968/1970 trans) *Pedagogy of the oppressed*, trans MB Ramos. London: Continuum.

Gardner, PR (2018) 'Ethnicity monopoly: Ulster-Scots ethnicity-building and institutional hegemony in Northern Ireland'. *Irish Journal of Sociology*, 26.2, 139–161.

Garivelli, D (2016) 'Why politicise the Scots language?'. *The Scotsman*, 9 Jan. [www.scotsman.com/news/opinion/dani-garavelli-why-politicise-the-scots-language-1-3996400].

Gillespie, A (2022) 'Scots language has a place in schools – but where exactly?'. *TES Magazine*, 31 May. [www.tes.com/magazine/analysis/general/scots-language-has-place-schools-where-exactly].

Glasgow University (2014) *Sounds of the City project: a real-time study of Glaswegian 2011–2014*. [soundsofthecity.arts.gla.ac.uk/]

González Castro, A (2019) *Manual d'autoajuda per a Catalanoparlants*. Barcelona:

Cossetània Edicions.

Görlach, M (2002) *A textual history of Scots*. Heidelberg: Universitätsverlag C Winter.

Grae, E (2024) Census makes clear case to invest in the Scots language. The National 24 May. [https://www.thenational.scot/politics/24344341.census-makes-clear-case-invest-scots-language/]

Graham, W (1977) *The Scots word book*. Edinburgh: The Ramsay Head Press.

Graham, W (1981) *The Talking Scots quiz book*. Ayr: Alloway Publishing.

Grant, A (2019) 'SNP conference calls for new quango to promote the Scots language'. *The Herald*, 14 Oct. [www.heraldscotland.com/news/17966932.snp-conference-calls-new-quango-promote-scots-language/].

Grant, G (2016) 'Made-up words on a 'website' betray the lunacy of promoting the Scots language'.

The Daily Mail (Scottish Edition), 25 March.

Grant, W and Dixon, JM (1921) *Manual of modern Scots*. Cambridge: Cambridge University Press. [archive.org/details/manualofmodernscoogranuoft/].

Grenoble, LA and Whaley, LJ (2006) *Saving languages: an introduction to language revitalization*. Cambridge: Cambridge University Press.

Grieve, CM ('Hugh MacDiarmid') ed (August 1922) *The Scottish Chapbook*, Vol I, No I. Montrose: CM Grieve.

Hagen, A (2002) *Urban Scots dialect writing*. Bern: Peter Lang.

Hall, S (2019a) 'Education'. In 'Scots language and culture – part 1' (online course). Milton Keynes: The Open University. [www.open.edu/openlearncreate/course/view.php?id=2705].

Hall, S (2019b) 'History and Linguistic Development'. In 'Scots language and culture – part 2' (online course). Milton Keynes: The Open University. [www.open.edu/openlearncreate/course/view.php?id=4190].

Hames, S (2013) 'On vernacular Scottishness and its limits: Devolution and the spectacle of 'voice''. *Studies in Scottish Literature*, 39.1, 201–222.

Hames, S (2016) 'Not nationality but language.' *Bella Caledonia*, 19 Feb.

[bellacaledonia.org.uk/2016/02/19/not-nationality-but-language/].

Hamilton, A, Kelman, J and Leonard, T (1976). *Three Glasgow Writers*. Glasgow: Molendinar.

Hance, M (2011) Ministerial Working Group. The Scots Language Centre.

[www.scotslanguage.com/articles/node/id/253/type/referance].

Hance, M (2016) 'Shrieking privilege'. *Bella Caledonia*.

[bellacaledonia.org.uk/2016/03/16/shrieking-privilege/].

Hands Up For Trad (2020) Winners announced for the Scots Language Awards 2020, Oct 2020.

[projects.handsupfortrad.scot/scotslanguageawards/winners-annoonced-for-the-scots-language-awards-2020/].

Harper, E (2022) Harper promotes use of Scots Language in Parliament. Official website, 21 March. [emmaharpermsp.scot/harper-promotes-use-of-scots-language-in-parliament/].

Hassan, G (2016) 'Does Glasgow have a chip on its shoulder?'. *Scottish Review*, 1 June.

Haugen, E (1966) *Language Conflict and Language Planning: The Case of Modern Norwegian*. Cambridge, MA: Harvard University Press.

Hay, K (2020a) ''They went absolutely mad for it' - Scottish poet overwhelmed by online response to her latest Scots poem'. *The Scotsman*, 24 Oct. [www.scotsman.com/

heritage-and-retro/heritage/they-went-absolutely-mad-it-scottish-poet-overwhelmed-online-response-her-latest-scots-poem-3012554].

Hay, K (2020b) "It's embarrassing to witness' - Top Scottish playwright condemns trolls for 'misogynistic' comments towards Scots poet'. *The Scotsman*, 18 Dec. [www.scotsman.com/heritage-and-retro/heritage/its-embarrassing-witness-top-scottish-playwright-condemns-trolls-misogynistic-comments-towards-scots-poet-3072487].

Hay, K (2021) 'Listen to Shetland poet's poem about her experiences with accent discrimination'. *The Scotsman*, 24 Mar. [www.scotsman.com/heritage-and-retro/heritage/listen-to-shetland-poets-poem-about-her-experiences-with-accent-discrimination-3177574].

Heather, A (2019) 'It's time ye jyned the Scots language renaissance'. *The National*, 26 Sep. [thenational.scot/news/17927034.time-ye-jyned-scots-language-renaissance/].

Heather, A (2020) 'How generations are joining forces to give the Scots language its proper place'. *The National*, 26 Apr. [www.thenational.scot/news/18405968.generations-joining-forces-give-scots-language-proper-place/].

Heather, A and Bircham, J (2018) *Whit's Scots Language?* (video). BBC Scotland, 10 Dec. [www.bbc.co.uk/programmes/p06v4zqr].

Hebditch, J (2021) 'Scots language 'in danger of dying out' as younger people stop learning it from parents'. *Daily Record*, 21 May. [www.dailyrecord.co.uk/news/scottish-news/scots-language-in-danger-dying-24155080].

Hendry, J (1993) 'No bad language'. *Fortnight*, 318, Supplement: Talking Scots, 20–23.

Herald, The (1998a) 'Claim of Scots tongue silenced'. 27 Jun. [www.heraldscotland.com/news/12260161.claim-of-scots-tongue-silenced/].

Herald, The (1998b) 'Speaking in tongues'. 14 Nov. [www.heraldscotland.com/news/12364160.speaking-in-tongues/].

Herald, The (2003) 'BBC approves list of words to promote Scots language on air'. 6 Dec. [www.heraldscotland.com/news/12423276.bbc-approves-list-of-words-to-promote-scots-language-on-air/].

Herald, The (2012) 'Booker winner Kelman backs referendum Yes vote'. 4 Apr.

Herald, The (2017) 'Herald View: Braw news that speaking Scots is helping pupils'. 2 Sep. [www.heraldscotland.com/opinion/15509437.herald-view-braw-news-that-speaking-scots-is-helping-pupils/].

Herman, A (2001) *How the Scots invented the modern world: the true story of how western Europe's poorest nation created our world & everything in It.* New York: Three Rivers Press.

Hinds, A (2021) 'A language of the soul: Poet Len Pennie on why Scots is more than just a dialect'. *The Sunday Post*, 11 May. [www.sundaypost.com/fp/poet-len-pennie/].

Hobsbawm, EJ (1990) *Nations and Nationalism Since 1780: programme, myth, reality.* Cambridge: Cambridge University Press.

Hodgart, J (2016) 'Scots and the Curriculum'. *Bella Caledonia* blog, 7 Sept. [bellacaledonia.org.uk/2016/09/07/scots-and-the-curriculum/].

Hodge, J (1996) *Trainspotting* [screenplay]. London: Faber and Faber.

Holborow, M (1999) *The politics of English.* London: Sage Publications.

Holmes, J (2008) *An introduction to sociolinguistics*, 3rd ed. London: Pearson Longman.

Horsbroch, D (2020a) 'Timelines of the Scots Language 1920-1990'. Scots Language Centre. [www.scotslanguage.com/articles/node/id/745/type/referance].

Horsbroch, D (2020b) 'Recommendations for Names of Countries, Nations, Regions & States in Scots'. Scots Language Centre, 24 Sep. [d3lmsxlb5a0r5x.cloudfront.net/library/document/Warld%20Names%20in%20Scots%202020%201.pdf].

Hoyer, A (2007) *The Scottishness of Oor Wullie*. PhD Thesis, Ruprecht-Karls Universität, Heidelberg.

Hunter, R (2022) 'Scots language: Ian Smart claims Scottish Government use Scots as 'racist' tool'. *The National*, 20 Aug. [www.thenational.scot/news/20679743.scots-language-ian-smart-claims-scottish-government-use-scots-racist-tool/].

Hyvik, JJ, Millar, RM and Newby, AG (2016) 'Language and nationalism in the nineteenth century: Nynorsk and Scots in comparative context'. *Scandinavica*, 55.2, 6–42.

Iosad, P (2016) 'What does the Scots language have to do with Scottish identity?'. *New Statesman*, 8 Jan. [www.newstatesman.com/politics/devolution/2016/01/what-does-scots-language-have-do-scottish-identity].

Jack, I (2017) 'Flattening in England, resurgent in Scotland: accents still shape our island life'. *The Guardian*, 21 Oct. [www.theguardian.com/commentisfree/2017/oct/21/england-scotland-accents-dialects-north-south].

Jackson, R and Niven, L (2000) *Language, Law and Liberty*. [media.scotslanguage.com/library/document/LanguageLawLiberty.pdf accessed 25.05.2017].

Jamieson, J (1808) *An etymological dictionary of the Scottish language*. Edinburgh: University Press. [archive.org/details/etymologicaldicto1jami].

Jenkins, J (2015) *Global Englishes: A resource book for students*. London: Routledge.

Jones, C (1995) *A language suppressed: the pronunciation of the Scots language in the 18th century*. Edinburgh: John Donald Publishers.

Jones, C (2002) *The English language in Scotland: an introduction to Scots*. East Linton: Tuckwell Press.

Joyce, J (1922) *Ulysses*. Paris: Sylvia Beach.

Judge, A (2007) *Linguistic policies and the survival of regional languages in France and Britain*. Basingstoke: Palgrave Macmillan.

Kaul, S (2009) *Eighteenth-century British Literature and Postcolonial Studies (Postcolonial Literary Studies)*. Edinburgh: Edinburgh University Press.

Kavanagh, P (2015) 'Why Scots is a language'. *Wee Ginger Dug* blog, 11 Sep. [weegingerdug.wordpress.com/2015/09/11/why-scots-is-a-language/].

Kavanagh, P (2016) 'Wee Ginger Dug: There's nae need tae cringe - Scots is oor mither tongue'. *The National*, 9 Jan. [www.thenational.scot/comment/14860001.Wee_Ginger_Dug__There___s_nae_need_tae_cringe___Scots_is_oor_mither_tongue/].

Kavanagh, P (2017) 'Looking under the bonnet of language', *Wee Ginger Dug* blog, 4 Sep.

Kavanagh, P (2018a) 'It's the Unionists who are politicising Scots – not us'. *The National*, 2 May.

[www.thenational. /news/16197727.unionists-politicising-scots---not-us/].

Kay, B (1986, revised 1993) *Scots: the mither tongue*. Edinburgh: Mainstream.

Keating, M (1996) *Nations against the state: the new politics of nationalism in Quebec, Catalonia and Scotland*. London: Macmillan Press.

Kelman, J (1994) *How Late It Was, How Late*. London: Minerva.

Kemp, J (2018) 'The Guid Scots Tongue – A Short History'. [www.jackiekemp.co.uk/2018/07/10/the-guid-scots-tongue-a-short-history/].

Kerswill, P (2003) 'Dialect levelling and geographical diffusion in British English'. In D

Britain and J Cheshire (eds), *Social Dialectology*, in honour of Peter Trudgill. Amsterdam: Benjamins, 223–243.

Kidd, C (2003) 'Race, empire, and the limits of nineteenth-century Scottish nationhood'. *The Historical Journal*, 46.4, 873–892.

Kilsyth Chronicle (1902) Kilsyth Burgh Academy: Distribution of certificates. 6 Dec.

Kirk, JM (2011) 'Scotland and Northern Ireland as Scots-speaking communities'. In JM Kirk and DP Ó Baoill (eds), *Sustaining minority language development: Northern Ireland, the Republic of Ireland, and Scotland*. Belfast Studies in Language, Culture and Politics Series 20. Belfast: Cló Ollscoil na Banríona, 193–205.

Kirk, JM (2013) 'Civil Service Scots: prose or poetry?'. In JM Kirk and I Macleod (eds), *Scots: Studies in its literature and language*. Amsterdam: Rodopi, 278–303.

Kloss, H (1967) 'Abstand languages and ausbau languages'. *Anthropological Linguistics*, 9.7, 29–41.

Kloss, H (1969) *Research possibilities on group bilingualism: A report*. Quebec: International Center for research on Bilingualism.

Knox, DL (2003) *Regional and national cultures in North-Eastern Scotland: tradition, language and practice in the constitution of folk cultures*. Doctoral thesis, Durham University. [etheses.dur.ac.uk/3655].

Kramsch, CJ (1998) *Language and Culture*. Oxford: Oxford University Press.

Kynoch, D (1994) *Teach yourself Doric: A course for beginners*. Aberdeen: Scottish Cultural Press.

Kynoch, D (1996) *A Doric dictionary*. Aberdeen: Scottish Cultural Press.

Kynoch, D (1997) *Doric for swots*. Aberdeen: Scottish Cultural Press.

Lauchlan, F, Parisi, M and Fadda, R (2012) 'Bilingualism in Sardinia and Scotland: Exploring the cognitive benefits of speaking a 'minority' language'. *International Journal of Bilingualism*, 17.1, 43–56.

Laurie, SS (1890) *Lectures on language and linguistic method in school*. Cambridge: Cambridge University Press.

Lawson, R, ed (2014) *Sociolinguistics in Scotland*. London: Palgrave Macmillan.

Learmonth, A (2021) 'Calls for a Scots language act as attacks on speakers increase'. *The National*, 24 Jan. [www.thenational.scot/news/19034578.calls-scots-language-act-attacks-speakers-increase/].

Leask, D (2015) 'Does speaking Scots really make you more likely to favour independence?'. *The Herald*, 8 June. [www.heraldscotland.com/news/13411968.Does_speaking_Scots_really_make_you_more_likely_to_favour_independence_/].

Leask, D (2016a) 'David Leask: Why do so many Scots cringe when they see the language of their neighbours written down?'. *The Herald*, 5 Apr. [www.heraldscotland.com/opinion/14403393.david-leask-why-do-so-many-scots-cringe-when-they-see-the-language-of-their-neighbours-written-down/].

Leask, D (2016b) 'Labour discovers a new Scottish language in its manifesto', *The Herald*, 27 April. [www.heraldscotland.com/news/14456251.Labour_discovers_a_new_Scottish_language_in_its_manifesto/].

Leask, D (2017) 'Cited in Politicisation "Tweetstorm"'. *Scotshaunbuik*, 6 Apr. [scotshaunbuik.co.uk/wp/politicisation-tweetstorm/].

Leask, D (2021) 'There is a vein of state nationalism within opposition to minority languages'. *The Herald*, 9 Aug. [www.heraldscotland.com/politics/19499453.david-leask-vein-state-nationalism-within-opposition-minority-languages/].

Lee, M (2021) 'Scots and Gaelic aren't Yes languages – here's why'. Blog post, 4 Apr.

[moadore.medium.com/scots-and-gaelic-arent-yes-languages-here-s-why-4345148d72a1].

Leith, D (1997) *A social history of English* (2nd ed). London: Routledge.

Leith, MS and Soule, DPJ (2012) *Political discourse and national identity in Scotland*. Edinburgh: Edinburgh University Press.

Leslie, JD (1943) 'Thinking shame of our own Scots tongue'. *The Daily Record*, 19 Jan.

Llamas, C and Watt, D, eds (2010) *Language and Identities*. Edinburgh: Edinburgh University Press.

Lo Bianco, J (2001) *Language and literacy policy in Scotland*. Glasgow: Scottish CILT. [www.scilt.org.uk/Portals/24/Library/publications/languageandliteracy/Language%20and%20literacy%20policy%20in%20Scotland_full%20document.pdf].

Lonely Planet (2017) Scotland. [www.lonelyplanet.com/Scotland].

Lorimer, WLL (1983 trans) *The New Testament in Scots*. Edinburgh: Canongate.

Macafee C (1987) 'Introduction' in *Nuttis Schell: Essays on the Scots Language Presented to AJ Aitken*, eds Macafee C and Macleod I. Aberdeen: Aberdeen University Press.

Macafee, C (1981) 'Nationalism and the Scots Renaissance now'. *English World-Wide* 2, 29–38.

Macafee, C (1983) *Varieties of English around the world: Glasgow*. Amsterdam: John Benjamins.

Macafee, C (2012) 'Rowin Back fae the Wilder Shores'. *Talk given to the Scots Language Society 40th Anniversary Collogue*. Edinburgh, 12 May. [www.scotslanguage.com/m/Scots_Language_Society_uid135/Caroline_Macafee audio recording, text via asls.arts.gla.ac.uk/Papers.html].

Macafee, C (2015) Commentary on Aitken, AJ (1980, 2015) 'New Scots: the problems'. In AJ Aitken (ed), Caroline Macafee, *Collected Writings on the Scots Language* (2015), Scots Language Centre. [d3lmsxlb5aor5x.cloudfront.net/library/document/aitken/New_Scots_the_problems.pdf].

Macafee, C (2016) 'Scots in the Census: validity and reliability'. The Scots Language Centre. [media.scotslanguage.com/library/document/Scots%20in%20the%20Census%20-%20validity%20and%20reliability.pdf].

Macaulay, RKS (1997) *Standards and variation in urban speech: Examples from Lowland Scots*. (Varieties of English Around the World, Volume 20). Amsterdam: John Benjamins.

Macaulay, RKS (2005) *Extremely common eloquence: Constructing Scottish identity through narrative*. Amsterdam: Rodopi.

Macdonald, K (2017) 'Scots dialects 'as good as a second language''. BBC Scotland News, 3 Nov. [www.bbc.com/news/uk-scotland-41844216].

MacEacheran, M (2021) 'Doric, a little-known form of North East Scots, is undergoing a pandemic-inspired renaissance'. BBC Travel, 22 Mar. [www.bbc.com/travel/article/20210321-scotlands-little-known-fourth-language].

Macfarlane, J (2012) 'Scots Wha Hae or Scots Who Have'. *Concept*, 3.1. [concept.lib.ed.ac.uk/article/view/2328].

Mackay, C (1888) *A dictionary of Lowland Scotch*. London: Whittaker & Co. [archive.org/details/dictionaryoflowloomackrich].

Mackie, A (1913) *Readings in modern Scots*. London: Chambers.

Mackie, R (2021a) '"You think your attacks don't hurt me, but they do" Scottish poet speaks out about being the victim of relentless online abuse'. *The Scotsman*, 8 Jan.

[www.scotsman.com/news/people/you-think-your-attacks-dont-hurt-me-they-do-scottish-poet-speaks-out-about-being-victim-relentless-online-abuse-3090524].

Mackie, R (2021b) 'Artists, poets and language lovers speak out as they face a torrent of online abuse for speaking Scots'. *The Scotsman*, 26 March. [www.scotsman.com/news/people/artists-poets-and-language-lovers-speak-out-as-they-face-a-torrent-of-online-abuse-for-speaking-scots-3180320].

Macleod, I and Cairns, P, eds (2017) *The Concise Scots English Scots Dictionary* 2nd edition (Scottish Language Dictionaries). Edinburgh: Chambers.

Macleod, I and Cairns, P, eds (2005) *The Essential Scots Dictionary (Scots-English/English-Scots)*. Edinburgh: Scottish Language Dictionaries.

MacMillan, A (1972) *The new Scots reader*. Edinburgh: Oliver & Boyd/Burns Federation.

Maguire, G (1987) 'Language revival in an urban neo-Gaeltacht'. In Gearoid MacEoin et al (eds),

Third International Conference on Minority Languages: Celtic papers, 72–88.

Maguire, W (2012) 'English and Scots in Scotland'. In R Hickey (ed), *Areal Features of the Anglophone World*. Berlin: Mouton de Gruyter, 53–78.

Massie, A (2004) 'Makkin a right mess o' the Scots language'. *The Scotsman*, 31 Jan.

[www.scotsman.com/lifestyle-2-15039/makkin-a-right-mess-o-the-scots-language-1-511921].

Massie, A (2016) 'Confidence in our nation speaks for itself'. *The Sunday Times*, 16 Feb.

[www.thetimes.co.uk/article/confidence-in-our-nation-speaks-for-itself-qddlf7605sk].

Máté, I (1996) *Scots Language. A Report on the Scots Language Research carried out by the General Register Office for Scotland in 1996*. Edinburgh: General Register Office (Scotland).

McArthur, C (1998) 'The exquisite corpse of Rab(elais) C(opernicus) Nesbitt'. In M Wayne (ed), *Dissident voices: the politics of television and cultural change*. London: Pluto Press.

McArthur, T (1998) *The English languages*. Cambridge: Cambridge University Press.

McCall, C (2002) 'Political transformation and the reinvention of the Ulster-Scots identity and culture'. *Identities*, 9.2, 197–218.

McClure, JD (1979) 'Scots: its range of uses'. In AJ Aitken and T McArthur (eds), *Languages of Scotland*. Edinburgh: Chambers, 26–48.

McClure, JD (1980) 'Developing Scots as a National Language'. In JD McClure, AJ Aitken and JT Low (eds), *The Scots Language*. Edinburgh: The Ramsay Head Press.

McClure, JD, ed (1983) *Scotland and the Lowland tongue: studies in the language and literature of Lowland Scotland* (in honour of David D Murison, with a foreword by AJ Aitken). Aberdeen: Aberdeen University Press.

McClure, JD (1988, revised 1997) *Why Scots matters*. Edinburgh: The Saltire Society.

McClure, JD (1995) *Scots and its literature*. Amsterdam: John Benjamins.

McClure, JD (1998) 'What is the Scots Language?'. In L Niven and R Jackson (eds), *The Scots Language: its Place in Education*. Dundee: In·House, 7–18.

McClure, JD (2000) *Language, poetry and nationhood: Scots as a poetic language from 1878 to the present*. Edinburgh: Tuckwell Press.

McClure, JD (2002) *Doric: the dialect of North-East Scotland*. Amsterdam: John Benjamins Publishing Company.

McClure, JD (2008) 'English in Scotland'. In M Matto and H Momma (eds), *A Companion to the History of the English Language*. Oxford: Wiley-Blackwell.

McClure, JD (2018) 'The Scots columns in *The National*'. In *Volume 6: Language on the move across domains and communities*. Selected papers from the 12th triennial Forum for Research on the Languages of Scotland and Ulster, Glasgow 2018. [www.abdn.ac.uk/pfrlsu/documents/Ch1_McClure.pdf].

McCrone, D (2009) *Understanding Scotland: The sociology of a nation*. Abingdon: Routledge.

McDermid, V (2021) 'Scotland and me: Val McDermid stands up for the Scots language'. *Financial Times*, 22 Apr. [www.ft.com/content/f5ee12a2-402f-4f39-91b6-1bb2c9767592].

McEwan-Fujita, E (2006) "Gaelic Doomed as Speakers Die Out'?: The Public Discourse of Gaelic Language Death in Scotland.' In Wilson McLeod (ed), *Revitalising Gaelic in Scotland: Policy, Planning and Public Discourse*. Edinburgh: Dunedin Academic Press, 279–293.

McEwan-Fujita, E (2011) 'Language Revitalization Discourses as Metaculture: Gaelic in Scotland from the Eighteenth to Twentieth Centuries'. *Language & Communication*, 31.1, 48–62.

McEwan-Fujita, E (2015) 'Anti-Gaelic bingo'. *Gaelic.co* blog. [gaelic.co/anti-gaelic-bingo/].

McEwan-Fujita, E (2018) 'Anti-Gaelic bingo revisited'. *Gaelic.co* blog. [gaelic.co/anti-gaelic-bingo-revisited/].

McGonigal, J (2013) 'Edwin Morgan, Hugh MacDiarmid and the Direction of the MacAvantgarde'. In E Bell and L Gunn (eds), *The Scottish Sixties: Reading, Rebellion, Revolution?*. Amsterdam and New York: Rodopi.

McIlvanney, W (2002) 'Reviving the Scots language'. *The Scotsman*, 18 Aug. [www.scotsman.com/news-2-15012/reviving-the-scots-language-1-1376160].

McKenna, K (2017) 'Only bampots will girn about BBC's poetic delight'. *The Guardian*, 1 Oct. [www.theguardian.com/commentisfree/2017/sep/30/bampots-girn-bbc-downpour-dialect-scots].

McKinlay, S (2013) 'Glasgow's 'EastEnders' accent shows the ties that bind across the border'. *The Guardian*, 10 Sep. [www.theguardian.com/commentisfree/2013/sep/10/glasgow-eastenders-accent].

McLeod, W (2019) 'The nature of minority languages: Insights from Scotland', *Multilingua - Journal of CrossCultural and Interlanguage Communication*, 38.2, 141–154. [www.pure.ed.ac.uk/ws/portalfiles/portal/92467493/_Multilingua_The_nature_of_minority_languages_insights_from_Scotland.pdf].

McMillan, J (2021) 'The Scotsman Sessions #232: Len Pennie', *The Scotsman*, 6 May. [www.scotsman.com/arts-and-culture/books/the-scotsman-sessions-232-len-pennie-3227085].

Meighan, C (2021) 'Miss PunnyPennie: Scots poet leaves Twitter after misogynistic abuse', *The National*, 2 Oct 2021. [www.thenational.scot/news/19620929.miss-punnypennie-scots-poet-leaves-twitter-misogynistic-abuse/].

Melchers, G and Shaw, P (2011) *World Englishes: an introduction* (2nd ed). London: Hodder Education.

Menzies, J (1991) 'An investigation of attitudes to Scots and Glasgow dialect among secondary school pupils'. *Scottish Language*, 10, 30–46. [www.arts.gla.ac.uk/STELLA/STARN/lang/MENZIES/menzie1.htm].

Meyerhoff, M (2006) *Introducing sociolinguistics*. London: Routledge.

Millar, R McColl, Barras, W and Bonnici, L (2014) *Lexical Variation and Attrition in the Scottish Fishing Communities*. Edinburgh: Edinburgh University Press.

Millar, R McColl (2005) *Language, nation and power: an introduction*. Basingstoke: Palgrave Macmillan.

Millar, R McColl (2006) 'Burying alive: unfocussed governmental language policy and Scots'. *Language Policy*, 5, 63–86.

Millar, R McColl (2007) *Northern and Insular Scots*. Edinburgh: Edinburgh University Press.

Millar, R McColl (2008) 'Dislocation: is it presently possible to envisage an economically based Language Policy for Scots in Scotland?'. In JM Kirk and D Ó Baóill (eds), *Language and Economic Development: Northern Ireland, the Republic of Ireland, and Scotland*. Belfast: Cló Ollscoil na Banríona.

Millar, R McColl (2011) 'Linguistic democracy?'. In J Kirk and D O Baoill (eds), *Sustaining Minority Language Communities: Northern Ireland, the Republic of Ireland, and Scotland*. Belfast Studies in Language, Culture and Politics Series, vol 20. Belfast: Clo Ollscoil na Banriona, 218–224. Reprint. [www.abdn.ac.uk/staffpages/uploads/enl097/Linguistic%20democracy_.].

Millar, R McColl (2018) *Modern Scots: an analytical survey*. Edinburgh: Edinburgh University Press.

Millar, R McColl (2020) *A sociolinguistic history of Scotland*. Edinburgh: Edinburgh University Press.

Miller, J (1998) 'Scots: a sociolinguistic perspective'. In L Niven and R Jackson (eds), *The Scots Language: its Place in Education*. Dundee: In House, 45–56.

Miller, P (2018) 'Poet: I have given up writing in my heartfelt language of Scots'. *The Herald*, 5 April. [www.heraldscotland.com/news/16138798.poet-given-writing-heartfelt-language-scots/].

Milroy, J and Milroy, L (1985, 1999) *Authority in language: Investigating Standard English*. Oxford: Routledge.

Muir, E (1936) *Scott and Scotland: the predicament of the Scottish writer*. London: George Routledge and Sons, Ltd.

Muirson, D (1977) *The guid Scots tongue*. Edinburgh: William Blackwood.

Munck, R (1986) *The difficult dialogue: Marxism and nationalism*. London: Zed Books.

Munro, M (1985) *The Patter: guide to current Glasgow usage*. Glasgow: Glasgow City Libraries and Archives.

Munro, M (1996) *The Complete Patter*. Edinburgh: Canongate Books.

Murdoch, S (1996) *Language Politics in Scotland*. Aberdeen: Aberdeen University Scots Leid Quorum. [citeseerx.ist.psu.edu/viewdoc/download?doi=10.1.1.558.1778&rep=rep1&type=pdf].

Murray, JAH (1873) *The dialect of the southern counties of Scotland: its pronunciation, grammar, and historical relations*. London: Philogical Society. [archive.org/details/cu31924026538938].

Nairn, T (1977, 2015) *The break-up of Britain*. Champaign, Illinois: New Directions in the Humanities.

Neuroscience News (2017) 'Brain treats dialect as language'. 6 Nov. [neurosciencenews.com/dialect-language-7882/].

Nicholson, C (2002) *Edwin Morgan: Inventions of modernity*. Manchester: Manchester University Press.

Niven, L (2001) *Scots: The Scots Language in education in Scotland (regional dossier series)*. Leeuwarden: Mercator-Education.

[www.mercator-research.eu/fileadmin/mercator/documents/regional_dossiers/scots_in_scotland.pdf].

Niven, L (2017) *Scots: The Scots Language in education in Scotland* (2nd Edition). Leeuwarden: Mercator-Education. [www.mercator-research.eu/fileadmin/mercator/documents/regional_dossiers/scots_in_scotland_2nd.pdf].

Niven, L and Jackson, R, eds (1998) *Scots language: Its place in education*. Dundee: In House.

Nothern Ireland Humand Rights Commission (2020) *Ulster Scots/Ulster British Provisions of the Northern Ireland Act 1998 (Amendment No 3)*. May 2020. [nihrc.org/uploads/publications/NIHRC_Amendment_No_3_Ulster_Scots_FINAL.PDF].

Northern Ireland Human Rights Commission (2022) *NIHRC Briefing on the Identity and*

Language (Northern Ireland) Bill. 15 Jun. [nihrc.org/publication/detail/nihrc-briefing-on-the-identity-and-language-northern-ireland-bill].

Nutt, K (2021) 'Language record broken at MSP swearing-in ceremony as Scottish Parliament opens'. *The National*, 14 May [www.thenational.scot/news/19301869.language-record-broken-msp-swearing-in-ceremony-scottish-parliament-opens/].

Ó Giollagáin, C, Camshron, G, Moireach, P, O Curnain, B, Caimbeul, I, MacDonald, B and Petervary, T (2020) *The Gaelic Crisis in the Vernacular Community 2020: A comprehensive sociolinguistic survey of Scottish Gaelic*. Aberdeen: Aberdeen University Press.

Ofcom (2019) *Children and parents: media use and attitudes report 2018*. 21 Feb. [www.ofcom.org.uk/research-and-data/media-literacy-research/childrens/children-and-parents-media-use-and-attitudes-report-2018].

Officer, D (2015) 'A wee scrieve oan Scots leid policy'. *Bella Caledonia* blog, 4 Jun. [bellacaledonia.org.uk/2015/06/04/a-wee-scrieve-oan-scots-leid-policy/].

Oor Vyce (2020) Campaign group. [www.oorvyce.scot/].

Open University (2019), 'The Scots language and culture – Part 1'. Milton Keynes: The Open University. [www.open.edu/openlearncreate/course/view.php?id=2705].

Orr, J (1942) 'The Scots vernacular' (letter). *The Scotsman*, 18 April.

Parsley, IJ (2012) *Ulster Scots: A short reference grammar*. Belfast: Ultonia Publishing/ Ulster Scots Academic Press.

Parsley, IJ (2017) 'Difference between Scots and Gibberish'. Blog post, 16 June 2017. [ianjamesparsley.wordpress.com/2017/06/16/difference-between-scots-and-gibberish/].

Paterson, TE (1925) *Scotch readings, recitations and sketches*. Edinburgh: John Menzies & Co.

Pattie, D (2007) 'Mapping the territory: modern Scottish drama'. In R D'Monté and G Saunders (eds), *Cool Britannia? British political drama in the 1990s*. Basingstoke: Palgrave.

Peterkin, T (2015) 'Holyrood launches drive to promote Scots language', *The Scotsman*, 10 September. [www.scotsman.com/news/politics/holyrood-launches-drive-to-promote-scots-language-1-3883171].

Phillipson, R (1992) *Linguistic Imperialism*. Oxford: Oxford University Press.

Purves, D (1997, 2002). *A Scots grammar: Scots grammar and usage*. Edinburgh: The Saltire Society.

Purves, G (2018) 'Retreat ti 'The Hertland'?'. By Erceldoune blog, 21 Apr. [graemepurves.wordpress.com/2018/04/21/retreat-ti-the-hertland/].

Rawsthorne, A (2016) 'Is a day out of Hawick a day wasted? A study of bidialectalism in young Hawick females'. *Lifespans & Styles: Undergraduate Working Papers on Intraspeaker Variation*, 2.1, 48–62.

Review of Scottish Culture Group (1998) *Scottish culture and the curriculum: A report to Scottish Consultative Council on the Curriculum*. Unpublished.

Richards, X (2020) 'Iona Fyfe asks Spotify to fix 'alarming' omission of Scots language'. *The National*, 17 Dec. [www.thenational.scot/news/18952242.iona-fyfe-asks-spotify-fix-alarming-omission-scots-language/].

Robertson, B and Rennie, S (1999, 2000) *Grammar Broonie*. Edinburgh: Polygon.

Robertson, G (2013) 'Speaking at: Scottish Independence Debate – 23rd September 2013, Abertay University'. Dundee: abertayTV. [www.youtube.com/watch?v=A50HTBvidgc quoted comments at 36:15).

Robertson, J, ed (1994) *A tongue in yer heid: A selection of the best contemporary short stories in Scots*. Edinburgh: B&W Publishing.

Robertson, J (2015) 'Lang looked for's come at last!'. Speech for Creative Scotland, 3 June. [www.creativescotland.com/__data/assets/word_doc/0006/31668/James-Robertsons-Speech.doc].

Robertson, K (2019) 'Doric film festival to celebrate 'crannies, colours and contermashes neuks''. *The Press and Journal*, 21 Sep. [www.pressandjournal.co.uk/fp/news/aberdeenshire/1845459/doric-film-festival-to-celebrate-crannies-colours-and-contermashes-neuks/].

Robinson, C (2012) *Modren Scots grammar*. Edinburgh: Luath Press.

Robinson, P (1997) *Ulster Scots: A grammar of the traditional written word and spoken language revised*. Belfast: The Ullans Press.

Rojals, M.(2016) 'El castellà és una llengua, el català és una polèmica'. Vilaweb news outlet, 6 Apr. [www.vilaweb.cat/noticies/el-castella-es-una-llengua-el-catala-es-una-polemica/].

Romaine, S (2000) *Language in society: An introduction to sociolinguistics* (2nd Ed). Oxford: Oxford University Press.

Ross, R (1997) 'No place for our native tongue?' *TES2* (Scottish curriculum). 24 Oct.

Royle, T (2011) *A time of tyrants: Scotland and the Second World War*. Edinburgh: Birlinn.

Ruaix i Vinyet, J (2011) *Diccionari de barbarismes*. Barcelona: Editorial Claret.

Scotch Education Department (1907) 'Memorandum on the teaching of English in Scottish primary schools, His Majesty's Stationery Office'. [hdl.handle.net/2027/uiug.30112069112909].

Scotland, J (1972) 'The centenary of the Education (Scotland) Act of 1872'. *British Journal of Educational Studies*, 20.2, 121–136. [www.tandfonline.com/doi/abs/10.1080/00071005.1972.9973339].

Scots Language Centre (2011) 'Census site brings in thousands of visitors'. [www.scotslanguage.com/articles/view/id/2425].

Scots Language Centre (2020) 'The Big Wiki Rewrite'. News item, 27 Aug. [www.scotslanguage.com/news/5724].

Scots Language Centre (2021a) *Report to the Committee of Experts on the European Charter for Regional or Minority Languages*. Jan 2021. [d3lmsxlb5a0r5x.cloudfront.net/library/document/Scots_Language_Centre_Report_ECRML_Committee_of_Experts_Jan2021_Web.pdf].

Scots Language Centre (2021b) 'Scots Language in the 2021 Scottish Parliament Election'. News item, 26 Apr. [www.scotslanguage.com/news/5824].

Scots Language Centre (undated a) 'Debased or Evolved? Glesca.'. [www.scotslanguage.com/Glesca/Debased_or_Evolved%3F].

Scots Language Centre (undated b) 'The Invisible Language. Glesca.'. [www.scotslanguage.com/Glesca/The_Invisible_Language].

Scots Language Centre (2021) *Scots Warks: Support and guidance for writing/ Uphaud an guidance for screivars*. [d3lmsxlb5a0r5x.cloudfront.net/library/document/Scots%20Warks_support%20and%20guidance%20for%20writing.pdf].

Scots Online (2020) Android Scots Dictionary App. [www.scots-online.org/downloads/android_dictionary.php].

Scots Spellin Comatee, The (1998) *Mensefu Scots Spellin for ti lairn an be lairnit: Report & recommends o the Scots Spellin Comatee*. (Nov 1996 – August 1998). [media.scotslanguage.com/library/document Scots%20Spellin%20Comatee%20recommends%20(RRSSC).pdf].

Scotsman, The (1924) 'The Scots language'. 3 Oct.

Scotsman, The (1932) 'The Scots vernacular: Mr Eric Linklater on its preservation'. 29 Oct.

Scotsman, The (1947) 'A Scotsman's log: Ane for yin'. 28 Apr.

Scotsman, The (1950) 'The Scots tongue: an Aberdeen plea for its encouragement'. 31 May.

Scotsman, The (1999) 'Row over final draft of culture in the curriculum'. 4 Feb.

Scotsman, The (2002) 'Ayes don't have it as sheriff bans Scots yes in court'. 20 Aug. [www.scotsman.com/news/ayes-don-t-have-it-as-sheriff-bans-scots-yes-in-court-1-617939].

Scotsman, The (2006) 'Jings, crivvens! Is Oor Wullie turning into Our William?'. 24 Jul.

Scotsman, The (2010) 'Blow to SNP as two-thirds say Scots is not a real language'. 14 Jan. [www.scotsman.com/news/politics/blow-to-snp-as-two-thirds-say-scots-is-not-a-real-language-1-786317].

Scotsman, The (2010) 'Scots fails to cross language barrier'. 14 Jan. [www.scotsman.com/news-2-15012/scots-fails-to-cross-language-barrier-1-786243].

Scottish Consultative Council on the Curriculum (1996) *The Kist/ A'Chiste*. Walton-on Thames: Thomas Nelson and Sons Ltd.

Scottish Consultative Council on the Curriculum (1998) *Scottish Culture and the Curriculum.* Report from Review Group [unpublished].

Scottish Education Department (1947) *Secondary Education: A Report of the Advisory Council on Education in Scotland.* (The Fyfe Report). Edinburgh: His Majesty's Stationery Office. [www.educationengland.org.uk/documents/fyfe1947/fyfe1947.html].

Scottish Executive (2000) *Revitalising Gaelic: A National Asset*. Edinburgh: Scottish Executive.

Scottish Executive (2007) *A strategy for Scotland's languages*. Edinburgh: Education Department Cultural Policy Division. [www2.gov.scot/resource/doc/163888/0044602.pdf].

Scottish Government (2010a) *Scots language: Ministerial Working Group report*, 30 Nov. [www.gov.scot/publications/report-ministerial-working-group-scots-language/].

Scottish Government (2010b) *Adult Literacies in Scotland 2020: Strategic guidance. Edinburgh: Scottish Government.* [www.gov.scot/publications/adult-literacies-scotland-2020-strategic-guidance/].

Scottish Government (2018) 'Annual spend on support for Gaelic since 1999: FOI release'. 1 May. Edinburgh: Scottish Government. [www.gov.scot/publications/foi-18-01112/].

Scottish Government (2018) 'Convention on the elimination of all forms of discrimination against women: position statement'. 2 May. [www.gov.scot/publications/scottish-government-position-statement-convention-elimination-forms-discrimination-against-women/pages/2/].

Scottish Government (2022) 'Gaelic and Scots and Scottish Languages Bill: Scottish Government commitments'. 24 Aug. [consult.gov.scot/education-reform/gaelic-and-scots-scottish-languages-bill/].

Scottish Government/Evans, R (2009) *Audit of current Scots language provision in Scotland.* Edinburgh: Scottish Government Social Research. [www.webarchive.org.uk/wayback/archive/20170701162406/ www.gov.scot/Publications/2009/01/23133726/12].

Scottish Government/TNS-BMRB (2010) *Public Attitudes Towards the Scots Language.* [www2.gov.scot/resource/doc/298037/0092859.pdf].

Scottish Labour Party (2016) 2016 Scottish Parliament election manifesto. [www.spokes.org.uk/wp-content/uploads/2016/03/Scottish-Labour-Manifesto-2016.pdf].

Scottish Language Dictionaries (2005) *The essential Scots dictionary: Scots-English, English-Scots.* Edinburgh: Edinburgh University Press.

Scottish Language Dictionaries (2017) *Concise Scots dictionary* (2nd Ed). Edinburgh:

Edinburgh University Press.

Scottish National Party (2021) *SNP 2021 Manifesto: Scotland's Future, Scotland's Choice.* 15 Apr. SNP: Edinburgh [www.snp.org/manifesto/].

Scottish Parliament, The (2023a) Scottish Languages Bill.

Scottish Parliament, The (2023b) Scottish Languages Bill: Explanatory Policy Memorandum, 12.

Scottish Parliament Information Centre, The (2024) 'Gaelic and Scots in Scotland: What does the census tell us?' 12 Aug.

[https://spice-spotlight.scot/2024/08/12/gaelic-and-scots-in-scotland-what-does-the-census-tell-us/]

Scottish Qualifications Authority (2013) Scottish Studies Award. [www.sqa.org.uk/sqa/64329.html].

Scottish Qualifications Authority (2014) Scots Language Award. [www.sqa.org.uk/sqa/70056.html].

Seenan, G (2005) 'Glaswegians throw the R away'. *The Guardian*, 14 Mar. [www.theguardian.com/uk/2005/mar/14/research.highereducation].

Shanks, P (2010) 'Early Kelman'. In S Hames (ed), *Edinburgh companion to James Kelman.* Edinburgh: Edinburgh University Press.

Shoemark, P, Sur, D, Shrimpton, L, Murray, I and Goldwater, S (2017) 'Aye or naw, whit dae ye hink? Scottish independence and linguistic identity on social media'. In *Proceedings of the 15th Conference of the European Chapter of the Association for Computational Linguistics*, Volume 1, Long Papers, 1239–1248. [www.aclweb.org/anthology/E17-1116/].

Siegel, J (1999) 'Stigmatized and standardized varieties in the classroom: Interference or separation?'. *TESOL Quarterly*, 33.4.

Small, M (2018) 'North by Northeast', *Bella Caledonia* blog, 26 Mar. [bellacaledonia.org.uk/2018/03/26/north-by-northeast/].

Smart, I (2022) 'We need to talk about "Scots"'. *iansmart* blog, 18 Aug. [ianssmart.blogspot.com/2022/08/we-need-to-talk-about-scots.html].

Smith, J and Durham, M (2012) 'Bidialectalism of dialect death? Explaining generational change in the Shetland Islands, Scotland'. *American Speech*, 87.1, 57–88.

Smith, L (2017) 'Our big slang theory? Well, for a start, Scots isn't slang'. *The Sunday Post*, Oct 9. [www.sundaypost.com/fp/our-big-slang-theory-well-for-a-start-scots-isnt-slangdefine-inspiration/].

Smith, MC (1913) 'The Boy in the Train' (poem). Available at the Scottish Poetry Library [www.scottishpoetrylibrary.org.uk/poem/boy-train/]

Smith, WW (1901) *The New Testament in braid Scots.* Paisley: Alexander Gardner (1904 edition). [archive.org/details/NTinBraidScots/page/n5].

Sobey, A (1993) 'Scots realpolitik. Supplement: Talking Scots'. *Fortnight*, 318 (Jun).

[www.jstor.org/stable/25554103].

Solé i Camardons, J (1988, 2012) *Sociolingüística per a joves del segle XXI.* Argentona: Voliana Edicions.

Stevenson, R (2011) 'Drama Language and Revival'. In I Brown (ed), *The Edinburgh companion to Scottish drama.* Edinburgh: Edinburgh University Press.

Stuart-Smith, J (2007) 'The influence of the media'. In C Llamas, L Mullany and P Stockwell (eds), *The Routledge Companion to Sociolinguistics* (1st ed). London: Routledge, 140–148.

Stuart-Smith, J (2018) 'Sound perspectives? Speech and speaker dynamics over a century of Scottish English'. In R Mesthrie and D Bradley (eds), *The Dynamics of Language: Plenary and Focus Lectures from the 20th International Congress of Linguists.* UCT Press: Cape Town, 74–92.

Stuart-Smith, J, Lawson, E and Scobbie, JM (2014) 'Derhoticisation in Scottish English: a sociophonetic journey'. In C Celata and S Calamai (eds), *Advances in sociophonetics*. Amsterdam: John Benjamins.

Tait, JM (2016) 'RAPAQ on Scots Orthography'. *Scots Threip*, undated. [sites.google.com/site/scotsthreip/ulsterography].

Tait, JM (2017) 'Robertsonianism'. *Scots Threip*, updated 25 Apr. [sites.google.com/site/scotsthreip/robertsonianism].

Tait, JM (2018) 'The 95% Rule'. *Scots Threip*, updated 11 Mar. [sites.google.com/site/scotsthreip/concepts/95-rule].

Tait, JM (2019) 'Some principles of expository Scots'. *Scots Threip*, updated 25 May. [sites.google.com/site/scotsthreip/development/principles].

Tett, L (2000) 'Excluded voices: class, culture, and family literacy in Scotland'. *Journal of Adolescent & Adult Literacy*, 44.2, 22–128.

Trainer, P (2021) 'Irvine Welsh on vernacular speech, Edinburgh and his new drama'. *The Herald*, 2 July 2021.

Trousdale, G (2010) *An introduction to English sociolinguistics*. Edinburgh: Edinburgh University Press.

Trudgill, P (1984) 'Standard English in England'. In P Trudgill (ed), *Language in the British Isles*. Cambridge: Cambridge University Press, 32–44.

Trudgill, P (2021a) 'The Swiss secret that could keep Britain together'. *The New European*, 17 Feb. [www.theneweuropean.co.uk/brexit-news-europe-news-switzerland-and-its-languages-7304514].

Trudgill, P (2021b) 'Not a real language? You've Scot to be joking'. *The New European*, 28 Mar. [www.theneweuropean.co.uk/brexit-news-is-scots-a-language-7820022/].

Tuson, J (1988) *Mal de llengües: A l'etorn dels prejudicis linguistics*. Barcelona: Empúries.

Ulster-Scots Academy (undated) The Ulster-Scots Academy website. [www.ulsterscotsacademy.com/].

Unger, JW (2010) 'Legitimating inaction: differing identity constructions of the Scots language'. *European Journal of Cultural Studies*, 13, 99–113.

Unger, JW (2013) *The discursive construction of the Scots language*. Amsterdam: John Benjamins.

University of Aberdeen (2018) 'Scots language workshop to encourage people to speak in their 'mither tongue''. News, 15 Aug. [www.abdn.ac.uk/news/12156/].

University of Cambridge (2016) 'The ability of children to speak any two dialects – two closely related varieties of the same language – may confer the same cognitive advantages as those reported for multilingual children who speak two or more substantially different languages (such as English and French)'. *University of Cambridge Research News*, 27 Apr. [www.cam.ac.uk/research/news/speakers-of-two-dialects-may-share-cognitive-advantage-with-speakers-of-two-languages].

Walters, S (2009) 'Walcome tae the Scottish Pairlament wabsite: The internet guide to Holyrood translated into 'Rab C Nesbitt' dialect'. *Mail on Sunday*, 15 Nov. [www.dailymail.co.uk/news/article-1227837/Walcome-tae-Scottish-Pairlament-wabsite-The-internet-guide-Holyrood--translated-Scots-dialect.html].

Warnecke, S (2019) '*Introduction*, Scots language and culture – part 1' (online course). Milton Keynes: The Open University.

Warrack, A (1911) *A Scots dialect dictionary*. Edinburgh: W and R Chambers. [openlibrary.org/books/OL24604531M/A_Scot's_dialect_dictionary].

Watson, R (1998) 'Postcolonial Subjects? Language, narrative authority and class in contemporary Scottish culture'. *The European English Messenger*, 7.1, 21–31.

Watson, R (2013) 'Scottish poetry: The scene and the sixties'. In L Gunn and E Bell (eds), *The Scottish sixties: Reading, rebellion, revolution?. SCROLL: Scottish Cultural Review of Language and Literature*, 20. Leiden: Brill.

Watt, I (2018) 'Outlander is boosting a renaissance of the Scots language – here's how'. *The National*, 23 Aug. [www.thenational.scot/news/16595101.outlander-boosting-renaissance-scots-language--/].

Weber, J-J (2015) *Language racism*. London: Palgrave Macmillan.

Wee, L (2011) *Language without rights*. Oxford: Oxford University Press.

Wells, JC (1982) *Accents of English*. Cambridge: Cambridge University Press.

Welsh, I (1993) *Trainspotting*. London: Secker and Warburg.

Wilson, J (1915) *Lowland Scotch as spoken in the lower Strathearn district of Perthshire*. Oxford: Oxford University Press. [archive.org/details/lowlandscotchas00wilsuoft].

Wilson, J (1923) *The dialect of Robert Burns as spoken in Central Ayrshire*. Oxford: Oxford University Press. [archive.org/stream/dialectofrobertb00wilsuoft].

Wilson, J (1926) *The dialects of Central Scotland*. Oxford: Oxford University Press.

Wilson, LC (2012) *Luath Scots language learner: an introduction to contemporary spoken Scots* (revised ed). Edinburgh: Luath Press.

Wilson, R (2017) 'Spellin oot thorny kinch fir language thought police'. *The National*, 6 Jul.

Wilson, R (2018) 'Ye need a gey thick skin tae scrieve in Scots!'. *The National*, 12 Apr. [www.thenational.scot/news/16152842.ye-need-gey-thick-skin-tae-scrieve-scots/].

Wilson, R (2019) 'We hae a new generation o bonnie young fechters fir Scots!'. *The National*, 24 Oct. [www.thenational.scot/news/17988845.hae-new-generation-o-bonnie-young-fechters-fir-scots/].

Winder, R (2004) 'Highly literary and deeply vulgar: If James Kelman's Booker novel is rude, it is in good company'. *The Independent*, 12 October.

Woehrling, J-M (2006) *The European Charter for Regional or Minority Languages - A critical commentary*. Strasbourg: Council of Europe. [book.coe.int/en/minorities/3575-pdf-the-european-charter-for-regional-or-minority-languages-a-critical-commentary.html].

Woods, J (2016) 'Letters to The National II: Principled objection to the project of promoting Scots'. *The National*, 1 Feb. [www.thenational.scot/news/14861018.letters-to-the-national-ii-principled-objection-to-the-project-of-promoting-scots/].

Woollaston, V (2016) 'Speaking SLANG is as good for your brain as being bilingual and spending just a week using a new language boosts attention span'. *Mailonline*, 27 Apr. [www.dailymail.co.uk/sciencetech/article-3561902/Speaking-SLANG-good-brain-bilingual-spending-just-week-using-new-language-boosts-attention-span.html].

Wright, S (2015) 'What is language? A response to Philippe van Parijs'. *Critical Review of International Social and Political Philosophy*, 18.2, 113–130. [researchportal.port.ac.uk/portal/files/3277637/Response_to_van_Parijs_Final.pdf].

Wright, S (2016) *Language policy and language planning: from nationalism to globalisation*. London: Palgrave Macmillan.

Wynne, A (2021) 'Scottish poet, 21, is accused of 'making Scottish people sound stupid''. *Mail Online*, 17 Jan. [www.dailymail.co.uk/femail/article-9156461/amp/Scottish-poet-21-accused-making-Scottish-people-sound-stupid.html].

Young, CPL (2012) '"The Broons" – how 'Scots' are they? (Part 2)'. *Scotslanguage.info* blog, 8 Sep. [scotslanguage.info/"the-broons"—how-'scots'-are-they-part-2/].

Young, CPL (2013) 'How to kill a story. Scots'. *Scotslanguage.info* blog, 27 Sep. [scotslanguage.info/how-to-kill-a-story/].

Young, CPL (2015a) 'Speakin Scots is apoleetical'. *Scotslanguage.info* blog, 16 February. [scotslanguage.info/speakin-scots-is-apolitical/].

Young, CPL (2015b) 'Creative Scotlan(d) maun dae better'. *Scotslanguage.info* blog, 7 June. [scotslanguage.info/creative-scotland-maun-dae-better/].

Young, CPL (2015c) 'The Scots scriever must have the write stuff'. *Scotslanguage.info* blog, 21 Jun. [scotslanguage.info/the-scots-scriever-must-have-the-write-stuff/].

Young, CPL (2017) 'The Bam Whisperer'. *The Scots Haunbuik*, blog 22 Nov. [scotslanguage.info/wp/the-bam-whisperer/].

Young, D (1946) '"Plastic Scots" and the Scottish literary tradition: An authoritative introduction to a controversy'. Glasgow: William MacLellan.

Zuckermann, G (2017) 'Language Revival Diamond'. Professor Ghil'ad Zuckermann website. [www.zuckermann.org/images/2017/diamond.jpeg].

Acknowledgements

Trying to make sense of such a controversial, contested and complex subject as the Scots language was always going to be a challenge. I have had to lean heavily on the insights of the small but determined group of Scots language scholars and activists who over the years have persevered with a cause rarely viewed as academically or politically fashionable. My grateful thanks to them are acknowledged by copious footnotes throughout the book. I hope I haven't misrepresented their views too grievously. My own reappraisal of Scots was sparked by Bob Fairnie's *Scots Tung Wittins* and refined by a decade of discussion on Facebook's Scots Language Forum, most notably in the early days with former Shetland language activist John M Tait, and latterly with countless others. As the book began to take shape, I am hugely indebted to all who provided encouragement and feedback on various drafts, including Susi Briggs, Michael Dempster, Andy Eagle, Bruce Eunson, Michael Everson, Jamie Fairbairn, Gavin Falconer, Michael Hance, Caroline Macafee, Derrick McClure, Duncan Sneddon and my good friend L Colin Wilson. Apologies if I've left anyone out. Many thanks to Gavin MacDougall for his faith in this project, Rachael Murray and Jennie Renton for their meticulous editing and layout, Amy Turnbull for the splendid cover and the entire team at Luath. Of course, none of this would have been remotely possible without the support of my wonderful wife Deb.

Luath Press Limited

committed to publishing well written books worth reading

LUATH PRESS takes its name from Robert Burns, whose little collie Luath (*Gael.*, swift or nimble) tripped up Jean Armour at a wedding and gave him the chance to speak to the woman who was to be his wife and the abiding love of his life. Burns called one of the 'Twa Dogs' Luath after Cuchullin's hunting dog in Ossian's *Fingal*. Luath Press was established in 1981 in the heart of Burns country, and is now based a few steps up the road from Burns' first lodgings on Edinburgh's Royal Mile. Luath offers you distinctive writing with a hint of unexpected pleasures.

Most bookshops in the UK, the US, Canada, Australia, New Zealand and parts of Europe, either carry our books in stock or can order them for you. To order direct from us, please send a £sterling cheque, postal order, international money order or your credit card details (number, address of cardholder and expiry date) to us at the address below. Please add post and packing as follows: UK – £1.00 per delivery address; overseas surface mail – £2.50 per delivery address; overseas airmail – £3.50 for the first book to each delivery address, plus £1.00 for each additional book by airmail to the same address. If your order is a gift, we will happily enclose your card or message at no extra charge.

Luath Press Limited
543/2 Castlehill
The Royal Mile
Edinburgh EH1 2ND
Scotland
Telephone: 0131 225 4326 (24 hours)
Email: sales@luath.co.uk
Website: www.luath.co.uk